International Law's Invisible Frames

International Law's Invisible Frames

Social Cognition and Knowledge Production in International Legal Processes

Edited by

ANDREA BIANCHI AND MOSHE HIRSCH

OXFORD
UNIVERSITY PRESS

OXFORD
UNIVERSITY PRESS

Great Clarendon Street, Oxford, OX2 6DP,
United Kingdom

Oxford University Press is a department of the University of Oxford.
It furthers the University's objective of excellence in research, scholarship,
and education by publishing worldwide. Oxford is a registered trade mark of
Oxford University Press in the UK and in certain other countries

First Edition published in 2021

Impression: 1

Published in the United States of America by Oxford University Press
198 Madison Avenue, New York, NY 10016, United States of America

British Library Cataloguing in Publication Data

Data available

Library of Congress Control Number: 2021935986

ISBN 978–0–19–284753–9

DOI: 10.1093/oso/9780192847539.001.0001

Printed and bound by
CPI Group (UK) Ltd, Croydon, CR0 4YY

Acknowledgements

Research projects may be triggered by a number of different considerations. This one was prompted by a genuine desire to bring together two distinct, yet closely inter-related, scholarly sensibilities in order to look afresh at international law and to unveil some of its invisible structures.

We crossed paths quite late, at least in person, our respective writings being well known to each other. After a warm personal encounter in Geneva, we decided to do a research project together. Our brainstorm sessions in Geneva and Manchester proved to be useful for understanding what we did not want to do. It was only at a cosy and pleasant dinner at the Miyako restaurant in Luxembourg City at the margin of a conference that social cognition, knowledge production, and invisible frames came together as a thread. They looked to us as a challenging intellectual task and a most interesting field of inquiry. Ever since, we have worked passionately on them and endeavoured to shed some light on their nature, multiple functions, and mutual interaction.

Besides a few general guidelines, we left the contributors a wide measure of discretion to write about the subject. We are grateful to them for their trust and generosity. The fact that other people believed in our intellectual joint venture motivated us even further to bring the project to completion. However different in our backgrounds and scholarly sensibilities, we both are very curious and remain committed to looking at international law as a distinctly human process. We humbly hope that the questions the book asks and the issues it raises might be of some interest to the members of our profession. How law is perceived, apprehended, and produced as a form of knowledge is a matter that seems to us particularly worthy of investigation. All the more so, given the still widespread professional reflex of looking at law as merely a set of rules.

Thanks are owed to the institutions and the people that made this project possible. We are particularly grateful to the Leonard Davis Institute for International Relations, the Harry and Michael Sacher Institute for Legislative Research and Comparative Law, and the Aharon Barak Center for Interdisciplinary Legal Research at the Hebrew University of Jerusalem for their generous financial support. Thanks also to Tal Mimran and Eden Negar, who assisted in organizing the workshop at the Hebrew University and made sure that everything ran smoothly. Heartfelt thanks also to Hiruni Alwishewa, who competently and skilfully led the editorial process in the last phase of the project.

Our gratitude goes out to Merel Alstein, John Louth, and Jack McNichol at Oxford University Press, who believed in the project since its inception and encouraged us to pursue it. To believe in the value of theory is a rare quality for law book publishers, particularly nowadays. The editors' hope is that the publisher's courage will be rewarded by readers.

Finally, it has been a great pleasure and a lot of fun working together. We hope it shows in the book.

AB and MH
Geneva and Jerusalem, January 2021

Table of Contents

II. MAKING KNOWLEDGE PRODUCTION VISIBLE: STRUCTURES, ACTORS, AND PROCESSES

Contributors

Anne van Aaken (Dr iur and MA Economics) is Alexander von Humboldt Professor for Law and Economics, Legal Theory, Public International Law, and European Law, University of Hamburg. She was Professor at the University of St Gallen, Switzerland from 2006 to 2018. She was Vice-President of the European Society of International Law and of the European Association of Law and Economics, and is the Chair of the EUI Research Council. She taught as a guest professor at numerous universities in Europe, Africa, Asia, and Latin America, as well as the USA and was a Global Law Professor at NYU 2016. She was a Fellow at the Institute for Advanced Study in Berlin in 2010 and 2011. She chairs the EUI Research Council, is general editor of the *Journal of International Dispute Settlement* (OUP), and a member of the editorial boards of, inter alia, the *American Journal of International Law* (CUP), *European Journal of International Law* (OUP), and *International Theory* (OUP). She has been consultant for the IBRD, OECD, UNCTAD, and GIZ. She is currently working on behavioural economics/psychology of International Law and International Legal Theory and has published widely on those topics.

Jean d'Aspremont is Professor of International Law at Sciences Po Law School. He also holds a chair of Public International Law at the University of Manchester. He is General Editor of the *Cambridge Studies in International and Comparative Law* and Director of *Oxford International Organizations* (OXIO). He is a member of the Scientific Advisory Board of the *European Journal of International Law* and series editor of the *Melland Schill Studies in International Law*. He writes on questions of international law and international legal theory.

Eyal Benvenisti is the Whewell Professor of International Law at the University of Cambridge, CC Ng Fellow in Law at Jesus College, and the Director of the Lauterpacht Centre for International Law. He is Visiting Professor of Law at the Hebrew University of Jerusalem and Global Visiting Professor at New York University School of Law. He is Member of the *Institut de droit international* and of the Israeli Academy of Sciences and Humanities. A Co-editor of the *British Yearbook of International Law*, he was on the Editorial Board of the *American Journal of International Law* from 2009 to 2018). He was Project Director of the 'GlobalTrust—Sovereigns as Trustees of Humanity' research project, funded by an ERC Advanced Grant (2013–18). As a Visiting Professor at the Faculties of Law at the universities of Yale, Harvard, Toronto, Columbia, Pennsylvania, and Michigan, he gave special courses at The Hague Academy of International Law (2013) and the Xiamen Academy of International Law (2017).

Ana Luísa Bernardino is a PhD candidate in International Law at the Graduate Institute of International and Development Studies, and a Departmental Lecturer in Public International Law at the University of Oxford. She is the recipient of the 2020 James Crawford Prize awarded for the best article published in the *Journal of International Dispute Settlement*. Previously, Ana was the LLM Programme Manager at the Graduate

Institute, having also served as Teaching Assistant to the International Law Department. She has collaborated in different capacities with a Lisbon-based law firm, the World Trade Organization, the United Nations International Law Commission, the International Centre for Trade and Sustainable Development, and the Portuguese Mission to the United Nations Office and other International Organizations in Geneva. Ana holds a master's in International Law from the Graduate Institute, Geneva, where she was awarded the Mariano Garcia Rubio Prize for the best master dissertation in international law.

Andrea Bianchi is Professor of International Law at the Graduate Institute of International and Development Studies, Geneva. He is the author and/or editor of *International Law Theories. An Inquiry into Different Ways of Thinking* (OUP, 2016); *Interpretation in International Law* (co-edited with Dan Peat and Matt Windsor, OUP, 2015); *Transparency in International Law* (co-edited with Anne Peters, CUP, 2013); and of a trilogy of books on terrorism for Hart Publishing: *Enforcing International Law Norms against Terrorism* (2004); *Counterterrorism: Democracy's Challenge* (co-edited with Alexis Keller, 2008); and *International Law and Terrorism* (co-authored with Yasmin Naqvi, 2011). He has also edited the following research collections: *Theory and Philosophy of International Law* (Edward Elgar Publishing, 2017); and *Non-State Actors in International Law* (Ashgate, 2009).

Tomer Broude is the Bessie and Michael Greenblatt QC Chair in Public and International Law at the Faculty of Law and Department of International Relations at the Hebrew University of Jerusalem. His research spans international economic law, behavioural analysis of public international law, and international cultural heritage law.

Harlan Grant Cohen is the Gabriel M. Wilner/UGA Foundation Professor in International Law at the University of Georgia School of Law and Faculty Co-Director of the Dean Rusk International Law Center. His scholarship and teaching focus on international law, international legal theory, US foreign relations law, global governance, and international trade, with a particular emphasis on sources, authority, and communities of practice. Cohen is a member of the Board of Editors of the *American Journal of International Law* and the American Law Institute. He currently serves as Chair of the American Society of International Law's International Legal Theory interest group.

Jan-Philip Elm (MA, HSG in Law and Economics and LLM (Stanford)) is a law clerk at the Cantonal and Commercial Court of St Gallen (in preparation for the Swiss bar exam) and doctoral student at the University of Hamburg, supervised by Prof Dr Anne van Aaken (University of Hamburg) and Prof Eyal Zamir (The Hebrew University of Jerusalem). His research interests lie at the intersection of law, economics, and psychology in international conflict and dispute resolution. He has completed the Visiting Research Fellowship at the Hebrew University of Jerusalem (as recipient of the DAAD Research Grant for Doctoral Candidates), as well as the Special Student Program at the Graduate School of Arts and Sciences (GSAS) at Harvard University. He has been a member of the organizing committee of the St Gallen Symposium and START St Gallen. Prior to the clerkship, he had worked as research assistant to Prof Dr Anne van Aaken at both the University of St Gallen (HSG) and the University of Hamburg and trained with two leading law firms in the field of international arbitration and litigation in Switzerland and the United Kingdom (UK).

Moshe Hirsch is the Von Hofmannsthal Professor of Law at the Hebrew University of Jerusalem and Co-director of the International Law Forum at the Hebrew University Law Faculty. A significant part of his publications involves theoretical and interdisciplinary research that draws, inter alia, on sociological theories, cognitive studies, political economy, game theory, and international relations theory. His recent publications include *Invitation to the Sociology of International Law* (OUP, 2015); *Research Handbook on the Sociology of International Law* (2018, co-edited with Andrew Lang); 'Cognitive Sociology, Social Cognition and Coping with Racial Discrimination in International Law' (*European Journal of International Law*, 2019); 'Social Movements, Reframing Investment Relations, and Enhancing the Application of Human Rights Norms in International Investment Law' (*Leiden Journal of International Law*, 2020); 'The Role of International Tribunals in the Development of Historical Narratives' (*Journal of History of International Law*, 2018); and 'Explaining Compliance and Non-Compliance with ICSID Awards: a Multiple Theoretical Approach' (*Journal of International Economic Law*, 2016).

Jan Klabbers studied international law and political science at the University of Amsterdam, and has been at the University of Helsinki since 1996, where he is currently professor of international law. He has written several books and a number of articles, many of them addressing the law of international organizations. To continue this line of work, he has been awarded an Advanced Grant by the European Research Council (2021–25). He has held invited visiting positions at a number of institutions of higher learning, including New York University School of Law, Sorbonne, and the Graduate Institute of International and Development Studies; he has been director of the Academy of Finland Centre of Excellence in Global Governance Research (2006–11), and held the Academy of Finland Martti Ahtisaari Chair from 2013 to 2018.

Shiri Krebs is an Associate Professor and HDR Director at Deakin University's Law School, and Co-lead, Law and Policy Theme at the Australian Government Cyber Security Cooperative Research Centre (CSCRC). She is an affiliated scholar at Stanford University's Center for International Security and cooperation (CISAC). Dr Krebs' research focuses on legal fact finding processes during armed conflicts and human–machine interaction in technology-assisted legal decision-making, at the intersection of law, science, and technology. Her scholarship has been published at leading international law and general law journals (eg the *Harvard National Security Journal*), and has been supported by a number of research grants. Her publications granted her several awards, including the Vice-Chancellor's Early Career Researcher Award for Career Excellence (Deakin University, 2019) and the 2016 American Society of International Law (ASIL) 'New Voices' award. Dr Krebs has taught in a number of law schools, including at Stanford University, University of Santa Clara, and the Hebrew University of Jerusalem, where she won the Dean's award recognizing exceptional junior faculty members. Krebs earned her doctorate and master's degrees from Stanford Law School with honours, as well as LLB and MA, both *magna cum laude*, from the Hebrew University of Jerusalem.

Doreen Lustig is a Senior Lecturer at Tel Aviv University Faculty of Law. She studies the history and theory of international law, global governance, and constitutional law. She is the author of *Veiled Power: International Law and the Private Corporation 1886-1980* (OUP, 2020).

Lustig was a Hauser Global Law School Fellow and an IILJ (Institute of International Law and Justice) Fellow at New York University School of Law. She is a member of the *European Journal of International Law* Editorial Board and the winner of the 2019 Zeltner Prize in the category of the junior legal scholar.

Mikael Rask Madsen is Professor of European Law and Integration and the Director of iCourts, the Danish National Research Foundation's Centre of Excellence of International Courts at the Faculty of Law, University of Copenhagen. Trained as both a lawyer and a sociologist, his research has long focused on the globalization of law and its consequences for international institutions such as international courts and the societal and professional transformations triggered by legal globalization. He is the author of more than 150 publications, including many books with leading publishers. His research has been recognized by a number of prizes, including the Elite Researcher Prize, the Carlsberg Research Prize, and the Prize for best article published in the *International Journal of Constitutional Law* (I.CON). Recent publications include *The Authority of International* (co-edited with KJ Alter and LR Helfer, OUP, 2018) , 'Between Universalism and Regional Law and Politics: A Comparative History of the American, European and African Human Rights Systems' (co-authored with A Huneeus, International Journal of Constitutional Law, 2018), and 'Backlash Against International Courts: Explaining the Forms and Patterns of Resistance to International Courts' (co-authored with P Cebulak and M Wiebusch, *International Journal of Law in Context*, 2018).

Tamar Megiddo is a lecturer (Assistant Professor) at the College of Law and Business, teaching public international law and technology, democracy, and the rule of law. She also serves as a research fellow at Tel Aviv University (TraffLab ERC research project) and at the University of Haifa (the Minerva Center for the Rule of Law under Extreme Conditions). Her research focuses primarily on public international law and law and technology. Her research addresses the role of non-elite, 'ordinary' individual people in the everyday practice of international law and the impact of technology on human freedom, democracy, and the rule of law. Her work has been published in leading academic journals including the *Harvard International Law Journal*, the *Yale Journal of International Law*, and *Theoretical Inquires in Law*.

Margherita Melillo is an Associate at the O'Neill Institute for National and Global Health Law of Georgetown University. Margherita completed her PhD at the European University Institute, where she focused her research on the role of evidence in the international law on tobacco control (from the Framework Convention on Tobacco Control to the *Australia – Plain Packaging* and *Philip Morris v Uruguay* disputes). Her thesis was awarded the 2021 Antonio Cassese Prize for the best thesis in international law by the European University Institute. Before her current position, and while she was working on the chapter for this book, Margherita was a Research Fellow at the Max Planck Institute Luxembourg for Procedural Law. Moreover, during her PhD, she was a visiting scholar at Columbia Law School and participated in the Centre for Studies and Research of the Hague Academy of International Law.

Akbar Rasulov teaches international law at the University of Glasgow. He holds degrees from universities in Uzbekistan, the United Kingdom, and the United States. His main research interests fall in the fields of international economic law, critical legal studies, and the history of international legal thought.

Jacob Livingston Slosser is a Carlsberg Postdoctoral Research Fellow at iCourts—The Danish National Research Foundation's Centre of Excellence for International Courts at the University of Copenhagen Law Faculty. His research focuses on the use of cognitive science to understand conceptual change in international law and the use of artificial intelligence in law. This focus is reflected in his published work and lectures on areas such as: the regulation of artificial intelligence in public administrative law; experimental and empirical approaches to legal linguistics; the force of precedent in the European Court of Human Rights; law and gender; and feminist legal theory. Jacob completed his PhD at the University of Kent Brussels School of International Studies, where he developed a proof of method for efficacy of analysing legal concepts through the use of cognitive linguistics.

Ingo Venzke is Professor of International Law and Social Justice at the University of Amsterdam and Director of the Amsterdam Center for International Law (ACIL). His monographs include *How Interpretation Makes International Law: On Semantic Change and Normative Twists* (OUP, 2012), which won the book award of the European Society of International Law (ESIL), and *In Whose Name? A Public Law Theory of International Adjudication* (together with Armin von Bogdandy, OUP, 2014). Recently, he edited *Contingency in International Law: On the Possibilities of Different Legal Histories* (together with Kevin Jon Heller, OUP, 2021). Ingo is Editor-in-Chief of the *Leiden Journal of International Law* (together with Eric de Brabandere). His main research interests lie in international economic law and different dimensions of sustainability.

Matthew Windsor is a Lecturer (Assistant Professor) in International Law and Co-Director of Postgraduate Research at the University of Reading School of Law, where he teaches courses on international trade, investment, and human rights law. Matthew holds a BA/ LLB(Hons) from the University of Auckland, an LLM from Columbia University, and a PhD from the University of Cambridge. He has published in a variety of leading journals, including the *Leiden Journal of International Law* and the *British Yearbook of International Law*, and is the co-editor (with Andrea Bianchi and Daniel Peat) of *Interpretation in International Law* (OUP, 2015). Matthew was previously a Junior Research Fellow in International Law at the University of Oxford, a litigation associate at the Open Society Justice Initiative in New York City (as the recipient of Columbia Law School's Leebron Human Rights Fellowship), and a judge's clerk at the Court of Appeal of New Zealand.

International Law's Invisible Frames: Introductory Insights

Andrea Bianchi and Moshe Hirsch

I The Project and Its Two Strands of Analysis

The underlying premise of the research project is that humans acquire and form their knowledge through cognitive processes (eg perception, interpretation, language). At the same time, that knowledge is processed and used via different mental channels to form a representation of reality. Law as a social process carried out by human beings is a stimulating object of investigation for those who would like to analyse social cognition and knowledge production processes. Understanding how psychological and socio-cultural factors (including cultural bias) can affect decision-making in an international legal process; identifying the groups of people and institutions that may shape and alter the prevailing discourse in international law at any given time; and unearthing the hidden meaning of the various mythologies that populate and influence our normative world, are all key factors to providing a better understanding of the invisible frames within which international law moves and performs.

Cognitive science is the interdisciplinary study of mental processes involved in the acquisition, classification, interpretation, and retention of knowledge in a human environment as well as the decision on the appropriate action to take on the basis of such operations. The point of departure is that we do not directly sense information, as cognitive processes mediate between sensory input from the environment and behaviour. For example, mental processes (such as perception and memory) filter in/out and colour incoming information. Cognitive processes involved in gaining and processing information in a human environment are explored by experts from a broad range of disciplines, including neuroscience, computational science, psychology, philosophy, anthropology, and sociology. The term 'social cognition' here embraces cognitive streams in social-psychological (including behavioural), sociological, philosophical, and social-anthropological approaches to human cognition (including cognitive biases).

Cognitive social-psychological[1] and cognitive sociological scholarships complement each other. While social psychology regularly focuses on individuals'

[1] In social psychological literature, the term 'social cognition' commonly refers to an important subfield in social psychology.

Andrea Bianchi and Moshe Hirsch, *International Law's Invisible Frames: Introductory Insights* In: *International Law's Invisible Frames*. Edited by: Andrea Bianchi and Moshe Hirsch, Oxford University Press. © Andrea Bianchi and Moshe Hirsch 2021.
DOI: 10.1093/oso/9780192847539.003.0001

mental processes (and generally acknowledges cultural influences), cultural issues are not centre stage of cognitive social-psychological studies. Cognitive sociology focuses on social groups (and their interactions vis-à-vis individuals) and underlines that socio-cultural factors affect how humans acquire and process information. While not ignoring universal cognitive processes (such as certain elements of neural processing) or the impacts of personal factors on mental processes, cognitive sociologists highlight the differences that define the thinking of people in various communities. The latter literature underscores that socio-cognitive patterns vary not only across distinct cultures but also within cultures, eg according to historical periods, social networks, and in accordance with social roles (like gender or professional roles). Socio-cognitive features are transmitted to new members of society via socialization, acculturation, social control, and other social processes. For example, people observe the world in an uneven fashion. One of the significant sets of factors influencing the process of perception is people's 'cognitive culture of attention', which is shaped by groups and social networks. Thus, norms of focusing and socialization affect patterns of attention to reality.[2]

The complex combination of neurological, psychological, and sociological factors influencing human cognition engenders certain *frames*, which in this book broadly refer to mental patterns (such as patterns of attention, language, metaphors, labels, biases, and structures of knowledge and knowledge production).[3] As Karen Cerulo explains: '[W]hile sociocultural factors may not determine how mental constructs are initially acquired, such factors may help us to understand why certain constructs become so widely shared among social actors while others do not.'[4] One of the central mental patterns is *schema* that pertains to multiple cognitive processes. Much of our stored knowledge is in the form of schema. Schemata constitute highly generalized knowledge structures and abstract guidelines and assist people in understanding the world and form expectations. They are both representations of existing knowledge and information-processing mechanisms. Schemata may be conceived as abstract generalizations derived from a collection of specific experiences or complex phenomena (such as group stereotypes or social roles). They influence the processing of information, allowing people to 'fill in the blanks' and make sense of new experiences. For example, they filter our perception and may create perceptual biases, as they can commit to memory 'facts' more elaborate than those we actually experience. Schemata and culture are often closely

[2] Eviatar Zerubavel, *Hidden in Plain Sight* (OUP 2015) 62–66; M Augoustinos, I Walker, and N Donaghue, *Social Cognition* (3rd edn, Sage Publications 2014) 20–21; WH Brekhus, *Culture and Cognition: Patterns in the Social Construction of Reality* (Polity 2015) 22, 25, 33; Eviatar Zerubavel, *Social Mindscapes: An Invitation to Cognitive Sociology* (Harvard University Press 1997) 22–25, 42.

[3] On frames and their effects in behavioural scholarship see Anne van Aaken and Jan-Philip Elm, 'Framing in and through Public International Law', ch 2 in this volume at section I.

[4] K Cerulo, 'Representation and Integration' in K Cerulo (ed), *Culture in Mind: Toward A Sociology of Culture and Cognition* (Routledge, 2002) 113, 118.

interrelated, and Paul DiMaggio explains that '[h]ighly schematic cognition is the realm of institutionalized culture'.[5]

The formation, interpretation, and implementation of international law interact with diverse socio-cognitive processes.[6] International law often affects the appearance of the social world as natural,[7] necessary, or just. Furthermore, international legal rules are affected by and influence culturally infused schemata, including the framing (and reframing) of certain global threats (such as climate change[8] or tobacco smoking[9]), image schemata (such as 'balancing'[10]), classification of social groups (such as 'states', 'racial' groups, or 'indigenous groups'), and certain types of behaviour (such as a 'terrorist act'). Likewise, the development of new legal practices or legal rules interacts with distinctive patterns of language,[11] motivated cognition,[12] and prevalent metaphors.

Similarly, socio-cognitive processes often influence the interpretation of international legal instruments and attribution of responsibility to a particular state or individual. And as discussed in recent behavioural literature, international legal decision-makers at all levels are susceptible to the influence of certain cognitive biases.[13] Socio-cognitive patterns are not uniformly shared by all groups and cognitive conflicts are frequent in the international legal community. This occasionally creates significant dividing lines in the international legal system. Challenging existing socio-cognitive patterns (such as prevailing categorizations)[14] may lead to ideological and legal changes.[15] Such socio-cognitive processes and divisions are also fundamentally involved in knowledge creation.

The way in which our knowledge of international law is formed may be worthy of a few additional comments. Traditional representations of international law look

[5] P DiMaggio, 'Culture and Cognition' (1997) 23 *Annual Review of Sociology* 263, 269. See also K Cerulo, 'Mining the Intersections of Cognitive Sociology and Neuroscience' (2010) 38 *Poetics* 115, 125–26; MW Eysenck and MT Keane, *Cognitive Psychology* (7th edn, Psychology Press, 2015), 436.

[6] Moshe Hirsch, 'Social Cognitive Studies, Sociological Theory, and International Law', ch 1 in this volume at section I.

[7] On the impact of legal rules on factual findings in the context of military investigatory process see Shiri Krebs, 'The Invisible Frames Affecting Wartime Investigations: Legal Epistemology, Metaphors, and Cognitive Biases', ch 7 in this volume at section I.

[8] On framing and international climate change negotiations see van Aaken and Elm (n 3).

[9] On labels (as visible frames) and the negotiations leading to the Framework Convention on Tobacco Control see Margherita Melillo, 'Labels as the Visible Part of International Law's Invisible Frames: the case of the Framework Convention on Tobacco Control as an "evidence-based" treaty', ch 8 in this volume at section 1.

[10] See Jacob Livingston Slosser and Mikael Rask Madsen, 'Institutionally Embodied Law: Cognitive Linguistics and the Making of International Law', ch 4 in this volume at section I.

[11] On interactions between language and international law see Slosser and Madsen (n 10).

[12] On motivated cognition and humanitarian intervention see Tomer Broude, 'Prosociality, International Law and Humanitarian Intervention', ch 5 in this volume at section II.

[13] See eg Krebs (n 7); Broude (n 12).

[14] For a challenge to the fundamental distinction between international law and the world see Jean d'Aspremont, 'A Worldly Law in a Legal World', ch 6 in this volume, section I.

[15] On the potential of critical legal theory to exposing unjust reality and contributing to changing the status quo see Ingo Venzke, 'Cognitive Biases and International Law: What's the Point of Critique?', ch 3 in this volume, section I.

at it as a social practice that scholarship should objectively apprehend and rationalize in their writings. An increasing number of international law scholars seem to have abandoned such simplistic view, and adhere instead to the vision that what we know as international law is produced by processes and mechanisms of a different nature. This book attempts to foreground the notion of 'knowledge production', an expression that could turn into an established term of art to connote the study of the mechanisms of producing knowledge in the field of international law, with due heed being paid to the forces at play and the actors involved in such processes.[16] Power structures, epistemic forces, and discursive policies—influenced as they are by theories and theoretical discourse—determine what is deemed to be an acceptable and competent thing to say about international law. The same structures and forces draw the contours of the policy that controls the discipline, and are reflected in accepted social practices.

The interactive conduct of the different actors involved in the dynamic processes that produce knowledge in the field provides food for thought. Just drawing on the examples given in the book, international organizations increasingly act as standard setters by producing benchmarks and indicators to measure and appraise certain phenomena.[17] Inevitably, such normative tools and techniques end up shaping the culture by which legal problems are addressed and strategies to tackle them are developed. Likewise, other players and epistemic forces may be at play in different domains. Institutions, rules, and normative policies do not come about by any natural or objective process. They often result from the initiative of norm entrepreneurs having specific goals and using certain strategies to attain their desired normative outcomes. Knowledge is moulded and produced. The circumstances, context, and actors involved in such processes should become an unavoidable subject of investigation for international legal scholarship.[18]

II The Interaction between Social Cognition and Knowledge Production

The way in which the relationship between social cognition and knowledge production can be envisaged may vary depending on what particular processes one emphasizes, or which specific disciplinary sensibility is set to play out in a given context. But one could also look at these two different strands of analysis as constituting a somewhat circular mechanism, some kind of 'cycle of knowledge', where

[16] See Andrea Bianchi, 'Knowledge Production in International Law: Forces and Processes', ch 9 in this volume, section II.

[17] See eg van Aaken and Elm (n 3).

[18] For an interesting study on the 'machinery' producing knowledge production within international organizations see the interesting study by Jan Klabbers, 'Reflections on the International Trade Union: International Organizations as Epistemic Structures', ch 11 in this volume at section II.

social cognition and knowledge production constantly feed input into each other, although not by regular and simple sequencing. By apprehending and processing sensory 'input' through mental processes (categorization, interpretation, memorization, and—most prominently—scheming), one acquires information, which is then fed into the dynamics of social processes where it is moulded and turned into an 'output' that we qualify as 'knowledge' of a given field or discipline. Such knowledge, in turn, becomes a *lens* through which we experience, process and organize reality. Perhaps not all knowledge production processes are based on social cognition mechanisms, but almost certainly the latter are always relevant to assessing the former.

While the idea of circularity may have some intellectual appeal and carry some explanatory force with it, it would be wrong to conceive of the process of interaction between social cognition and knowledge production as a linear one. It is rather one made of discontinuities, ruptures, and irregularities, despite occasional patterns and instances of overlap. It suffices to think of *metaphors* to see how what is being used to grasp reality by making associations through comparison in a figure of speech often directs—if not coerces—our way of thinking about the legal world and its multifaceted forms.[19] Metaphors may help decipher what might be difficult to understand otherwise. In doing so they prompt a certain reflex or create a bias that contributes to forming our knowledge about a legal institution, a rule or a legal process. Likewise, by *framing* a legal issue in a certain way a court may direct the outcome of a case, simply by deciding to emphasize certain facts or channelling them into a particular set of rules, or by giving a particular interpretation of a principle or a rule in a given legal regime. Analogous considerations apply to using *narratives*, or in constructing story-telling in legal processes.[20] They are both ways of persuading or justifying legal outcomes that determine our vision of the law as a whole or of a specific legal issue. Finally, in the example of the effects of textbooks it is almost impossible to determine whether it is an apt illustration of social cognition—the way in which we learn about international law—or rather of knowledge production, as our understanding of what international law is and how it is used is hugely affected by our studying textbooks in our university years.[21]

Ultimately, the collection of essays gathered in this book aims at providing some illustrations of how social cognition and knowledge production affect our understanding and representation of international law, more than foregrounding a full-fledged theoretical framework. The overarching idea is that there is no unmediated access to knowledge and that knowledge is mentally and socially constructed. The other noticeable feature that social cognition and knowledge production share is

[19] See Harlan Grant Cohen, 'Metaphors of International Law', ch 12 in this volume at section II.

[20] See Matthew Windsor, 'Counterstorytelling in International Economic Law', ch 13 in this volume at section II.

[21] From this perspective see the intriguing essay by Ana Luísa Bernardino, 'Going By the Book—What International Law Textbooks Teach Us Not To Learn', ch 16 in this volume at section II.

that they are often invisible processes that take place without us being fully aware that they are at play.[22]

The problem with these unconscious processes is that it is far from easy to provide the profession with 'ears for the unheard of' to borrow from Nietzsche's well-known suggestive expression.[23] To go against common wisdom or to start talking about law and legal processes in a manner which is not conventional, borrowing concepts and categories from other disciplinary fields or branches of knowledge, are all exercises to which lawyers are traditionally averse. Most importantly, their salience to the discipline is doubtful given the very fact that such processes are either hidden or present features that often go unnoticed. Therefore, to prove that there is value in unearthing them implies 'a change of level' in the analysis that not everyone might be able or willing to accept.[24]

III Invisibility and Its Consequences

The duplicitous character of invisibility is apparent when one looks at philosophical and literary texts. Plato in *The Republic* tells the story of Gyges, a Lydian shepherd who finds a ring which can make him invisible.[25] He then decides to take advantage of the ring and he wears it, thus becoming invisible. He then 'seduced the king's wife and with her aid set upon the king and slew him and possessed his kingdom'.[26] According to Plato, no man is so virtuous as to resist the lust for power and pleasure, if they can be so easily obtained: '[e]veryman, when he supposes himself to take the power to do wrong, does wrong'.[27] The parable of Gyges might

[22] One of the characteristic features of social-cognitive studies is the 'dual mode system', ie the distinction between automatic (taking place below the level of consciousness) and deliberate processes that demands consciousness. Socio-cultural features permeate into automatic and deliberate cognitive processes but automatic cognitive processes rely heavily on culturally available mental structures (prominently schemata) and provide default assumptions about the characteristics of people, places, objects or events. For further details see M Hirsch, 'Cognitive Sociology, Social Cognition and Coping with Racial Discrimination in International Law' (2019) 30 *European Journal of International Law* 1319, 1329–30 and the references therein.

[23] Friedrich Nietzsche, *Thus Spoke Zarathustra: A Book for All and None* (Adrian Del Caro and Robin Pippin (eds), Adrian Del Caro (tr), CUP 2006) 15: 'I shall sing my song to lonesome and twosome hermits, and for him who still has ears for the unheard of, I shall make his heart heavy with my happiness.'

[24] Michel Foucault, *Power/Knowledge: Selected Interviews and Other Writings 1972-1977* (Colin Gordon and others (trs), Pantheon Books 1980), talking about history at 50–51: 'The making visible of what was previously unseen can sometimes be the effect of using a magnifying instrument ... But to make visible the unseen can also mean a change of level, addressing oneself to a layer of material which had hitherto had no pertinence for history and which had not been recognized as having any moral, aesthetic or historical value.'

[25] Plato, *The Republic, Vol I, Books 1–5* (Loeb Classical Library No 276) (Paul Shorey (ed), Harvard University Press 1937) Book 2, 117 ff.

[26] ibid 119.

[27] ibid 121.

have inspired H. G. Wells in his well-known dark novel *The Invisible Man*, where invisibility presents itself again as pretext for violence and aberration.[28]

In Tolkien's saga *The Lord of the Rings*, the Ring of Power provides those who wear it with invisibility, but at the same time it corrupts their moral values and makes them detectable by the dark forces.[29] Frodo almost always risks his life and with it the fate of Middle Earth every time he wears the ring either to hide himself or to invoke the ring's power. Once again invisibility is associated with dark power, and dark power corrupts and makes one amenable to evil. Harry Potter's cloak of invisibility could be seen as representing something altogether different. Presented to Harry by Dumbledore (as Harry's father's belonging),[30] the cloak of invisibility allows Harry to protect himself several times against evil, but also to carry out minor misdemeanours in and around Hogwarts. At the same time, the cloak of invisibility is also one of the Deathly Hallows that together with the others—the elder wand and the resurrection stone—will make the beholder the Master of Death. The link between power and invisibility is invariably present. Whether invisibility protects the good-hearted or hides the evil character of the story, it invariably draws one's attention. Its duplicitous character is both charming and scary, like anything else whose real existence is only left to imagination.

If the literary references that we have just hinted at may elicit mild amusement in the reader, the realization that the structures that determine our understanding of international law may be hidden from our view could be a reason for concern. The express acknowledgement made by our research project that social cognition and knowledge production mechanisms often constitute the unseen structures of international law could even be qualified as 'scary'. Indeed, those who like thrillers and horror movies can tell you how the 'unseen' is infinitely scarier than gruesome scenes of bloodshed—Stephen King's style. If the invisibility feature spurred our initial curiosity, our scholarly duty consists of subjecting the alleged invisibility of certain international law frames to intellectual scrutiny. Exposing and focusing attention on unnoticed structures may constitute a vital element of social, cognitive, and legal change.[31] With a view to shedding light on these frames, a few questions might be in order.

[28] HG Wells, *The Invisible Man* (Harper & Prothers 1897). For a particularly beautiful edition see the recent 100th Anniversary Collection paperback edition, published in 2019 by Sea Wolf Press, with illustrations from Louis Strimpl, which appeared in the 1912 French edition *L'homme invisible*.

[29] JRR Tolkien, *The Lord of the Rings* (50th Anniversary edn, Harper Collins 2004) 50.

[30] JK Rowling, *Harry Potter and the Philosopher's Stone* (Bloomsbury 1999) 148.

[31] On law's complicity in perpetuating some instances of injustice see Venzke (n 15). Social cognitive literature indicates that people are more likely to sift to deliberate cognition and override well-established schemata where, for example, their attention is attracted to a problem, when they are motivated to do so, or when their routines are disrupted. See eg Karen Cerulo, 'Mining the Intersections' (n 3) 117; Susan Fiske and Shelley Taylor, *Social Cognition: From Brain to Culture* (3rd edn, Sage Publications 2018) 51; Augoustinos and others (n 2) 77–78.

IV Investigative Questions about Invisibility

The first question to be asked is: *why* are these frames unseen? Sometimes they are hidden from view deliberately, on purpose because some actors do not want them to be seen, as this might jeopardize their vested interests, their reputation, and their symbolic capital. Yet, another possibility is that the fact that they are unseen may be a matter of perspective. They cannot be seen from where the observer is positioned. Inevitably, every theoretical perspective highlights some factors while obscuring or eclipsing others. The traditional standpoint of doctrinal analysis makes it difficult to see processes and mechanisms that do not come under the traditional disciplinary field of view. At other times, however, these structures are so conspicuous that they can hardly be noticed, and the fact they are not visible does not depend on their being hidden.[32] Quite to the contrary, they stand before our eyes, but we are incapable of seeing them either because we do not expect them to be there, or because our eyes and our minds have not been trained to focus our attention on them, and to see them where they conspicuously stand.

As Foucault used to say, it is the specific duty of an intellectual to draw people's attention to the conspicuous structures of society and power relations that they are unable or unwilling to see.[33] Finally, invisibility may be due to the fact that certain processes have been integrated into our professional *habitus*. They have become a second skin to us, a reflex that comes naturally and that is never called into question. Most of the time we accept the framing of a case by the International Court of Justice or any other international court or tribunal in deference to their authority, without questioning whether alternative options in terms of interpretation or judicial policy might have been available to them.

Secondly, one should wonder *whose* task it is to make these unseen frames visible. Here the answer is quite straightforward in our view. It is scholarship in its current variety of approaches and sensibilities that can help us see beyond the 'form' of positive law, read through the lines of received doctrinal wisdom, analyse societal processes, challenge our beliefs, and guide us through the complexity of multi-faceted phenomena with the precious help of insights drawn from other disciplines as well. Long gone are the days in which academic work was merely meant to mimic the 'official discourse' in order to legitimize and reproduce what practitioners do.[34] Although this tradition still persists in certain circles, the

[32] Zerubavel, *Hidden in Plain Sight* (n 2).

[33] 'What I look for are not secrets, hidden relations that are more silent or more profound than the consciousness of people. I try rather to define relations that are on the surface of discourse; I try to make visible what is invisible only because it's too much on the surface of things!' Michel Foucault, *The Punitive Society: lectures at the Collège de France, 1972-1973* (Palgrave Macmillan 2015) 289.

[34] 'What I mean by 'official discourse' is the self-representation made by the social agents engaged in the practice of international law. In other words, it is the way in which state officials, government lawyers, international civil servants, international judges and everyone else taken up with 'doing law' or 'doing things with law' at the international law level represent themselves and what they are doing.' (Andrea Bianchi, *International Law Theories: An Inquiry Into Different Ways of Thinking* (OUP 2016) 33.

contemporary generation of international lawyers is better read, more intellectually curious, and infinitely more self-reflective than the previous ones, including ours. Nowadays, scholars and legal professionals alike are not necessarily content with doing things with positive law and legal technique. Many of them are interested in actively thinking how the law works and do not shy away from asking challenging questions or using analytical tools that clearly come from outside the discipline. Our whole project in this book is to undertake this type of research that has little to do with disciplinary boundaries, particularly when these can be an impediment to understanding or making visible the unseen structures and mechanisms that explain how international law works.

Thirdly, one may legitimately wonder: *what* is it that is unseen or gets overlooked? In this context the metaphor of the play comes in handy to illustrate our intellectual and physical limits about what we cannot see and what we do not want or wish to see. Indeed, in watching a play the spectator may just want to look at the actors on stage and to listen to what they say. But for people who are interested in the production of the play, it is easy to realize that what happens on the stage is not all there is to the play. They would know that many more people are involved in making the play actually possible and that many activities need to be performed before, during, and after the performance. They would know that even if the actors seem to behave spontaneously, there is a script, produced by scriptwriters, on the basis of which the actors act. The production of a play is a complex machinery which entails many activities being performed by professionals having different skills. It is not just about what actors do on stage. Likewise, law is not just about clear and straightforward rules being applied by judges and decision-makers. What we know as international law is produced by the interaction of social cognition and knowledge production mechanisms. Social practices and intellectual processes are influenced by theoretical discourses that shape our understanding of what international law is and how it works. There are many processes of a different nature that preside over the making of the law, its interpretation, and its implementation. Some of these processes and some of the people involved in them are unseen by most observers, but they should not be invisible to scholars and researchers.

To think about these issues is not like applying the set of skills we have learnt and acquired through legal and academic socialization. It is not about finding a solution to a problem by technical means.[35] Nor is it about ascertaining some unquestionable 'truth' in a legal dispute, or about finding *the* correct legal answer to a legal query. Scholarly inquiries must set out to investigate in which power structures the prevailing discursive policies are grounded, and by what epistemic forces

[35] Even though technology may have a role to play in knowledge production processes at the normative level (see the chapter by Tamar Megiddo, 'Knowledge Production, Big Data. and Data-driven Customary International Law', ch 15 in this volume at section II.

they have been shaped.[36] The very same forces and structures determine what is an acceptable and competent thing to say about international law and what is not. In other words, they draw the contours of the politics that controls the discipline and the accepted social practices of international law.

But *how* can one detect such invisible structures and make them visible? Mostly by and with the tools of the trade. By analytical investigations that ask the right questions and do not shy away from challenging the things that are taken for granted or go without saying in the profession. By exercising critical thinking and refusing to remain entrapped in the traditional canons that are by definition 'traditionally' not called into question.[37] Any scholarly inquiry presupposes a choice of theoretical presuppositions and methodology. Some of these theories are better than others at asking certain questions, and one should not hesitate to shift the focus of one's analysis and use them in order to test or question their explanatory force. Theories and methods can become prisons from which it becomes hard to escape if adhered to too strictly. Similar considerations apply to disciplines that are not just different ways of approaching and creating knowledge, but also social groups with a strong bond of identity and membership, the comfort of which it is difficult to abandon. Yet for research projects such as this, the challenge of using concepts and categories borrowed from other disciplines, or using particular intra-disciplinary sensibilities to pursue new lines of inquiry, seem to be key to bringing to light the invisible frames of international law.

V By Way of Conclusion: The Three Us

Ultimately, our intellectual exercise could be summarized as primarily concerned with three Us: (i) to *unveil*, ie to bring to the surface and/or to make visible the hidden or often unnoticed processes by which our understanding of international law is formed; (ii) to *understand*, ie to better grasp the mechanisms that allow us to apprehend and intellectually represent the social practice of international law; (iii) to *unlearn* some of the presuppositions that activate automatic cognitive processes and inform our beliefs that most of the time remain largely unquestioned. To unlearn what one thinks they know is probably the most difficult. To abandon long-established convictions and override automatic mental reflexes, to cast doubts on things one has always taken for granted, causes us to feel strange and somewhat

[36] See the interesting study on the politics and economics of the discipline's knowledge production processes in the chapter by Akbar Rasulov, 'The Discipline as a Field of Struggle: the Politics and Economics of Knowledge Production in International Law', ch 10 in this volume at section II.

[37] An interesting example is the way in which international humanitarian law has constructed and represented itself for a long time, the historical and political circumstances of which are called into question by Eyal Benvenisti and Doreen Lustig, 'Revisiting the Memory of Solferino: Knowledge Production and the Laws of War', ch 14 in this volume at section II.

estranged from our colleagues and the profession. The sense of insecurity that comes with an impending doubt that is just about to transform the way in which we look at what we do and at why we do it in a certain way may be unpleasant, and yet it is necessary to start the quest for alternative paradigms. The act of unlearning requires courage, patience, and a great deal of determination. It demands a fine balance between humbleness and self-assurance. To unlearn is tantamount to be willing to relinquish one's credo and set of beliefs, and to set aside—if need be—disciplinary common wisdom and predominant intellectual representations. To go above and beyond all of this, intellectual curiosity and serious engagement with both tradition and innovation are indispensable qualities to undertake the task of modifying socio-cognitive lenses successfully, seeking new discoveries, and forming our understanding of knowledge on a different basis.

SECTION I

SOCIAL COGNITION: FOREGROUNDING INFORMATION PROCESSING AND RECONTEXTUALIZING INTERNATIONAL LAW

1

Social Cognitive Studies, Sociological Theory, and International Law

*Moshe Hirsch**

I Introduction

The 'cognitive revolution' (during the 1950s) and the establishment of 'cognitive science' (during the 1970s) have generated far-reaching changes in several disciplines, prominently psychology, neuroscience, linguistics, computer science, and philosophy.[1] In recent decades, cognitive science has made inroads into research work and theoretical scholarship in many other fields, such as economics, political science, anthropology, international relations, and law. This chapter presents some key insights from social-cognitive studies, analyses the effect of the new literature on some prominent theoretical trends in sociological theory, and discusses a possible change in the way we conceive international criminal law (and ensuing legal change).

Cognitive science is the interdisciplinary study of mental processes involved in acquiring, classifying, and interpreting knowledge in human environment, and in deciding what action might be appropriate. Human cognition is explored by experts from diverse disciplines, including neuroscience, psychology, sociology, computational science, philosophy, and anthropology. The term '*social* cognitive studies' refers in this work to the confluence of research strands in some disciplines exploring interactions between human cognitive processes and socio-cultural factors, such as social psychology (including 'social cognition' in psychological literature), cognitive sociology, cultural psychology, cognitive anthropology, and philosophy of mind. Although there are some significant differences between

* I am very grateful to Anne van Aaken (University of Hamburg Law Faculty), Ilan Yaniv (Hebrew University Department of Psychology), and Yahli Shereshevsky (Hebrew University, Cyber Security Research Centre) for their insightful comments on earlier drafts of this chapter. Thanks also to Jiries Elias for excellent research assistance.

[1] On the first decades of the 'cognitive revolution' and 'cognitive studies' see George A Miller, 'The Cognitive Revolution: a Historical Perspective' (2003) 7(3) *Trends in Cognitive Sciences* 141; Howard E Gardner, *The Mind's New Science: A History of The Cognitive Revolution* (Basic Books 1985) 28–38; William Bechtel, Adele Abrahamsen, and George Graham, 'Cognitive Science: History' in NJ Smelser and PB Baltes (eds), *International Encyclopaedia of the Social & Behavioral Sciences* (Pergamon 2001) 2154; Kathleen Galotti, *Cognitive Psychology: In and Out of the Laboratory* (6th edn, Sage Publications 2018) 10–13.

Moshe Hirsch, *Social Cognitive Studies, Sociological Theory, and International Law* In: *International Law's Invisible Frames*. Edited by: Andrea Bianchi and Moshe Hirsch, Oxford University Press.
DOI: 10.1093/oso/9780192847539.003.0002

the methodologies and theories employed by researchers from these disciplinary streams, there are also substantial similarities and overlap; these studies complement each other and can be applied in international law scholarship.

While social-psychological literature traditionally highlights individuals as the basic unit of analysis,[2] recent publications in the sphere of 'social cognition' (a branch of social psychology) acknowledge that individuals' mental processes are also influenced by cultural features.[3] Thus, for example, Fiske and Taylor explain in their influential book on social cognition that '[m]any of the central assumptions about how people think about other people turn out to be culturally bound'.[4] As for sociological literature, in recent years there has been growing scholarly interest in studying 'cognitive sociology', and researchers often draw on social psychological studies. This strand in sociological scholarship is more focused on social groups (and their interactions vis-à-vis individuals) and underscores that sociocultural factors affect how individuals and communities process information. From this perspective, human information processing varies cross-culturally, historically, and within cultures. Zerubavel (one of the leading scholars in this field) explains: '[s]ociety, in short, plays a major role in organizing our "optical" predispositions. Indeed, many of the mental lenses through which we come to "see" the world are actually *socio*mental lenses grounded in particular social environments'.[5]

Thus, cognitive research streams in social psychology and sociology explore various interactions between cognitive processes and social behaviour, and since they complement each other, it is desirable that international law scholars should draw on both rich literatures. The formation, interpretation, and implementation of international law interact with diverse socio-cognitive processes, and drawing on the confluence of these research strands (as well as related disciplines exploring human cognition) is likely to enrich our understanding of international law in real-life situations.

Section II introduces some core insights gained from social-cognitive studies pertinent to international law. Section III analyses certain consequences of the new socio-cognitive scholarship on three prominent theoretical divides cutting across the sociological literature: (i) the structure–agency debate that revolves around the question of the extent to which the social structure (eg norms) constrains people in society; (ii) the consensus–conflict divide relating to the consensual or conflictual nature of social relations; and (iii) the positivist–interpretative debate, which focuses on the objective–subjective nature of reality. Social cognitive studies may

[2] See eg Martha Augoustinos, Iain Walker, and Ngaire Donaghue, *Social Cognition* (3rd edn, Sage Publications 2015) 6.

[3] Susan Fiske and Shelley Taylor, *Social Cognition: From Brain to Culture* (3rd edn, Sage Publications 2017) 17, 27–28; Augoustinos and others (n 2) 6–7, 288–89; Ziva Kunda, *Social Cognition: Making Sense of People* (2nd edn, A Bradford Book 2000) 515–60.

[4] Fiske and Taylor (n 3) 27. See also Galotti (n 1) 396.

[5] Footnote omitted. Eviatar Zerubavel, *Social Mindscapes: An Invitation to Cognitive Sociology* (Harvard University Press 1997) 22, 31.

generate diverse changes in the ways we understand international law, and such conceptual changes are likely to prompt some legal changes. Section IV illustrates the potential effects of socio-cognitive studies on international law by focusing on international criminal law. In light of the growing awareness to the constraining nature of socio-cognitive processes on individuals, this section suggests that international criminal tribunals should consider such socio-cognitive effects at the sentencing stage.

II Some Core Principles of Social Cognitive Studies

This section briefly introduces some major principles arising from recent social cognitive psychology and cognitive sociology that are pertinent to international law.[6] As discussed in the following sections, these principles could cast new light on well-known debates in social theory as well as on the ways we conceive international law.

(i) *Intermediary mental processes*: Friedman states: '[s]trictly speaking, what human beings see, feel, taste, touch, and smell is not the world per se but a version of the world their minds have created.'[7] The point of departure of social cognitive studies is that people do not directly sense information; cognitive processes *mediate* between sensory input from the environment and behaviour[8]—and they are 'the stuff ... which is found between input and output.'[9] Thus, for example, cognitive processes (such as attention, categorization, and memory) filter in/out, interpret, and store incoming information. Such processes construct in the mind mental representations (prominently schemata) that organize our knowledge and expectations about various social objects in our environment.[10] What we perceive is constructed not solely from observed data but also from the context and meaning attributed to the data (also influenced by our already existing mental representations).[11]

(ii) *Limited cognitive resources and heuristics*: Humans frequently come across ample information but they possess limited cognitive capacity to process such data. Exposed to the constant flow of sensory stimuli, cognitive processes (such as attention) are commonly selective and inherently imply the exclusion of some

[6] The concepts of 'priming' and 'schema' are discussed in Sections III and IV below.

[7] Asia Friedman, *Blind to Sameness* (University of Chicago Press 2013) 20.

[8] Fiske and Taylor (n 3) 13, 16; Augoustinos and others (n 2) 20.

[9] Gardner (n 1) 38.

[10] Augoustinos and others (n 2) 20–21; Karen Cerulo (ed), *Culture in Mind: Toward A Sociology of Culture and Cognition* (Routledge 2002) 113–121.

[11] Gordon Moskowitz, *Social Cognition: Understanding Self and Others* (1st edn, The Guilford Press 2005) 64. See also Stanislas Dehaene, *Consciousness and the Brain* (Penguin Books 2014) 60–62. On reconstruction in cognitive sociology see Piet Strydom, 'Understanding and Explaining Cognitive Sociology' (2012) 6 ff. Researchgate https://www.researchgate.net/publication/301276276_Understanding_and_Explaining_in_Cognitive_Sociology (accessed 31 August 2020).

information.[12] To cope with large amounts of information from different channels and make decisions under uncertain circumstances, people resort to heuristics ('rules of thumb')—to reduce complex situations to simpler and manageable ones.[13] Kahneman defines heuristics as 'a simple procedure that helps find adequate (though often imperfect) answers to difficult questions'.[14] These mental shortcuts provide quick guidelines but may lead to systemic errors.[15]

One of the basic heuristics is the 'representative heuristic' that refers to the generation of assessments about the probability of some event by matching information about the particular event against an existing representative category of events.[16] The assumed probability that something is true is judged by how much it resembles one of the alternatives being considered by the person[17] (occasionally based on partial information or stereotypes).[18] Although this rapid method is imperfect (and frequently leads to errors), people are often insensitive to more reliable factors affecting the actual probability of the specific event (such as the size of the sample). For example, when people are asked to assess whether a particular person is a farmer or a librarian, and presented with some information about this person's personality traits (eg shyness, obsession about details) as well as the base rate of such occupations in the population (eg 80% of the people in the specific population are farmers/librarians)—it is common to base estimated probabilities on the representativeness of those personality traits (shyness/obsession about details), and neglect information regarding the proportion of librarians/farmers in the population or the sample size.[19]

(iii) *Culture in mind*: Cognitive processes are influenced by neurological, psychological, socio-cultural, and other factors. Cognitive sociological scholarship and cross-cultural psychological literature highlight the impact of socio-cultural aspects on cognitive processes and social construction of reality.[20] Cognitive sociologists emphasize the differences that define the thinking of people in various

[12] See eg Eviatar Zerubavel, *Hidden in Plain Sight: The Social Structure of Irrelevance* (Oxford University Press 2015) 2–3.

[13] Fiske and Taylor (n 3) 15, 188–9; See also Hans Eysenck and Mark Keane, *Cognitive Psychology* (7th edn, Psychology Press 2015) 141–42, 441–42. On the human need to save time and cognitive energy see also Jens Rydgren, 'The Power of the Past: A Contribution to a Cognitive Sociology of Ethnic Conflict' (2007) 25(3) *Sociological Theory* 225, 28.

[14] Daniel Kahneman, *Thinking Fast and Slow* (Penguin 2012) 98.

[15] Galotti (n 1) 314; Moskowitz (n 11) 141–42; Fiske and Taylor (n 3) 189; Kahneman (n 14) 130.

[16] Fiske and Taylor (n 3) 189–92.

[17] Moskowitz (n 11) 142–43.

[18] Kahneman (n 14) 146–53.

[19] Fiske and Taylor (n 3) 189–92; Moskowitz (n 11) 142–44; Kahneman (n 14) 146–53. See also Galotti (n 1) 317–19.

[20] Wayne Brekhus, *Culture and Cognition: Patterns in the Social Construction of Reality* (Polity 2015) 1; Zerubavel (n 12) 31, 22; Fiske and Taylor (n 3) 27; Galotti (n 1) 396. On the mutual links between culture and cognitive processes see also Richard Nisbett and Ara Norenzayan, 'Culture and Cognition' in Douglas Medin (ed), *Steven's Handbook of Experimental Psychology* (vol. 2, 3rd. edn, Wiley 2002) 561, 62.

communities.[21] A series of experiments have consistently shown that people from different cultural systems have different perception and attention patterns.[22] For example, cross-cultural psychological studies point out that East Asians and Westerners perceive the reality and think about it in different ways. When people from Japan and the U.S. were presented with an animated vignette of underwater scenes, participants from the U.S. started their statements by mentioning salient objects far more frequently than participants from Japan did. In contrast, Japanese participants began by mentioning information about the field almost twice as often as Americans did. Nisbett and Masuda conclude from this and additional studies that East Asians attend to the field more than do Westerners, and that Westerners pay more attention to focal objects. Attention to focal objects encourages categorization, application of rules, and causal attribution in terms of these focal objects. Attention to the field encourages noticing relationships and change, and prompts causal attribution in terms of the context and distal forces.[23]

It is noteworthy that socio-cognitive patterns vary not only across distinct cultures but also within cultures; eg according to historical periods, sub-cultures, social networks, and in accordance with social roles (like gender or professional roles).[24] Such socio-cognitive characteristics are transmitted to new members of society via social mechanisms, such as socialization or language, and are enforced via social control mechanisms.[25]

(iv) *Dual mode system and automatic cognitive processes*: One of the emblematic features of social-cognitive studies is the distinction between automatic and deliberate processes.[26] Automatic cognitive processes can occur below the level of consciousness while deliberate thought demands consciousness.[27] *Automatic*

[21] Cerulo (n 10) 113, 18; Friedman (n 7) 16–17; Eviatar Zerubavel, 'Cognitive Sociology: Between the Personal and the Universal Mind' in Wayne H. Brekhus and Gabe Ignatow (eds), *the Oxford Handbook of Cognitive Sociology* (OUP 2019) 31, 37–38.

[22] Richard Nisbett and Takahiko Masuda, 'Culture and Point of View' (2003) 100(19) *Proceedings of the National Academy of Sciences* 1163; Shinobu Kitayama and Ayse Uskul, 'Culture, Mind, and the Brain' (2011) 64 *Annual Review of Psychology* 419, 435–36. For a summary of numerous cross-cultural cognitive studies regarding the influence of culture on cognitive processes see Galotti (n 1) 396 ff.

[23] Nisbett and Masuda (n 22) 1169.

[24] See eg Zerubavel (n 5), 33; Asia Friedman, 'Toward a Sociology of Perception: Sight, Sex, and Gender' (2011) 5(2) *Cultural Sociology* 187.

[25] See eg Zerubavel (n 12) 62–66; Zerubavel (n 5) 14–15; Rydgren (n 13) 228. On learning mental representations see Augoustinos and others (n 2) 20–21. On socialization of language and social values see Anne Fernald and Hiromi Morikawa, 'Common Themes and Cultural Variations in Japanese and American Mothers' Speech to Infants' (1993) 64 *Child Development* 637.

[26] This feature is particularly innovative in cognitive sociological literature (compared to traditional sociological literature). See eg Stephen Vaisey, 'Motivation and Justification: A Dual-Process Model of Culture in Action' (2009) 114(6) *American Journal of Sociology* 1675; Omar Lizardo and others, 'What Are Dual Process Models? Implications for Cultural Analysis in Sociology' (2016) 34(4) *Sociological Theory* 287; Stephen Vaisey and Margret Frye, 'The Old One-Two: preserving Analytical Dualism in Cognitive Sociology' in Donal Carlston (ed), *The Oxford Handbook of Social Cognition* (OUP 2013) 10.

[27] On several degrees of automatic processing see Fiske and Taylor (n 3) 34. On the criteria of cognitive processing see Galotti (n 1) 90. On the distinctive 'signatures' of conscious thoughts see Dehaene (n 11) 115–59.

cognition involves rapid, effortless, and unintentional processes of information,[28] essentially activating some well-learned set of associations or responses that have developed through the repeated activation of memory.[29] *Deliberate cognition* involves slow, well-thought, and measured cognitive processing.[30] Although most of our thoughts and behaviours tend to be automatic or have automatic components,[31] people tend to overestimate the extent to which their thoughts control actions and the extent they *can* control their thoughts.[32]

Cognitive experts have highlighted the special properties ('signatures') of conscious thinking. Conscious processes amplify sensory stimuli, combine multiple types of information and synchronize them in a coherent fashion; they take place in multiple regions of the brain, lagging behind developments in the external world.[33]

Socio-cultural features permeate automatic and deliberate cognitive processes.[34] Automatic cognitive processes rely heavily on culturally available mental structures (prominently schemata)[35] and provide default assumptions about the characteristics of people, places, objects, or events.[36] When engaged in deliberate thought, people may reject and override their automatic schemata (including stereotypes) or biases, thus leading them to actively search for characteristics and connections rather than assume them.[37] As discussed below, under some circumstances (such as high motivation), people are more likely to shift to deliberate cognition.[38]

(v) *Inter-group relations and social identity*: Inter-group relations literature reveals the significant effects of social identity on individuals' cognitive processes and behaviour.[39] Human beings strive to belong to social groups and have the

[28] Karen Cerulo, 'Mining the intersections of Cognitive Sociology and Neuroscience' (2010) 38 *Poetics* 115, 117; Fiske and Taylor (n 3) 34, 40; Kunda (n 3) 266 ff.

[29] Patricia Devine, 'Stereotypes and Prejudice: Their Automatic and Controlled Components' (1989) 56 *Journal of Personality and Social Psychology* 5, 6.

[30] Cerulo, 'Mining the intersections' (n 28) 117.

[31] T Wheatley and DM Wegner, 'Automaticity of Action, Psychology of' in *International Encyclopedia of the Social & Behavioral Sciences* (Elsevier, 2001) 991. See also Dehaene (n 11) 13.

[32] Fiske and Taylor (n 3) 61. See also Dehaene (n 11) 47, 79–80.

[33] On these properties of conscious processes and additional ones see Dehaene (n 11) 115–60; Eysenck (n 13) 684–705.

[34] Malia Mason and Michael Morris, 'Culture, Attribution and Automaticity: A Social Cognitive Neuroscience View' (2010) 5 *Social Cognitive and Affective Neuroscience* 292, 293, 300–302. See also Ann Swidler, *Talk of Love: How Culture Matters* (University of Chicago Press 2001) 99–107.

[35] Schemata constitute highly generalized knowledge structures and abstract guidelines, and they assist people in understanding the world and forming expectations. They are both representations of existing knowledge and information-processing mechanisms. See International Law's Invisible Frames: Introductory Insights [in this volume], Section A (and the references therein).

[36] P DiMaggio, 'Culture and Cognition' (1997) 23 *Annual Review of Sociology* 263, 269; Cerulo, 'Mining the intersections' (n 28) 117; Kahneman (n 14) 135; Yuki Shimizu, Hajin Lee, and James S Uleman, 'Culture as Automatic Processes for Making Meaning: Spontaneous Trait Inferences' (2017) 69 *Journal of Experimental Social Psychology* 79.

[37] Cerulo, 'Mining the intersections' (n 28) 117. See also Kahneman (n 14) 135.

[38] See section II(vii) below.

[39] Social identity has been explored in both sociological and social psychological literatures. Although the two perspectives on identity present some differences regarding their origin, orientation, and language, there are also substantial similarities. Jan Stets and Peter Burke, 'Identity, Theory and Social Identity Theory' (2000) 63 *Social Psychology Quarterly* 224, 224, 228, 234.

tendency to differentiate themselves by group membership.[40] Empirical studies have persuasively demonstrated that once people identify with a particular social group, they are likely to view in-group members more positively, and grant them favourable treatment compared with that granted to out-group members.[41] This discriminatory tendency is also discerned in settings characterized by the absence of any history of intergroup contact or conflict.[42]

People tend to believe that their group has a 'better human essence' than other groups,[43] allowing them to sympathize less with people belonging to other groups.[44] Generally, in-group members are believed to be trustworthy, cooperative, peaceful, and honest; whereas outgroup members are often perceived as untrustworthy, competitive, quarrelsome, and dishonest.[45] Group affiliation also tends to affect the radius of one's 'moral circle',[46] suggesting that members of a particular group readily excuse unfair acts if the transgressors belong to the subjects' group.[47] Although group identity tends to generate certain discriminatory biases, these tendencies are not uniform, and cultural variations across social groups influence the type and extent of discrimination along certain lines.[48]

(vi) *Motivation, affect, and cognition*: Recent social cognitive studies underline the role of motivation and affect in a broad range of mental processes, and both factors are integrated at every stage of research in this field.[49] Motivation influences mental processes, such as the preference for a particular interpretation that reduces anxiety or enhances self-esteem.[50] The term 'affect' refers here to moods, emotions, and evaluations.[51] Cognitive processes occasionally influence affect. For instance,

40 Marilynn Brewer, *Intergroup Relations* (2nd edn, Open University Press 2003, reprinted in 2009) 103, 20; Elliot Aronson, *The Social Animal* (11th edn, Worth Publishers 2012) 27–28. See also Richard Jenkins, *Social Identity* (4th edn, Routledge 2014) 120 ff. On social identity and international law see Moshe Hirsch, *Invitation to the Sociology of International Law* (OUP 2015) 104 ff.

41 Walter Stephan and Cookie Stephan, *Intergroup Relations* (Westview Press 1996) 92–93; Brewer (n 40) 43 ff. See also Jenkins (n 40) 8.

42 Brewer (n 40) 45; see also at 26.

43 BP Cortes and others, 'Infrahumanization or Familiarity? Attribution of Uniquely Human Emotions to the Self, the Ingroup, and the Outgroup' (2005) 31(2) *Personality and Social Psychology Bulletin* 243, 251. See also Eva Krumhuber and others, 'Real or Artificial? Intergroup Biases in Mind Perception in a Cross-Cultural Perspective' (2015) 10(9) *PLoS One* 1 https://www.ncbi.nlm.nih.gov/pmc/articles/PMC4567265/pdf/pone.0137840.pdf (accessed on 31 August 2020).

44 Fiske and Taylor (n 3) 314.

45 Brewer (n 40) 51. See also Fiske and Taylor (n 3) 54.

46 On 'moral circle' and social identity see Stefano Passini, 'What do I Think of Others in Relation to Myself?' (2013) 23 *Journal of Community and Applied Psychology* 261.

47 Piercarlo Valdesolo and David DeSteno, 'Moral Hypocrisy, Social Groups and the Flexibility of Virtue' (2007) 18(8) *Psychological Science* 869, 870.

48 Group affiliation does not necessarily result in negative attitudes vis-à-vis out-group's members, and the content of such attitudes can be either positive (eg admiration) or negative. See eg on the 'stereotype content model' and cross-cultural variances, Susan Fiske, 'Intergroup Biases: A Focus on Stereotype Content' (2015) 3 *Current Opinion in Behavioural Sciences* 45; Amy Cuddy and others, 'Stereotype Content Model Across Cultures: Towards Universal Similarities and Some Differences' (2009) 48 *British Journal of Social Psychology* 1, 3, 22–23.

49 Fiske and Taylor (n 3) 16; Augoustinos and others (n 2) 23.

50 Fiske and Taylor (n 3) 238–40. See also Galotti (n 1) 375, 389.

51 Fiske and Taylor (n 3) 368, 372; Eysenck and Keane (n 13) 636.

emotional arousal often follows cognitive discrepancy (eg remembering information that disconfirms existing schema) or disruption of an ongoing cognitive process.[52] On the other hand, emotional moods (such as feeling cheerful) influence numerous aspects of human cognition, including attention, learning, memory, and judgment.[53] 'Mood congruency' affects memory, and people are inclined to better remember material whose valence fits their current mood state. For example, people recall positive material while they are in a positive mood, and sometimes recall negative material while in a negative mood.[54] Some scholars argue that affect and cognition are not separated and that affect has a primary role in human mental processes.[55]

(vii) *Socio-cognitive change*: Cognitive processes not only reflect humans' cultural systems but also tend to sustain and reproduce cultural patterns. Such deeply ingrained socio-mental processes may explain (at least partially) why certain harmful socio-cognitive biases (such as racial or gender biases) are relatively stable over time.[56] Although social cognitive changes are possible, cognitive psychology literature suggests that that such changes ordinarily do not respond rapidly to environmental or socio-cultural changes.[57] While the psychological and biological approaches to cognition emphasize long-term changes, sociological approaches are more attuned to the dynamic character of socio-cultural patterns. Social change has been at the heart of sociology since its inception; and the general assumption is that changes occur in all domains of social life.[58] Thus, while cognitive processes are commonly not subject to rapid modification, they are not immune to change.

Socio-cognitive change is significantly discussed in the literature concerning automatic biases towards people belonging to disadvantaged groups. This scholarship reveals that people who are aware of their negative racial stereotype but believe it is inappropriate and mistaken ('low-prejudice' individuals)—and who wish

[52] Fiske and Taylor (n 3) 282–83 see also in 385–86.

[53] Eysenck and Keane (n 13) 648. See also Fiske and Taylor (n 3) 398.

[54] Fiske and Taylor (n 3) 402. See also Eysenck and Keane (n 13) 652. On the influence of affect on judgments see Fiske and Taylor (n 3) 402, 406, 411. See also Eysenck and Keane (n 13) 655.

[55] Fiske and Taylor (n 3) 367, 420. See also John Sonnett, 'Priming and Framing' (2009) *Oxford Handbook of Cognitive Sociology* 226, 234.

[56] On interactions between socio-cognitive processes and racial discrimination see eg Moshe Hirsch, 'Cognitive Sociology, Social Cognition and Coping with Racial Discrimination in International Law' (2019) 30 *European Journal of International Law* 1319, 1331 ff. On the social perception of gender differences see Friedman (n 24) 196–99.

[57] Cognitive *psychological* literature takes into account dynamic cognitive processes but the prominent functional–evolutionary approach in this scholarship emphasizes slow adaptation-functional processes (aimed at managing challenges relating, for example, to, self-protection, disease avoidance, etc.). Steven Neuberg and Mark Schaller, 'Evolutionary Social Cognition' in Eugene Borgida and John Bargh (eds), *APA Handbook of Personality and Social Psychology, vol. 1* (American Psychological Association, 2015) 2; Cecilia Heyes, 'New Thinking: The Evolution of Human Cognition' (2012) 367 *Philosophical Transactions of the Royal Society* 2091, 2093–94. On evolutionary processes in human cognition see also Galotti (n 1) 21.

[58] George Ritzer and Wendy Murphy, *Introduction to Sociology* (5th edn, Sage Publications 2020) 468 ff; Jay Weinstein, *Social Change* (3rd edn, Rowman & Littlefield 2010) 9–10; John Macionis, *Sociology* (14th edn, Pearson 2012) 561 ff.

to inhibit automatically activated cues—may override and replace such automatic activation with non-prejudiced ideas and responses.[59] Additional studies show that people in society are more likely to shift to deliberate cognition (and override stereotypic thinking) where, for example, they are motivated to do so, where routines are disrupted, or when encountering disconfirming information.[60]

III Sociological Theoretical Debates and Social-cognitive Studies

The increasing attention paid by sociologists (and experts from additional social sciences) to new insights arising from social cognitive studies is likely to influence certain trends in sociological theory. This section briefly explores some likely effects of social cognitive literature on three major theoretical debates in sociological theory. The three prominent sociological theoretical divides discussed here relate to: (i) the structure–agency debate concerning the relationship between individuals and society; (ii) the consensus–conflict divide relating to different perspectives concerning the consensual or conflictual nature of society; and (iii) the positivist–interpretative debate focused on the objective (empirical) or subjective (including inter-subjective) nature of reality. Each of these divides constitutes a theoretical continuum along which people's and experts' positions are located.

(i) *The structure–agency continuum*: One of the central debates in sociological literature revolves around the relationship between individuals and social structures. The central question here is how and to what extent does the social structure (including norms, values etc.) constrain people in society? Or, alternatively: does most behaviour result from social forces beyond individuals' control? Generally, the sociological perspective assumes that individuals' behaviour and their normative choices are significantly affected by socio-cultural factors and processes.[61] Individuals, however, also influence their social structure. In addition, cultures equip people with a 'tool kit' of resources, enabling them to construct strategies of action.[62]

Agency-oriented approaches emphasize the active and creative aspects of human behaviour, while structure-oriented approaches underline the

[59] Devine (n 29) 14–15. Kunda (n 3) 326–27. See also Lorella Lepore and Rupert Brown, 'Category and Stereotype Activation: Is Prejudice Inevitable?' (1997) 72(2) *Journal of Personality and Social Psychology* 275.

[60] Cerulo, 'Mining the Intersections' (n 28) 117; Fiske and Taylor (n 3) 51; Brekhus (n 20) 29–30; Augoustinos and others (n 2) 77–78; Irene V Blair, 'The Malleability of Automatic Stereotypes and Prejudice' (2002) 6 *Personality and Social Psychology Review* 242, 243.

[61] See eg Richard Schaefer, *Sociology Matters* (5th ed, McGraw-Hill 2011) 2–3; Macionis (n 58) 2–3; Reza Banakar and Max Travers, 'Introduction' in Reza Banakar and Max Travers (eds), *An Introduction to Law and Social Theory* (Hart Publishing 2002) 1–3; Shaun Hargreaves Heap and others, *The Theory of Choice: a Critical Guide* (Wiley-Blackwell 1992) 63–64.

[62] Swidler (n 34) 82–83, 104–17.

constraining nature of social structures on individuals (prominently through socialization and social control processes).[63] Generally, theories belonging to the *macro*-sociology tradition (generally focusing on large-scale social patterns, such as the social system as a whole and its functions) tend to emphasize the constraining power of social structures on individual choices. Individuals are largely perceived here as 'bearers' of social patterns. *Micro*-sociology theories (highlighting the role of individuals and small groups in society) tend to view social structures, like a society itself, as constituted and changed by interactions between individuals. Human beings are not viewed here as the product (or victims) of the social system, but rather as active agents whose choices are not determined by social patterns.[64]

Although sociologists embrace various approaches to the structure-agency debate, *cognitive* sociological scholarship (as well as social-cognitive studies in general) tends to pay more attention to socio-cultural *structures*, and the ways cultural patterns constrain individuals' mental processes (prominently concerning schemata or frames).[65] From this perspective, people are socialized (eg via learning a language) to particular socio-cognitive patterns and socially pressured to follow these socio-mental patterns (such as norms of attention).[66] This constraining character is particularly notable in the 'embodied cognitive' approach (influenced by Bourdieu's scholarship) in sociological literature.[67] The tendency to emphasize the restraining effects of socio-cultural patterns is related to increasing attention paid in recent literature to the unconscious nature of mental processes, underlining that many cognitive processes are undertaken below conscious awareness.[68]

[63] Anthony Giddens and Phillip Sutton, *Sociology* (7th edn, Polity Press 2013) 86; James Fulcher and John Scott, *Sociology* (4th edn, OUP 2011) 53. See also George Ritzer and Jeffrey Stepnisky, *Sociological Theory* (9th edn, McGraw-Hill 2013) 510.

[64] On the structure–agency debate see Ritzer and Stepnisky (n 63) 488–89; Ritzer and Murphy (n 58) 24–25; Giddens and Sutton (n 63) 86–87; Banakar and Travers (n 61) 4–5; Sharon Hays, 'Structure and Agency and the Sticky Problem of Culture' (1994) 12(1) *Social Theory* 57.

[65] For a discussion on the structural feature of Goffman's frame analysis see Norman Denzin and Charles Keller, 'Frame Analysis Reconsidered' (1981) 10(1) *Contemporary Sociology* 52, 52–60. On frame analysis and changes in international investment law see Moshe Hirsch, 'Social Movements, Reframing Investment Relations, and Enhancing the Application of Human Rights Norms in International Investment Law' (2020) 34(1) *Leiden Journal of International Law* 127, 133–140.

[66] See eg Friedman (n 7) 22. See also Zerubavel (n 12) 62–66; Zerubavel (n 5) 14–15; Rydgren (n 13) 228; Augoustinos and others (n 2) 20–21; Fernald and Morikawa (n 25) 639–40.

[67] On the embodied cognitive approach in cognitive sociology see Wayne Brekhus and Gabe Ignatow, 'Cognitive Sociology and the Cultural Mind: Debates, Directions and Challenge' in Wayne H. Brekhus and Gabe Ignatow (eds), *the Oxford Handbook of Cognitive Sociology* (OUP 2019) 1, 15–16, 11. On embodied cognition and Bourdieu's writings see Omar Lizardo, 'Pierre Bourdieu as Cognitive Sociologist' in Wayne H Brekhus and Gabe Ignatow (eds), *the Oxford Handbook of Cognitive Sociology* (OUP 2019) 65, 70–75.

[68] On the limited attention paid by classical sociological streams to dual-process process see Jacob Strandell, 'Bridging the Vocabularies of Dual-Process Models of Culture and Cognition' in Wayne H. Brekhus and Gabe Ignatow (eds), *the Oxford Handbook of Cognitive Sociology* (OUP 2019) 193, 194. See also Vaisey and Frye (n 26) 101.

The notion of *activated actor* highlights unconscious effects of 'priming',[69] and further reinforces the constraining nature of socio-cognitive processes on individuals. The notion of 'priming' refers to the enhanced tendency of people who have been recently exposed to a certain stimulus to perceive certain objects (or enhancing the prospect for adopting a certain interpretation of those objects).[70] Recent literature emphasizes the influence of an exposure to certain stimuli on the activation of certain mental representations (eg some categories), often outside conscious awareness. Individuals may be primed by rhetorical elements, imagery, and/or subconscious stimuli. Thus, the activation of social representations (eg stereotypes) and their application are more likely to follow exposure to various types of information.[71] Certain *cultural* features (eg cues relating to a group orientation or gender classification) may prime individuals and influence their propensity to activate some social categories and stereotypes.[72]

The increasing attention devoted to the influence of socio-cultural factors on mental processes (particularly with regard to unconscious processes) tends to highlight the *constraining effects* of socio-cultural patterns on individual thoughts and behaviour, and inclines to diminish the significance of human agency in social life. This inclination in social cognitive literature supports a shift towards the structural pole of the agency–structure continuum. The impact of this changing conception of the relations between individuals and social groups on international criminal law is addressed in Section IV(ii).

(ii) *The positivist—interpretative continuum*: Sociological streams may also be classified according to their positivist or interpretative orientation. The *positivist approach* (notably embraced in Comte's early writings) views the social world as an objective and argues that the sociological discipline is similar to the natural sciences. Proponents of this tradition advocate the application of scientific methods in exploring social phenomena, similar to those adopted in positivist social science. Such scientific analysis should be open to objective enquiry, involving testing

[69] See eg Fiske and Taylor (n 3) 16; Augoustinos and others (n 2) 80–81. See also Dehaene (n 11) 56–58.

[70] Saul Kassin, Steven Fein and Hazel Rose Markus, *Social Psychology* (7th edn, Wadsworth 2008) 116. Masson defines 'priming' as the phenomenon whereby the identification of an object (or word) can be enhanced either through the presentation of a related stimulus or through a prior processing episode involving that object or word. Michael EJ Masson, 'Priming, Cognitive Psychology of', *International Encyclopaedia of the Social & Behavioural Sciences* (2001) 12042.

[71] Daniel C Molden, 'Understanding Priming Effects in Social Psychology' (2014) 32 *Social Cognition* 1, 3; Kunda (n 3) 22. On priming and the activation of schemata and collective memory see DiMaggio (n 36) 274–75. See also Fiske and Taylor (n 3) 35–37. Carl Palmer, 'Which Cues Matter? The Implications of Stereotype Appeals and Explicit Predispositions for Group-Centric Issue Opinion' (2010) 3 SSRN http://ssrn.com/abstract=1664772 (accessed 31 August 2020). See also Fiske and Taylor (n 3) 78. On the impact of priming on the automatic activation of gender stereotypes see eg Irene Blair and Mahzarin Banaji, 'Automatic Stereotyping' (1996) 70 *Journal of Personality and Social Psychology* 1142.

[72] See eg Beth Morling and Takahiko Masuda, 'Social Cognition in Real Worlds: Cultural Psychology and Social Cognition' in Susan Fiske and C Neil Macrae (eds), *Sage Handbook of Social Cognition* (Sage Publications 2012) 434, 440–41. As to priming and gender representations see Augoustinos and others (n 2) 80.

hypotheses by empirical observations, quantitative measurement, requiring value neutrality, and separation between values and scientific examination.[73]

The *interpretative* tradition in sociology (prominently developed by Weber) focuses on explaining social phenomena through the understanding which individuals adopt in a particular social context. This approach also emphasizes the difference between natural and human sciences but argues that sociology is distinctively concerned with humans engaging in social life. Social reality is not viewed here as an object exterior to humans but rather as a *subjectively* lived construct, and humans are considered as being engaged in constant mental activity; they subjectively experience everyday reality, and mentally internalize that reality. Interpretative sociology regards meaning and action as the prime objects of sociology. The interpretations that individuals attach to social patterns are important because they significantly influence behaviour.[74] Max Weber viewed sociology itself as 'a science which attempts the interpretative understanding of social action in order thereby to arrive at a causal explanation of its course and effects'.[75] From this perspective, sociology aims to study social behaviour by interpreting individuals' actions in the social world and the ways in which individuals attribute meaning to social phenomena. Thus, for Weber, social action itself occurs 'when and in so far as the acting individual attaches a subjective meaning to it'.[76]

Social cognitive research work often employs scientific methods but it clearly diverges from the positive-objective conception of social behaviour. The above-discussed assumptions of social cognitive studies include the suppositions that people do *not* objectively sense their environment, that humans' cognitive mechanisms (eg attention, categorization etc.) actively process information—inter alia, according to personal moods and various socio-cultural factors. This point of departure in social cognitive literature points out that sensory objects are not self-evident and that they constantly undergo interpretation and meaning construction.[77] The inter-subjective interpretative nature of many cognitive processes arises, for example, from studies showing that socio-cognitive patterns vary not only across cultures but also within cultures; eg according to historical periods and in accordance with social roles (like gender). These different inter-subjective approaches to reality are also reflected in common cognitive *biases* shared by

[73] Michele Dillon, *Introduction to Sociological Theory* (2nd edn, Blackwell 2010) 21; Martin Hollis, *The Philosophy of Social Science* (CUP 2011) 41–43; Ritzer and Stepnisky (n 63) 108; 'Positivism' in John Scott (ed), *Oxford Dictionary of Sociology* (4th edn, OUP 2014) 579–81; 'Positivism' in *Penguin Dictionary of Sociology* (4th edn, Penguin 2000) 269–70.

[74] 'Interpretation (interpretive sociology)' in Oxford Dictionary of Sociology (n 73) 368; Dillon (n 73) 21–22; Malcolm Waters, *Modern Sociological Theory* (Sage Publications 1994) 12, 15; Norman Denzin, *Symbolic Interactionism and Cultural Studies* (Wiley-Blackwell 1992) 49, 25; Véronique Mottier, 'The Interpretive Turn: History, Memory, and Storage in Qualitative Research' (2005) 6 *Forum: Qualitative Social Research*.

[75] Max Weber, *The Theory of Social and Economic Organization* (Martino Fine 1947) 88.

[76] ibid 21, 88.

[77] See eg Friedman (n 7) 4–5.

different communities.[78] Thus, social cognitive literature distinctly highlights that people perceive and process information in subjective and inter-subjective manners—clearly signalling a shift towards the interpretative pole of the positivist–interpretative continuum.

(iii) The consensus—conflict continuum: The third prominent dichotomy in sociological theory relates to the emphasis placed by social theorists on the consensual or conflictual features of society and its stratification. Social conflict theorists argue that societies are marked by inequalities, and that social groups struggle to gain control over various resources. Thus, politically and culturally dominant groups impose their will on subordinate groups in society. Such approaches underline the ubiquitous nature of power relations and exploitation in societies. From this perspective, the social order is based on manipulation and control by dominant groups. Consensual theories downplay the role of social struggles and power relations, tending to stress the integrated conception of society as well as the harmonious effect of shared values. The latter approaches underline the importance of consensus over basic values as essential for a stable and harmonious society.[79]

One of the main fields in social cognitive literature[80] addresses inter-group relations and identity, paying significant attention to prejudice, stereotypes, and discrimination between members of different groups. Inter-group scholarship underlines that people who identified with social groups are prone to develop mistrustful attitudes and discriminatory practices vis-à-vis members of outgroups. This discriminatory tendency also exists in settings characterized by the absence of any history of intergroup contact or conflict.[81] People belonging to a certain group (eg an ethnic group) tend to harmonize their beliefs with those held by most members of the group.[82] One of the significant explanations for inter-group bias and discrimination lies in power differentiation and competition between social groups. Social groups are often embedded in hierarchical relations, with some groups accorded more power than others. The need for self-esteem and positive distinctiveness interacts with enduring power differences, and it affects the degree of inter-group discrimination and the forms it takes.[83] Some scholars argue that numerous inter-group conflicts have their basis in competition for power and scarce resources (such as money or natural resources).[84]

[78] See section II(iii) above.

[79] On the consensus–conflict debate see Ritzer and Stepnisky (n 63) 237–38; Giddens and Sutton (n 63) 91; Banakar and Traverse (n 61) 3–4; Waters (n 74) 219–20.

[80] Issues relating to inter-group prejudice and discrimination are mostly developed in social psychology literature on identity; and sociological identity literature is more concerned with other (less-conflictual) features of identity groups. On cognitive conflicts in cognitive sociological literature see eg Zerubavel (n 5) 12, 22, 44, 97; DiMaggio (n 36) 271, 275–77; Rydgren (n 13) 225.

[81] See Section II (vi) above.

[82] Rydgren (n 13) 236 and see the references therein.

[83] See Brewer (n 40) 55 and see the references therein. See also Stephan and Stephan (n 41) 39. On social dominance orientation and its correlation with biases see Fiske and Taylor (n 3) 309–10.

[84] Stephan and Stephan (n 41) 144 and see the references therein.

Regardless of the sources of inter-group prejudice and discrimination, discriminatory treatment is often sustained by biased cognitive processes[85] that constitute fertile ground for further social tensions and conflicts. Inter-group relations literature is mainly concerned with internal struggles (eg along religious, racial, or gender lines) but conflicts are occasionally linked to international conflicts.[86] This literature foregrounds tensions, discrimination and struggles between social groups and suggests a change towards the conflictual pole of the consensus–conflict continuum.

As discussed below, some of the above-cited trends in sociological theory can affect the ways we conceive international law and may suggest certain changes in this field.

IV A Socio-Cognitive Perspective on International Criminal Law

The formation, interpretation, and implementation of international law interact with diverse socio-cognitive processes. International legal rules, for example, are affected by and influence culturally-infused schemata, notably the framing of certain global threats (such as climate change)[87] during negotiations or classification of social groups (such as 'states' or 'indigenous groups'). Similarly, the development of new international legal concepts is influenced by patterns of language[88] and prevalent metaphors.[89] Socio-cognitive processes often influence the interpretation of international legal instruments. And as amply shown in recent behavioural international law scholarship, international legal decision-makers are susceptible to the influence of certain cognitive biases.[90]

Significant changes in social theory may herald changes in international legal theory, and such changes may influence, for example, the interpretation of international legal instruments. To illustrate such potential changes, this section addresses a potential change of the above-cited socio-cognitive studies for the way we conceive international criminal law, and suggests some changes in the interpretation of the Statute of the International Criminal Court (ICC).

[85] Hirsch, 'Cognitive Sociology' (n 56) 1331 and see the references therein.

[86] See eg Brewer (n 40) 111 ff; Rydgren (n 13) 235 ff.

[87] See Anne van Aaken and Jan-Philip Elm, 'Framing in and Through International Law', ch 2 in this volume, section III(1).

[88] See eg Jacob Livingston Slosser and Mikael Rask Madsen, 'Institutionally Embodied Law: Cognitive Linguistics and the Making of International Law', ch 4 in this volume, at section II.

[89] See eg Harlan Grant Cohen, 'Metaphors of International Law', ch 12 in this volume, at section II.

[90] Anne van Aaken, 'Behavioral International Law and Economics' 55 *Harvard International Law Journal* (2014) 421, 439 ff; Tomer Broude, 'Behavioral International Law' (2015) 163 *University of Pennsylvania Law Review* 1099, 1136 ff; Susan D Franck and others, 'Inside the Arbitrator's Mind' (2017) 66 *Emory Law Journal* 1117, 1176.

(i) *International criminal law as multi-socio-cognitive field*: International criminal law is intertwined with socio-cultural issues[91] and international criminal law legal proceedings are often infused with socio-cognitive processes. International criminal law is inherently nested in multicultural settings. National criminal legal systems occasionally exhibit certain multicultural features, but the intensity of such factors is significantly higher in international criminal law. The enhanced multicultural character of international criminal proceedings is conspicuous, for example, in the different cultural backgrounds of the members of the staff of tribunals (including judges) as well as in inter-cultural features that often characterize interactions between defendants and judges. International criminal law tribunals' particular vulnerability to inter-cultural misunderstandings pertains not only to cultural differences (such as different norms) but also to socio-cognitive differences relating, for example, to fact-finding.

On the socio-cognitive level, international criminal law judges are frequently required to process volumes of information and selectively focus on the 'relevant' facts, attaching particular meaning to defendants' behaviour (including interpreting a speech in a different language).[92] Assessing the credibility of witnesses is particularly challenging in multicultural trials, and judges occasionally need, for example, to detect the meaning of a gaze (direct or averted) of a witness socialized in a different cultural system.[93] Although the involvement of distinct socio-cognitive systems is visible to some observers, it may constitute a 'blind spot' for some international criminal law decision-makers who habitually function in a multi-cultural environment.

The multi-socio-cognitive perspective on international criminal law is consistent with the pluralist approach to international law[94] but it turns the spotlight

[91] On diverse interactions between ICL and cultural issues see eg WL Cheah, 'International Criminal Law and Culture' in Kevin Heller and others (eds), *Oxford Handbook of International Criminal Law* (OUP 2020) 748; Gregor Maučec, 'The Power of Culture and Judicial Decision-Making at the International Criminal Court' in Julie Fraser and Brianne McGonigle Leyh (eds), *Intersection of Law and Culture at the International Criminal Court* (Edward Elgar Publishing 2020); Jessica Almqvist, 'The Impact of Cultural Diversity on International Criminal Proceedings' (2006) 4 *Journal of International Criminal Justice* 745; Ilias Bantekas, 'The Anthropological Dimension of International Crimes and International Criminal Justice' in I Bantekas, E Mylonaki (eds), *Criminological Approaches to International Criminal Law* (CUP 2014) 240.

[92] On ascertaining the meaning of speeches by the International Criminal Court for Rwanda see Richard Ashby Wilson, 'Expert Evidence on Trial: Social Researchers in the International Criminal Courtroom' (2016) 43 *American Ethnologist* 730, 735–37. See also Maučec (n 91) 14–16.

[93] On the perception of eye contact by people from different cultural backgrounds see Jari K Hietanen, 'Eye Contact Perception in the West and East: A Cross-Cultural Study' (2015) 10(2) *PLoS One* 1. On the social context of direct gaze see Antonia F de C Hamilton, 'Gazing at Me: The Importance of Social Meaning in Understanding Direct-Gaze Cues' (2016) 371 *Philosophical Transactions of The Royal Society B Biological Sciences* 1, 3 https://royalsocietypublishing.org/doi/pdf/10.1098/rstb.2015.0080 (accessed on 31 August 2020).

[94] For a perceptive discussion on the pluralist approach to international law see Andrea Bianchi, *International Legal Theories: An Inquiry into Different Ways of Thinking* (OUP 2016) 227–45. On pluralism in international criminal law see Elies van Sliedregt and Sergey Vasiliev (eds), *'Pluralism' in International Criminal Law* (OUP 2014) 3.

onto the deeper socio-cognitive dimension of this approach. The pluralist perspective on international law prominently refers to the plurality of legal orders (both state-based and non-state-based rules) and social norms applying to a particular behaviour.[95] The socio-cognitive conception of international criminal law highlights that people involved in international criminal proceedings are socialized into different sets of socio-cognitive patterns (such as norms of attention or culturally-infused schemata) and are commonly pressured to conform with these cognitive patterns. Some of these invisible patterns seep into people's deeper cognitive system (eg through language) and are involved in the construction of lenses through which they (defendants, judges etc.) perceive and interpret reality. These socio-cognitive effects are occasionally overlooked by some actors who routinely participate in international criminal law proceedings.

(ii) *Socio-cognitive constraints and employing multi-focal lens*: The considerable emphasis which international criminal law doctrine places on *individual* liability implicitly assumes a substantial measure of human agency and free will;[96] and it stands in contrast to the growing realization that individuals are often deeply influenced by socio-cognitive structures prevailing in their social groups.[97] Social cognitive studies concerning the limited choice available to humans bring to the fore the dilemma concerning the role of the defendant's socio-cognitive background at the sentencing stage.

Diverse socio-cognitive differences can be involved in the commission of international crimes and we bring here only three brief examples. Launching an attack where it would knowingly cause excessive incidental loss of life or injury to civilians (compared to the anticipated military advantage) constitutes a war crime.[98] Military commanders' calculations of the expected collateral damage to civilians (and civilian targets) are susceptible to the influence of several cognitive heuristics, prominently 'availability bias'.[99] The notion of 'availability heuristic' refers to the tendency of people to judge probabilities based on how quickly instances or risks come to their mind.[100] Accordingly, people's assessments of probabilities are

[95] See eg Paul Schiff Berman, A Pluralist Approach to International Law (2007) 32 *Yale Journal of International Law* 301, 302; Bianchi (n 94) 227.

[96] See eg Carsten Stahn, *A Critical Introduction to International Criminal Law* (CUP 2019) 157, 419–20. On the move from state civil agency to individual criminal agency in international criminal law see Kirsten Ainley, 'Responsibility for Atrocity: Individual Criminal Agency and the International Criminal Court' in John T Parry (ed), *Evil, Law and the State: Perspectives on State Power and Violence (At the Interface/Probing the Boundaries)* (Rodopi BV 2006) 143, 144–46. On the links between free will and general criminal responsibility see Alan Brudner, *Punishment and Freedom: A Liberal Theory of Penal Justice* (OUP 2009) 59.

[97] See Section III(ii) above. For an insightful discussion on religiously driven harmful activities under Anglo-American *tort* law see Guido Calabresi, *Ideals, Beliefs, Attitudes, and the Law* (Syracuse University Press 1985) 47–53.

[98] Rome Statute of the International Criminal Court (adopted 17 July 1998, entered into force 1 July 2002) 2187 UNTS 90, art 8(2)(b)(iv).

[99] Luke A Whittemore, 'Proportionality Decision Making in Targeting: Heuristics, Cognitive Biases, and the Law' (2016) 7 *Harvard National Security Journal* 577, 619–20.

[100] Fiske and Taylor (n 3) 192; Kahneman (n 14) 138; ibid 619; Galotti (n 1) 315–17.

influenced, inter alia, by their prior experience, familiarity with or memories of previous events (influenced, eg by the mass media's coverage of certain events).[101] The latter factors and risk perceptions are likely to be affected, inter alia, by the particular decision-maker's distinctive culture concerning the specific risk.[102] Thus, proportionality assessments undertaken by different military commanders can be influenced by their distinctive cultural systems. The second example of socio-cognitive differences is related to crimes against humanity. Under certain circumstances, non-violent discriminatory practices against people belonging to an ethnic or religious group is considered a crime against humanity.[103] As noted previously, such discriminatory treatment often involves inter-group categorization and negative stereotypes predominating in the defendant's social group,[104] and those socio-cognitive patterns may be involved in the commission of certain crimes against humanity. The final example concerns directing attacks against a hospital bearing the required distinctive emblem (which constitutes a war crime).[105] Combatants from certain societies are not familiar with the meaning attached to legally-recognized emblems used to mark medical units (and the prominent ones are widely associated with religious symbols);[106] and such misunderstandings[107] may be involved in attacks on medical units.[108]

The increasing awareness to the constraining effects of socio-cognitive patterns on individuals (and the previously mentioned shift on the structure-agency continuum) sheds new light on appropriate punishment imposed on convicted persons. Recognizing the deeper influence of cultural patterns may attract enhanced attention to the relatively under-explored cultural defence[109] in international criminal law scholarship,[110] and bolster the case for its formal application regarding the

[101] See eg Fiske and Taylor (n 3) 192–94.

[102] Cass R Sunstein, 'Precautions against What: The Availability Heuristic and Cross-Cultural Risk Perception: Risk and the Law' (2005) 57 *Alabama Law Review* 75, 87–93.

[103] See ICC Statute (n 98) arts 7(1)(h) and 7(2)(g).

[104] On cognitive aspects involved in discrimination against disadvantaged groups see section II(v) above.

[105] ICC Statute (n 98) art 8(2)(b)(ix).

[106] See eg ICRC, Study on the Use of the Emblems (ICRC, 2001) 37 https://www.icrc.org/en/doc/assets/files/publications/icrc-001-4057.pdf (accessed 31 August 2020). IFRC, The Emblem Debatehttps://www.ifrc.org/en/who-we-are/the-movement/emblems/the-emblem-debate/ (accessed 21 February 2021).

[107] Such mistakes are more prone to happen following changing emblems; ibid 37.

[108] According to Triffterer and Ambos, the defence of mistake of fact (under art 32 of the ICC Statute) may apply to such situation. Otto Triffterer and Kai Ambos (eds), *The Rome Statute of the International Criminal Court: A Commentary* (3rd edn, Beck/Hart Publishing 2016) 1170. Where this defence is not applied to the particular defendant, the tribunal may consider the defendant's relating socio-cognitive background and address the legally recognized emblem as a mitigating factor during the sentencing stage.

[109] For a concise discussion on arguments for and against the cultural defence in international criminal law see Noelle Higgins, *Cultural Defences at the International Criminal Court* (Routledge 2018) 10–19; Alison Dundes Renteln, 'Cultural Rights and Culture Defense: Cultural Concerns' in *International Encyclopaedia of the Social & Behaviour Science, vol 5* (1st edn, Elsevier, 2001) 491, 492–93.

[110] On the scant attention paid in international criminal law scholarship to the cultural defence see Higgins (n 109) 2. See also Alison Dundes Renteln, 'Cultural Defenses in International Criminal

punishment. While a similar question arises in domestic criminal legal systems, socio-cognitive differences are particularly intensified in international criminal law.[111] The term 'cultural defence' is used here in the narrow sense, referring to socio-cognitive considerations raised by the defendant at the sentencing stage. In light of the intensified conception of socially-constrained individuals, we are of the view that where it is credibly proven that the particular crime directly involves distinctive socio-cognitive patterns prevailing in the defendant's community—it is desirable that international criminal law tribunals adopt a broad interpretation of some provisions of the ICC law[112] and consider the socio-cultural background of the particular defendant as a mitigating or aggravating factor at the sentencing stage.

The rationales for punishment in international criminal law jurisprudence are mixed and the principal justifications mentioned in case law are deterrence, personal retribution, public condemnation ('expressivism'), and rehabilitation.[113] International criminal law tribunals generally consider the objectives of deterrence and retribution as the primary objectives of punishment.[114] The growing realization that cultures significantly constrain humans' default cognitive systems involved in the commission of certain crimes weakens the justification for personal retribution, and may reduce the punishment in certain cases. The constraining force of socio-cognitive processes, however, does not diminish the significance of the other rationales for criminal punishment, prominently deterrence. Thus, where international criminal law tribunals are convinced that the objective of deterrence is paramount, they may legitimately take into account the defendant's distinctive socio-cognitive background but impose the full penalty (eg with regard to crimes involving mass atrocities or violent persecution). Still, even in the latter cases, where socio-cognitive biases that are directly related to the crime dominate the defendant's cultural system, the element of retribution in the sentencing formula

Tribunals: A Preliminary Consideration of the Issues' (2011) 18 *Southwestern Journal of International Law* 267, 274–75.

[111] See section IV(i) above.

[112] The prominent provisions of the ICC law relating to sentencing are art 78(1) of the Statute, and r 145 of the Rules of Procedures and Evidence. ICC Statute (n 98) art 78(1) provides: 'In determining the sentence, the Court shall, in accordance with the Rules of Procedure and Evidence, take into account such factors as the gravity of the crime and the individual circumstances of the convicted person.' On art 78(1) of the ICC Statute and r 145 of the Rules of Procedure and Evidence in this context see Higgins (n 109) 36–38.

[113] Sergey Vasiliev, 'Punishment Rationales in International Criminal Jurisprudence: Two Readings of a Non-Question' (2019) in Florian Jeßberger and Julia Geneuss (eds), *Why Punish Perpetrators of Mass Atrocities? Purposes of Punishment in International Criminal Law* (CUP 2020) 45, 54–72; Mirko Bagaric and John Morss, 'International Sentencing Law: In Search of a Justification and Coherent Framework' (2006) 6 *International Criminal Law Review* 191, 206ff; Barbora Hola, 'International Sentencing' in *Encyclopedia of Criminology and Criminal Justice, vol 5* (Springer 2014) 2643–47.

[114] See eg Vasiliev (n 113) 62, 70, 73; Hola (n 113) 2648.

is weakened. As Blackmore explains with regard to the concern that realizing the absence of free will would undermine moral responsibility:

> Rather than punishing people because they are bad, we would ask what good it would be. We might still lock people up to deter them and others from committing crimes or to protect everyone else, and such a basis for law would arguably be fairer and more compassionate.[115]

Since the rationale for considering the defendant's cultural background lies in the significant constraining nature of certain socio-cognitive patterns, the punishment can be either mitigated or aggravated, according to the particular circumstances. For example, the socio-cognitive background might constitute an aggravating factor where the defendant exercised significant measure of agency, diverged from socio-cognitive patterns prevailing in her/his social groups, and took an active role in the development of the diverging socio-cognitive pattern facilitating the particular crime (eg inter-group prejudice and hostility).

Persistent overlooking of socio-cognitive variations between different defendants or marginalizing these differences at the sentencing stage can be explained (at least partly) by the 'fundamental attribution error'[116] and it conveys an assumption of cultural uniformity.[117] The latter assumption may reflect either tacit or strategic inattention[118] by judges. Practical or official ignorance of perpetrators' distinctive socio-cognitive background can also be explained by 'representative heuristic' or 'availability heuristic' (discussed above) among judges; indicating their tendency to generate inferences or assessments based on the apparent resemblance of the particular criminal event (or expected risk) to their own cultural representative category of criminal events or risks.[119] Rather than implicitly relying on a single cultural context and overlooking socio-cognitive heterogeneity, the

[115] Susan Blackmore, *Consciousness: A Very Short Introduction* (2nd edn, OUP 2017) 98.

[116] The 'fundamental attribution error' refers to explaining other people's behaviour by overestimating the influence of other individuals' stable traits, and underestimating the influence of external factors (such societal norms or socialization) A large empirical literature demonstrates that the fundamental attribution error is stronger in Westerns than in non-Western cultures; Fiske and Taylor (n 3) 166, 179–81. See also Kassin (n 70) 107 ff.

[117] As Cotterrell explains (while discussing the 'cultural' defence): "If law is gendered, the parallel claim that law is 'cultured', in the sense of being powerfully shaped by certain cultural assumptions, may raise even more difficult practical problems for legal regulation. *This is because law has typically assumed the uniformity of culture and so avoided considering it. But in contemporary conditions of considerable . . . cultural diversity such a position may no longer be tenable* (emphasis added). Roger Cotterrell, *Law, Culture and Society* (Ashgate 2006) 100.

[118] For a discussion on the views of Goffman and Bourdieu regarding tacit and strategic inattention see Brekhus (n 20) 24–28; Zerubavel (n 12) 22–23.

[119] On the link between cultural factors and representative heuristic see Roy R Spina and others, 'Cultural Differences in the Representativeness Heuristic' (2010) 36(5) *Personality and Social Psychology Bulletin* 583, 593–96. On the link between availability heuristic and cultural systems see Sunstein (n 102) 87–93.

multi socio-cognitive reality in international criminal law calls for employing a multi-focal lens and attending to the differences between distinct socio-cognitive systems.[120]

IV Concluding Remarks

The image of international legal decision-makers emerging from socio-cognitive studies is significantly different from the prevalent view among diverse actors operating in this field. The socio-cognitive perspective on international law underlines that sensory objects are not 'objectives' or self-evident, and that their internalization in legal decision-makers' minds always involves mediating mental processes (such as perception, categorization, and interpretation). Limited cognitive resources available to such decision-makers (including military commanders, national decision-makers, or international adjudicators) often lead them to utilize heuristic shortcuts (although occasionally involving some biases). These cognitive processes and heuristics are frequently influenced by socio-cultural patterns (such as norms of attention or stereotypes) prevailing in the decision-makers' social groups, and often below their conscious level. The increasing awareness to the constraining influence of default socio-cognitive systems on individual decision-makers tends to diminish the significance of human agency in real social life situations. On the theoretical level, the latter tendency in socio-cognitive literature supports a shift towards the structural pole of the agency–structure continuum.

Equipped with insights drawn from socio-cognitive and sociological theoretical literatures, this chapter explored the field of international criminal law, emphasizing its intensified multi-cognitive character and the significant effects of socio-mental patterns on defendants and additional actors in this sphere (such as adjudicators and prosecutorial staff). This discussion suggests that where it is credibly proven that the particular crime directly involves a distinctive socio-cognitive pattern predominant in the defendant's community, it is desirable that the tribunal considers the defendant's socio-cognitive background as a mitigating or aggravating factor at the sentencing stage. Future studies in this field may explore additional socio-cognitive patterns and their interactions with diverse international legal rules and concepts, including international arbitration, state responsibility, and human rights. Such studies may broaden our understanding of international legal behaviour and offer some legal strategies to cope with some new challenges faced by contemporary international law.

[120] On multi-focal attention and its benefits see Zerubavel (n 12) 75–77.

2

Framing in and through Public International Law

Anne van Aaken[*] *and Jan-Philip Elm*

I Introduction

The rational choice assumption, widely used in international relations and international legal scholarship, stipulates that rational actors should and do make the same decision independent of the way the decision problem is framed. Not doing so would be contrary to the independence and the invariance axioms of rational choice theory as a result of inconsistent decision-making,[1] and challenge the objectivity of public international law. In contrast, social psychology has a long tradition in acknowledging that 'everyday human behavior, especially social behavior, becomes explainable and predictable only when we know, or can accurately guess, the subjective interpretations and beliefs of the people involved'.[2] The recognition of the relativity of judgment has also found support in decision-making theory because the relativist view in psychology—usually studied in decision-making theory under the heading of 'framing effects'—has been shown to have objective (ie systematic) behavioural and motivational consequences.[3] Frames function as psychological lenses through which people make sense of each other, the issues they face, and the choice options available to them.[4] There are arguably no 'right' or 'wrong' frames, but which frame bears an effect has important implications for how individuals ultimately behave.[5]

* I gratefully acknowledge the support of the Alexander-von-Humboldt Foundation.

1 For an introduction into the von Neumann-Morgenstern utility theorem see John von Neumann and Oskar Morgenstern, *Theory of Games and Economic Behavior* (Princeton University Press 1944). Whereas the independence axiom holds that a choice is independent of irrelevant alternatives, the invariance axiom holds that the ranking of choice options is invariant to alternative but logically equivalent ways of eliciting the same preference.

2 Lee Ross and Richard E Nisbett, *The Person and the Situation: Perspectives of Social Psychology* (McGraw-Hill 1991) 60.

3 ibid 63.

4 Deepak Malhotra, *Negotiating the Impossible: How to Break Deadlocks and Resolve Ugly Conflicts (Without Money or Muscle)* (Berrett-Koehler Publishers 2016) 11.

5 ibid.

Anne van Aaken and Jan-Philip Elm, *Framing in and through Public International Law* In: *International Law's Invisible Frames*. Edited by: Andrea Bianchi and Moshe Hirsch, Oxford University Press. © Anne van Aaken and Jan-Philip Elm 2021. DOI: 10.1093/oso/9780192847539.003.0003

Some framing effects occur 'when different ways of describing the same choice problem change the choices that people make, even though the underlying information and choice remain essentially the same'.[6] This obviously plays a role when a decision-maker faces an explicit choice. For example, experimental research shows that individuals make different choices depending on whether the very same choice options are framed in terms of either gains or losses.[7] Yet framing also plays a more subtle role when a given problem description influences the decision-maker's—mostly unconscious—choice of how to address a broader problem, that is, by making certain aspects of an information set more salient, to the detriment of others. For example, describing a problem of hate speech as an issue of free speech leads individuals to primarily base their opinions on free speech as opposed to public safety considerations (even though they are essentially not forced to do so).[8] Whereas the former can be referred to as 'equivalency' framing, which includes gain-loss framing effects as widely studied in behavioural law and economics, the latter is dubbed 'issue' (or 'emphasis') framing and emerges from research in political communication.[9]

Framing effects—both in terms of equivalency and issue framing—address the discrepancy between normative claims and positive observations in the study of judgment and choice: whereas normative analysis is concerned with the nature of rationality and the logic of decision-making as it should be, positive analysis is concerned with individuals' beliefs and preferences as they (really) are.[10] On the one hand, the standard model of rational choice theory proceeds from the simple requirement that observed choices ought to be consistent with each other. Framing effects, on the other hand, amount to a violation of the axioms of rational choice theory. Experimental evidence is supportive of the existence of framing effects.

The independence and invariance axioms—and with it the objectivity of public international law—has long been a mantra in international legal scholarship. Framing effects therefore shine a new light on the study of public international law. On the one hand, both equivalency and issue framing bear the potential of triggering preference reversals in individual choice, which has important implications for several areas in public international law, most notably

[6] Richard Cookson, 'Framing Effects in Public Goods Experiments' (2000) 3 *Experimental Economics* 55.

[7] See Daniel Kahneman and Amos Tversky, 'Prospect Theory: An Analysis of Decision under Risk' (1979) 47 *Econometrica* 263.

[8] See Thomas E Nelson, Rosalee A Clawson, and Zoe M Oxley, 'Media Framing of a Civil Liberties Conflict and Its Effect on Tolerance' (1997) 91 *American Political Science Review* 567.

[9] See James N Druckman, 'Political Preference Formation: Competition, Deliberation and the (Ir) relevance of Framing Effects' (2004) 98 *American Political Science Review* 672.

[10] Daniel Kahneman and Asmos Tversky, 'Choices, Values, and Frames' (1984) 39 *American Psychologist* 341.

international adjudication. On the other hand, framing effects may also change individuals' beliefs about others' beliefs in strategic interactions (such as international treaty-making), which is of high interest to international legal scholars. Given that framing effects cannot be captured by standard game theory as conventionally used in rationalist international scholarship,[11] those who rely exclusively on rationalist approaches to public international law are missing important phenomena likely to influence outcomes. Challenges to the rational choice assumption such as framing effects have only recently entered the research agenda of a few international legal scholars.[12] Yet at the same time framing effects have been greatly impactful in the study of political science (both at the domestic and international level) and appear to confirm long-held constructivist views in international relations theory.[13] International legal scholars, policy-makers, and practising lawyers are therefore bound to benefit from studying framing effects as it refines our understanding of the mechanics underlying much of public international law.

In this chapter, we examine the implications of framing effects for preference and belief formation, shedding light on knowledge production processes and social cognition in specific settings in public international law.[14] The first part of the chapter sketches out the experimental evidence of equivalency and issue framing, shows how it has already been incorporated both explicitly and implicitly in neighbouring disciplines to public international law, and untangles the difference between preference reversals and a change in beliefs (section II). Without claiming to be exhaustive, the second part (section III) identifies four typical situations in public international law where framing effects play an important role in social cognition and knowledge production processes: (1) international negotiations ('how law comes into being'), (2) international adjudication ('how law is interpreted and shaped'), (3) global performance indicators ('how soft law shapes behavior'), and (4) norm framing ('how law shapes solutions to problems'). The last part concludes (section IV).

[11] For a discussion on the use of standard game theory in public international law and international relations theory see eg Duncan Snidal, 'The Game Theory of International Politics' (1985) 38 *World Politics* 25.

[12] See eg Anne van Aaken, 'Behavioral International Law and Economics' (2014) 55 *Harvard International Law Journal* 421 (2014); Tomer Broude, 'Behavioral International Law' (2015) 163 *University of Pennsylvania Law Review* 1099; Eyal Zamir and Doron Teichman, *Behavioral Law and Economics* (OUP 2018) 423–31 with further references; see also Emilie M Hafner-Burton and others, 'The Behavioral Revolution and International Relations' (2017) 71 *International Organization* 1. For a discussion on the unit of analysis problem see Anne van Aaken and Tomer Broude, 'Introduction to Special Issue "The Psychology of International Law"' (2019) 30 *European Journal of International Law* 1225.

[13] *See* Anne van Aaken, 'An Experimental Approach to International Legal Theory' (2019) 30 *European Journal of International Law* 1237.

[14] See the introduction by Andrea Bianchi and Moshe Hirsch in this book.

II Evidence of Framing Effects

A Equivalency Framing

Gain-loss framing effects, arguably the best-known form of equivalency framing, originate from prospect theory.[15] Experimental evidence shows that perceived differences based on a change in the framing of the very same available choice options—that is, from gains to losses—can trigger preference reversals in choices made by individuals in violation of rationalist assumptions. When facing a given decision problem, individuals categorize available choice options as potential gains and losses in relation to a salient reference point (eg the status quo or expectations) and systematically pick either the risk-averse option when the decision problem is framed in terms of gains and the risk-seeking option when the decision problem is framed in terms of losses.[16] The underlying value function associated with prospect theory is sharply kinked at the reference point in the sense that it is concave in the domain of gains and convex in the domain of losses, while steeper for losses than for gains by factor of about two-to-one.[17] Simply put, a loss looms larger than an equivalent gain.

Insights from prospect theory have been used in political science scholarship under the heading of 'political psychology'. It has been studied in the context of voting and public opinion, political campaigning, policy-making, coalition bargaining, and a variety of other topics.[18] In the international realm, political psychologists have heavily drawn on prospect theory and associated gain-loss framing effects to formalize foreign policy-makers' decision-making.[19] They have examined how risk preferences vary as a function of whether foreign policy-makers face decision problems either framed in terms of gains or losses.[20] One the one hand, with respect to loss frames, political psychology claims that foreign policy-makers exhibit a tendency to adopt risk-seeking behaviour (eg by resorting to preemptive action) to prevent the deterioration of their international positions.[21] Prominent examples include the failed rescue mission of the American hostages in Iran under President Carter in 1980.[22] In the domain of gains, on the other hand, foreign

[15] See Kahneman and Tversky (n 7).

[16] ibid.

[17] ibid 279.

[18] See eg Jack S Levy, 'Applications of Prospect Theory to Political Science' (2003) 135 *Synthese* 215.

[19] James Davis (ed), *Psychology, Strategy and Conflict* (Routledge 2013).

[20] See eg Barbara Farnham, *Avoiding Losses, Taking Risks: Prospect Theory and International Conflict* (University of Michigan Press 1994); Rose McDermott, *Risk-Taking in International Politics: Prospect Theory in American Foreign Policy* (University of Michigan 1998).

[21] See eg Jack S Levy, 'Prospect Theory and International Relations: Theoretical Applications and Analytical Problems' (1992) 13 *Political Psychology* 286.

[22] See Rose McDermott, 'Prospect Theory in International Relations: The Iranian Hostage Rescue Mission' (1992) 13 *Political Psychology* 237; for further examples see Audrey McInerney, 'Prospect Theory and Soviet Policy Towards Syria, 1966–1967' (1992) 13 *Political Psychology* 265; Barbara

policy-makers appear more likely to accept the status quo.[23] Examples include NATO's hesitation in the 1990s to expand into parts of Eastern Europe in view of Russia's weaknesses.[24]

B Issue Framing

Issue framing refers to 'situations where, by emphasizing a subset of potentially relevant considerations, a speaker leads individuals to focus on these considerations when constructing their opinions'.[25] As compared to equivalency framing, issue framing does not involve logically equivalent ways of making the same statement and appears to occur via distinct psychological processes.[26] The latter is not a violation of the invariance axiom.[27] In contrast to earlier studies that explained issue framing in terms of either altering the content of beliefs or temporary priming,[28] it has been shown that issue framing influences opinion not primarily by targeting belief content, but rather by selectively enhancing the relative importance an individual assigns to specific beliefs with respect to the issue at hand.[29] Whether employed consciously or not, issue framing allows individuals to filter information to make some aspects of a broader problem more salient than others and therefore has the potential to change the way individuals deliberate and what they believe to be important,[30] particularly if promulgated by sources that individuals deem credible.[31] Furthermore, experimental research shows that the 'lens' through which subjects view a given question changes their attitudes on a broad range of related questions.[32] In international politics, for example, describing a protectionist

Farnham, 'Roosevelt and the Munich Crisis, Insights from Prospect Theory' (1992) 13 *Political Psychology* 205.

[23] James M Goldgeier and Philip E Tetlock, 'Psychology in International Relations Theory' (2001) 4 *Annual Review of Political Science* 71.

[24] ibid.

[25] See Druckman (n 9) 672; see also James N Druckman, 'On the Limits of Framing Effects: Who Can Frame?'(2001) 63 *Journal of Politics* 1041, 1042.

[26] Druckman (n 9) 672.

[27] ibid 673.

[28] See eg Shelly Chaiken, Wendy Wood, and Alice H Eagly, 'Principles of Persuasion' in E Tory Higgins and Arie W Kruglanski (eds), *Social Psychology: Handbook of Basic Principles* (Guilford Press 1996); Benjamin I Page and Robert Y Shapiro, *The Rational Public* (University of Chicago Press 1992); Donald R Kinder and Lynn M Sanders, *Divided by Color: Racial Politics and Democratic Ideals* (University of Chicago Press 1996) 174.

[29] See Thomas E Nelson and Zoe M Oxley, 'Issue Framing Effects on Belief Importance and Opinion' (1999) 61 *Journal of Politics* 1040; Thomas E Nelson, Zoe M Oxley, and Rosalee A Clawson, 'Toward a Psychology of Framing Effects' (1997) 19 *Political Behavior* 221.

[30] See Nelson and Oxley (n 29).

[31] See James N Druckman, 'Using Credible Advice to Overcome Framing Effects' (2001) 17 *Journal of Law, Economics, & Organization* 62.

[32] See Dennis Chong and James N Druckman, 'Framing Theory' (2007) 10 *Annual Review of Political Science* 103.

trade policy as an issue of national security by a head of state may cause people to base their opinions primarily on security threats as opposed to adverse economic implications.[33] Also, foreign engagements by the United States may be framed as either tools for promoting American interests abroad, a waste of taxpayers' money, or humanitarian gestures directed at the needy of the world.[34]

Issue framing has also been demonstrated in strategic interactions by showing that describing a prisoner's dilemma game in two different ways—either as a 'Wall Street Game' or 'Community Game'—had an influence on players' choices to either cooperate or defect, leading to more cooperation in the latter case as compared to the former.[35] Intuitively, this does not seem surprising: whereas 'Wall Street' emphasizes one's individual self-interest, 'community' is generally associated with the collective interest of a particular group. In other words, players' beliefs about other players' most probable choice to either defect or cooperate can be represented as a function of the label of the game.[36] Plenty of other examples are relevant to public international law: it has been shown that reframing an ultimatum game as a product of resource scarcity generates higher offers and fewer rejections,[37] reframing negotiations as occurring in an international setting rather than a business context increases cooperation,[38] and reframing a prisoner's dilemma as a trust game has equally been reported to enhance cooperation.[39] This is in stark contrast to what standard game theory would predict; that is, the Nash equilibrium in the prisoner's dilemma game is to defect. Both conditions in the experiments involved alternative wordings, but objectively equivalent material incentives. Experimental research thereby exposes the shortcomings associated with overemphasizing the role of material payoffs in human decision-making.

Rationalist international relations theory has already incorporated, albeit not explicitly through the lens of framing effects, the issue of changes in beliefs and how this affects behaviour. On the one hand, both realist and institutionalist scholars assume that international actors select the best option among available alternatives based on payoff structures that focus exclusively either on security concerns or material interests, respectively.[40] On the other hand, constructivists claim

[33] See Anne van Aaken and Jürgen Kurtz, 'Beyond Rational Choice: International Trade Law and the Behavioral Political Economy of Protectionism' (2019) 22 *J Journal of International Economic Law* 601.

[34] Nelson and Oxley (n 29) 1041.

[35] See Varda Liberman, Steven M Samuels, and Lee Ross, 'The Name of the Game: Predictive Power of Reputations Versus Situational Labels in Determining Prisoner's Dilemma Game Moves' (2004) 30 *Society of Personality and Social Psychology Bulletin* 1175; see also Tore Ellingsen and others, 'Social Framing Effects: Preferences or Beliefs?' (2012) 76 *Games and Economic Behavior* 117.

[36] Liberman, Samuels, and Ross (n 35) 1182.

[37] See Colin F Camerer, *Behavioral Game Theory: Experiments in Strategic Interaction* (Princeton University Press 2003) 75.

[38] See Richard J Eiser and Kum-Kum Bhavnani, 'The Effect of Situational Meaning on the Behaviour of Subjects in the Prisoner's Dilemma Game' (1974) 4 *European Journal of Social Psychology* 93.

[39] See Brian Skyrms, *The Stag Hunt and the Evolution of Social Structure* (CUP 2004).

[40] Jeffry A Frieden, David A Lake, and Kenneth A Schultz, *World Politics: Interests, Interactions, Institutions* (3rd edn, WW Norton & Company 2016) xxviii.

that international institutions—conceptualized as interpretative frameworks—can be transformative as a result of defining identities and shaping action.[41] Unlike institutionalists, for example, constructivists depart from the overemphasis on material interests and focus on the causal effects of non-material aspects such as ideas, culture, and norms: 'what actors want is not fixed and predetermined, but a function of their culture, prevailing ideas, and identity, or the conception of who they are'.[42] Considering that constructivists treat belief formation as a function of external forces, elements such as learning effects, shared understanding, and social norms become important in determining the behaviour of international actors.[43] In particular, the language and rhetoric used to construct social reality—that is, the framing of beliefs—are essential to predict outcomes in strategic settings.

C Preference Reversals versus a Change in Beliefs

Whereas preferences reflect what individuals want (to increase their utility), beliefs relate to what individuals think (about others' beliefs and actions). In the context of strategic interactions, beliefs center on players' beliefs about other players' choices, which then again depend on the latter players' beliefs about the former players' choices (and so forth). In standard game theory, the process of tracing back interdependent decision-making up to the very first choice to either cooperate or defect is commonly referred to as backward induction.[44] If players are assumed to be mere payoff maximizers, payoffs alone represent preferences. However, recent work in psychological game theory—supported by experimental evidence—shows that preferences also depend on features of beliefs about behaviour, which are determined by strategic analysis (eg kindness-based reciprocity).[45] In other words, players' beliefs about other players' choices are endogenous variables of the underlying strategic setting.[46] As a result, backward induction alone cannot be used to figure out a player's optimal choice independently of beliefs.[47] To make an expected-utility maximizing choice, a player thus must consult their beliefs about the probability of the other player to either cooperate or defect.[48] A given model of

[41] ibid xxxi; see also John G Ruggie, *Constructing the World Polity: Essays on International Politics* (Routledge 1998); Alexander Wendt, *Social Theory of International Politics* (CUP 1999).

[42] Frieden, Lake, and Schultz (n 40) xxxi.

[43] See eg Alexander Wendt, 'Constructing International Politics' (1995) 20 *International Security* 73.

[44] See eg Andreu Mas-Colell, Michael D Whinston, and Jerry R Green, *Microeconomic Theory* (OUP 1995) 277.

[45] See Pierpaolo Battigalli and Martin Dufwenberg, 'Belief-Dependent Motivations and Psychological Game Theory' (2020) CESifo Working Papers No 8285, 1, 3 https://www.cesifo.org/en/publikationen/2020/working-paper/belief-dependent-motivations-and-psychological-game-theory (accessed 21 June 2020).

[46] ibid.

[47] ibid 9.

[48] ibid.

standard game theory (such as the prisoner's dilemma game) can thereby be transformed into a psychological game by extending standard payoff-based utilities by belief-dependent utilities.[49] As the independence and invariance axioms also apply to belief formation, a player's beliefs about the probability of the other player to either cooperate or defect should not vary on how the underlying strategic setting is framed. Yet belief-based framing matters. As shown above, both equivalency framing and issue framing, which may reasonably be assumed to apply to strategic settings as much as to public opinion, bear the potential of triggering preference reversals and influencing individuals' beliefs about others' beliefs. The causal link between framing effects and resulting behaviour thereby becomes clear: framing effects cause a change in beliefs, and as beliefs are factored into preferences, beliefs, in turn, shape resulting behaviour.[50]

To gain a better understanding of how framing effects shape public international law, it is important to distinguish between preference reversals and a change in beliefs, even if difficult in practice. On the one hand, preference reversals (eg triggered by loss aversion) are more long-lasting and impact compliance with a given treaty, for example, to a larger extent. A change in beliefs, on the other hand, is a matter of interaction between international actors, such as whether other signatories to the treaty are expected to comply or not. In practice, both preference reversals and a change in beliefs may be intertwined.

III Applications in Public International Law

As compared to international legal scholarship, neighbouring disciplines differ in their research focus. Perhaps most importantly, both political psychology and most international relations scholarship attribute minor importance to international legal norms, if any. Furthermore, political psychology predominantly concentrates on international security concerns, which form only a small part of public international law. Also, whereas public international law has focused for a long time on collective unitary actors (eg sovereign states), political psychology uses prospect theory predominantly to explain the behaviour of single elite decision-makers. However, in view of the Cuban Missile Crisis, for example, it becomes clear that elite decision-makers (including former President Kennedy) do not make important decisions on their own.[51] A detailed overview of experimental research on group decision-making would go beyond the scope of this chapter. The issue, however, is crucial as behavioural decision theories are most germane

[49] ibid 4.

[50] Martin Dufwenberg, Simon Gächter, and Heike Hennig-Schmidt, 'The Framing of Games and the Psychology of Play' (2011) 73 *Games and Economic Behavior* 459; Battigalli and Dufwenberg (n 45).

[51] See eg Robert F Kennedy, *Thirteen Days: A Memoir of the Cuban Missile Crisis* (WW Norton & Company 1969).

'to situations in which an individual makes choices among several alternatives presented by an external environment'.[52] In general, how findings from behavioural and experimental research—primarily tested in the context of individual decision-making—unfold within groups greatly depends on a wide array of factors: group characteristics, decision-making procedures, the object of decision, and the decision task,[53] while furthermore taking into account that public international law offers many instances of advice-taking, which differs from group decision-making in subtle ways.[54] However, it has been shown that groups could be more vulnerable to framing effects than individuals.[55] Groups may amplify framing effects because of the high likelihood for initial framing effects at the individual level to interact, in potentially destructive ways, with processes of social influence.[56] Given the required fine-tuning of decision-making processes to counter framing effects, there is little reason to believe that governmental bodies form an exception.[57] Yet international courts may fare better in introducing counter-frames if they have diversity requirements, such as the International Court of Justice.[58] Diversity leverages counter-factual mindsets, which may foster deliberative efforts among international judges as well as arbitrators and thus reduce the influence of framing effects.[59]

In what follows, we identify four typical situations in public international law where framing effects play an important role in social cognition and knowledge production processes, which happen in those instances simultaneously—international

[52] van Aaken, 'Behavioral International Law and Economics' (n 12) 439.

[53] Christoph Engel, 'The Behaviour of Corporate Actors: How Much Can We Learn from the Experimental Literature?' (2010) 6 *Journal of Institutional Economics* 445; Steven R Elliot and Michael McKee, 'Collective Risk Decision in the Presence of Many Risks' (1995) 48 *Kyklos* 541; Patrick R Laughlin and Alan L Ellis, 'Demonstrability and Social Combination Processes on Mathematical Intellective Tasks' (1986) 22 *Journal of Experimental Social Psychology* 177; see also Zamir and Teichman (n 12) 120–24; Eyal Zamir, *Law, Psychology, and Morality: The Role of Loss Aversion* (OUP 2015) 37.

[54] Zamir and Teichman (n 12) 123–24.

[55] Norbert L Kerr, Robert J MacCoun, and Geffrey P Kramer, 'Bias in Judgment: Comparing Individuals and Groups' (1996) 103 *Psychological Review* 687; Timothy W McGuire, Sara Kiesler, and Jane Siegel, 'Group and Computer-Mediated Effects in Risk Decision Making' (1987) 52 *Journal of Personality and Social Psychology* 917; Paul W Paese, Mary Bieser, and Mark E Tubbs, 'Framing Effects and Choice Shifts in Group Decision Making' (1993) 56 *Organizational Behavior and Human Decision Processes* 149.

[56] Cass R Sunstein and Reid Hastie, *Wiser: Getting Beyond Groupthink to Make Groups Smarter* (Harvard Business Review Press 2015) 52, 75.

[57] ibid.

[58] See Statute of the International Court of Justice (26 June 1945) 33 UNTS 933 art. 9. More generally on diversity in international arbitration in comparison with courts: Susan Franck, 'The Diversity Challenge: Exploring the 'Invisible College' of International Arbitration' (2015) 53 *Columbia Journal of Transnational Law* 429.

[59] See Adam D Galinsky and Laura J Kray, 'From Thinking About What Might Have Been to Sharing What We Know: The Effects of Counterfactual Mind-Sets on Information Sharing Groups' (2004) 40 *Journal of Experimental Social Psychology* 606; Laura J Kray and Adam D Galinsky, 'The Debiasing Effect of Counterfactual Mind-Sets: Increasing the Search for Disconfirmatory Information in Group Decisions' (2003) 91 *Organizational Behavior and Human Decision Processes* 69; see also Jan-Philip Elm, 'Behavioral Insights into International Arbitration: An Analysis of How to De-Bias Arbitrators' (2016) 27 *American Review of International Arbitration* 125–27.

negotiations, international adjudication, global performance indicators, and norm framing—pointing out whether it refers rather to equivalency or issue framing.

A How Law Comes into Being: International Negotiations

Much of public international law comes into being through negotiations between sovereign states. International negotiations thereby primarily address legal processes that underlie the creation of substantive public international law. In so doing, international negotiations become critical for both social cognition and knowledge production processes at the international level. The influence of framing effects in international negotiations is therefore of utmost importance in understanding the creation of public international law, in particular in the domain of treaty-making. At the same time, the existence of framing effects also implies the need for a different kind of knowledge production: the development and dissemination of behaviourally informed negotiation practices.

It has been shown that actively manipulating the setting of the negotiation—that is, by framing each negotiator's problem description either in terms of gains or losses—resulted in different outcomes.[60] Whereas negotiators whose problem description was framed in terms of losses showed little willingness to make concessions, negotiators in the positive frame condition reached more successful outcomes.[61] These findings suggest that negotiating parties tend to become risk-seeking if they enter the negotiation process considering what they have to lose while they could just as well reach a mutually beneficial compromise by primarily focusing on what they could gain. However, even though the previous set of findings is good news for integrative settings that aim at maximizing joint surplus, public international law is nevertheless also prone to distributive concerns. In these situations, negatively framed negotiators appear to outperform their positively framed peers.[62] As framing effects generally determine whether a negotiator tends to claim value rather than create value,[63] a risk-seeking negotiator should

[60] Margaret A Neale and Max H Bazerman, 'The Effects of Framing and Negotiator Overconfidence on Bargaining Behaviors and Outcomes' (1985) 28 *Academy of Management Journal* 34; in the context of settlement negotiations see Jeffrey J Rachlinski, 'Gains, Losses, and the Psychology of Litigation' (1996) 70 *Southern California Law Review* 113; Russell Korobkin and Chris Guthrie, 'Psychological Barriers to Litigation Settlement: An Experimental Approach' (1994) 93 *Michigan Law Review* 107; Linda Babcock and others, 'Forming Beliefs About Adjudicated Outcomes: Perceptions of Risk and Reservation Values' (1995) *15 International Review of Law and Economics* 289.

[61] Neale and Bazerman (n 60) 44; see also Max H Bazerman, Thomas Magliozzi, and Margaret A Neale, 'Integrative Bargaining in a Competitive Market' (1985) 35 *Organizational Behavior and Human Decision Processes* 294.

[62] See Linda Chang, Mandy M Cheng, and Ken T Trotman, 'The Effect of Framing and Negotiation Partner's Objective on Judgments About Negotiated Transfer Prices' (2008) 33 *Accounting, Organizations & Society* 704.

[63] See generally David A Lax and James K Sebenius, *The Manager as Negotiator: Bargaining for Cooperation and Competitive Gain* (The Free Press 1986).

have a higher propensity to resort to threatening tactics. It follows that risk-averse negotiators—because of their reluctance to engage in risky tactics—might be susceptible to exploitation from those risk-seeking negotiators who are willing to employ them.[64] In an ideal scenario, different frames should therefore be used alternately throughout the negotiation process depending not only on whether a given issue is either integrative or distributive in nature but also to align negotiators' attitudes among themselves in order to achieve cooperative gains while at the same time assert their interests.

A comparison between the United Nations Framework Convention on Climate Change (UNFCCC) negotiations in Copenhagen and Paris shows that gain-loss framing effects play a role in international treaty-making. In contrast to Copenhagen, Paris triggered a collective shift in international climate action by framing UNFCCC negotiations not in terms of economic burdens associated with coordinated climate action but in terms of opportunities with respect to economic growth and development.[65] The negotiations in Copenhagen, in contrast, reinforced the developed-developing world framing divide and long-lasting disputes over who ought to take responsibility for mitigating the adverse consequences of climate change, how to share the burden associated with respective policies, and the amount and type of financing on behalf of developed states.[66] At the same time, the manipulability of a given (loss) frame is not unlimited: some situations display particularly resilient frames,[67] which appears likely to apply to the immense costs associated with climate action. Perceived reference points outside the laboratory are determined by a wide array of psychological, historical, social, and legal factors.[68] Even though preference reversals caused by gain-loss framing effects undeniably play a role in the comparison of UNFCCC negotiations, the magnitude of their impact thus remains debatable. A meta-analysis shows that although framing effects exist, their size may be nonetheless small to moderate.[69] However, prior to the negotiations in Paris, 185 States submitted nationally endorsed climate action plans (referred to as Intended Nationally Determined Contributions, INDCs), thereby circumventing long-lasting disputes over how to share the costs of climate action. In comparison to the negotiations in Copenhagen, INDCs thus provided an additional signal. Both theoretical and experimental studies show

[64] Andrea Caputo, 'A Literature Review of Cognitive Biases in Negotiation Processes' (2012) 24 *International Journal of Conflict Management* 385.

[65] Jean A Garrison, 'Overcoming Obstacles in Global Climate Action from Copenhagen to Paris: Issue Framing as a Tool to Understand Opportunities for Policy Change' (2017) KFG Working Paper No 81 https://www.polsoz.fu-berlin.de/en/v/transformeurope/publications/working_paper/wp/wp81/WP_81_Garrison_WEB.pdf (accessed 21 June 2020).

[66] ibid 7.

[67] Zamir (n 53) 7.

[68] ibid 211.

[69] See Anton Kühberger, 'The Influence of Framing in Risky Decisions: A Meta-Analysis' (1998) 75 *Organizational Behavior and Human Decision Processes* 23.

that using expectations as the reference point (as opposed to the status quo) may offer better explanations and predictions about behaviour.[70] Although debatable, one may argue that the introduction of INDCs not only solved disputes over how to split the costs of climate action but as a result also succeeded in changing the reference expectation in that states expected that the negotiations in Paris would successfully pave the way to an agreement rather than not, thereby highlighting the reputational 'losses' associated with the prospect of not belonging to the 'green club' of signatories of the agreement.[71]

International negotiations, aside from competing (distributional) views with respect to the selection of a particular set of Pareto-efficient solutions, are also characterized by competing narratives.[72] These narratives—that is, alternative issue frames—determine the definition of the negotiation problem, the choice options to be considered, and influence the set of choices ultimately made.[73] Different frames thereby compete for the attention of the targeted audience, and relative salience of the messages conveyed decides upon which frame dominates the other.[74] Put differently, the most effective frames focus on specific attributes and are based on salient issues and experiences that link the negotiation problem to vivid instances of everyday life.[75]

The UNFCCC negotiations in Paris provide evidence for issue framing in action. The presence of 140 world leaders at the launch of the conference, each giving compelling speeches, provided an opportunity for framing the negotiations in terms of need for immediate collective action given the salience of recent natural disasters,[76] that is, an issue of resource scarcity. In fact, experimental evidence suggests that the salience of 'dangerous' thresholds—such as the adverse effects of climate change as per the 2 degrees Celsius limit of global warming—can turn climate negotiations into a cooperative game.[77] Threshold uncertainty, in contrast, can be detrimental to cooperation.[78]

[70] Zamir (n 53) 8; see also Botond Kőszegi and Matthew Rabin, 'A Model of Reference-Dependent Preferences' (2006) 121 *Quarterly Journal of Economics* 1133; Botond Kőszegi and Matthew Rabin, 'Reference-Dependent Risk Attitude' (2007) 97 *American Economic Review* 1047.

[71] Regarding INDCs and associated expectations see also Lavanya Rajamani and Jutta Brunnée, 'The Legality of Downgrading Nationally Determined Contributions under the Paris Agreement: Lessons from the US Disengagement' (2017) 29 *Journal of Environmental Law* 537.

[72] See Garrison (n 65).

[73] ibid; see also text accompanying n 36 ff.

[74] ibid; for an introduction into salience theory in behavioural economics see Pedro Bordalo, Nicola Gennaioli, and Andrei Shleifer, 'Salience Theory of Choice Under Risk' (2012) 127 *Quarterly Journal of Economics* 1243.

[75] ibid.

[76] See Garrison (n 65).

[77] See Scott Barret and Astrid Dannenberg, 'Climate Negotiations Under Uncertainty' (2012) 109 *Proceedings of the National Academy of Sciences of the United States of America* 17372.

[78] ibid; see also Astrid Dannenberg and others, 'On the Provision of Public Goods with Probabilistic and Ambiguous Thresholds' (2015) 61 *Environmental and Resource Economics* 365.

B How Law Is Interpreted and Shaped: International Adjudication

Adjudication is knowledge production in two areas: facts and law. Whereas the facts are usually case-specific, the law is not, but frames future decisions by precedent or argument, usually by making one issue salient while under-emphasizing other, equally important aspects. That is, it is an application of issue framing.[79] Whereas law itself is a frame, we are more concerned with how legal interpretation creates frames that ultimately justify adjudicatory decision-making as well as future reasoning in international adjudication. We pick two examples of high salience that relate to public international law: the recent Advisory Opinion by the International Court of Justice (ICJ) relating to the separation of the Chagos Archipelago from Mauritius in 1965 (Chagos) and the decision of the European Court of Human Rights (ECtHR) in *James and Others v United Kingdom*,[80] which either possibly turn out (in the *Chagos* case) or already were (in the *James and Others* case) very influential in subsequent case law of international adjudication.

The 2019 Advisory Opinion of the ICJ in *Chagos* framed the debate about treaties concluded during colonial times.[81] The United Kingdom (UK) excised the Chagos Islands from the British colony of Mauritius in 1965, after reaching an agreement with the representatives of the Mauritian colonial government. The UK paid Mauritius £3 million in recognition of the detachment of the Chagos Islands and committed to cede the islands back to Mauritius when 'no longer needed for defence purposes'.[82] The ICJ held that the separation of the Chagos Islands was contrary to Mauritius's right to self-determination and that, accordingly, the decolonization of Mauritius was not completed in accordance with public international law.

One key problem was the exercise of discretion to give an opinion, namely whether, in answering the questions posed by the UN General Assembly, the ICJ would in essence decide on a bilateral dispute between states over territorial sovereignty, which one of them (the UK) did not consent to. The ICJ acknowledged that

[79] The existence of cognitive biases and heuristics in adjudication is now well documented see eg Chris Guthrie, Jeffrey Rachlinski, and Andrew J Wistrich, 'Inside the Judicial Mind' (2001) 86 *Cornell Law Review* 777; Susan Franck and others, 'Inside the Arbitrator's Mind' (2017) 66 *Emory Law Journal* 1115.

[80] *James and Others v United Kingdom* App no 8793/79 (ECtHR, 21 February 1986); *Legal Consequences of the Separation of the Chagos Archipelago from Mauritius in 1965* (Advisory Opinion) [2019] ICJ Rep 95 ff https://www.icj-cij.org/public/files/case-related/169/169-20190225-ADV-01-00-EN.pdf (accessed 21 June 2020).

[81] ibid; for a discussion of the Advisory Opinion see Diane Marie Amann, 'Legal Consequences of the Separation of the Chagos Archipelago from Mauritius in 1965' (2019) 113 *American Journal of International Law* 784.

[82] Chagos Advisory Opinion (n 80) [50].

there would be a compelling reason to decline if an advisory opinion 'would have the effect of circumventing the principle that a State is not obliged to allow its disputes to be submitted to judicial settlement without its consent'.[83] It got around that problem by framing the issue as one of decolonization and self-determination,[84] issues in which the UN General Assembly has a longstanding interest—thereby allowing it to proceed—instead of one of sovereignty where it would have needed to decline to give an opinion.[85] Dissenting Judge Donoghue viewed the issue as a 'quintessentially bilateral ... dispute over territorial sovereignty'[86] since '[t]he questions of decolonization and sovereignty cannot be separated'.[87] The Advisory Opinion of the ICJ may have implications for further cases, such as military bases in Cyprus (UK)[88] and the Comorian island of Mayotte (France).[89] It can be expected that the Advisory Opinion in *Chagos* will continue to frame future debates and cases.

Another prominent example of influential framing in public international law has been the use of democratic theory by investment tribunals. Several tribunals have claimed that the interests of foreign investors ordinarily will not be represented within the political processes of the host state and investors therefore deserve heightened protection from policy decisions that adversely affect their investment.[90] In several cases, this has served as an argument to decide in favour of foreign investors. How has this inequality frame—and as a result, special protection in favour of foreign investors—come about?

In *James and Others*, the ECtHR had to decide on protection of a foreign investor in an expropriation case. It argued that

[83] ibid [85], quoting *Western Sahara* (Advisory Opinion) 1975 [33] https://www.icj-cij.org/public/files/case-related/61/061-19751016-ADV-01-00-EN.pdf (accessed 21 June 2020).

[84] Chagos Advisory Opinion (n 80) [88]. This follows other Advisory Opinions using the 'compelling reason' argument to establish jurisdiction, such as *Accordance with International Law of the Unilateral Declaration of Independence in Respect of Kosovo* (Advisory Opinion) [2010] ICJ Rep 403 ff [30] https://www.icj-cij.org/public/files/case-related/141/141-20100722-ADV-01-00-EN.pdf (accessed 21 June 2020); *Legal Consequences of the Construction of a Wall in the Occupied Palestinian Territory* (Advisory Opinion) [2004] ICJ Rep 136 ff [44] https://www.icj-cij.org/files/case-related/131/131-20040709-ADV-01-00-EN.pdf (accessed 21 June 2020).

[85] Similarly see Marko Milanovic, 'ICJ Delivers Chagos Advisory Opinion, UK Loses Badly' *EJIL:Talk!* (25 February 2019) https://www.ejiltalk.org/icj-delivers-chagos-advisory-opinion-uk-loses-badly/ (accessed 21 June 2020).

[86] *Legal Consequences of the Separation of the Chagos Archipelago from Mauritius in 1965* (Dissenting Opinion of Judge Donoghue) [2019] (n 80) 261 [1], [5]–[8], [21] https://www.icj-cij.org/public/files/case-related/169/169-20190225-ADV-01-06-EN.pdf (accessed 21 June 2020).

[87] ibid [16].

[88] Constantinos Yiallourides, 'Islands, Sovereignty and the Right to Return: An Analysis of the Chagos Islands ICJ Advisory Opinion Request' (2018) *JTMS* 1.

[89] UNGA Res 31/4 (21 October 1976) UN Doc A/RES/31/4 and subsequent resolutions up to and including UNGA Res 49/19 (6 December 1994) UN Doc A/RES/49/19 on the 'Comorian island of Mayotte', subsequently integrated into France as an overseas *département* in 2011 following a referendum in 2009.

[90] For an excellent critique see David Schneiderman, 'Investing in Democracy? Political Process and International Investment Law' (2010) 60 *Univ Tor LJ* 909.

> [e]specially as regards a taking of property effected in the context of a social reform, there may well be good grounds for drawing a distinction between nationals and non-nationals as far as compensation is concerned. To begin with, non-nationals are more vulnerable to domestic legislation: unlike nationals, they will generally have played no part in the election or designation of its authors nor have been consulted on its adoption.[91]

For this result, it also relied on the *travaux préparatoires*, which show that in cases of social reform there was a consensus that foreigners had to be compensated whereas nationals did not in all circumstances, and there was good reason for this given the historical context. ECtHR case law indeed shows that in the context of social reform or land reform, full compensation was not owed to nationals.[92]

The first investment tribunal to refer to *James and Others* was the *Tecmed* Tribunal. When the tribunal took up this citation in the context of proportionality analysis, it skipped the first part of the sentence, namely 'as regards a taking of property effected *in the context of a social reform*' (emphasis added), thus depriving the citation of its context of wide-scale social reform expropriation.[93] Weighing into the tribunal's proportionality analysis was 'that the foreign investor has a reduced or nil participation in the taking of the decisions that affect it, partly because investors are not entitle[d] to exercise political rights reserved to the nationals of the state, such as voting for the authorities that will issue the decisions that affect such investors'.[94] It thus engaged in a general theory of the disadvantage of foreign investors who are subject to regulation in host states, framing the situation as one of disenfranchisement, that is, inequality of (democratic) influence of foreign investors as compared to national property owners, and suggested investment protection as an inequality-reducing device. Such issue framing made the participatory element of political rights salient to the detriment of other means of influence of foreign investors.

The *Tecmed* Tribunal's perception of inequality is factually unfounded because foreign investors often have even more influence than national ones, surely more than regular national private property owners unless in the context of social reform. The literature on corporate political activity and business risk suggests that foreign corporate actors can and do shape host state domestic policy.[95]

[91] *James and Others* (n 80) [63].

[92] Anne van Aaken, 'Direct Expropriation: The Legal Landscape in Europe' in Hojun Lee, Ilya Somin, and Iljoong Kim (eds), *Shifting the Paradigm for Sustainable Development: Eminent Domain and Property Rights* (CUP 2017) 67–92.

[93] *Técnicas Medioambientales Tecmed SA v United Mexican States* (2003) ICSID Case No ARB (AF)/00/2 [122].

[94] ibid.

[95] Kathleen A Rehbein, 'Foreign-Owned Firms Campaign Contributions in the United States: An Exploratory Study' (1995) 23 *Policy Stud J* 41; Schneiderman (n 92) 931.

It even goes further and shows that foreign business may contribute to regime change, where the common underlying motive is 'to establish, promote, and defend the right of Americans to do business around the world'.[96] This is not meant to say that foreign influence is necessarily bad in single instances, indeed it can be efficiency enhancing,[97] yet it is to say that foreign investors' political influence is clearly not negligible, which means that inequality in political influence as compared to regular nationals is not a factual pattern to be relied on in legal interpretation. Furthermore, if 'exit' or 'entry' are complements to 'voice',[98] then foreign investors clearly voted with their feet to step into the host country. Regular national citizens cannot do that. This living myth has nevertheless framed the scholarly discussion for a long time[99] and several tribunals have taken up the argument.[100] Framing the problem as an inequality issue has thus worked very well (even though it was based on misinformed facts). As the *Lemire* Tribunal held:

> this unequal treatment is not without justification: justice is not to grant everyone the same, but suum cuique tribuere. *Foreigners, who lack political rights, are more exposed than domestic investors to arbitrary actions of the host State and may thus, as a matter of legitimate policy, be granted a wider scope of protection.*[101]

There are several other examples in investment law in which the original, and 'wrong' (ie annulled or heavily criticized) decision keep on influencing subsequent jurisprudence.[102]

[96] Stephen Kinzer, *All the Shah's Men: An American Coup and the Roots of Middle East Terror* (John Wiley & Sons 2003) 3; this view receives econometric support by Arindrajit Dube, Ethan Kaplan, and Suresh Naidu, 'Coups, Corporations and Classified Information' (2008) 126 *Quarterly Journal of Economics* 1375.

[97] Toke S Aidt and Facundo Albornoz, 'Political Regimes and Foreign Intervention' (2011) 94 *J Dev Econ* 192.

[98] See Albert Hirschman, *Exit, Voice and Loyalty* (CUP 1970).

[99] See eg August Reinisch and Ursula Kriebaum, 'Property, Right to, International Protection' *Max Planck Encyclopedia of Public International Law* [48] https://deicl.univie.ac.at/fileadmin/user_upload/i_deicl/VR/VR_Personal/Reinisch/Publikationen/Propertyright_int_protec.pdf (accessed 19 October 2019); Pasquale de Sena, 'Economic and Non-Economic Values in the Case Law of the European Court of Human Rights' in Pierre-Marie Dupuy, Francesco Francioni, and Ernst-Ulrich Petersmann (eds), *Human Rights in International Investment Law and Arbitration* (OUP 2009) 211.

[100] *Pac Rim Cayman LLC v Republic of El Salvador* (2016) ICSID Case No ARB/09/12; *Pac Rim Cayman LLC v Republic of El Salvador* (Republic of El Salvador's Counter-Memorial on the Merits) (10 January 2014) [270] (fn 406)https://www.italaw.com/sites/default/files/case-documents/italaw3040.pdf; *International Thunderbird Gaming Corporation v United Mexican States* (Separate Opinion Thomas Wälde) 1 December 2005 [4] (fn 3) https://www.italaw.com/sites/default/files/case-documents/ita0432.pdf (accessed 21 June 2020).

[101] *Joseph Charles Lemire v Ukraine* (2011) ICSID Case No ARB/06/18 [57] (emphasis added).

[102] Wolfgang Alschner, 'Correctness of Investment Awards: Why Wrong Decisions Don't Die' (2019) 18 *LPICT* 345.

C How Soft Law Shapes Behaviour: Global Performance Indicators

Global performance indicators[103] are not strictly public international law but may exhibit more behavioural force than classical international hard law via issue and equivalency framing. Starting from the 1990s, there has been a global trend in the use of indicators as a governance technique.[104] Intergovernmental organizations, non-governmental organizations (NGOs), private firms, and even states (mainly the United States) have begun regularly to package and distribute information on the relative performance of states, ranging from the World Bank's Ease of Doing Business Index, the Financial Action Task Force Blacklist, and the Sustainable Development Goals, to the Transparency Perception Index by Transparency International. Such global performance indicators are ever more analysed by public international law and international relations scholars[105] given that they are powerful governance tools for shaping the behaviour of states and framing issues in the national as well as the international realm. However, the legitimacy of global performance indicators is sometimes questioned given the risk of abuse.[106]

Global performance indicators are intended to generate easily digestible knowledge on the performance of states in selected issue areas. Global performance indicators use comparative information to influence policy and governance through the pressure of comparison.[107] There is evidence that global performance indicators influence discourse, standards, and measurement, and that they also change actions. They may alter policy priorities, also with unintended consequences, for example by shifting resources to measurable proxies used to compute indicators. For example, it was found that countries gravitate toward primary education enrolment rates (which is targeted by the Millennium Development Goals) and away from secondary (which is not), but that these effects are mitigated as accountability rises.[108] Next to material interests and reputation creation via global performance indicators, Kelley and Simmons argue that 'the social process of GPI influence

[103] For a definition (there are several) see Kevin E Davis, Benedict Kingsbury, and Sally E Merry, 'Introduction: Global Governance by Indicators' in Kevin E Davis and others (eds), *Governance by Indicators: Global Power through Quantification and Rankings* (OUP 2012) 3, 6; OECD, *Handbook on Constructing Composite Indicator: Methodology and User Guide* (OECD 2008) 13 www.oecd.org/std/42495745.pdf (accessed 21 June 2020).

[104] Morag Goodwin, 'The Poverty of Numbers: Reflections on the Legitimacy of Global Development Indicators' (2017) 13 *Intl JLC* 487; Marta Infantino, 'Global Indicators' in Sabino Cassese (ed), *Research Handbook on Global Administrative Law* (Edward Elgar Publishing 2017) 349.

[105] Judith G Kelley, *Scorecard Diplomacy: Grading States to Influence Their Reputation and Behavior* (CUP 2017); Judith G Kelley and Beth A Simmons, 'Politics by Number: Indicators as Social Pressure in International Relations' (2015) 59 *Am J Political Sci* 1146; Judith G Kelley and Beth A Simmons, 'Introduction: The Power of Global Performance Indicators' (2019) 73 *International Organization* 491.

[106] David Nelken and Mathias Siems, 'Introduction: Global Social Indicators: Constructing Transnational Legitimacy' (2017) 13 *Intl JLC* 438.

[107] Kelley and Simmons 'Introduction: The Power of Global Performance Indicators' (n 105).

[108] James H Bisbee and others, 'The Millennium Development Goals and Education: Accountability and Substitution in Global Assessment' (2019) 73 *International Organization* 547.

begins with their ability to frame issues': 'naming an issue, coining a vocabulary for describing it, and creating categories for its assessment, promulgators hope to affect discourse and ultimately policy'.[109] Whereas in some cases, the promulgators collect new data, in others existing data are presented in ways that prioritize new objectives; yet in all cases they draw attention to some issues by making them salient and not others. Only by naming an issue and coining a vocabulary for describing it, as well as by creating categories for its assessment, they affect discourse and ultimately policymaking. Global performance indicators can be well fought over and criticized, a sign for their importance not least because of framing the issue and performance at hand. Furthermore, it may well be that global performance indicators also rely on gain-loss framing effects since they often are issued annually and a decline in the ranking would activate loss aversion, potentially leading to risky policy choices on behalf of governments.[110]

D How Law Shapes Solutions to Problems: Norm Framing

Norm framing has been analysed (and welcomed) in many instances at the national and international level but mostly without drawing on psychological insights such as equivalency or issue framing.[111] It works particularly well under conditions of uncertainty and fluidity, that is, in situations where opinions can easily be influenced through framing. It is also utilized in instances where an area of public international law is weak in the sense that it lacks international courts to strengthen its effectivity or to mobilize more actors. It is often used to advance a (normative) agenda.

One well researched example is the problem of human trafficking,[112] where issue frames have changed over time. Historically, the victim protection frame linked trafficking to prostitution, as illustrated by the international treaties of the first half of the 20th century[113] and was seen as a matter of protecting the vulnerable from exploitation and an immoral life, typically of a sexual nature, often de-emphasizing the autonomy and rights-bearing nature of the trafficked individual. This was the predominant frame through at least until the 1950s, but by the late 1990s, the victim protection frame was weakened by differences in opinion over

[109] Kelley and Simmons 'Introduction: The Power of Global Performance Indicators' (n 105) 495.

[110] For different reactions of governments in order to avoid reputational and material losses due to a downgrading in ranking see Alexander Cooley and Jack Snyder, *Ranking the World* (Cambridge University Press 2015) 3.

[111] Gwendolyn Leachman, 'Legal Framing' (2013) 61 *SLPS* 25.

[112] Mojca Pajnik, 'Media Framing of Trafficking' (2019) 12 *Intl Fem J Politics* 45.

[113] International Agreement for the Suppression of the 'White Slave Traffic' (adopted 18 July 1904, entered into force 18 July 1905) 1 LNTS 83; International Convention for the Suppression of the Traffic in Women and Children (as amended by the 1947 Protocol) (adopted 30 September 1921, entered into force 15 June 1922) 9 LNTS 415.

the acceptability of 'sex work'. It has been shown that framing the issue as a 'crime issue' was crucial for reaching a consensus, given that human trafficking sits somewhat in between combatting transnational crime and international human rights (if analysed through the lens of UN General Assembly Resolutions). The 'crime-fighting' frame generates more support than a 'human rights' frame, especially in the crucial period leading up to the adoption of the Protocol to Prevent, Suppress and Punish Trafficking in Persons in 2000.[114] This may be attributed to both issue framing and equivalency framing because crime—more specifically, the prospect of criminal sanctions—is likely to induce loss aversion.

Another example where human rights frames elevate a problem beyond its legal scope *strictu sensu* is corruption.[115] For a long time, international and regional organizations had stressed the negative impacts of corruption on human rights without identifying corruption itself as a violation of human rights. It had mainly been framed as an issue of economic criminal law and although it was stressed that it was not a victimless crime, the victims were not made salient. Lately, however, this tendency has begun to shift in favour of human rights both in the academic discourse as well as in international human rights courts.[116]

Anne Peters has proposed to use international human rights law as a lens for analysing corrupt acts or omissions, arguing that this would close the 'implementation gap' of anti-corruption law.[117] While she sets out the legal ways of doing so, Kevin Davis starts earlier and analyses the added value of doing so by stressing that human rights analysis plays a valuable role in anti-corruption efforts to the extent that it helps produce information about the incidence in the first place.[118] It does so because international human rights regimes have considerably more capacity for fact-finding by various actors, not least international human rights activists. Moreover, human rights frames highlight the moral significance of corruption since international human rights can be interpreted as statements about moral priorities, thereby inducing states to give higher priority to combating corruption that result in human rights violations rather than to combating other forms of corruption.[119] He thus alludes to classical framing mechanisms, albeit not mentioning the underlying psychological phenomena.

[114] Volha Charnysh, Paulette Lloyd, and Beth A Simmons, 'Frames and Consensus Formation in International Relations: The Case of Trafficking in Persons' (2015) 21 *Eur J Intl Relat* 323.

[115] Jimena Reyes, 'State Capture Through Corruption: Can Human Rights Help?' (2019) 113 *American Journal of International Law Unbound* 331.

[116] *Ramírez Escobar y otros v Guatemala*, Inter-American Court of Human Rights Series C No 351 (9 March 2018).

[117] Anne Peters, 'Corruption as a Violation of International Human Rights' (2018) 29 *European Journal of International Law* 1251.

[118] Kevin Davis, 'Corruption as a Violation of International Human Rights. A Reply to Anne Peters' (2018) 29 *European Journal of International Law* 1289.

[119] ibid.

IV Conclusion

The objectivity of public international law has long been a mantra in international legal scholarship. As such, it was assumed that subjects of public international law make the same decision independent of the way a given decision problem is framed. However, experimental evidence supports the existence of framing effects, both in terms of equivalency and issue framing. Framing effects therefore shine a new light on the study of public international law by providing a more finely grained understanding of how different actors in public international law make sense of international legal regimes and what this implies for resulting behaviour.

In particular, framing impacts social cognition as well as knowledge production processes in public international law through various channels: in the context of international negotiations, state representatives and other actors involved (such as NGOs) bring to the negotiation table not only a 'way of looking' at the issues at stake but also produce knowledge and information, which influence both their beliefs (eg about others' beliefs) and ultimately their behaviour. When judicial bodies issue decisions, they produce knowledge about legal interpretation and facts but also frame the issues at hand in a decisive way for the general public and subsequent judicial decisions. Global performance indicators also impact both social cognition and knowledge production. They frame issues by providing salience and may give rise to equivalency framing and induce loss aversion, both of which bear the potential to shape policymaking. Issue framing also plays a role in the generation of international legal norms, which had already long been discussed in constructivist thought.[120] However, this debate also raises important follow-up questions, namely with respect to the actors who provide and use frames and those exposed to those frames and thus to the broader question of authority and authority-wielding bodies in public international law and their legitimacy.

Hitherto, those insights have not been studied through the lens of psychological research and have been entirely neglected by rationalist approaches. By illuminating the differences between equivalency framing and issue framing as well as preference reversals and a change in beliefs, international scholars, policymakers, and practising lawyers can better understand what is going on—be it at the negotiation table, in courtrooms, or governmental bodies—and become aware of their own frames and those of others.

[120] See nn 43 ff.

3
Cognitive Biases and International Law: What's the Point of Critique?

*Ingo Venzke**

I Introduction

One of the main aims of critique is to work towards progressive change. What are some of critical scholarship's assumptions about how that change should happen? And do they hold? In the present chapter, I discuss three characteristic traits of critical scholarship: first, exposing law as part of the problem; secondly, emphasizing indeterminacy; and, thirdly, revealing contingencies in the course of international law. Many such practices are well received, some might even seem quaint. If the hope to facilitate progressive change is a common denominator for much critical work, it is less clear, how such change should happen, and what critical work does about that. What are reasons to hope that critique somehow matters?

Many of those reasons can be located squarely within dynamics of social cognition and knowledge production.[1] Critique can unveil and counteract a variety of dynamics that render the present state of affairs more natural, necessary, and just. Those dynamics forestall progressive change simply because they render such change impossible and undesirable.[2] This is arguably critique's most classic and most characteristic feature as I see it, working against alienation to unveil and regain a political understanding of the social world. It is only possible to change what is neither natural nor without alternative.[3] Critique thus also offers alternative understandings and suggests that some things indeed need to be unlearned.[4]

* I thank Andrea Bianchi, Moshe Hirsch, Yahli Shereshevsky, and all the participants of the International Law Forum at the Hebrew University of Jerusalem, 4–5 December 2019, for their valuable comments.

[1] On the importance of foregrounding those dynamics see Bianchi and Hirsch in this volume.

[2] Duncan Kennedy, *A Critique of Adjudication (Fin de Siècle)* (Harvard University Press 1997) 241.

[3] Max Horkheimer, 'Traditional and Critical Theory' in Max Horkheimer (ed), *Critical Theory: Selected Essays* (Continuum 2002) 204, arguing that critique must unravel an understanding of 'senseless wretchedness [as] an unchangeable force of nature, a fate beyond man's control'. Rainer Forst, 'Gerechtigkeit nach Marx' in Rainer Forst (ed), *Normativität und Macht* (Suhrkamp 2015) 183.

[4] See Bianchi and Hirsch in this volume on the programme of unveiling, understanding, and unlearning.

Ingo Venzke, *Cognitive Biases and International Law: What's the Point of Critique?* In: *International Law's Invisible Frames*. Edited by: Andrea Bianchi and Moshe Hirsch, Oxford University Press. © Ingo Venzke 2021.
DOI: 10.1093/oso/9780192847539.003.0004

While its strategic targets vary, critique has overall remained vague as to how change should happen, and how it should happen with the help of critique.[5] Sometimes critical scholarship has taken comfort in abstract declarations of faith: critique *is* the practical work. Or it has remained self-assertively agnostic, suggesting that it is just not possible to further support its assumptions—at least not in a way that would be considered 'empirical'.[6] Some might then consider the question of how critique matters, perhaps reflecting a concern for practical impact, to be hearsay. There are good reasons for critique to resist the pull towards practical relevance, especially as it may then also be pushed to offer neat solutions. The need to offer workable, implementable insights tends to limit, if not distort, the analysis of the underlying problem—often abstracting from root causes, flattening the context, and leading to a rather *un*critical understating of what the issue is.[7] The question of how change should happen through critique, however, is neither new, nor necessarily blasphemous.[8]

A while ago, David Trubek drew attention to the absence of any account, as he saw it, of how critique in law is expected to unfold its effects in practice.[9] While debates have evolved, many critical scholars continue to fear, that diving further into that question of *how* change should happen, could pull critique onto the terrain of empirical methods and their supposed commitment to positivism—that is, in short, the belief according to which facts are the arbiters about truth claims.[10] Critical thinking would, also in brief, point out that facts are not just out there but the products of our own making, and thus somewhat unreliable.[11] Much more could be said on those theoretical commitments and remnants of the classic

[5] Fleur Johns, 'Critical International Legal Theory' in Jeffrey L Dunoff and Mark A Pollack (eds), *International Legal Theory: Foundations and Frontiers* (Cambridge University Press 2021) (arguing that critical scholarship 'has sometimes overstated the power of its own diagnoses ... overestimated the newness of, and the emancipatory potential associated with, its "revalations"—the bringing to light of historical contingency perhaps especially').

[6] Kennedy (n 2); Duncan Kennedy, 'The Structure of Blackstone's Commentaries' (1979) 28 *Buffalo Law Review* 209, 220. I am bracketing what empirical may mean for just a moment. It is itself a contentious term. See nn 8–10 below.

[7] Susan Marks, 'Human Rights and Root Causes' (2011) 74 *Modern Law Review* 57.

[8] Also see Thomas Kern, Thomas Laux, and Insa Pruisken, 'Critique and Social Change: An Introduction' (2017) 42 *Historical Social Research* 7.

[9] David M Trubek, 'Where the Action Is: Critical Legal Studies and Empiricism' (1984) 36 *Stanford Law Review* 575, 610. I am using the notion of critique in a broad sense to refer to work informed by critical theories, which is notably more than critical legal studies alone, for a markers of such a broader understanding and its still distinctive features, consider the classic distinction by Horkheimer (n 3); for a sense of legal critique beyond critical legal studies as it is mostly known from debates centred in the US, consider for example Christoph Menke, 'Law and Violence' (2014) 22 *Law and Literature* 1; Andreas Fischer-Lescano, 'Radikale Rechtskritik' (2014) 47 *Kritische Justiz* 171

[10] See the classic exchanges in Theodor W Adorno and others, *Der Positivismusstreit in der Deutschen Soziologie* (Luchterhand 1969).

[11] See eg Reymong Geuss, *The Idea of a Critical Theory* (Cambridge University Press 1981); Seyla Benhabib, *Critique, Norm, and Utopia: A Study of the Foundations of Critical Theory* (Columbia University Press 1986).

Positivismusstreit—as well as the rather commonplace caricatures often rendered of the respective other.[12]

Still now, divides between critical scholarship and more recent socio-psychological work run deep, in particular as the latter has developed further under the heading of behavioural economics, again—rightly and wrongly—conveying a commitment to positivism that critical scholars reject. While critique lost faith in rationality and drew attention to its pathologies, economics continued to stick to assumptions of rationality, something that neither the emphasis on bounded rationality nor the behavioural turn has changed.[13] It is also the case that emerging experimental research in international law is placed—and in fact places itself—within that rationalist tradition.[14] What the behavioural turn has done, to be sure, is to highlight the many ways in which human action deviates, especially due to cognitive and emotional dynamics, from what could be considered rational. 'Who would have ever thought otherwise?', the critic might righteously claim in reaction, pointing to a long-standing practice of critical scholarship to draw out every individual's situatedness, paralleled with an emphasis on collective, structural biases.[15]

I will try to largely side-step these protracted divides, without wanting to downplay the importance of the related and anyway much more nuanced debates. I only note that some empirical—better: empiricist—legal studies assume a simplistic positivism that is indeed difficult to defend, but many others do not, and it would be critical work's own loss if it disregarded those more promising studies' insights. I thus indeed join the current project in its programme of bringing social cognition closer together with the classically critical work on the production of knowledge.

Social-psychological and related cognitive-sociological work has made great strides in understanding the dynamics that render the present state of affairs more natural, necessary and just, and what to do about that. In spite of scepticism in some quarters, there is a rich critical tradition that has linked up closely with such

[12] Adorno and others (eds), *Der Positivismusstreit in der deutschen Soziologie* (Fn 10).

[13] Cf Andrea Bianchi and Anne Saab, 'Fear and International Law-Making: An Exploratory Inquiry' (2019) 32 *Leiden Journal of International Law* 351.

[14] See Jeffrey L Dunoff and Mark A Pollack, 'Experimenting with International Law' (2017) 28 *European Journal of International Law* 1317; Jean Galbraith, 'Treaty Options: Towards a Behavioral Understanding of Treaty Design' (2013) 53 *Virginia Journal of International Law* 309; Anne van Aaken, 'Behavioral International Law and Economics' (2014) 55 *Harvard International Law Journal* 501; Tomer Broude, 'Behavioral International Law' (2015) 163 *University of Pennsylvania Law Review* 1099. Eyal Zamir and Doron Teichman, *Behavioral Law and Economics* (Oxford University Press 2018) 423–430.

[15] Outi Korhonen, 'New International Law: Silence, Defence of Deliverance?' (1996) 7 *European Journal of International Law* 1. Johns (n 10)) (emphasizing critique's concern 'with understanding and addressing the persistence of bias'). Cf Anne van Aaken, 'Rationalist and Behavioralist Approaches to International Law' (2018) https://ssrn.com/abstract=3237033. (arguing that '[a]lthough behavioral economics has a rationalist starting point concerning its pedigree and methods, it hints at insights which were long proposed by constructivist scholars'); Moshe Hirsch, 'The Sociological Perspective on International Law' in Jeffrey L Dunoff and Mark A Pollack (eds), *International Legal Theory: Foundations and Frontiers* (Cambridge University Press 2020).

work. The oeuvre of Theodor W Adorno still serves as a towering example. While it is not geared towards legal practices, let alone international law, it testifies to the closely linked concerns of critical theory and socio-psychological research.[16] The driving question of much of Adorno's thinking was, after all: Why do people not seek knowledge, even if they could?[17] Why do they let themselves be deceived and even seek deception? Perceptions and beliefs are main targets of much critique, especially in law, and it thus makes good sense to continue to open up towards socio-psychological work.

I will focus on points of contact related to three of critical scholarships' main traits. First is the emphasis on exposing the complicity of law as part of the problem (section IIA). Critique here finds support in research on omission and confirmation biases (section IIB) as well as in psychological dynamics that respond to people's strong longing for a just world, seen as a world in which things happen for a reason. In particular, system justification theory lends itself for close conversations with critical work in law as it emphasizes the role of ideology in stabilizing attitudes towards the social world (section IIC). Secondly, I turn to the well-received work of revealing law's indeterminacy (section IIIA), the practical aims of which resonate with research on hindsight bias and counterfactual thinking (section IIIB). That research shows, in particular, how different kinds of reasoning impact perceptions of what is likely and what is just (section IIIC). Thirdly, I will discuss the search of contingency in international law's past, which also finds support in studies on hindsight bias (section IV). I will close with an outlook. While there are many points of contact between critical legal research and social psychology, and underlying concerns are sometimes quite similar, frictions do remain. More transgressing research should probe how exactly law is weaved into beliefs about our social world and how those beliefs can possibly change (section V).

II Exposing Complicity

A The Law as Part of the Problem

A first characteristic trait of critical scholarship is that it draws attention to law's complicity in injustice, that the law is also part of the problem. It is an integral part of such arguments that they place emphasis on the (unequal) distribution of

[16] His *Negative Dialectics*, while difficult to penetrate for its philosophical richness, is ripe with insights about different psychological reasons for self-deception, many of which could be described as the working of ideology. Theodor W Adorno, *Negative Dialectics* (Routledge 1990). The psychology is most upfront in Theodor W Adorno and others, *The Authoritarian Personality* (Harper & Row 1950), the outcome of Adorno's collaborations at UC Berkeley.

[17] The context for this question was the experience of indifference during the Holocaust. Bluntly, why did Germans in Frankfurt or elsewhere not want to know what happened to their Jewish neighbours during the Nazi-regime?

payoffs and, generally, on the question of who wins and who loses. While there are abundant examples to support this point, it suffices to draw attention to international economic law's prohibition on certain import restrictions, subsidies or capital controls, all of which play a part in favouring developed countries and 'their' economic actors over developing countries who tend to be on the receiving end of the bargain, facing the constraints of international law when they might try to build-up an internationally competitive industry or reap benefits of foreign investment, for example.[18] Who would be surprised? Of course, powerful actors have a relatively strong imprint on the law and manage to align it better with their interests and convictions.

Arguments about law's complicity in perpetuating some instances of injustice not only targets prohibitions of the law but also emphasizes its enabling function, i.e. what it authorizes and allows. An example is the fact that trade law allows developed countries to arrange their tariff schemes in a way that continues to reserve valuable economic activity for them, while leaving less profitable business for others.[19] Those tariff schemes are part and parcel of the fact that companies located in Germany make almost twice as much money by re-exporting roasted coffee than all of Africa makes with harvesting it.[20] It remains necessary to hammer the point that this is not an expression of a natural comparative advantage but the result of factors including a series of politico-legal arrangements like tariff schemes that prevent producers outside Europe to enter the market with roasted coffee. A similar dynamic is at play when it comes to fancy chocolate products that yield a significant profit while harvesting cacao beans supports a living. A steep tariff on processed cacao keeps it out of the European market and cacao-producing countries out of that more lucrative part of the production chain.[21] Labour conditions surely vary significantly along that chain too. Similar stories could be told many times over with reference to other products and other fields of life. In their more detailed versions, they would include transnational ownership structures and value chains, among other things. The core point remains: all of that is crucially made possible by legal arrangements.

[18] Cf Nicolás M Perrone and David Schneiderman, 'A Critique of International Economic Law: Depoliticization, Inequality, Precarity' in Emilios Christodoulidis, Ruth Dukes, and Marco Goldoni (eds), *Research Handbook on Critical Legal Theory* (Edward Elgar Publishing 2018); David Kennedy, *A World of Struggle: How Power, Law and Expertise Shape Global Political Economy* (Princeton University Press 2016).

[19] See, classically, Immanuel Wallerstein, *Historical Capitalism: With Capitalist Civilization* (Verso 1983).

[20] Calestous Juma, 'How the EU Starves Africa into Submission' (2015) https://www.belfercenter.org/publication/how-eu-starves-africa-submission.

[21] Cf Monika Hoegen, 'High Duties Keep Food Imports from Poor Countries out of Europe' (2010) http://www.dw.com/en/high-duties-keep-food-imports-from-poor-countries-out-of-europe/a-5127705.

Now, the hope of exposing the complicity of law in injustice tends to be, with grand ambition, that it may contribute to progressive change. What are some of the reasons for such a hope? I wish to stress at this stage that the conditions and possibilities of social change are of course incredibly varied as well as contested across disciplines. They also work at different levels of abstraction. I continue to limit myself to drawing out specific points of contact between critical work in international law and social psychology.

III Omission and Confirmation Biases

A first relevant socio-psychological dynamic that underpins people's attitudes and behaviour is their frequent omission bias. According to this bias, an act of commission tends to be judged more severely than an omission to act, even if the consequences of both are the same. Differences in the assessments are associated with the belief that omissions do not *cause* outcomes.[22] The omission bias is part of dynamics that underlie a more general bias towards the status quo.[23] With regard to critique in international law, it is thus important to counter the view, for instance, that some are poor and others are rich not because the rich omitted to help the poor, but because they actively contribute to the fact that they remain rich, and the poor remain poor, and that they have also been doing that through international law. Critique re-describes what is happening so that what may seem like acts of omission come to be understood as acts of commission.

Approaching the core of critical theory, a combination of psychological dynamics supports the need to continuously draw attention to instances and patterns of injustice, even if it that is not followed by suggestions for a solution. Highlighting instances and patterns of injustice that irritate prevailing narratives counters confirmation biases as well as more general social dynamics that present the world as just. It is well-documented that people tend to rely on information which is consistent with their preconceptions.[24] The conformation bias extends to the information that people seek out in the first place, the interpretation of pieces of information and which information is remembered down the line. This is fairly well known and relevant, but also fairly unspecific to critique. More to the point are the dynamics that render the world just.

[22] Mark Spranca, Elisa Minsk, and Jonathan Baron, 'Omission and Commission in Judgment and Choice' (1991) 27 *Journal of Experimental Social Psychology* 76.

[23] Ilana Ritov and Jonathan Baron, 'Status-Quo and Omission Biases' (1992) 5 *Journal of Risk and Uncertainty* 49.

[24] PC Wason, 'On the Failure to Eliminate Hypotheses in a Conceptual Task' (1960) 12 *Quarterly Journal of Experimental Psychology* 129. For the legal context see Kevin Jon Heller, 'The Cognitive Psychology of Circumstantial Evidence' (2006) 105 *Michigan Law Review* 241, 292.

A The Longing for Justice

1 Just world theory

Just world theory posits that people have a strong motivation to believe that they live in a world that is in principle just. Therefore, they seek to find reasons for what would otherwise seem unjust—reasons suggesting that people get what they deserve or deserve what they get.[25] Melvin Lerner argued in his pioneering work that this belief in a just world has a functional, motivational basis. A world in which actions have predictable and appropriate consequences enables people to act and pursue their plans within it.[26] Several studies have shown how people find reasons for others' unfavourable situation, their poverty or their illness, just as they find reasons for their own favourable situation, turning luck or privilege into merit.[27] There is a strong, everyday longing for reasons that explain and justify what may otherwise seem unjust. The businesswomen can, for instance, step over a homeless person sleeping at her doorstep with relative ease when she thinks that this person had a fair chance in life but blew it.

Just world theory places emphasis on predictable action and their consequences, on a degree of individual control over life-circumstances. Such a belief that life-circumstances are of 'our' making may be fairly common for the powerful few, but is rare among the disenfranchised many.[28] This has been borne out in further research, showing that relative to the middle-class, members of the lower economic strata have a significantly weaker sense of personal control over their circumstances and, as a result, are more likely to explain social events in situational rather than systematic terms.[29] It requires further explanation, however, that those individuals and groups that are also systematically disenfranchised and disfavoured by the rules of the game still frequently believe in the justice of those rules.

2 System justification theory

System justification theory purports to offer that explanation, focusing especially on people's overall motivation to defend and justify the system even if it disfavours them.[30] The theory predicts that system justification is a strong motivational factor

[25] Vicky M Wilkins and Jeffrey B Wenger, 'Belief in a Just World and Attitudes Toward Affirmative Action' (2014) 42 *Policy Studies Journal* 325; Melvin J Lerner and Carolyn H Simmons, 'Observer's Reaction to the "Innocent Victim": Compassion or Rejection?' (1966) 4 *Journal of Personality and Social Psychology* 203. See already Zick Rubin and Letita Anne Peplau, 'Who Believes in a Just World' (1975) 31 *Journal of Social Issues* 65.

[26] MJ Lerner, *The belief in a just world: The fundamental delusion* (Plenum Press 1970). Cf Adrian Furnham, 'Belief in a Just World: Research Progress over the Past Decade' (2003) 34 *Personality and Individual Differences* 795;

[27] Lerner and Simmons (n 25).

[28] Susan Marks, 'False Contingency' (2009) 62 *Current Legal Problems* 1, 14.

[29] Antony SR Manstead, 'The Psychology of Social Class: How Socioeconomic Status Impacts Thought, Feelings, and Behaviour' (2018) 57 *British Journal of Social Psychology* 267.

[30] See the recent debate on the occasion of system justification theory's 25th anniversary in (2019) 58 *British Journal of Social Psychology* 263 ff.

for defending system outcomes in addition to ego and group justifications. It has found that self-interest (ego justification) or ingroup favouritism (group justification) both fall short of explaining many social phenomena, such as the fact that those who are most disadvantaged by a social system may end up becoming its most ardent supporters. In short, it has been shown that people find it easier to attribute their disadvantageous position to their own 'objective' shortcomings rather than to the injustice in the social system.

At the heart of system justification theory is once more the need to ease cognitive dissonance resulting from evident inequality that cries out for reasons. Denying reasons is precisely part of critical scholarship. System justification theory further highlights how winners believe themselves to be deserving and losers to be undeserving for their laziness or lack of intelligence, for instance. Remarkably, those who are disfavoured by the social system, too, tend to rationalize their situation on behalf of the social system, for example, believing that they did not work or study hard enough.[31] Stereotypes and ideologies supply ready-made rationalizations that support and justify the social system.[32] System justifications, in sum, provide a palliative function to curb feelings of discontent and anger with a system that would otherwise not only seem (and be) unjust, but also be hard and frustrating to change.[33] It is cognitively and motivationally less onerous to blame oneself than the social system. Strikingly, and consistent with system justification theory, such effects are more pronounced among the poorest and in cases of the greatest inequality, leading to the fact that a bottom-up drive towards social change is weakest where it is needed most.[34] At the same time, it remains crucial not to overlook the contestation and resistance that does exist, not to think, for example, that international investment law has been in a legitimacy crisis only once Western host states were on law's receiving end. Such a view would belittle earlier contestations and rightly prompt charges of Eurocentrism.

3 System justification theory and the role of ideology

System justification theory squares with critical (legal) theory's emphasis on the role of ideology in maintaining the status quo while fending off critique. It is in this vein that both Shirley Scott and Susan Marks have studied international legal practices as ideology.[35]

[31] Gary Blasi and John T Jost, 'System Justification Theory and Research: Implications for Law, Legal Advocacy, and Social Justice' (2012) 94 *Ideology, Psychology, and Law* 1119, 1130.

[32] John T Jost and others, 'Social Inequality and the Reduction of Ideological Dissonance on Behalf of the System: Evidence of Enhanced System Justification among the Disadvantaged' (2003) 33 *European Journal of Social Psychology* 13; Blasi and Jost (n 31) at 1127.

[33] John T Jost, 'A Quarter Century of System Justification Theory: Questions, Answers, Criticisms, and Societal Applications' (2019) 58 *British Journal of Social Psychology* 263.

[34] PJ Henry and Andrea Saul, 'The Development of System Justification in the Developing World' (2006) 19 *Social Justice Research* 365.

[35] Shirley V Scott, 'International Law as Ideology: Theorizing the Relationship between International Law and International Politics' (1994) 5 *European Journal of International Law* 313; Susan Marks, *The Riddle of All Constitutions. International Law, Democracy and the Critique of Ideology* (Oxford University

They have both drawn on John Thompson's seminal work, whose conception of ideology,

> calls our attention to the ways in which meaning is mobilized in the service of dominant individuals and groups, that is, the ways in which the meaning constructed and conveyed by symbolic forms serves, in particular circumstances, to establish and sustain structured social relations from which some individuals and groups benefit more than others, and which some individuals and groups have an interest in preserving while others may seek to contest.[36]

Free market ideology is one of the leading cases in point, and a main target of criticism. With reference to the above examples from trade, it may be recalled that comparative advantages on the market typically do not arise in the absence of law, but through law and legal privileges. Similarly, as long as economic law is deemed to be about increasing welfare through efficiency gains, its key role in distributing, rather than creating, value gets lost.[37] The workings of ideology can contribute to leading the have-nots away from contesting the social system, thus stabilizing the rules of the game and allowing those rules to be mobilized in the service of the haves. Several studies in international law have zoomed in on particular parts of practice, focusing on international law not only *as* ideology, but in service of another ideology, be it service of particular great powers,[38] specific promises of progress,[39] or grand schemes of (neo-)liberalism or capitalism.[40]

The practice of exposing the complicity of international law in contributing to instances and patterns of injustice—of seeing it as part of the problem—thus counters a combination of powerful cognitive and social psychological dynamics that render the world seemingly just. The persistence of those dynamics and the cognitive effects they produce demands that critique be repeated, rubbed in, as it were.

Press 2000). Also see China Miéville, *Between Equal Rights: A Marxist Theory of International Law* (Brill 2005). Grietje Baars, *The Corporation, Law and Capitalism: A Radical Perspective on the Role of Law in the Global Political Economy* (Brill 2019).

[36] John B Thompson, *Ideology and Modern Culture: Critical Social Theory in the Era of Mass Communication* (Polity Press 1990) 72–73.

[37] Ingo Venzke, *International Law and the Spectre of Inequality* (Amsterdam University Press 2019); Nicolas Lamp, 'How Should We Think about the Winners and Losers from Globalization? Three Narratives and Their Implications for the Redesign of International Economic Agreements' (2019) 30 *European Journal of International Law* 1359.

[38] Nico Krisch, 'International Law in Times of Hegemony: Unequal Power and the Shaping of the International Legal Order' (2005) 16 *European Journal of International Law* 369.

[39] Martti Koskenniemi, 'The Ideology of International Adjudication and the 1907 Hague Conference' in Yves Daudet (ed), *Topicality of the 1907 Hague Conference, the Second Peace Conference* (Nijhoff 2008) 127–52.

[40] BS Chimni, 'Marxism and International Law: A Contemporary Analysis' (1999) 34 *Economic and Political Weekly* 337; Akbar Rasulov, 'A Marxism for International Law: A New Agenda' (2018) 29 *European Journal of International Law* 631.

It is not, as is sometimes suggested, that critique, if once expressed, it is done, or that it is at best a first step before the real work begins. Omission and confirmation biases, just world, and system justification theories are too powerful.

IV Revealing Indeterminacy at any Moment

A Law's Indeterminacy (Once More, Briefly)

A second characteristic feature of critique is that it draws attention to law's indeterminacy. Duncan Kennedy has shown for private law how decisions oscillate between party autonomy and mandatory rules, and David Kennedy as well as Martti Koskenniemi have done so similarly for the structure of international legal argument, which they see to be caught between apology (linked to state consent) and utopia (linked to some transcendent idea of justice).[41] The main techniques for exposing the indeterminacy of specific choices have been those of structuralism,[42] in particular deconstruction—peeling off layers of argument to expose the arguably groundless choice between antagonistic principles and to retain a sense that a choices could also have gone the other way. In Jacques Derrida's drastic formulation, deconstruction *is* freedom, the possibility to take full responsibility for one's decisions that cannot be derived from anything or anywhere.[43]

Even if one does not buy into that full theoretical package, the critique of legal decisions' determining forces—be it in politics, economics, morality, or another terrain—has a strong tradition.[44] Part of that tradition is to keep the legal form free from outside interference. The critical Hans Kelsen subscribed to that programme, among others, not in defence of an implausible pseudo-formalism, as is sometimes suggested, but in favour of keeping open a space for choice within the law.[45]

The main point of practicing this technique—of revealing the indeterminacy of legal decisions—has always been twofold, to show that it could have been otherwise, and to start an inquiry into why it was not.[46] If the law does not determine

[41] David Kennedy, 'Theses about International Law Discourse' (1980) 23 *German Yearbook of International Law* 353; Martti Koskenniemi, *From Apology to Utopia: The Structure of International Legal Argument* (Cambridge University Press 2005).

[42] Martti Koskenniemi, 'What Is Critical Research in International Law?' (2016) 29 *Leiden Journal of International Law* 727.

[43] Jacques Derrida, 'Force of Law: The "Mystical Foundation of Authority"' (1990) 11 *Cardozo Law Review* 920.

[44] Jochen von Bernstorff and Ingo Venzke, 'Ethos, Ethics and Morality in International Relations' in Rüdiger Wolfrum (ed), *Max Planck Encyclopedia of Public International Law* (Oxford University Press 2010).

[45] Jochen von Bernstorff, *The Public International Law Theory of Hans Kelsen: Believing in Universal Law* (Cambridge University Press 2010); Ernesto Laclau, *Emancipation(s)* (Verso 1996); Ingo Venzke, 'Legal Contestation about "Enemy Combatants": On the Exercise of Power in Legal Interpretation' (2009) 5 *Journal of International Law & International Relations* 155.

[46] See Ingo Venzke, 'What If? Counterfactual (Hi)Stories of International Law' (2018) 8 *Asian Journal of International Law* 403.

its interpretation, what does? These two sides of critique stand in a mutually supportive relationship, but they also pull into different directions. On the one hand, the critical argument suggests that an inquiry into why a legal decision went this way and not the other way must first expose how, legally, very different decisions were indeed possible. Law *as* ideology, the argument goes, hides the 'real' reasons. Law's spell must first be undone, its indeterminacy be exposed, before deeper understanding and critique is possible. On the other hand, however, exposing indeterminacy is placed into the service of freedom and responsible action—it *could* have been otherwise, not only legally, but 'really', practically.[47] That latter argument is tangibly more difficult as it needs to counter the forces that in practice close down interpretative choices.

B Hindsight Bias and Counterfactual Thinking

There is a point to exposing indeterminacy that is backed up by social-psychological research but largely overlooked. It emerges from attention to the bias of hindsight and the potential of counterfactual thinking. Baruch Fischhoff notably placed his classic study on the phenomenon of hindsight bias within the context of historiography's problematic tendency to rationalize what has happened, thereby leading to 'creeping determinism',[48] as he put it; that is, to 'an impression that it really could not have happened otherwise'.[49] This was a couple of decades before Roberto Unger and Duncan Kennedy charged 'rationalizing legal analysis' with contributing to the creation of 'false necessity' (Unger),[50] or beliefs in the 'false determinacy' (Kennedy) of legal decisions.[51]

Research on the phenomenon of hindsight bias not only resonates strongly with Unger's as well as Kennedy's understanding of the problem, but also with their suggested solutions. In a classically critical fashion, Kennedy has placed his bets on deconstruction as an aide to expose legal decisions' indeterminacy,

[47] On this difficulty see, Genevieve Painter, 'Contingency in International Legal History: Why Now?' in Ingo Venzke and Kevin Jon Heller (eds), *Contingency in International Law: On the Possibility of Different Legal Histories* (Oxford University Press 2021).

[48] Baruch Fischhoff, *Hindsight ≠ Foresight: The Effect of Outcome Knowledge on Judgment Under Uncertainty* (1975) 1 *Journal of Experimental Psychology: Human Perception and Performance* 288, 288 (speaking of 'creeping determinism' through hindsight bias 'in contrast to philosophical determinism, which is the conscious belief that whatever happens has to happen); Scott A Hawkins and Reid Hastie, 'Hindsight: Biased Judgments of Past Events After the Outcomes Are Known' (1990) 107 *Psychological Bulletin* 311, 313 (speaking of creeping determinism as 'the tendency to perceive a reported outcome as virtually inevitable').

[49] Georges Florovsky, 'The Study of the Past' in Ronald H Nash (ed), *Ideas of History, vol 2* (EP Dutton 1969) 351–69 at 369; quoted in Fischhoff (n 48) 288.

[50] Roberto Mangabeira Unger, *False Necessity: Anti-Necessitarian Social Theory in the Service of Radical Democracy* (Verso 2001).

[51] Kennedy (n 2).

and inconsistencies in the legal order more generally. In theory and practice, underlying principles could also be flipped around to offer outcomes pointing in the opposite direction, according to Kennedy. Respect for autonomy (or sovereignty) could serve as a perfectly plausible basis for respecting individual choices just as well as overriding them.[52] Unger, in turn, advocates institutional imagination in order to counter any resignation to the present order of things.[53] Social-psychological research that has rather extensively tested the effect of counterfactual thinking to work against hindsight bias, however, has gone unrecognized.

Hindsight bias refers to the excessively higher assessment of a certain outcome's likelihood ex post when compared to ex ante.[54] It may make perfect sense to update one's likelihood assessments of an outcome ex post, for instance when the ex ante likelihood of a certain outcome was thought to be zero and then it happened. More generally, it is possible to learn from what has happened and to adjust likelihood assessments in that light. However, likelihood assessments tend to be biased, exaggerated in hindsight beyond such 'reasonable' adjustments.[55] At this point, where learning stops and exaggeration begins, the presumption flares up that unbiased, rational beliefs and action are indeed possible.[56] Even if that occasional presumption is problematic, research on hindsight remains insightful and relevant for critical thinking.

It has been shown in further detail how several specific psychological dynamics—both motivational and cognitive—sustain the bias of hindsight. A first set of reasons once more connects to people's well-documented desire to live in a world that is relatively certain, predictable and just.[57] Echoing the *Dialectics of Enlightenment*, Hannah Arendt for instance noted the strong appeal of theories that explain the world in terms of general laws. In her view, '[p]eople find such theories in order

[52] For a more concrete and detailed argument see, Kennedy, 'The Structure of Blackstone's Commentaries' (n 6). See more generally on the role of antagonisms in critical scholarship, Ingo Venzke, 'The Practice of Interpretation in International Law: Strategies of Critique' in Jeffrey L Dunoff and Mark A Pollack (eds), *International Legal Theory: Foundations and Frontiers* (Cambridge University Press 2020).

[53] Roberto Mangabeira Unger, *What Should Legal Analysis Become?* (Verso 1996). See also Isabel Feichtner, 'Critical Scholarship and Responsible Practice of International Law. How Can the Two Be Reconciled?' (2016) 29 *Leiden Journal of International Law* 979.

[54] Fischhoff (n 48); Baruch Fischhoff, 'For Those Condemned to Study the Past: Heuristics and Biases in Hindsight' in Daniel Kahneman, Paul Slovic, and Amos Tversky (eds), *Judgment Under Uncertainty: Heuristics and Biases* (Cambridge University Press 1982) 335 (. Also see Hawkins and Hastie (n 48) 311; Neal J Roese and James M Olson, 'Counterfactuals, Causal Attributions, and the Hindsight Bias: A Conceptual Integration' (1996) 32 *Journal of Experimental Social Psychology* 197.

[55] Fischhoff, 'For Those Condemned to Study the Past' (n 54).

[56] On the distinction between hindsight bias and leaning from the past see Stephen J Hoch and George F Loewenstein, 'Outcome Feedback: Hindsight and Information' (1989) 15 *Journal of Experimental Psychology: Learning, Memory, and Cognition* 605.

[57] Neal J Roese and Kathleen D Vohs, 'Hindsight Bias' (2012) 7 *Perspectives on Psychological Science* 411.

to get rid of contingency and unexpectedness'.[58] What happens must happen for a reason.[59]

Secondly, individuals want to be seen as though they knew all along what would happen.[60] Adapting the argument for the field of international law by way of example, as experts of their métier, it is plausible that international lawyers want to think that they knew judicial outcomes all along, or that they at least want to be seen that way. Acknowledging a mistaken expectation ex ante about the ICJ's decision in *Jurisdictional Immunities*, for instance, does not square well with claims to being an expert of international law. As a result of these motivational reasons for hindsight bias, people come to hold mistaken beliefs about the state of the world or about the subjective capacity to foresee outcomes.[61] Motivational dynamics may thus lead to the fact that people wrongly remember their ex ante likelihood assessments.[62]

C Beliefs in Likelihood and Desirability

System justification theory offers another insight when it comes to beliefs about law's determinacy, showing that whatever is perceived to be next to necessary is for that reason also believed to be more desirable, thus supporting the practice of exposing indeterminacy from a different angle.[63] Research in the context of the US Presidential elections in 2000, for instance, showed how the desirability of either the Democrat or Republican candidate increased across party affiliations when their victory became more likely—they were seen as 'sweet lemons'—and how that desirability decreased when their chances for success waned—'sour grapes'.[64] Other research has likewise found that people indeed resign themselves to what they believe to be inescapable—they are adjusting their normative beliefs about what *should be* the case to what *is* (and is bound to

[58] Hannah Arendt, interviewed by Roger Errera in October 1973, excerpts published in *New York Review of Books* (26 October 1973) 18.

[59] Jeffrey J Rachlinski, 'A Positive Psychological Theory of Judging in Hindsight' (1998) 65 *University of Chicago Law Review* 571, 582–83; Melvin J Lerner and Dale T Miller, 'Just World Research and the Attribution Process: Looking Back and Ahead' (1978) 85 *Psychiatry Bulletin* 1030; Jennifer D Campbell and Abraham Tesser, 'Motivational Interpretations of Hindsight Bias: An Individual Difference Analysis' (1983) 51 *Journal of Personality and Social Psychology* 605.

[60] See in particular Barry R Schlenker, *Impression Management: The Self-Concept, Social Identity, and Interpersonal Relations* (Brooks/Cole 1980).

[61] Roese and Vohs (n 57).

[62] See Linda L Carli, 'Cognitive Reconstruction, Hindsight, and Reactions to Victims and Perpetrators' (1999) 25 *Personality and Social Psychology Bulletin* 966.

[63] Jost (n 33) 285.

[64] Blasi and Jost (n 31); Aaron C Kay, Maria C Jimenez, and John T Jost, 'Sour Grapes, Sweet Lemons, and the Anticipatory Rationalization of the Status Quo' (2002) 28 *Personality and Social Psychology Bulletin* 1300.

remain so).[65] Beliefs in a legal decision's apparent necessity and their justice are thus closely aligned.

Overall, drawing attention to arguments about the law's indeterminacy may seem quaint, but persistent cognitive biases testify to its continued relevance. Counterfactual thinking—thinking how it could have been otherwise—impacts attitudes towards the law because it can decrease perceptions of both likelihood and desirability.[66]

V Recovering Contingency in the Course of International Law

A third trait of critique is that it works historically to expose not only the complicity of the law in patterns of injustice but also past possibilities for a different law.[67] This work is related to revealing the law's indeterminacy in a moving present, but is less focused on specific decisions and more so on broader legal developments. The question is both whether a certain development could have gone another way at any particular moment—within and against the context—and whether this would actually have made a difference in the long run.[68] There are several modes of such historical scholarship.[69] It may proceed in an archaeological fashion in the sense of—as Foucault put it—'grasp[ing] the implicit systems which determine our most familiar behavior without our knowing it ... the constraint they impose upon us'.[70] The present state of affairs is not necessary, look at the past, it *was* different! But circumstances of course change. Knowing that the earth rotates around the sun can hardly be unlearned, nor could God easily be brought back to life to offer a basis for international law. Much of critical scholarship thus echoes a genealogical, rather than archaeological, mode of inquiry. It is concerned not with a sequence of different dominant belief systems, but with underlying conflicts within each system, and with transitions between systems. Genealogical inquiry seeks to unearth

[65] Justin P Friesen and others, 'System Justification: Experimental Evidence, Its Contextual Nature, and Implications for Social Change' (2019) 58 *British Journal of Social Psychology* 315.

[66] Other moderating and conditioning factors are of course relevant, in particular the perceived difficulty of thinking how it could have been otherwise. As might be expected, both likelihood and desirability assessments of what actually happened in fact increase when participants' find it very difficult to think of counterfactual possibilities.

[67] Nils Gilman, 'The New International Economic Order: A Reintroduction' (2015) 6 *Humanity: An International Journal of Human Rights, Humanitarianism, and Development* 1. Cf Ingo Venzke, 'Possibilities of the Past? The Histories of the NIEO and the Travails of Critique' (2018) 20 *Journal of the History of International Law* 263.

[68] Ingo Venzke, 'Situating Contingency in the Path of International Law' in Ingo Venzke and Kevin Jon Heller (eds), *Contingency in International Law: On the Possibility of Different Legal Histories* (Oxford University Press 2021).

[69] Cf Painter (n 47).

[70] John K Simon, 'A Conversation with Michel Foucault' (1971) 38 *Partisan Review* 192, 201, quoted in David Garland, 'What Is a "History of the Present"? On Foucault's Genealogies and Their Critical Preconditions' (2014) 16 *Punishment and Society* 365, 369.

past conflict, to emphasize heterogeneity, to reveal the power relations on which outcomes depend and, overall, to remind us of the contingency of the present.[71] 'Experience has taught me', Foucault wrote, 'that the history of various forms of rationality is sometimes more effective in unsettling our certitudes and dogmatism than is abstract criticism'.[72] What exactly is being unsettled and how?

While some international legal histories have indeed set out to reveal a sense of contingency that has been lost, most of them continue to be written in a way that loses such a sense of how it could have been otherwise.[73] When pushed, few authors would subscribe to a teleological understanding of history, to an understanding of history that is aimed at a specific finality.[74] They still convey precisely such a sense when they embed developments of humanitarian or criminal law into narratives of progress, for instance.[75] They recognize that there are deviations, but the course is still set—and needs to be set firmly in order not to swerve yet again.[76] Accounts that critique international law as a relentless tool of imperialism and other forms of domination also occasionally convey such a sense that it could not have come about differently—thinking that it could have been different only suggests that one has still not fully grasped all the penetrations of power.[77]

Accounts of contingency further struggle to break through standards of the profession and its narrative style.[78] On another occasion, I have argued how contingency is lost in Douglas Irwin's authoritative history on US trade policy: the demise of the International Trade Organization in the 1940s was tragic and the establishment of the North Atlantic Free Trade Organization (NAFTA) in the 1990s came as

[71] Michel Foucault, 'Nietzsche, Genealogy, History' in Paul Rabinow (ed), *The Foucault Reader* (Pantheon 1984) 76, at 82: 'The search for descent is not the erecting of foundations: on the contrary, it disturbs what was previously thought immobile; it fragments what was thought unified; it shows the heterogeneity of what was imagined consistent with itself.' See also M Dean, *Critical and Effective Histories: Foucault's Methods and Historical Sociology* (Routledge 1994).

[72] Michel Foucault, 'Politics and Reason (1979)', reprinted in LD Kritzman (ed), *Michel Foucault: Politics, Philosophy, Culture: Interviews and Other Writings, 1977–1984* (Routledge 1988) 83, quoted in Garland (n 70) 373.

[73] Samuel Moyn, 'From Situated Freedom to Plausible Worlds' in Ingo Venzke and Kevin Jon Heller (eds), *Contingency in International Law: On the Possibility of Different Legal Histories* (Oxford University Press 2021).

[74] For a lasting critique of this position see Karl R Popper, *The Poverty of Historicism* (Routledge 1957).

[75] Thomas Skouteris, *The Notion of Progress in International Law Discourse* (Asser 2010).

[76] Cf Geoff Gordon, 'The Time of Contingency in International Law' in Ingo Venzke and Kevin Jon Heller (eds), *Contingency in International Law: On the Possibility of Different Legal Histories* (Oxford University Press 2021).

[77] Mohsen al Attar, 'Subverting Eurocentric Epistemology: The Value of Nonsense when Designing Counterfactuals' in Ingo Venzke and Kevin Jon Heller (eds), *Contingency in International Law: On the Possibility of Different Legal Histories* (Oxford University Press 2021); Painter (n 47), arguing that for some, 'analysis of contingency weakens the claim that international law's telos has been relentlessly imperial'.

[78] Moyn (n 73). Cf Jean d'Aspremont, 'The Critical Attitude and the History of International Law' (2019) 1 *Brill Research Perspectives in International Legal Theory and Practice* 1.

a surprise. But frequent fore- and back-shadowing produces a clear story line that did not allow for a different path.[79]

There are other reasons for why contingency continuously gets lost. Here I only want to draw out three ways in which recovering a sense for possibilities resonates with psychological insights, drawing together many of the points of the previous sections.[80] First, research on the reasons for hindsight bias has placed particular emphasis on cognitive dynamics according to which people integrate outcome knowledge into pre-existing explanatory schemes, fitting them into a coherent narrative. This practice leads them to attribute outcomes to the factors they know, frequently making those factors more important than they are.[81] This is precisely the dynamic that Fischhoff emphasized when he wrote of 'creeping determinism'[82]—the rushed attribution of outcomes to known factors.[83] The push of critique to reveal past possibilities has, like counterfactual thinking about specific decisions, the potential of countering such a cognitive bias, trying to keep the mind open for longer.[84] Secondly, I have highlighted many of the dynamics that lead to closely aligning assessments of likelihood and desirability. Revealing contingency may thus also works to regain a political understanding of social conditions to orient and motivate action. Relatedly, third, asking about how international law could have been otherwise (*vel non*), takes the analysis of why something happened further, often exposing agency that had remained nebulous.

VI Outlook

There are many reasons why a lot of critical research is deeply sceptical about social-psychological research, especially as it developed under the mantle of behavioural economics. Such scepticism targets the commitment to the possibility of unbiased, objective, and rational action, as well as the arguably rather late recognition that such rationality is often just not the norm. Scepticism extends to

[79] Venzke, 'Situating Contingency' (n 68), with reference to DA Irwin, *Clashing Over Commerce: A History of US Trade Policy* (University of Chicago Press 2017).

[80] Also see Janne Nijman, 'An Enlarged Sense of Possibility for International Law: Seeking Change by Doing History' in Ingo Venzke and Kevin Jon Heller (eds), *Contingency in International Law: On the Possibility of Different Legal Histories* (Oxford University Press 2021), linking up to the psychoanalytically informed work of Paul Riceur, among others.

[81] NJ Roese and JM Olson, 'Counterfactuals, Causal Attributions, and the Hindsight Bias: A Conceptual Integration' (1996) 32 *Journal of Experimental Social Psychology* 197; Richard Ned Lebow, *Forbidden Fruit: Counterfactuals and International Relations* (Princeton University Press 2010); D Wasserman, RO Lempert, and R Hastie, 'Hindsight and Causality' (1991) 17 *Personality and Social Psychology Bulletin* 30.

[82] Baruch Fischhoff, 'Hindsight ≠Foresight: The Effect of Outcome Knowledge on Judgment Under Uncertainty' (1975) 1 *Journal of Experimental Psychology: Human Perception and Performance* 288.

[83] Compare the emphasis on *schema* in Bianchi and Hirsch, in this volume.

[84] Richard Ned Lebow, 'Counterfactual Thought Experiments: A Necessary Teaching Tool' (2007) 40 *The History Teacher* 153.

the related methods of inquiry, especially those that build on questionable positivism.[85] But certainly not all of social psychology can be cast asides like that. There is, to be sure, a strong tradition of combining insights. Such a tradition would invite the emerging body of experimental studies in international law to look beyond the law's practical operation towards its social effects: how is law weaved into beliefs about what can and cannot change of our present condition?

[85] For such scepticism see Kennedy, *A Critique of Adjudication (Fin de Siècle)* (n 2).

4
Institutionally Embodied Law: Cognitive Linguistics and the Making of International Law

Jacob Livingston Slosser and Mikael Rask Madsen

I Introduction

For some, international legal practice can be understood as a set of institutions in a continual power struggle that is often reconciled by an appeal to certainty regarding the meaning of legal categories as developed in a body of case law.[1] However tempting this certainty may be in its pragmatism, it is short sighted in its completeness. What is needed are supplementary approaches to the nature of legal categories that explain the creation and interpretation of law from a cognitive point of view that does not disregard the institution, but marries the two. Methods derived from cognitive linguistics are, in this regard, well-suited to the task of understanding the practice of international law as, what we term, an *institutionally embodied law*. This is a practice centred on category building, developing prototypes, analogies, and metaphors: conceptual projections that are based on the same or similar embodied experiences shared by judges and their interlocutors as cognitive beings.[2] We anchor ourselves with the argument that this is reflected in the law's 'deep structure' and, thus, can be read in the texts of its canon. We ask, what are the linguistic dynamics of categorization and how does legal language mediate the power dynamics of a situated institution? We answer these questions by exploring law as *institutionally embodied.* We make use of the notion of a situated institution, namely, that choices and understanding about and of legal concepts are made *somewhere.* We structure this contextual understanding by expanding the remit of what that *somewhere* means to the entity situated within it—what could be called the *somebody*—and make use of the scholarship that promotes embodied cognition. By merging the social and linguistic readings of legal interpretation we

[1] Nico Krisch, 'International Law in Times of Hegemony: Unequal Power and the Shaping of the International Legal Order' (2005) 16 *European Journal of International Law* 369.

[2] See generally Gabriel Ignatow, 'Theories of Embodied Knowledge: New Directions for Cultural and Cognitive Sociology?' (2007) 37 *Journal for the Theory of Social Behaviour* 115.

Jacob Livingston Slosser and Mikael Rask Madsen, *Institutionally Embodied Law: Cognitive Linguistics and the Making of International Law* In: *International Law's Invisible Frames.* Edited by: Andrea Bianchi and Moshe Hirsch, Oxford University Press. DOI: 10.1093/oso/9780192847539.003.0005

look for a thicker analysis of the behaviour of legal-institutional actors in terms of the formation of legal categories, beyond just institutional power or cognitive bias.

The chapter considers the social and linguistic dynamics of categorization by melding an institutional power-based view with a cognitive realist perspective to investigate international law's invisible frames. It also responds in spirit to the first and second of Paul DiMaggio's three challenges to cognitive sociologists emanating from his classic 'Cognition and Culture', left still largely unanswered.[3] Namely, how schemata form institutional logics and how actors negotiate those logics. We use the margin of appreciation as laid out by the *Cyprus* case,[4] a classic of European human rights jurisprudence, as an example of an institution riddled by a puzzle of legitimacy and diplomacy making use of embodied concepts—the invisible frames that proliferate throughout the life of the institution. As pointed out in the introduction to this volume, invisible does not always mean hidden. Often what is thought of as the banal, obvious, irrelevant, simplistic, or miscategorized can suffice for the invisibility of certain features that make up thought and action. We first layout the basics of cognitive linguistics and how it can be applied to rule-interpretation. We cover the bare minimum of cognitive linguistics as methodological tools to investigate the underlying conceptual structure of legal principles. We cover the basic premises on which to expand judicial behaviour beyond politics and the politics embedded within category building itself, namely, categorization and conceptual projection. We then use the example of margin of appreciation to outline our conception of *institutionally embodied law*. We supply our example European Court of Human Rights (ECtHR) to give life to this theory in a generalizable format and to promote further research in the paradigm of cognitive legal studies.

II Legal Interpretation and Cognitive Linguistics

Section II describes first, the general applicability and strength of a cognitive approach to law. It then gives a brief primer on three major tenets of cognitive linguistics and how they can be applied as methodological tools to understand how legal categories can be seen as embodied categories that proliferate through case law. These tenets are: the image schema, frames, and conceptual metaphor. This is, by necessity, nowhere near an exhaustive list. Other useful concepts include prototype theory,[5] conceptual

[3] Paul DiMaggio, 'Culture and Cognition' (1997) 23 *Annual Review of Sociology* 263, 278.

[4] *Greece v United Kingdom*, App no 176/56 (26 September 1958) Report of the Commission (*Cyprus case* or *Cyprus*).

[5] E Rosch and B Lloyd (eds), *Cognition and Categorization* (Lawrence Erlbaum 1978); Eleanor Rosch and Carolyn B Mervis, 'Family Resemblances: Studies in the Internal Structure of Categories' (1975) 7 *Cognitive Psychology* 573; Eleanor Rosch, 'Cognitive Representations of Semantic Categories' (1975)

blending,[6] and idealized cognitive models,[7] among others. Here we seek mainly to highlight what can be used from even the more basic tenets of cognitive approaches. The benefits are, in our view, twofold. First, is the understanding of that which comes from 'outside' the law and how concepts constructed outside of the law inform the interpretation of 'legal' terms. Secondly, is the ability of these ideas to effect interpretation in a path dependant nature negotiated by coherence. We return to both of these in the following section.

A Cognitive Linguistics and Law

Human beings are faced with an insurmountable project of sorting out information from cues coming from our environment. To provide a shortcut for this overload, information is sorted into concepts; delineated categories from which we can make heuristic choices about the world. It is a cognitive strategy for a mind that is overwhelmed by raw input. Many disciplines have attempted to sort through the minutiae of category-making and have made little headway. Philosophy, linguistics, law, among others, have been dominated for two millennia by category membership being defined through a measure of necessary and sufficient conditions and amodal reasoning. This classical understanding implies that categories fit in a binary system. Something is either in or out as a member. Although useful for building and maintaining truth value in logical systems, this binary system is not how people seem to construct and make use of categories in everyday life. Categories are blurred (fuzzy) where membership is graded by fit (radial), and members do not all necessarily share all the same attributes.[8] The role and make-up of categories goes beyond just membership. At the forefront of taking up the challenge of categorical fuzziness is the field of cognitive linguistics.

Cognitive linguistics was born out of a frustration with a formal linguistic approach that was not plausible based on emerging findings from the cognitive science of the 1960s and 1970s. Its main founders (Ronald Langacker, George Lakoff, Mark Turner, Ray Jackendoff, Gilles Fauconnier, among others) investigated how the systematic structure of language can be paired with the systematic structure of thought. Although its scholars range among various strains of linguistics, Cognitive Linguistics shares two main commitments, outlined by George Lakoff

104 *Journal of Experimental Psychology: General* 192; Eleanor Rosch, 'Cognitive Reference Points' (1975) 7 *Cognitive Psychology* 532.

[6] Gilles Fauconnier and Mark Turner, *The Way We Think: Conceptual Blending and the Mind's Hidden Complexities* (Basic Books 2008); Gilles Fauconnier and Eve Sweetser, *Spaces, Worlds, and Grammar* (University of Chicago Press 1996).

[7] Steven L Winter, *A Clearing in the Forest: Law, Life, and Mind* (University of Chicago Press 2001).

[8] A point famously made by Wittgenstein; see Ludwig Wittgenstein, *Philosophical Investigations* (4th edn, John Wiley & Sons Ltd 2009).

in 1990: the 'Generalization Commitment' and the 'Cognitive Commitment'.[9] The Generalization Commitment stipulates that any theory of language must contain 'general principles that are responsible for all aspects of human language'.[10] Unlike the formal theoretical approaches to language where different functions of language are allocated to different 'modules' of the brain, the Generalization Commitment looks for the underlying principles in language formation and function. The Cognitive Commitment is an adherence to the principle that theories of language must comport with evidence from studies of the mind and brain.

The major underlying premise of cognitive linguistics (more technically, the subfield of cognitive semantics) is that humans think and make meaning in conceptual structures: containers that act as reference points to other knowledge, where 'linguistic units serve as prompts for an array of conceptual operations and the recruitment of background knowledge'.[11] These structures are anything but binary, varying in form (eg image schemata, frames, mental spaces, prototypes, idealized cognitive models) and interaction (eg mapping, blending, systematicity, analogies, and metaphors). The binding principle is that these concepts are defined by their *embodied* nature. That is, that 'we have a species-specific view of the world due to the unique nature of our physical bodies ... [and] our construal of reality is likely to be mediated in large measure by the nature of our bodies'.[12] Embodiment informs our notions of both tangible things and their abstract extensions. Thus, our reasoning is not regulated by a strict adherence to rule based maxims that define category membership but are understood through a systematic extension of our lived experience. These embodied conceptual structures are not purely subjective (in some solipsistic notion), but they are mediated by the habitus of human interaction.[13]

Unlike the cognitive approach, legal interpretation traditionally relies on the binary categorical structure. This takes on one form at the level of interpreting the meaning of a single word. For instance, whether something falls within the notion of 'private and family life', 'home' or 'correspondence', in the sense of Article 8 of the European Convention on Human Rights (ECHR or Convention).[14] This can be highly counterintuitive as to how all of these instances are members of the same category. This takes on a second form in applying general principles to a particular case (eg maxims, rules, principles, etc.). These principles are meant to behave independently (or at least be justified independently). There is a presumption of

[9] George Lakoff, 'The Invariance Hypothesis: Is Abstract Reason Based on Image-Schemas?' (1990) 1 *Cognitive Linguistics* 39.

[10] Vyvyan Evans and Melanie Green, *Cognitive Linguistics: An Introduction* (L Erlbaum 2006) 27.

[11] This is often regarded as the encyclopaedic nature of meaning. See ibid 160–62.

[12] ibid 45.

[13] We discuss this notion in section III.A.

[14] See eg Maris Burbergs, 'How the Right to Respect for Private and Family Life, Home and Correspondence Became the Nursery in Which New Rights Are Born' in Eva Brems and Janneke Gerards (eds), *Shaping Rights in the ECHR* (Cambridge University Press 2013).

applying something which is built within the law as a principle that has the clarity of a binary, in-or-out category. This is most clearly demonstrated when a judgement professes imperatives such as a particular circumstance is a case of category A occurring (eg humiliating treatment) which demands the use of category/principle/etc. X (eg ECHR Article 3 meaning of 'degrading' and its case law) which *must* be understood to mean Y (eg 'the humiliation or debasement involved must attain a particular level ... other than that usual element of humiliation'[15] from punishment in general). This imperative is invoked due to the normative force of objective justification.

To use Neil MacCormick's words, 'when is it justifiable to apply this category in our explanation of events, and how [should we] apply it?'.[16] The search for an objective standard is aimed at constructing law in a way which allows it to exist outside of human construction. MacCormick, among the many who have searched for this standard, does not ignore the humanity of a judge or their decision. It is precisely their human fallibility and subjectivity in decision-making they are trying to circumvent by constructing an objective notion of the law. It is an attempt to justify the law by way of a cognitive linguistics-like generalizability commitment:

> There is, I submit, no justification without universalization; motivation needs no universalization; but explanation requires generalization. For particular facts—or particular motives—to be justifying reasons they have to be subsumable under a relevant principle of action universally stated.[17]

If this premise is true, then it is incumbent on the legal theorist to understand those generalizations and their applications to particular circumstances. For MacCormick, the defeasibility (in the Popperian sense) of universal principles is the best recourse to provide justification for the outcomes of legal reasoning. A generalization, or a principle derived from a common set of particulars, must allow itself to be tested over and over again to define its boundaries, core assumptions, and ultimately its ability to be falsified, if it hopes to be a justified generalization. It will ultimately be refined to categorical maxims of membership. However, this is a double-edged sword. Any single case, once classified as an instance of 'x', allows (in fact even calls for) some inductive reasoning along the lines of; *if x then y*, or *x has a value of y*, *x exists in a set of premises that leads to y*, etc. The particular exists in a larger conceptualization of the universal principle, and that principle dictates (at least in part) the inductive reasoning that follows from it. MacCormick uses the death of Cleopatra as an example of this logic:

[15] *Tyrer v United Kingdom*, App no 5856/72 (25 April 1978) § 30.

[16] Neil MacCormick, 'Particulars and Universals' in Zenon Bankowski (ed), *The Universal and the Particular in Legal Reasoning* (Ashgate Publishing 2006) 17.

[17] ibid 19.

> [w]hat enables us so to conceptualize the death of Cleopatra is that the particular fact of the biting snake belongs as minor premise in an argument of which the major premise is a hypothesis culled from the snake-venom theory and the conclusion is the death.[18]

The particulars in each case test our notions of the 'snake-venom theory of death' so that the general principle can be honed to fit more and more circumstances, making us more assured of its justified content, and by extension increasing our trust that the law is just, or a decision or interpretation of a statute or precedent was, if not certainly *correct*, at least reasonable or justifiable. It requires containing the principle within a set of criteria, often in the form of necessary and sufficient conditions, to see where it fits within the law. It is a decision claiming that circumstance *A* is a case of *x*.

This practice of category building—one that allows for the justification of the application of law to a particular circumstance—relies on a set of prior assumptions, background knowledge, institutional settings, present day conditions, etc. However, the act of categorization as traditionally theorized by legal scholars often aims so squarely on objective justification, that it risks ignoring the cognitive mechanisms by which it is built, and relegating the process to an unknown or relying on abstract generalizations that have their only grounding in philosophy, ethics, or an appeal to the coherence of law. Coherence, in this regard, does not mean that there is one correct reading, but rather that each reading affects the coherence of an overall structure: it is coherent 'with the background system of acceptances, reasonings and preferences, conceived as an all-embracing theory'.[19] Coherence, as a legal concept, aims to provide a 'consistency in adjudication'[20] as well as the oft-argued role of legitimating the entire enterprise of legal reasoning.[21] Coherence, in this sense, is considered for its normative force. A judgment, if coherent to its larger whole and consistent with its background assumptions and precepts, provides a judge, law maker, and/or citizen a knowability about the law and its likely outcomes. Traditional legal scholarship accepts that there is this greater structure to conceptual knowledge than simple definitions—that concepts 'hang together'—but it usually stops short of digging into the minutiae of how categories (even legal ones) are built, referred to, stretched, and eventually cohere. This is the strength of the cognitive approach. The cognitive linguistic understanding

[18] ibid.

[19] Zenon Bankowski and James MacLean, 'Introduction' in Zenon Bankowski (ed), *The Universal and the Particular in Legal Reasoning* (Ashgate Publishing 2006) xx.

[20] ibid.

[21] In this respect see the discussion in, among various others, Joseph Raz, *The Authority of Law* (Clarendon Press 1979); Joseph Raz, *Ethics in the Public Domain* (Clarendon Press 1994); Andrei Marmor, *Interpretation and Legal Theory* (Hart Publishing 2005); Ken Kress, 'Legal Reasoning and Coherence Theories: Dworkin's Rights Thesis, Retroactivity, and the Linear Order of Decisions' (1984) 72 *California Law Review* 369.

of categories is the main entry point for interpreting the law and investigating its actors. This is not to say that this is the only factor to consider in explaining the behaviour of international (or national) legal actors. However, given that we are talking about the actions and judgements of human beings, we propose that the study of law should reflect critically on the basic commitments of cognitive linguistics in terms of comporting with findings in cognitive science and be generalizable across a legal institution.

B Tools for Empirical Analysis of Category-making

In what follows, we describe the basic tenets of cognitive linguistics relevant to this chapter and its empirical study. The point of entry is the *image schema*. An image schema is a conceptual representation of action or physical relationships with which we understand both concrete and abstract concepts. These include 'rudimentary concepts like CONTACT, CONTAINER, and BALANCE, which are meaningful because they derive from and are linked to human pre-conceptual experience: experience of the world directly mediated and structured by the human body'.[22] For instance, in a legal setting, we understand a notion of a balancing test because of the lived experience of BALANCE that entails EQUILIBRIUM, WEIGHT, VERTICALITY, etc. For example, when the court engages in a test of proportionality, this direct physical knowledge of balance underwrites the notion of *weighing* reasons against one another. When taking into consideration, '[t]he *gravity* of the offence' or 'offences of a *certain minimum gravity*' or giving a consideration '*[s]pecial weight*' or judging '*[w]eighty* reasons' the *weight* and *gravity* of abstract legal reasoning only makes sense given the interpreters' knowledge of a bodily sense of BALANCE and EQUILIBRIUM.[23]

A second integral concept are *frames*. The terms schema, frame, script, domain, and idealized cognitive model, have over the last decades been used somewhat interchangeably over the last few decades .[24] Here we make a distinction between *schema* in the general sense as defined in the introduction which might be used interchangeably with the term *frame*,[25] and *image schema* which we use according to Mark Johnson as 'a recurring, dynamic pattern of our perceptual interactions

[22] Evans and Green (n 10) 46.

[23] Selections from *S and Marper v United Kingdom*, App nos 30562/04 and 30566/04, (4 December 2008) § 125, § 34, § 108, § 82, respectively.

[24] For some history and disambiguation see Alan Cienki, 'Frames, Idealized Cognitive Models, and Domains' in Dirk Geeraerts and Hubert Cuyckens (eds), *The Oxford Handbook of Cognitive Linguistics* (Oxford University Press 2010); also see the introductory chapter to this volume.

[25] See Charles Fillmore's definition in Charles J Fillmore and Collin Baker, 'A Frames Approach to Semantic Analysis' in Bernd Heine and Heiko Narrog (eds), *The Oxford Handbook of Linguistic Analysis* (Oxford University Press 2009).

and motor programs that gives coherence and structure to our experience'.[26] Image schemata represent the basics of force, motion, and space, and are innately perceptual. Frames operationalize and organize image schematic concepts into a systematic representation by 'relat[ing] the elements and entities associated with a particular culturally embedded scene from human experience'.[27] It is here that frames have a persuasive power, where 'it is frequently possible to show that the same "facts" [with] different framings, framings which make them out as different "facts"'.[28] Frames organize relationships in what Gilles Fauconnier terms *mental spaces*. Mental spaces are 'very partial assemblies constructed as we think and talk for purposes of local understanding and action' containing the basic 'elements [of concepts]'.[29] These spaces and their inner structures are used to map their systematic attributes and relationships to understand and give meaning to other spaces. This system is what MacCormick was referring to above with the snake-venom theory of death.

The mere mention of a word can evoke an entire frame, for example where '"buy", "sell", "cost", "goods", "advertise", "credit", etc. make sense only in terms of a frame ... of a commercial transaction that relates them together as a meaningful, social activity'.[30] In legal practice we can see this for instance when the ECtHR (or, 'the Court') invokes a frame through reading into the purpose of the Convention rather than a strictly literal meaning of the terms given in an article. For example in *Airey*,[31] the Court assessed the idea of protection of Article 6 rights must be 'effective' when stating that 'The Convention is intended to guarantee not rights that are theoretical or illusory but rights that are practical and effective'.[32] Effectiveness has a social meaning that does not just live within the law itself but evokes a meaning that is understood in a frame of 'duty' as a positive action.[33] In this framing, the law takes from the wider sense of duty and the relationships of actors that frame requires, and ports it to a legal obligation of positive protection. There is no mention of 'duty' in the Convention, yet it is an operative word in distinguishing the meaning of effective protection, where 'fulfilment of a duty under the Convention on occasion necessitates some positive action on the part of the

[26] Mark Johnson, *The Body in the Mind: The Bodily Basis of Meaning, Imagination, and Reason* (University of Chicago Press 1987).

[27] Evans and Green (no 10) 85.

[28] Charles J. Fillmore, 'Frame semantics' in *Linguistics in the morning calm* (Hanshin 1987) 111–37, 125

[29] Gilles Fauconnier, 'Mental Spaces,' in *Oxford Handbook of Cognitive Linguistics*(Oxford University Press 2010) 351.

[30] Steven L Winter, 'Frame Semantics and the 'Internal Point of View" in Michael Freeman and Fiona Smith (eds), *Law and Language* (Oxford University Press 2013) 117.

[31] *Airey v Ireland*, App no 6289/73 (9 August 1979).

[32] ibid § 24.

[33] See here Winter's (non-exhaustive) distinction of six frames for law: 'law as authority', 'law as social obligation', 'law as moral imperative', 'law as social mechanism', 'law as strategic tool', and 'law as social identity'. Winter (n 30) 123–4.

State; in such circumstances, the State cannot simply remain passive'.[34] The Court also invokes the idea of *law as a process* frame in the form of the metaphorical extension of the image schema SOURCE-PATH-GOAL. The Court distinguishes effectiveness as a measure of arriving at a place, where 'legal *impediments*' must not produce a 'positive *obstacle* placed in [one's] *way*'.[35] Effectiveness is informed by a spatial notion of arriving *at* access to a court. This is of course just one way of framing spatial relationships. As we will see in the *Cyprus case* below, the Court extends the concrete spatial framing to the abstract metaphorical frame of CLOSE IN SPACE IS CLOSE IN MIND. Spatial proximity in this frame highlights the highly metaphoric nature of category building; in fact, '[t]hings that are similar along nearly any dimension can be described as close, and things that are dissimilar as far apart. For example, '[t]hese two shades of blue aren't identical, but they're close', or '[t]he opposing candidates' stances on the issue couldn't be farther apart'.[36] This is true even when literally presenting abstract nouns at different distances from each other on a computer screen: '[w]hen stimuli appeared closer in physical space, they were judged to be "closer" in participants' mental similarity space, as well'.[37]

This framing is a particularly good example of the third relevant tenet: the conceptual projection from one mental space to another epitomized by *conceptual metaphor* and *analogy*. These types of conceptual projections port meaning from a SOURCE domain to a TARGET domain. This is seen above in the construction ACCESS TO A COURT IS A JOURNEY. Another example is the common occurrence of the conceptual metaphor LAW IS A STRUCTURE, where LAW is the target domain and STRUCTURE is the source. The idea that an in interference with a right must be *laid down with precision* and have a legal *basis* or *foundation*, ports the qualities of what we expect from a strong structure to be the same of the law: the law's ability to protect is understood in this conceptual metaphor by way of an appeal to the strength and properties of strong structures. Our understanding of the abstract notion of what the law requires can be influenced by the understanding of a concrete frame of attributes.[38] Harlan Grant Cohen's contribution to this volume displays the multiple levels at which these metaphors play a role in international law. Like Cohen and the field of cognitive linguistics, we understand the role of conceptual metaphor to be more than a mere rhetorical device used

[34] *Airey v Ireland* (n 31) § 25.

[35] ibid (emphasis added).

[36] Daniel Casasanto, 'Similarity and Proximity: When Does Close in Space Mean Close in Mind?' (2008) 36 *Memory & Cognition* 1047, 1047.

[37] ibid 1053.

[38] See Jacob Livingston Slosser, 'Components of Legal Concepts: Quality of Law, Evaluative Judgement, and Metaphorical Framing of Article 8 ECHR' (2019) 25 *European Law Journal* 593; John Gibbons, *Language and the Law* (Routledge 2014); Stefan Larsson, *Conceptions, Categories and Embodiment: Why Metaphors Are of Fundamental Importance for Understanding Norms* (Ashgate Publishing 2013).

as flourish. It highlights and undergirds conceptual structure.[39] Conceptual metaphor (with its siblings in metonymy and analogy) highlight the systematicity of the cognitive approach to conceptual structure. This basic structure and functions among concepts allow for the categorization that the law requires to define words and principles. Conceptual metaphors, as one type of conceptual projection, present a specific structure that entails its own inferences and suggests its own paths of reasoning. As Slosser, among others, has previously developed, 'there can be no application of a general category without a prior acceptance of some underlying premise that frames subsequent judgements. Once framed, judgments can, and do, fall prey to over reliance on category membership or, in the least, to arriving at the kinds of conclusions that are deducible from their framing'.[40]

A salient demonstration of this is evident in the *metaphoric fit hypothesis*. It proposes that when participants are asked to evaluate the fitness of a proposed solution to a given problem they will one, favour solutions that are congruently framed to the problem, and two, disfavour misfit solutions of neutral, literally framed alternatives.[41] Previous work has explored this notion through the Court's assessment of a contracting state's 'quality of law' with regards to Article 8 where, 'The law is assessed for its ability to balance the protection of individual rights with the rights of a State to implement measures, within a certain margin of appreciation'.[42] Through a number of examples it found 'three different instances consistent with the metaphoric fit hypothesis': one, 'congruency [between frames] of the judgment and the competing arguments', as summarized by the Court; two, 'the congruency [between frames] of the judgment and its cited precedent'; and three, 'congruency of dissents to their own precedent choices and the rejection of the incongruent frames of the majority opinion'.[43]

The formula of a conceptual metaphor, with its target and source domains, is an expression of the framed mental spaces that compare and use constitutive elements from those spaces to construct a coherent linkage. Coherence here can be understood not as the comparison of the definitions of different categories, but as the interaction between the make-up and background schemata of complex constitutive spaces that depend significantly on the two categories being compared, and an embodied nature to their abstract attributes. The conceptual metaphor bridges the connection made by framed spaces that allows the conceptual transfer of its formative elements in such a way that metaphors may be judged on fitting an interpreter's own model in varying degrees. It is this dynamic that we rely on to establish a notion of an *embodied law*. Understanding, interpreting and implementing a legal

[39] See eg Lucas Keefer and others, 'Embodied Metaphor and Abstract Problem Solving: Testing a Metaphoric Fit Hypothesis in the Health Domain' (2014) 55 *Journal of Experimental Psychology* 12.
[40] Slosser (n 34) 2.
[41] Keefer and others (n 39); Slosser (n 34).
[42] Slosser (n 34) 11.
[43] ibid 23.

principle means understanding the legal and non-legal frames and embodiment they invoke. The appeal to coherence to the Court's previously laid out conceptual structures produces a path dependant structure of case law. Put simply, path dependence is the idea that preceding events can have 'lock-in effects'[44] dictating a specific outcome. Path dependence

> operates through the gradual building of legal rules upon one another over time. Not only does an earlier decision influence the later decisions of courts, but it also influences them in a particular way: It makes it more likely that courts will choose to resolve similar legal dilemmas in a similar manner.[45]

The metaphoric fit hypothesis (as one example) and the likelihood that the Court reproduces its own interpretations by framing certain values, provides intriguing evidence of this type of path dependence. The next section outlines how the historical development of the Court and its social dynamics laid the foundation for the framing of rights and duties that the Court would continue to perpetuate and rely on for interpretation. It synthesizes the law-making of the early ECtHR with the particular process of category making which the institution ultimately rests on. The categories it focuses on are the 'margin of appreciation', 'dynamic interpretation', 'practical and effective' rights, and finally the notion of 'fundamental rights'.

III From the Embodied Concept to the Embodied Institution

A The Institution

The ideal setting to investigate the interaction between the concepts of embodied law versus 'traditional' legal category making, and the social/political processes that negotiate the application of those categories in institutional practice, is a court whose very founding, design, and progression is characterized by political negotiation, or what Mikael Rask Madsen has previously described as 'legal diplomacy'.[46] It is for this reason we have chosen the European Court and Commission of Human Rights as they were 'constructed at the "crossroads" of other pre-existing

[44] Stefan Larsson, *Conceptions in the Code: How Metaphors Explain Legal Challenges in Digital Times* (Oxford University Press 2017) 151. On path dependence see Oona A Hathaway, 'Path Dependence in the Law: The Course and Pattern of Legal Change in a Common Law System' (2000) 86 *Iowa Law Review* 601.

[45] Hathaway (n 44) 127.

[46] Mikael R Madsen, 'The Protracted Institutionalization of the Strasbourg Court: From Legal Diplomacy to Integrationist Jurisprudence' (2011) 2 *The European Court of Human Rights between Law and Politics* 43, 44.

fields, ranging from national law on related matters to national politics and diplomacy'.[47] Legal diplomacy here should be understood as encompassing the process where, particularly in the early life of the system, 'the objective of providing justice to individuals was carefully balanced with both national and geopolitical interests'[48] of which the end result is margin of appreciation in conceptual terms. The early life of the Court and Commission was confronted by a highly tenuous objective: to somehow reconcile the notion,

> that human rights were at one and the same time both too integrated into national law and politics to be entirely entrusted to a new European court and too important to the idea of European integration to remain a question of national politics and law.[49]

This paradoxical set up was approached with the appointment of judges who were steeped in the culture of both law and politics/diplomacy and relied upon for their ability to negotiate this balance in the Commission and Court's early life. Consequently, this led to a court that was little productive. In its first ten years, 'it had only delivered ten judgments, and of those only a handful found violations' of the Convention, even with a significant number of applications being lodged.[50] The Commission fared somewhat better but lacked the legal teeth of the Court and produced recommendations that needed political action to be effective.

This restrictive nature changed dramatically in the 1970s with landmark cases that shifted the balance from one of integration of sovereign nation-states to the institutionalized conception of fundamental individual rights before the Court through changing notions of 'effective rights', assessing violations in light of 'present day conditions'.[51] It has been offered that these changes may be explained by the change of judges that made up the Court. But this does not bear itself out in analyses that consider the make-up of the Court's judges, at least in terms of political commitments, ideology, national background etc. except that different judges' preferences for how the abstract notions of human rights should be applied to particular cases.[52] Judge selection and presumed political bias do not seem to sway

[47] Mikael Rask Madsen, '"Legal Diplomacy": Law, Politics and the Genesis of Postwar European Human Rights' in SL Hoffman (ed), *Human Rights in the Twentieth Century: A Critical History* (Cambridge University Press 2011) 63.

[48] Madsen (n 45) 44.

[49] ibid 45. For a full history see AW Brian Simpson, *Human Rights and the End of Empire: Britain and the Genesis of the European Convention* (Oxford University Press on Demand 2004).

[50] Madsen (n 45) 51.

[51] Mikael Rask Madsen, 'The Challenging Authority of the European Court of Human Rights: From Cold War Legal Diplomacy to the Brighton Declaration and Backlash' (2016) 79 *Law & Contemporary Problems* 153.

[52] Erik Voeten, 'Politics, Judicial Behaviour, and Institutional Design' in Jonas Christoffersen and Mikael Rask Madsen (eds), *The European Court of Human Rights between Law and Politics* (Oxford University Press 2011).

judgments to any significant degree in the Strasbourg context. However, it may be the case that 'even if judges are not systematically swayed by political considerations, they may well be influenced on highly sensitive cases'.[53] Other theories about this shift are based on the geopolitics of the time, that the widening view of global human rights apparatuses allowed the Court more room to expand its jurisprudence.[54] This more nuanced view adopts the complex nature of the intermingling and the complex nature of how knowledge is constituted by the shift in cultural understandings and the cognitive models that come with them. This description of the background dependent nature of an approach to notions in human rights jurisprudence of the Court underlines the need for a mechanism that explains the interaction from the individual to an institution. This we suggest is the strength of merging the social and cognitive approaches. Understanding the dynamics of this minute scale of 'legal diplomacy', we can look at the practices of how issues like integration and sovereignty are mediated: through the linguistic practices of applying legal principles.

Studying 'legal diplomacy' is more than the influence of politics on law (or the reverse), but as a position of reflexivity (in the Bourdieusian sense).[55] Its aim is to understand the institutionalization of the Court as a process of dynamic construction from not just a purely politicized view but one of indistinct combinations of national and international practices that make use of 'the import-exports of capitals, ideas, practices or symbolic resources between ... interdependent socio-legal levels'.[56] This recruitment and intermingling of both national and international fields clash with the determinate and structured traditional legal separation among its own disciplines. Much like the approach to concepts in cognitive linguistics and its comparison with traditional legal category making, the reflexive sociology of international courts abandons the notion of distinct boundaries created for the ease of empirical study.[57] But empirical work can demonstrably be done. The indeterminate, while more complex, should not be abandoned for the sake of easier choices, when in fact those 'easy' choices are informed by more complex behaviour. Bourdieu's own work in fact can be seen as sympathetic if not wholly pioneering to the complexity of category making relying on embodiment.[58] The embodied

[53] ibid 76.

[54] See eg Stuart A Scheingold, *The Politics of Rights: Lawyers, Public Policy, and Political Change* (University of Michigan Press 2010).

[55] See Mikael Rask Madsen, 'Transnational Fields: Elements of a Reflexive Sociology of the Internationalisation of Law' (2006) 29 *Retfærd. Nordisk Juridisk Tidsskrift* 34; Salvatore Caserta and Mikael Madsen, 'Sociology of International Adjudication' (Social Science Research Network 2019) SSRN Scholarly Paper ID 3398906 https://papers.ssrn.com/abstract=3398906 .

[56] Madsen (n 55) 24.

[57] Mikael Rask Madsen, 'Sociological Approaches to International Courts' in Karen Alter, Cesare PR Romano, and Yuval Shany (eds), *Oxford University Press Handbook of International Adjudication* (Oxford University Press 2014)

[58] Omar Lizardo, 'Pierre Bourdieu as Cognitive Sociologist' in Wayne H Brekhus and Gabriel Ignatow (eds), *The Oxford Handbook of Cognitive Sociology* (OUP 2017).

institution perspective connects to that of the 'embodiment of the cognitive unconscious',[59] where the environment in which one acts relies on conceptions built by embodied notions (as in habitus), and those concepts are reflected back into the institutions. This is particularly important when considering the actions and reasoning often thought of as deliberate or separate from body and place such as legal or moral reasoning. As Lizardo points out, missing (or dismissing) the concept of embodiment when understanding cultural material (which as a thoroughly culturally embedded text, the law is no better example), one risks overlooking the multitudes of otherwise hidden linguistic meanings on which such reasoning is based, and erroneously over magnifies reasoning qua reasoning's importance in thought and action.[60]

This section should disabuse us of the notion that the messy, or directly non-causal cannot, and therefore should not be studied. Marrying the two approaches de-silos individuals, nations, and international institutions by concentrating on the fundamental conceptual structures that travel within and in-between them. As a short illustration, we look at the seminal *Cyprus case*[61] to show how the particular process of law making as an embodied concept sets the foundation for the institutional conception of its own categories. In this case, the margin of appreciation.

B The Margin of Appreciation in the *Cyprus case*

The Commission's report in the *Cyprus case* displays the invention of the principle of the margin of appreciation which would become the legal stand-in for legal diplomacy for years to come at the Court. In its first case, the Commission encountered two NATO allies 'at the height of both the Cold War and decolonization'[62] in Greece and the United Kingdom. The case concerned the emergency derogation of ECHR rights under Article 15 in a situation of martial law.

There are multiple displays of the Commission's spatial conceptions at play in *Cyprus*. First, is the construction of the relationship of the UK law to the Convention. Here the Commission is measuring the shape and positioning of the two entities where the UK law must *conform* with Article 15.[63] *Conform*, works to set up the metaphorical frame of GOOD LAW IS GOOD FIT. This frame triggers the image schematic understanding of *shape* and *container*. Pairing those image schemata with one of an agent in the same space coveys a malleable object paired

[59] ibid 7.

[60] ibid 9.

[61] *The Cyprus Case* (n 4).

[62] Mikael Rask Madsen, 'The Challenging Authority of the European Court Of Human Rights: From Cold War Legal Diplomacy to The Brighton Declaration and Backlash' (2016) 79 *Law & Contemporary Problems* 141, 147.

[63] *Cyprus* (n 4) 326 ('In deciding whether the Detention of Persons Law, in these circumstances, conformed with the requirements of Article 15').

with a wilful agent to manipulate it, in this case, the UK government. It constrains the perspective of the interpreter to that of an object-agent relationship where conformity can be expected. A more process or naturalistic frame, for instance, would not necessarily contain this type of agent-object relation and conformity would be a matter of natural predilection, perhaps easier to forgive (or at least attribute responsibility) than an agentive choice.

Similarly, constructions such as *under* ('derogation of the Convention *under* Article 15'[64]), presents a common (in legal thought) VERTICALITY frame where the UK being *under* the law relies on both an image schema of up-down orientation (a construction shown to have an effect decision making[65]) and one of weight and gravity. The weight schema does the heavy conceptual lifting (to speak metaphorically) in the frame of GOOD REASONS/IMPORTANCE IS HEAVY in 'the Commission had to *bear in mind*', which is overtly metaphorical or 'to *weigh* in each case',[66] which is not. Weight as a metaphor is also at work in the '*suppression* of one of the most fundamental rights guaranteed by the Convention'[67] where the weight and verticality frames combine to easily assist the listener to understand where rights stand in vertical space and that the force used to hold them down may be considered heavy handed. Perhaps of most importance is the framing the Commission employs on the margin of appreciation itself.

Although the case was eventually resolved outside the purview of the Commission, the report spells out the notion of a margin of appreciation given to states:

> [it] was *a matter of course* that the Government concerned was *in a better position* than the Commission to know all relevant facts and *to weigh in each case* the, different *possible lines of action* for the purpose of countering an existing threat to the life of the nation. Without *going as far* as to recognise a presumption in favour of the necessity of measures taken by the Government, the Commission was of the opinion, nevertheless, *that a certain margin of appreciation* must be conceded to the Government.[68]

First are the invocations to horizontal space in 'far-reaching measure', 'strictly required', and of course the 'margin' itself. But perhaps the most telling of the spatial framing is the notion of POSITION and MOVEMENT highlighted by the italics above. The reasoning 'it was a matter of course' that the Commission could hardly deviate from a given trajectory without good reason relies on an intuitive

[64] ibid.

[65] For review see Luca Cian, 'Verticality and Conceptual Metaphors: A Systematic Review' (2017) 2 *Journal of the Association for Consumer Research* 444.

[66] *Cyprus* (n 4) 326.

[67] ibid.

[68] ibid (emphasis added).

Newtonian physics of inertia. The Commission's reasoning that given the 'better position' of the UK government invokes a background frame of CLOSE IN SPACE IS CLOSE IN TRUTH, and that it is only right that the 'possible lines of action' could be assessed rightly be the closer viewer. This notion of the margin of appreciation, a wording not found in the Convention, was later thoroughly institutionalized and expanded within this notion of space when considering for instance, *wide* versus *narrow* margins to be considered. This was institutionalized not only through the interpretation of this notion in case law but reified time and again, through means as official as the Brighton Declaration or as decentralized as any textbook written on the subject. They all rely on a concrete notion of space and its intuitive physics as a frame to make sense of the abstract legal principle. This notion of truth via proximity is parallel to the work of cognitive linguistics on the idea of similarity via closeness, where close in space means close in mind. Similarity here, concerns the ability to generalize and to categorize. While the Commission may have had many diplomatic reasons to develop a notion of the margin of appreciation in *Cyprus*, it did so in a distinct way: proximity. Experiment after experiment has displayed evidence that a notion of proximity equates to similarity (or closeness is strength of effect[69]) and therefore 'better' judgment helps the Court in legitimising its novel margin of appreciation as a line of reasoning anyone could intuitively accept. The Court relies on a notion of spatial closeness that, due to its embodied and highly generalizable nature, fixes a well understood (or at least generally accepted and understandable) outcome. This proximity conception would continue throughout the Court's subsequent case law, institutionalising a specific embodied concept of proximity, space, and image schematic frames that those concepts entail.[70] This notion is obviously not restricted to the construct of the margin of appreciation. In its life, the Court displays many of the features found in cognitive linguistics that represent not simply rhetorical crutches but specific institutionalized frames. It highlights the conceptual power to cement an embodied concept into a social institution.

The way the notion of margin of appreciation has developed in recent years suggests that these inherent *impensées* of the notion are still operative. In fact, we can observe a proliferation in the usage of the margin of appreciation, notably since around 2010–12, where an upsurge of references to margin of appreciation has been found.[71] Some scholars have questioned the logical coherence of the notion in its growing use across many fields, arguing that it has become merely a tool for

[69] Boyoun Chae, Xiuping Li, and Rui Zhu, 'Judging Product Effectiveness from Perceived Spatial Proximity' (2013) 40 *Journal of Consumer Research* 317.

[70] For empirical work in this regard see Slosser (n 34).

[71] Mikael Rask Madsen, 'Rebalancing European Human Rights: Has the Brighton Declaration Engendered a New Deal on Human Rights in Europe?' (2018) 9 *Journal of International Dispute Settlement* 199.

disguising incrementalism.[72] Others have argued that the upsurge in margin of references is a response from the Court to two different yet ultimately related the system is facing, namely a too great number of pending cases which has caused a large backlog of cases and a growing political critique of the Court as being too invasive in national political matters, an argument often using the backlog of cases as (questionable) evidence of the overall expansionist tendencies of the Court.[73]

The political critique is interesting with regard to our analysis. It found its formal articulation in the 2012 Brighton Declaration the message of which can be summarized as the following:

> The Brighton Declaration most of all seeks to induce change in the balance between European and national institutions in the protection of human rights. Although the Declaration at times seems to look in several directions at once, its main message is that national institutions, ranging from courts and human rights institutes to parliaments, should play a more substantial role in interpreting and developing the European Convention on Human Rights.[74]

What is basically projected with the Brighton Declaration (and repeated in the 2018 Copenhagen Declaration with slightly more specific wording) is an idea of subsidiarity, a notion not usually used by the Court itself but rather known from EU law. In the EU context, subsidiarity implies that decisions should be made as *close* as possible to the citizens. However, in those areas where EU has exclusive competences or where action is more effectively taken at regional level, subsidiarity does not apply. In the Strasbourg context, subsidiarity projects even more precisely and explicitly the idea of proximity than margin of appreciation. While there is no evidence that the Court itself has opted to use this language, preferring seemingly to rely on its doctrine of margin of appreciation, the basic idea of proximity has been bolstered by this political intrusion with the Court. Now featuring in the preamble of the Convention (Protocol 15), proximity is supposed to be the guiding principle of the system thereby institutionalising the inherent but less formalized legal diplomacy of the earlier periods of the system.

One could argue that the member state governments are kicking in an open door, considering the notion is found in the very first case before the European Commission of Human Rights, but that would be to downplay political signalling of this move. This upsurge in the number of references to margin of appreciation since the Brighton Declaration certainly suggests that the message has had some empirical effects. It also has a political dimension—that the Court shall leave some

[72] Janneke Gerards, 'Margin of Appreciation and Incrementalism in the Case Law of the European Court of Human Rights' (2018) 18 *Journal of Human Rights Law Review* 495.

[73] Basak Cali, 'Coping with Crisis: Towards a Variable Geometry in the Jurisprudence the European Court of Human Rights?' (2018) 35 *Wisconsin Journal of International Law* 237; Madsen (n 71).

[74] Madsen (n 71) 200.

space to local political (as well as legal) solutions. This institutionalized deference to national political and legal institutions has in fact received renewed attention in recent years. Judges at the Court have worked hard to distil a workable doctrine that combines proximity in its legal and political dimensions with monitoring the respect of the convention. Known as the process-based review, the Court has explicitly embarked on adapting its approach to the (new) age of subsidiarity.[75]

IV Conclusion

Although many questions remain about the internal dynamics of the force of framing, it is clear that there is an inescapable resemblance between the premises of cognitive linguistics and the writing of ECtHR judgments. As an institution, the Court's interpretative approach allowed for more fluid understandings of its principles and the power of conceptual framing could do more work. Through choices mediated by political and social pressures, the Court reproduces that which is within the law. The Court, however, is not reproducing merely legal categories, but rich concepts underpinned by their bodily grounding (embodied) and socially constructed (institutionalized) background. It is in this way that we come to not just embodied law, but an *institutionally embodied law* that marries the study of both the social dynamics that allow for more or less dynamic interpretations and the mechanisms by which they work. Future research should employ both levels of analysis to understand the actors in and around courts for what they are: not just jurists, but cognitive beings.

[75] Robert Spano, 'The Future of the European Court of Human Rights—Subsidiarity, Process-Based Review and the Rule of Law' (2018) 18 *Human Rights Law Review* 473; Robert Spano, 'Universality or Diversity of Human Rights? Strasbourg in the Age of Subsidiarity' (2014) 14 *Human Rights Law Review* 487.

5

Prosociality, International Law, and Humanitarian Intervention

*Tomer Broude**

I Introduction

A significant insight of behavioural economics and social psychology, well established through years of experimental research, is that individuals often display 'social preferences', that is, other-regarding or non-self-interested motivations and choices in their decisions. Contrary to the assumptions and indeed expectations of rational choice theory, people may have only 'bounded selfishness' in the decisions they make, caring not only about their own payoffs and well-being, but also about those of others. Outside of a purely rationalist frame, it is perhaps not so surprising that in their behaviour, people may be driven by considerations such as fairness and equity.[1] However, such actions may also be considered as a part of human rationality. Sometimes, people may even be willing to sustain costs in order to enable greater benefits—or losses—to others, and to society at large. This so-called 'prosocial' behaviour, takes several forms and stems from different motivations, and may change under differing circumstances. Indeed, an ongoing research field relates to the measurement of individual prosociality[2] and the extent to which it derives from personal traits such as empathetic tendencies, or from situational determinants, both notable in experimental 'Ultimatum', 'Dictator', 'Trust', and other games (explained below).[3] In any case, prosocial behaviour departs from basic rational choice assumptions about raw 'pro-self' decision-making. For present

* Thanks to Anne van Aaken, Andrea Bianchi, Moshe Hirsch, Doron Teichman, Eyal Zamir for very helpful comments. Thanks also to Yuval Abramovich for excellent research assistance. The usual disclaimer applies.

[1] Colin F Camerer and Ernst Fehr, 'Measuring Social Norms and Preferences Using Experimental Games: A Guide for Social Scientists' in Joseph Henrich (ed), *Foundations of Human Sociality: Economic Experiments and Ethnographic Evidence from Fifteen Small-Scale Societies* (Oxford University Press 2004). See Zamir

[2] Rachel Baumsteiger and Jason T Siegel, 'Measuring Prosociality: The Development of a Prosocial Behavioral Intentions Scale' (2018) 101 *Journal of Personality Assessment* 305.

[3] Steven D Levitt and John A List, 'What Do Laboratory Experiments Measuring Social Preferences Reveal about the Real World?' (2007) 21 *The Journal of Economic Perspectives* 153, 155; Eyal Zamir and Doron Teichman, *Behavioral Law and Economics* (Oxford University Press 2018) 102–104.

Tomer Broude, *Prosociality, International Law, and Humanitarian Intervention* In: *International Law's Invisible Frames.* Edited by: Andrea Bianchi and Moshe Hirsch, Oxford University Press. © Tomer Broude 2021.
DOI: 10.1093/oso/9780192847539.003.0006

purposes, it can be understood as an element of social cognition, in the broad sense of the latter term.[4]

Is the study of prosociality relevant to public international law, and if so, how? This chapter explores this question, on a broad, tentative and theoretical basis. Section II below provides a non-exhaustive survey of elements and problems relating to bounded self-interest and prosociality as generally identified in human behaviour. The subsequent section III briefly discusses the interaction between prosociality and legal analysis in general, and devotes some attention to structural considerations in researching prosociality and international law, in particular the level of analysis problem. I argue that at the levels of individual and elite decision-making regarding international law, and also when aggregated into the state level of analysis, the same characteristics and conditions of prosociality identified in personal interactions may apply to decisions made with respect to international issues, making them worthy of further contemplation and rigorous research. Section IV focuses on one area in which the perspective of prosociality may enrich the discussion of a contested issue in international law and the problems such a perspective raises, namely humanitarian intervention. The concluding section V raises some questions regarding the efficacy of the exercise of seeking prosocial behaviour that relates to international law. Can the prosociality of states be measured? Which other areas of international law bear analytical relation to prosociality? And can (or should) the design of international law encourage prosociality by states and other international actors?

II Bounded Self-interest and Prosociality: Some Parameters

Prosocial behaviour can generally be defined as the tendency of actors to act for the benefit of others and of society, even at a cost to themselves. Following the classical typology of boundedness in behavioural economics,[5] prosociality is perhaps the greatest challenge to the rational choice *Homo Oeconomicus* model, because it contests not the cognitive rationality of decisions (bounded rationality),[6] or the ability to carry them through, particularly in intertemporal contexts (bounded willpower, including myopic decisions)[7] but the very assumption of egotism and the self-serving utility functions of actors (bounded self-interest, or bounded selfishness). Because prosocial decisions that run counter to assumed egotistic self-interest

[4] Moshe Hirsch, 'Social Cognitive Studies, Sociological Theory, and International Law', ch 1 in this volume.

[5] Sendhil Mullainathan and Richard H Thaler, 'Behavioral Economics' in *International Encyclopedia of the Social & Behavioral Sciences* (Pergamon 2001).

[6] Herbert A Simon, 'A Behavioral Model of Rational Choice' (1955) 69 *The Quarterly Journal of Economics* 99.

[7] George F Loewenstein, 'Frames of Mind in Intertemporal Choice' (1988) 34 *Management Science* 200.

are deliberate, manifestations of bounded self-interest are deeply entangled with questions of morality, in ways perhaps more obvious and acute than expressions of bounded rationality or willpower.[8] The very terms selfish/selfless and antisocial/prosocial are value-laden and carry judgmental, sometimes controversial baggage.

Here it may be useful to distinguish between descriptive questions about prosociality—when and under which circumstances do actors behave prosocially, that is, intentionally sacrificing part of one's self-interest in favour of another's goal or a social one; and normative ones—when is it desirable that actors do so. The former is essentially an empirical question. The latter includes empirical dimensions but depends on whose utility and well-being is considered to be at stake: that of the actor, her counterparts, or society more generally.

Focusing here on the descriptive, at either level, however, prosociality is intertwined with perceptions and theories of fairness and equity in the distribution of resources. People are sensitive to both substantive and procedural fairness. They will feel unfairly treated if the proportion between their rewards (such as financial income), and their inputs (such as work effort) is lower than the respective proportion accorded to others.[9] Importantly, 'people are distressed not only when they are treated less favorably than they feel they deserve, but also—albeit to lesser extent—when they are treated more favorably'.[10] Perceived unfairness can lead to action aimed at rebalancing, such as decreased contribution or increased unethical behaviour.[11] Fairness and equity are both empirically evident on an experimental basis in the strands of research relating to the 'Ultimatum' game (where one person is tasked with dividing a sum of money between herself and a second person; and the second person may either accept the distribution or reject it, thus defeating the entire disbursement); and the 'Dictator' game (in which one party unilaterally determines the distribution). In both games,[12] a large proportion of subjects make choices that diverge from rational choice expectations,[13] opting for distributive outcomes that are more fair, or rejecting unfair ones. Furthermore, some research shows that people care not only about allocative outcomes, but also—indeed sometimes even more so—about the fairness of allocative procedures.[14]

[8] But see Eyal Zamir, *Law, Psychology and Morality: The Role of Loss Aversion* (Oxford University Press 2015) 177 ff, discussing the moral implications of loss aversion.

[9] J Stacy Adams, 'Toward an Understanding of Inequity' (1963) 67(5) *Journal of Abnormal and Social Psychology* 422; Elaine Walster, Ellen Berscheid, and G William Walster, 'New Directions in Equity Research' (1973) 25 *Journal of Personality and Social Psychology* 151.

[10] Zamir and Teichman (n 3) 102.

[11] ibid.

[12] For an overview see Christoph Engel, 'Dictator Games: A Meta Study' (2011) 14 *Experimental Economics* 583.

[13] For discussion of structural application to international law and institutions, Anne van Aaken, 'Behavioral Aspects of the International Law of Global Public Goods and Common Pool Resources' (2018) 112 *American Journal of International Law* 67.

[14] Robert Folger and others, 'Effects of "Voice" and Peer Opinions on Responses to Inequity' (1979) 37 *Journal of Personality and Social Psychology* 2253.

On the complex backdrop of fairness and equity, prosocial behaviour takes more specific (yet still highly variegated) shapes of helping others—intervening in emergency situations that affect others, volunteering one's time to others' causes, donating money to charity and so on. Such behaviour is the essence of prosociality. It is often associated with the concept of altruism or selflessness, but this only highlights the key questions of diverging personalities and differing motivations for prosocial conduct.

Regarding *personality*, considerable research efforts and outputs have attempted to associate prosociality with differences among the so-called 'big-five' personality attributes (extraversion, agreeableness, openness, conscientiousness, and neuroticism).[15] Among these, not unpredictably, agreeableness is considered the most determinative of prosocial behaviour.[16] Altruistic and cooperative personalities have been identified as showing greater concern for the common good than do individualists and competitors.[17] A sense of responsibility, affective and other-oriented empathy as well as helpfulness, are affiliated with prosociality.[18] Some of these observations may be question-begging, but to be sure, recent years have seen much more nuanced research regarding personality, especially with respect to child development.[19]

Regarding *motivation*, prosocial actions will forever be suspect of being non-altruistic,[20] and somehow self-serving, even when these actions help others.[21] A reasoned approach to this question finds a heterogeneity of considerations and motivations, often positively or negatively incentive-based, towards prosocial behaviour: altruistic, expectations of specific and general reciprocity, self-respect and self-imagery, social reputation concerns,[22] and even deep-seated self-preservation concerns (such as increased organ donation commitments when exposed to information on mortality).[23]

[15] John M Digman, 'Personality Structure: Emergence of the Five-Factor Model' (1990) 41 *Annual Review of Psychology* 417.

[16] William G Graziano and Nancy Eisenberg, 'Agreeableness: A Dimension of Personality' in John Johnson and Stephen Briggs (eds), *Handbook of Personality Psychology* (Elsevier 1997).

[17] P van Lange and others, 'Development of Prosocial, Individualistic, and Competitive Orientations: Theory and Preliminary Evidence' (1997) 73 *Journal of Personality and Social Psychology* 733.

[18] Louis A Penner and others, 'Measuring the Prosocial Personality' in James N Butcher and Charles D Spielberger (eds), *Advances in Personality Assessment, vol 10* (LEA 1995); Melvin A Eisenberg, 'Why There Is No Law of Relational Contracts' (2000) 94 *Northwestern University Law Review* 805.

[19] Laura M Padilla-Walker and Gustavo Carlo (eds), *Prosocial Development: A Multidimensional Approach* (Oxford University Press 2014).

[20] C Daniel Batson, 'Prosocial Motivation: Is It Ever Truly Altruistic?' (1987) 20 *Advances in Experimental Social Psychology* 65.

[21] Francesca Gino, Shahar Ayal, and Dan Ariely, 'Self-Serving Altruism? The Lure of Unethical Actions That Benefit Others' (2013) 93 *Journal of Economic Behavior and Organization* 1.

[22] Roland Bénabou and Jean Tirole, 'Incentives and Prosocial Behavior' (2006) 96 *The American Economic Review* 1652.

[23] Gadi Hirschberger, Tsachi Ein-Dor, and Shaul Almakais, 'The Self-Protective Altruist: Terror Management and the Ambivalent Nature of Prosocial Behavior' (2008) 34 *Personality and Social Psychology Bulletin* 666.

Important in any discussion of prosocial motivations is the well-documented phenomenon of 'motivated reasoning', closely related to cognitive confirmation bias—the propensity to interpret information in ways that confirm pre-existing opinions.[24] People may tend to interpret events, decisions and actions in manners that portray them, both to themselves, and to others, as moral and prosocial—both *ex ante* and *ex post*, as justifications for otherwise selfish decisions. This tendency has recently been identified as a possible balancing function between theoretical, egoistic, rationality and actual, prosocial choices.[25]

Several additional demonstrations of prosocial behaviour are noteworthy. One relates to the spontaneous expression of mutual trust, as shown through variations of the so-called 'Trust' game. Like in the Ultimatum and Dictator games, one subject is given an asset, which she may either keep to herself or share in whole or in part with a second subject. If shared, the value of the asset increases, and the second subject may choose to return some of the gains to the first subject.[26] From a selfish, rational choice perspective, both subjects would be expected to refrain from sharing, thus constraining mutual gain. Nevertheless, extensive experimentation shows that both subjects tend to share, trusting that their counterpart will reciprocate. While this indicates a link between trust, investment and economic growth, such links may be highly contingent on the environment in which decisions are made.[27]

Other important prosociality research addresses the degree to which people will tend to come to the emergency assistance of others in distress, in varying situational circumstances, in particular the 'bystander effect'. Going back to Darley and Latané,[28] experimental research shows that although people will generally come to the aid of others when presented with the situation on their own, their tendency to intervene decreases in the presence of others, that is, shifting from empathy to apathy as they become passive actors or 'bystanders'. While the effect is well recognized, research now focuses on understanding its reasons, including personality traits of the (non-) responder.[29]

[24] Raymond S Nickerson, 'Confirmation Bias: A Ubiquitous Phenomenon in Many Guises' (1998) 2 *Review of General Psychology* 175.

[25] Eyal Zamir, 'Refounding Law and Economics: Behavioral Support for the Predictions of Standard Economic Analysis' (2020) 16 *Review of Law and Economics* 1.

[26] For an overview see Noel D Johnson and Alexandra A Mislin, 'Trust Games: A Meta-Analysis' (2011) 32 *Journal of Economic Psychology* 865.

[27] Paul J Zak and Stephen Knack, 'Trust and Growth' (2001) 111 *The Economic Journal* 295; and Fabrice Murtin, Lara Fleischer, and Vincent Siegerink, 'Trust and Its Determinants: Evidence from the Trustlab Experiment' OECD Statistics Working Papers No 2018/02, with a broad cross-country experiment on trust games.

[28] John M Darley and Bibb Latané, 'Bystander Intervention in Emergencies: Diffusion of Responsibility' (1968) 8 *Journal of Personality and Social Psychology* 377.

[29] Ruud Hortensius and Beatrice Gelder, 'From Empathy to Apathy: The Bystander Effect Revisited' (2018) 27 *Current Directions in Psychological Science* 249.

To be sure, this is only a partial survey of prosociality research. Other psychological factors and elements include moods (positive moods may increase prosociality and vice versa, but distress, shame and guilt may also do so, to a varying extent),[30] and identity and social categories, such as gender, age, and group belonging impacts upon prosocial behaviour.[31] It is a complex, dynamic and to large extent messy area of study in both social psychology and behavioural economics, restricting the ability to draw straightforward conclusions regarding law and policy.

III Prosociality, the Law, and International Contexts

A Prosociality and the Law

With this overall messiness in mind, what does prosociality mean for law? Even before delving into potential implications for international law, with its additional complications, this question appears to be significantly undertheorized and under-researched. Lynn Stout, a leading proponent of the relevance of prosociality to legal design 'appealing not to selfishness, but instead to the force of conscience',[32] surveying the field in 2014, described only a few selected yet important strands of research on prosociality and the law in general.[33]

The first strand, perhaps the most systemically important, addresses the connection between prosocial behaviour and negative incentives (fines and other forms of punishment) as components of legal regulation of behaviour. The general argument and line of thinking here, is that it may not always be necessary or even desirable to introduce such negative incentives where prosocial tendencies exist. For example, in some settings, in which prosocial norms are already internalized, people might spontaneously impose social sanctions on norm violators, even at personal cost to themselves ('altruistic punishment').[34] Indeed, the imposition of fines may even be counterproductive, if it is understood as a legitimizing price for non-conformity with a rule, that 'crowds out' a prosocial convention, such as in the Gneezy and Rustichini[35] field experiment on imposing fines on late pick-up

[30] David A Schroeder and William G Graziano, 'The Field of Prosocial Behavior: An Introduction and Overview' in David A Schroeder and William G Graziano (eds), *The Oxford Handbook of Prosocial Behavior* (Oxford University Press 2015) 22.
[31] George A Akerlof and Rachel E Kranton, 'Economics and Identity' (2000) 115 *The Quarterly Journal of Economics* 715.
[32] Lynn A Stout, *Cultivating Conscience: How Good Laws Make Good People* (Princeton University Press 2011) 5 .
[33] Lynn A Stout, 'Law and Prosocial Behavior' in Eyal Zamir and Doron Teichman (eds), *The Oxford Handbook of Behavioral Economics and the Law* (Oxford University Press 2014).
[34] Ernst Fehr and Simon Gächter, 'Altruistic Punishment in Humans' 415 *Nature* 137 (2002).
[35] Uri Gneezy and Aldo Rustichini, 'A Fine is a Price' (2000) 29 *The Journal of Legal Studies* 1. But see Cherie Metcalf and others, 'Is a Fine Still a Price? Replication as Robustness in Empirical Legal Studies' (2020) 63 *International Review of Law and Economics* 1.

of children from kindergarten: the monetary sanction was absorbed, hence backfiring, and lateness became more common and acceptable. This may apply to positive incentives as well—in certain settings, people who have been offered material incentives considered to be insufficient and unfair may perform worse than those not offered a material incentive at all.[36]

A second strand, primarily in the context of tort law, addresses the propensity of people to exercise care in avoiding negligence causing harm to others, even when those who are injured or harmed are generally undercompensated by them, and/or when the tortfeasor bears little or no costs (i.e., when the cost of negligence is not internalized).[37]

A third strand of thinking about prosociality and the law relates to contract law, in particular highly incomplete contracting, in which it is argued that the success of the contractual transaction depends not on the letter of the contract but on the relations between the parties—the not uncontroversial concept of 'relational contracting'.[38]

The fourth area in which prosociality and its effects on law are evident is corporate law, in particular the construction of the duties of fiduciary directors, who are encouraged to exercise their duties of care without applying penalties and imposing material costs.[39] In corporate governance, large *ex ante* material rewards to corporate executives and employees may actually decrease desired prosocial activity and decisions, leading to less cooperative and unethical conduct, and even to illegal decisions.[40] Notably, these observations relate to individual behaviour in the *intra*-corporate context, but with implications for the corporate actor as well. Moreover, some experimental research suggests that individual agents will display a significant decrease in fairness concerns when they bargain towards maximizing profit for a corporate principal.[41]

While each of these interactions of prosociality with public and private law at the domestic level—not very robust in themselves—may have international analogues, they are not easily transported to the international law level. Indeed, the latter discussion of corporate law indicates the most significant problem in doing so, even within the realm of theoretical application and the development of hypotheses, namely, the level or unit of analysis problem. Whose self-interest and selfishness are bounded, and which actors may display prosociality at the international level?

[36] Metcalf and others (n 35).

[37] Stout (n 32) 157–64; Stout (n 33) 204–206.

[38] Ian R Macneil, 'Relational Contract Theory: Challenges and Queries' (2000) 94 *Northwestern University Law Review* 877; Stout (n 32) 206–207.

[39] Margaret M Blair and Lynn A Stout, 'Trust, Trustworthiness, and the Behavioral Foundations of Corporate Law' (2001) 149 *University of Pennsylvania Law Review* 173; Edward B Rock, 'Saints and Sinners: How Does Delaware Corporate Law Work?' (1997) 4 *UCLA Law Review* 1009.

[40] Lynn A Stout, 'Killing Conscience: The Unintended Behavioral Consequences of "Pay For Performance"' (2014) 39 *Journal of Corporate Law* 525.

[41] Kent Greenfield and Peter Kostant, 'An Experimental Test of Fairness Under Agency and Profit Constraints' (2003) 71 *George Washington Law Review* 983.

B Levels of Analysis: The International Prosocial Actor?

The level or unit of analysis issue has been discussed at some length elsewhere, with respect to behavioural analysis of international law in general.[42] The issue arises mainly from the dissonance between the premises of behavioural economics, based mainly on experimental observations of individual human behaviour, and the generally statist structure of international law. This gap between methodological individualism and methodological statism[43] can be bridged in several ways, either theoretically[44] or through empirical research on state behaviour[45] or individual conduct associated with international law.[46] When one considers prosociality and bounded self-interest, additional problems arise. For example, pro- *which* society?—a question that goes to the core of international legal conceptions of the 'international community', for example.[47] More directly related to the level of analysis problem—*whose* self-interest is it that may be bounded? *Which* are the internationally relevant actors who may act beyond their own self-interest? Below are some initial thoughts in this regard.

First, there is the level of analysis of states and their corollaries. Rationalist approaches equate states to *homo economicus* and adopt assumptions of rationality, including self-interest.[48] Nevertheless, it cannot be assumed in earnest that states share the same degree of self-interest, however defined, in their decisions, across the board. Some states may be more prosocial than others, some circumstances may bring out state-egotism more than others. Moreover, states are corporate, collective actors, and their attitudes to international law may aggregate the relative prosociality (including cultural tenets) of the individual and group decision-makers involved. This may be analogous to corporate commercial enterprises which have been shown to act in fairness[49] but may also bring out the decrease in fairness and ethical considerations when acting for a collective.

Groups are not limited to states, of course, and may include quasi-states, would-be-states, communities and other non-state actors, such as international

[42] Tomer Broude, 'Behavioral International Law' (2015) 163 *University of Pennsylvania Law Review* 1099, 1121–30; Anne van Aaken, 'Behavioral International Law and Economics' (2014) 55 *Harvard International Law Journal* 421, 441–49; Anne van Aaken and Tomer Broude, 'The Psychology of International Law: An Introduction' (2019) 30 *European Journal of International Law* 1225.

[43] Broude (n 42) 1121.

[44] Tamar Megiddo, 'Methodological Individualism' (2019) 60 *Harvard International Law Journal* 601.

[45] Jean Galbraith, 'Treaty Options: Towards a Behavioral Understanding of Treaty Design' (2013) 53 *Virginia Journal of International Law* 309.

[46] Tomer Broude and Inbar Levy, 'Outcome Bias and Expertise in Investigations under International Humanitarian Law' (2019) 30(4) *European Journal of International Law* 1303 .

[47] Bruno Simma and Andreas L Paulus, 'The "International Community": Facing the Challenge of Globalization' (1998) 9 *European Journal of International Law* 266.

[48] Andrew T Guzman, *How International Law Works: A Rational Choice Theory* (Oxford University Press 2008).

[49] Zamir and Teichman (n 3) 103; Daniel Kahneman, Jack L Knetsch, and Richard Thaler, 'Fairness as a Constraint on Profit Seeking Entitlements in the Market' (1986) 76 *American Economic Review* 728).

governmental and non-governmental organizations. There is evidence of aggregation of individual prosociality in the form of planned, ongoing activities by groups of people, such as communal volunteerism.[50] Individuals with prosocial tendencies may better bring them into practice when they are backed-up by a like-minded community. This aggregation has been enhanced by online platforms, such as crowdfunding.[51]

Another unit or level of analysis is that of so-called elite decision-makers—individuals and small decision-making groups who ultimately determine the positions and conduct of states and other collective actors. These include state leaders, negotiators who act as agents of the state (or equivalent actors), public officials, and policy-makers who may or may not display prosocial preferences, either as expressions of their own attributes, or as reflections of their position vis-à-vis their principal. For example, Zamir and Sulitzeanu-Kenan show that public officials are driven both by self-interest and the public good.[52] Kertzer and Rathbun[53] conclude, on the basis of laboratory experiments and historical cases studies, that there are prosocial and pro-self approaches to international negotiations, and that in conformity with individual behaviour, prosociality is better attuned to avoiding bargaining failure, by being both more generous despite asymmetrical power, and not hesitant in applying negative reciprocity to punish a counterpart's pro-self behaviour. It has also been shown that personal values that relate to prosociality feed into foreign policy preferences between 'militant internationalism' and 'cooperative internationalism'.[54] Getting closer to international law,[55] has recently shown that (*in casu*, German), politicians with a high degree of cosmopolitanism have a (pro-)social approach to compliance with international law, whereas those with a low degree of cosmopolitanism have a more egotistic approach.

The final level of analysis is that of the individual, engaged somehow in activity that interacts with international law: the judge or arbitrator, the advocate, the soldier, the customs official, the immigration officer, the administrator. The role of the individual in international law is often forgotten or at least underestimated.[56] In

[50] Mark Snyder and Allen M Omoto, 'Volunteerism: Social Issues Perspectives and Social Policy Implications' (2008) 2(1) *Social Issues and Policy Review* 1.

[51] John P Berns and others, 'Dynamics of Lending-Based Prosocial Crowdfunding: Using a Social Responsibility Lens' (2020) 161 *Journal of Business Ethics* 169. More generally on the issue of aggregation in political psychology and international relations see Ross James Gildea, 'Psychology and Aggregation in International Relations' (2020) 26 *European Journal of International Relations* 166.

[52] Eyal Zamir and Raanan Sulitzeanu-Kenan, 'Explaining Self-Interested Behavior of Public-Spirited Policy Makers' (2018) 78(4) *Public Administration Review* 579.

[53] Joshua D Kertzer and Brian C Rathbun, 'Fair Is Fair: Social Preferences and Reciprocity in International Politics' (2015) 67 *World Politics* 613.

[54] Brian C Rathbun and others, 'Taking Foreign Policy Personally: Personal Values and Foreign Policy Attitudes' (2016) 60 *International Studies Quarterly* 124.

[55] A Burcu Bayram, 'Due Deference: Cosmopolitan Social Identity and the Psychology of Legal Obligation in International Politics' (2017) 71(S1) *International Organization* S137.

[56] But see Anne Peters, *Beyond Human Rights: The Legal Status of the Individual in International Law* (Cambridge University Press 2016) 5; Sergio Puig, 'Social Capital in the Arbitration Market' (2014) 25 *European Journal of International Law* 387; Broude and Levy (n 46); Megiddo (n 44).

each of these positions, individuals may display elements of bounded self-interest, either on their own behalf or on behalf of their principal, the state or other collective (although as noted, acting as an agent may promote egotistic decisions on behalf of the principal).

The next section will discuss some of these issues with respect to a 'prime suspect' for examination through the prosocial lens, namely, the question of humanitarian intervention.

IV Prosociality and Humanitarian Intervention in International Law and Relations: An Open Roster of Issues

A Prosocial Motivation Regarding Humanitarian Intervention

Humanitarian intervention is undoubtedly one of the most contentious concepts in international law. Simply put, on one hand stands the moral imperative to prevent or end horrific and wholesale violations of fundamental human rights; on the other hand, however, because these violations are taking place in the territory of another state, key principles of the prohibition of the use of force, state sovereignty and non-intervention in internal affairs may be at stake, as well as international peace and stability.[57] International law vacillates on the balance to be struck, not only due to the ethical questions involved—the overarching tension between 'legitimacy' and 'legality'[58]—but because of the real concern that humanitarian interventions may in practice be mere pretexts for political intrusions aimed at the promotion of the national interests of the intervenor or broad geopolitical objectives, such as 'regime change' or the 'war on terror'.

Without purporting to rehearse the doctrinal issues regarding humanitarian intervention, let alone exhaust them, some points may be mentioned to the extent that they relate to prosociality. First, there is the distinction between intervention with or without consent of the state in whose sovereign territory the intervention takes place. Some of the aforementioned concerns might be allayed if the intervention is so consented to, but this is still a very thorny issue,[59] which does not

[57] The literature on humanitarian intervention in international law and international relations is vast. Selected points of departure are JL Holzgrefe and Robert O Keohane, *Humanitarian Intervention: Ethical, Legal and Political Dilemmas* (Cambridge University Press 2003); and Nigel S Rodley, 'Humanitarian Intervention' in Mark Weller (ed), *The Oxford Handbook of the Use of Force in International Law* (Oxford University Press 2015). For a historical study see Mark Swatek-Evenstein, *A History of Humanitarian Intervention* (Cambridge University Press 2020).

[58] Patrick Macklem, 'Humanitarian Intervention and the Distribution of Sovereignty in International Law' (2008) 22 *Ethics & International Affairs* 369.

[59] Eliav Lieblich, *International Law and Civil Wars: Intervention and Consent* (Routledge 2013).

necessarily overcome scepticism regarding the bona fides of the intervenor.[60] Secondly, there is the (at least formally) legitimating impact of approval by collective security decisions, such as by the UN Security Council. Here too, the questions of personality and motivation remain open, especially when the intervening party has the capacity to generate its own requisite authorization. Thirdly, there is a relatively clear requirement to comply with all rules of *jus in bello* in the execution of the intervention, both morally and legally (while the rules themselves are not necessarily clear). Such abidance, at least efforts made to do so, may be indirect indications of the prosociality of the intervenor. Fourth, there is the ongoing discourse regarding the characterization of humanitarian intervention not only as a right but as a duty, namely, the scope and nature of the inchoate concept of the 'Responsibility to Protect' (R2P, for short), albeit subject to similar constraints. R2P in itself (discussed briefly below, in context) is difficult to see as panacea for the questions of personality and motivation with respect to humanitarian intervention.

Much of the debate over humanitarian intervention in both international law and international relations thus hinges on the characterization of the motivation for the forcible military action—in doctrinal terms, whether the objective is humanitarian (itself a pliable term). It is an interesting case for the exploration of prosociality, that this chapter can only illuminate briefly. For example, the concepts of 'motivated reasoning' and 'motivated cognition'[61] suggest that states' motivations to intervene will affect their inward assessment and outward depiction of the legality of the intervention. Moreover, some rational choice analysis of humanitarian intervention has included the possibility that the welfare of the state being intervened in is actually a part of the utility function of the intervenor and society at large,[62] to be weighed against the costs of intervention. This would appear to be a strong expression of motivated reasoning, selectively incorporating the welfare of others as part of the rational choice calculus, while ignoring the phenomenon of bounded self-interest. This framing is a far cry from contemplating the possibility that intervention is enabled *inter alia* by bounded self-interest or by altruism that is not a component of the intervenor's own utility, although these questions can be seen as two sides of the same coin: on one hand, states may justify their self-serving actions as humanitarian for self-motivated reasons; on the other hand, they may take prosocial action for humanitarian reasons not fully aligned with their own interests.

[60] For a broad critical approach see Anne Orford, *Reading Humanitarian Intervention: Human Rights and the Use of Force in International Law* (Cambridge University Press 2009).

[61] See n 24.

[62] Eric A Posner and Alan O Sykes, 'Optimal War and Jus Ad Bellum' (2004) 93 *The Georgetown Law Journal* 993, 1115.

B The Prosociality of Individual Defence of Others and Humanitarian Intervention

When viewed through the lens of prosociality, the issue of humanitarian intervention appears roughly analogous to questions relating to measures taken by individuals in providing emergency assistance to others in domestic settings. Persons using force to stop an assault against a helpless victim are placing themselves at both immediate physical risk and potentially may face longer-term costs, such as legal defence of their actions—the defence of others is not an easy legal excuse to establish for otherwise tortuous or criminal actions, in many jurisdictions.[63] Similarly, states using force to end severe human rights violations clearly incur the great costs of military action, placing their own soldiers and possibly their own civilians at risk, and there always exists the risk of failure, and international opprobrium.

There is, however, at least one crucial difference between individual assistance to others in grave danger, and state-based humanitarian intervention.[64] It is easier to accept that individual emergency responders do not have ulterior motives, even if they have time to deliberate whether and how to intervene. The chance individual responder in the defence of others is likely thrown into an entirely unexpected situation, usually with no prior acquaintance with the people she will try to assist. One study of individual civilian emergency intervenors in North America[65]—'Carnegie Hero Medal Recipients', who risked their lives to save that of others, eg a 60-year old man who witnessed the unprovoked stabbing of a 15-year old girl, engaged with the attacker, and was stabbed himself—demonstrated that such 'extreme altruists' act overwhelmingly through intuitive rather than deliberative decision-making. They have no immediate interests in the risky action they take, other than to come to the assistance of others.

In contrast, states, as corporate actors facing humanitarian intervention decisions may have long-term factual familiarity, historical complicity (such as colonial pasts) and current political interests vis-à-vis a humanitarian crisis. They have time to contemplate and deliberate and even justify through their own domestic—and international—collective decision-making processes. Thus, in this context the issue of the motivation for humanitarian interventions, which is of course very difficult to assess, conceptually and empirically,[66] appears to be very significant, not

[63] Darrell AH Miller, 'Self Defense, Defense of Others, and the State' (2017) 80 *Law and Contemporary Problems* 85; Otto Spijkers, 'Bystander Obligations at the Domestic and International Level Compared' (2014) 6 *Goettingen Journal of International Law* 47.

[64] For additional discussion of the comparison see Spijkers (n 63).

[65] David G Rand and Ziv G Epstein, 'Risking Your Life without a Second Thought: Intuitive Decision-Making and Extreme Altruism' (2014) 9 *PLoS One* 1.

[66] Fernando R Tesón, 'Humanitarian Intervention: Loose Ends' (2011) 10 *Journal of Military Ethics* 192. Tesón notes three conceptual distinctions that make such an exercise difficult, even before considering the empirical ones: direct intention versus oblique intention, foreseen versus willed action, and intention versus motive.

necessarily for an evaluation of the international legality of an intervention (although this is advocated by some, eg through the concept of R2P)[67] but for an assessment of the extent to which it is an expression of prosociality.

C Can Prosocial Motivation for Humanitarian Intervention Be Measured?

If motivation for humanitarian intervention is a key issue, how can it be measured? A core empirical study of the main international military interventions by Western states during the 1990s and 2000s[68] researched through qualitative and quantitative methods the very question of motivation—what is the relative weight of altruism versus national interest in decisions to intervene or not? There, this question is framed on the background of the debate between political 'realists', on the one hand, who argue that in order for humanitarian intervention to succeed it must be based first of all on the national interest of the intervenor; and liberal cosmopolitanists, on the other hand, who view altruistic intervention as morally justified in itself. Interestingly, two of the parameters that the study used to gauge altruism were defined not at the unit of analysis of the state or the humanitarian crisis in question, but at the unit of analysis of the elite decision maker, at the highest level, including state leaders. One such parameter analysed the number of reliable leadership statements of empathy, the depth of empathy expressed, and their credibility; the second analysed the political interest of the leader, such as public pressure to intervene (or not), diversion of attention from domestic issues, and relevance to upcoming elections.[69] Thus, with respect to the controversial Kosovo intervention of 1999, for example, the study concluded that it was motivated equally by self-interest and altruism, but with strong geopolitical interests at stake for NATO member states, and political interests of President Bill Clinton in diverting domestic attention from the Monica Lewinsky scandal, while no personal feelings of moral obligation to intervene were found. The analysis of the US non-intervention in Rwanda in 1994 concluded that it displays 'the lowest level of self-interest' and that 'Altruism alone does not trigger intervention'.[70]

[67] International Commission on Intervention and State Sovereignty, 'Report of the International Commission on Intervention and State Sovereignty: The Responsibility to Protect'; Alexander J Bellamy, 'Motives, Outcomes, Intent and the Legitimacy of Humanitarian Intervention' (2007) 3 *Journal of Military Ethics* 216.

[68] Andreas Krieg, *Motivations for Humanitarian Intervention: Theoretical and Empirical Considerations* (Springer 2013).

[69] ibid 90–92.

[70] ibid 110.

A more recent study[71] covered a larger dataset of about 40 cases of military intervention (from 1964 to 2016), in order to test and challenge narrow definitions of humanitarian military intervention that in the authors' view restrict important comparative empirical research. Thus, for example, a definition that excludes interventions with 'target' government consent or a UN Security Council mandate, significantly reduces the number of cases that can be studied; and definitions that rely on a certain threshold of actual mass violence exclude early interventions that prevented such escalation. Regarding motivation, the important issue for present purposes, the study shows that in the dataset there are no cases in which additional motives (i.e., beyond the purpose of saving others, such as political or economic motivations) can be ruled out—even in the case of the 1992 US intervention in Somalia. Other factors that cast doubt on what may be called altruistic motivation, such as assumptions that unilateral interventions or those conducted by former colonial powers in their prior territories must lack humanitarian purpose, leave only a handful of cases to examine.

These studies (which are inevitably not free from methodological and theoretical difficulties) confirm that decisions to launch a humanitarian intervention may include strong elements of altruism, but that such considerations are neither sufficient nor necessary conditions for action. A measure of self-interest in intervention—of states or leaders—is almost always present. This is indeed very different from the altruistic impulses that motivate risky life-saving interventions at the individual level. If one contemplates more recent cases of military intervention, in Libya, Syria and Yemen, it is difficult to avoid similar conclusions. According to critics, 'liberal hawks' in the West use and abuse the language of humanitarianism to justify politically-motivated interventions.[72] Analyses of US involvement simply ignore possible altruistic motivations,[73] or argue that Russia learned from earlier cases that humanitarian arguments are merely political pretexts for political-driven actions.[74]

Other empirical research has reached quite different conclusions, however. Choi[75] draws on an even larger dataset of US interventions in 153 countries between 1981-2005. Importantly, the gap in the dataset size is the result of a much broader definition, that includes delivery of food and medical aid and logistical support by military action, including when recipient state consent has been given,

[71] Matthias Dembinski, Thorsten Gromes, and Theresa Warner, 'Humanitarian Military Interventions: Conceptual Controversies and Their Consequences for Comparative Research' (2019) 26 *International Peacekeeping* 605.

[72] Paul Dixon, '"Endless Wars of Altruism"? Human Rights, Humanitarianism and the Syrian War' (2017) 23 *The International Journal of Human Rights* 819.

[73] Jeffrey S Lantis, 'Advocacy Coalitions and Foreign Policy Change: Understanding US Responses to the Syrian Civil War' (2021) 6(1) *Journal of Global Security Studies* 1.

[74] Samuel Charap, Elina Treyger, and Edward Geist, 'Understanding Russia's Intervention in Syria' (RAND Corporation 2019).

[75] Seung-Whan Choi, 'What Determines US Humanitarian Intervention?' (2013) 30(2) *Conflict Management and Peace Science* 121.

thus relaxing many of the definitional limits discussed above. For the study of prosociality in international law and relations, this makes sense, in that it expands the pool of cases in which a state takes costly and potentially risky action to assist others, in other states (even though the research mentioned focused on one intervening state, the US). The study finds that such interventions are primarily motivated by humanitarian concerns rather than national interest, making them more prosocial in nature. While here too, the conclusions should be taken with a grain of salt, they do suggest that prosociality is a driver of some state action.

D Prosociality and Its Interactions with the Legality of Interventions

A relevant yet underexplored question is the relationship between the prosocial elements of humanitarian intervention and its formal legality. The aforementioned studies of state motivations for intervention suggest that prosocial motivations exist, but that their implementation is partly guided by legality—perhaps more so than self-interest. As a hypothesis, states may be inclined towards prosocial humanitarian intervention, but refrain from carrying it out due to legal constraints. Conversely, when legality is secured, such as through the beneficiary state's consent or UNSC mandate, prosociality is set free. This in itself may not be an argument for reducing the legal constraints on humanitarian intervention, but it adds another consideration to the usual frameworks of debate.

To be sure, the legality of humanitarian intervention on the basis of recipient state consent, even when considered to include disaster aid and assistance, can hardly be taken for granted. There have been many instances in which states have rejected offers of international humanitarian aid and disaster relief, for various reasons.[76] In some cases, such as Myanmar under the military junta in 2008 in the wake of cyclone Nargis, one of the justifications for the regime's refusal was the overt claim that it constituted coercive humanitarian intervention, reflecting a distrust of the prosocial motivations of aid providers. At the same time, proponents of such intervention developed arguments in favour under the label of R2P.[77] Nevertheless, states avoided unapproved assistance activity, despite the increasing human costs of the refusal, again suggesting that legal structures may impede the exertion of prosocial tendencies.

Such legal restraints on prosocial behaviour are more generally noteworthy because of the formulation of R2P itself, which arguably goes beyond *permitting*

[76] Charlotte Dany, 'Failed Cooperation in Times of Natural Disasters: Explaining the Rejection of Humanitarian Aid' (2020) 20 *International Relations of the Asia-Pacific* 193.

[77] Julian Junk, 'Testing Boundaries: Cyclone Nargis in Myanmar and the Scope of R2P' (2015) 30 *Global Society* 78 (2015).

prosocial behaviour through humanitarian intervention, towards prescribing and *requiring* it (ideally but not exclusively through collective action). It is safe to say that at this stage R2P in this sense has not cohered into an accepted legal norm, despite strong bases of legitimacy made by a spectrum of actors, from the ICISS Report,[78] via the 2005 World Summit, to academic celebrations.[79] Why, therefore, has the international system avoided the establishment of a prosocial obligation? To this observation one can add the decision of the International Court of Justice (ICJ) in the 2007 *Genocide* case,[80] which restricted the treaty-based duty to prevent genocide according to 'various parameters', such as the capacity to influence effectively the perpetrators, taking into account geographical distance and political influence—and the limitations of international law.[81]

The standard explanation for this hesitance in creating such prosocial requirements and the trend to limit them is, as before, the fear of abuse by national interests in altruistic skin (obviously also in contravention of the sovereignty of the state intervened in). However, the psychology of prosociality suggests an additional explanation, namely, the concern that a requirement along the lines of R2P would be too onerous a commitment for the vast majority of states. Studies of individual decision making, across cultures, have demonstrated that just as there is 'prosocial punishment' there are also circumstances of 'antisocial punishment', in which highly prosocial people are punished or criticized by the larger group,[82] in order to reduce their excessive prosociality that creates competitive costs for others—sometimes called 'do-gooder derogation'.[83] The analogy here is imperfect, of course, but the dynamic is similar. Prosocial norms may be discouraged because most actors simply cannot (or will not) incur the costs of performing them.

E Additional Factors: The Bystander Effect, and Non-state/ Individual Actors

This discussion does not exhaust the ways in which the study of prosociality and bounded self-interest can relate to our understanding of humanitarian intervention. An additional question worthy of research is whether the 'bystander effect' mentioned in Section II above—people's tendency to refrain from emergency

[78] ICISS Report (n 67).

[79] Alexander J Bellamy and Timothy C Dunne (eds), *The Oxford Handbook of the Responsibility to Protect* (Oxford University Press 2016).

[80] *Application of the Convention on the Prevention and Punishment of the Crime of Genocide (Bosnia and Herzegovina v. Serbia and Montenegro)* Merits, Judgment of 26 February 2007.

[81] ibid para 430.

[82] Simon Gächter and Benedikt Herrmann, 'Reciprocity, Culture and Human Cooperation: Previous Insights and a New Cross-Cultural Experiment' (2009) 364 *Philosophical Transactions of the Royal Society* 791.

[83] Aleta Pleasant and Pat Barclay, 'Why Hate the Good Guy? Antisocial Punishment of High Cooperators Is Greater When People Compete To Be Chosen' (2018) 29 *Psychological Science* 868.

intervention in the presence of others, especially when action is already being taken—applies somehow to states. One possible international manifestation of this phenomenon is the problem of diffuse or shared responsibility, eg between governments among each other or between governments and an international organization, such as the UN—the problem of 'many hands.[84] While so far legal research on shared responsibility has focused on *ex post* responsibility in the doctrinal meaning, it may bear strongly on the ex ante sense of obligation to act in situations of need. As Nollkaemper[85] writes, in particular reference to the ICJ *Genocide* case, '[t]he principle of "responsibility to protect" assigns obligations to protect human populations from mass atrocities to a plurality of states or organizations—it may then be difficult to determine which of the actors indeed had to act'. In real time, an actor whose decisions involve international law (state, government, military commander etc.) may consider itself relieved of a responsibility to act if it believes others are already acting, or that the responsibility is the other actors's. Substantiating such a hypothesis requires, of course, qualitative and qualitative empirical research beyond the ambition of this chapter.

Finally, it may be useful to consider the role of other actors engaged with humanitarian intervention, from a prosociality perspective. Returning to the level of analysis issue, consider the conduct of individuals. On one hand, it has been pointed out that humanitarian intervention creates moral dilemmas not only for states but for the soldiers called into action,[86] and the decisions made may ultimately hinge on the prosociality of the participants in the intervention. On the other hand, soldiers participating in combat in humanitarian intervention may easily display the bystander effect, with respect to wrongdoing in their own military unit (eg the case of soldiers refraining from stopping a Somali youth being beaten in a Canadian Army camp in 1993).[87] The role of leaders and their personal involvement has already been discussed above, but elite decision making groups may also be key players in decisions to intervene, such as the 'institutionalized' human rights cadre in the US State Department.[88]

[84] Dennis F Thompson, 'Moral Responsibility of Public Officials: The Problem of Many Hands' (1980) 74 *The American Political Science Review* 905; André Nollkaemper, 'The Duality of Shared Responsibility' (2018) 24 *Contemporary Politics* 524.

[85] Nollkaemper (n 84) 530.

[86] Fernando R Tesón, 'The Liberal Case for Humanitarian Intervention' in JL Holzgrefe and Robert O Keohane (eds), *Humanitarian Intervention: Ethical, Legal and Political Dilemmas* (Cambridge University Press, 2003); Daniel Baer, 'The Ultimate Sacrifice and the Ethics of Humanitarian Intervention' (2011) 37 *Review of International Studies* 301.

[87] George Shorey, 'Bystander Non-Intervention and the Somalia Incident' (Winter 2000) *Canadian Military Journal* 19.

[88] Seung-Whan Choi and others, 'Human Rights Institutionalization and US Humanitarian Military Intervention' (2020) 46(4) *Journal International Interactions: Empirical and Theoretical Research in International Relations* 606.

The role of non-state actors is also an important factor. For example, Murdie and Peksen[89] show that 'shaming' by human rights organizations—a direct appeal to the prosociality of states—increases the likelihood of humanitarian intervention. This echoes to some extent the so-called 'CNN Effect' of media framing, which may drive political decisions, including humanitarian intervention[90] (but see Anderson and Brakstad,[91] who find that media narratives can also reinforce the bystander effect of polities). Humanitarian agencies on the ground in crisis and conflict areas may attain political influence and display a bystander effect, driven by their own goals,[92] which may lead them to turn a blind eye to human rights violations beyond their mandate. The prosociality or altruism of humanitarian workers is also an issue to be considered, such as its potential trade-off with professionalism.[93]

V Ways Forward: Understanding—and Encouraging—Prosociality in International Law

The discussion of humanitarian intervention demonstrates some of the strengths and limitations of adopting prosociality and bounded self-interest as a framework for analysis of actor behaviour within international law. It is, however, only the tip of an iceberg. The questions that have been discussed are extensions of the not unfamiliar problems associated with humanitarian intervention, such as mixed motivations and the bystander effect.

Many other international legal phenomena could benefit from research in this direction, and will display different interactions with prosociality. Thus, to mention a few, the duty of non-recognition of unlawful situations; obligations erga omnes (most recently covered by the ICJ in the 2019 *Chagos Archipelago* Advisory Opinion),[94] and the scope of the right to invoke them by states other than the injured state; collective sanctions in security and economic contexts; dispute settlement in multilateral settings, such as the WTO, and the role of courts and tribunals

[89] Amanda Murdie and Dursun Peksen, 'The Impact of Human Rights INGO Shaming on Humanitarian Interventions' (2014) 76 *The Journal of Politics* 215.

[90] Eytan Gilboa, 'The CNN Effect: The Search for a Communication Theory of International Relations' (2005) 22 *Political Communication* 27.

[91] Kjell Føllingstad Anderson and Ingjerd Veiden Brakstad, 'The Impossibility to Protect? Media Narratives and the Responsibility to Protect' (2016) 9(3) *Genocide Studies and Prevention: An International Journal* 96.

[92] Stephen L Esquith, 'The Political Responsibility of Bystanders: The Case of Mali' (2013) 9 *Journal of Global Ethics* 377.

[93] Gilles Carbonnier, 'Reason, Emotion, Compassion: Can Altruism Survive Professionalisation in the Humanitarian Sector?' (2015) 39(2) *Disasters* 189.

[94] *Legal Consequences of the Separation of the Chagos Archipelago from Mauritius in 1965*, Advisory Opinion of 25 February 2019.

more generally as fora of prosociality in international law;[95] participation in international organizations (including the conduct of delegations); cooperation in environmental regimes; individual defences in international criminal law; the absence of reciprocity as a requirement in international humanitarian law—these and many others can all be enriched by direct or indirect resort to the study of prosociality.

Beyond particular legal issues and issue areas that may lend themselves well to prosociality analysis, in this concluding section I would like to flag—no more than that—three broader questions that may merit further exploration and research, especially under the general theme of social cognition.

First, while most of the discussion of humanitarian intervention has focused on *motivation* (i.e., altruism versus national self-interest), a significant part of the study of prosociality deals with *personality*. We have seen this with respect to leaders, public officials and soldiers as examples. As noted, the measurement of prosociality among human beings is an ongoing area of research in behavioural science.[96] This leads inevitably to the question of whether the prosociality of states (and other corporate international actors) can be measured and compared? We know that some states have varying reputations of prosociality, but are these reputations true and accurate? Resorting to the use of different well-developed indices more often employed by researchers of international political economy (such as the KOF Globalization Index)[97] may be useful in this regard.

Secondly, while most of the discussion herein has been descriptive and explanatory, based on research that seeks to illuminate the motivations for prosocial behaviour, there hovers in the background the normative and design questions. Can (or should) the design of international law encourage prosociality of states and other international legal actors? Is prosociality always desirable? Does it lead to optimal outcomes—or only in some cases and circumstances?

Thirdly, in these times of backlash against international law and the rise of populism, the role of fairness and more so of perceived unfairness in the preferences of states and constituencies, that lead to antisocial, non-cooperative policies, must be explored in depth. This has already been explored initially in the particular context of international trade,[98] mainly within a bounded rationality framework. From a political psychology perspective, the effects of perceived unfairness and inferiority

[95] Sivan Shlomo Agon and Eyal Benvenisti, 'The Law of Strangers: The Form and Substance of Other-Regarding International Adjudication' (2018) 68 *University of Toronto Law Journal* 598.

[96] Baumsteiger and Siegel (n 2).

[97] https://kof.ethz.ch/en/forecasts-and-indicators/indicators/kof-globalisation-index.html (Swiss Economic Institute).

[98] Anne van Aaken and Jurgen Kurtz, 'Beyond Rational Choice: International Trade Law and the Behavioral Political Economy of Protectionism' (2019) 22 *Journal of International Economic Law* 601.

on entire national regimes are evidently very deep, placing democracy and the international order at risk.[99]

In sum, prosociality in international law and relations may be an aspiration; in any case it is worthy of deeper and more detailed contemplation. This chapter invites its incorporation into the research of issues in international law.

[99] Ivan Krastev and Stephen Holmes, *The Light That Failed: A Reckoning* (Allen Lane 2019).

6
A Worldly Law in a Legal World

Jean d'Aspremont[*]

Most of international legal thought and practice rests on a distinction between international law and the world to which international law applies. One commonly distinguishes between international law and the world to which international law applies when seeking to ground international law in practice, explicating the origin of international law, appreciating the impact of international law on global actors, elucidating the actual formation and functioning of international law, historicizing international legal discourses and international legal institutions, and even when shedding light on the world-making role of international law. Most international legal thought and practice is informed, in this sense, by what is called here a form of ontological dualism whereby the actuality, historicity, and materiality of international law is distinct from the actuality, historicity, and materiality of the world to which international law applies.

This chapter questions the ontological dualism that dominates international law and shows that, notwithstanding this common ontological dualism, international law and the world to which it applies are better construed as having no distinct actuality, historicity, and materiality because *international law exists nowhere else than in the world to which it applies and the world to which international law applies exists nowhere else than in international law*. This chapter argues accordingly that the relationship between international law and the world to which it applies should be understood in totalizing rather than dualistic terms.

The claim developed in this chapter, that one should dispense with mainstream ontological dualism and that the relationship between international law and the world to which it applies should be understood as a totality, is not another quibbling about arcane and oft-discussed ontological questions about international law. In fact, the claim made here serves a greater purpose, which is to demonstrate that the pre-discursive categories and intelligibility frameworks that govern international lawyers' cognition of the world—which the editors of this volume include in their understanding of frames[1]—are not visible or invisible, seen or unseen, noticeable

[*] The author wishes to thank Matilda Gillis for her assistance.

[1] On the notion of frame see Andrea Bianchi and Moshe Hirsch, 'Introductory Insights' in this volume. Compare with the notion of frame of Nelson Goodman, *Ways of Worldmaking* (Hackett Publishing 1978) 2–3.

Jean d'Aspremont, *A Worldly Law in a Legal World* In: *International Law's Invisible Frames*. Edited by: Andrea Bianchi and Moshe Hirsch, Oxford University Press. © Jean d'Aspremont 2021. DOI: 10.1093/oso/9780192847539.003.0007

or unnoticeable, conspicuous or undiscernible. From the perspective adopted in this chapter, international law's pre-discursive categories and intelligibility frameworks are part of the totality constituted by international law and the world to which it applies. That is, those pre-discursive categories and intelligibility frameworks have no actuality, historicity and materiality of their own that could let them be observed, captured, unveiled, fathomed, seen, or noticed.[2]

The chapter starts by formulating a few observations on the ontological dualism that dominates international legal thought and practice as well as the scrutiny such ontological dualism has been subjected to in international legal scholarship (section I). It goes on to explain two common illustrations of this ontological dualism, namely the constant quest for a grounding of international law in worldly practice (section II) and the wide recognition of the world-making performances of international law (section III). It then develops its main argument by showing how the relationship between international law and the world to which it applies is better construed as forming a totality where international law exists nowhere else than in the world to which it applies, and where that world exists nowhere else than in international law (section IV). Drawing on this argument, the last section provides a few observations on the epistemological consequences of dispensing with the ontological dualism that dominates international legal thought and practice, especially with respect to the (im)possibility of observing, capturing, unveiling, fathoming, seeing, or noticing the pre-discursive categories and intelligibility frameworks that govern international lawyers' cognition of the world (section V).

I Discourse and the World: Preliminary Remarks

It must first be acknowledged that the ontological dualism that dominates international legal thought, whereby international law is held as distinct from the world it applies to, is all but idiosyncratic. It actually reflects the very common transcendence of the *word* from the *world* inherited from the Enlightenment.[3] It permeates most modern discourses which are all commonly detached from the world they discuss.[4] International law does not stand out in its articulation of a

[2] At this stage, it will be of interest to the reader that, in developing such argument, the following considerations draw on (but do not transpose) some of the well-known lessons of post-structuralist literary studies. See generally Jacques Derrida, *De la Grammatologie* (Editions de Minuit 1967); Jacques Derrida, *L'écriture et la différence* (Editions du Seuil 1967); Jacques Derrida, *The Beast and the Sovereign, vol 1* (University of Chicago Press 2011); Roland Barthes, 'La mort de l'auteur' in Roland Barthes, *Le bruissement de la langue* (Seuil 1984) 61.

[3] See generally Michel Foucault, *Les mots et les choses* (Gallimard 1966) 58; see also Bruno Latour, *Nous n'avons jamais été modernes: Essai d'anthropologie symétrique* (La Découverte 1997) 24; Emmanuel Levinas, *Altéritéet transcendence* (Fata Morgana 1995) 17. This is not to say that dualism is unknown to pre-modern thought. See Jacques Le Goff, 'L'homme médiéval' in Jacques Le Goff (ed), *L'Homme médiéval* (Editions du Seuil 1989) 15.

[4] Foucault (n 3) 14, 58, and 70–72.

strict distinction between itself and the world to which it applies. As far as international law is concerned, the success of such ontological dualism is not difficult to fathom. In fact, the distinction between international law and the world to which it applies is a condition of the very existence of international law as a discourse. Indeed, international law can only be a discourse about the world as long as it is distinct from the world it discusses.[5] In other words, international law is bound to define itself by not being the very world to which it applies and which it discusses.[6] If international law cannot be distinct from the world it applies to, it can simply not discuss that world. International law thus owes its existence as a matter of discourse about the world to its very distinctiveness from the world. It is therefore no surprise that such ontological dualism pervades international legal thought and practice. As will be examined in section II below, this ontological dualism has manifested itself in the common discursive necessity to ground international law in the actual world—which 20th century international lawyers have come to call 'practice'.[7] More recently, as is discussed in section III below, this ontological dualism came to inform the prolific literature on the world-making performances of international law and the study of the ways in which international law constitutes the world to which it applies.

It must also be stressed that this chapter's engagement with the ontological dualism of international legal thought and practice is not entirely unprecedented. In recent decades, the dialectics at work in ontological dualism has drawn some attention. Following the mobilization of tools from structuralism,[8] and the popularization of findings made in the 1970s[9] and early 1980s[10] about the tensions in interpretive activity between the world that is perceived and the world that is wanted, some international legal theorists turned their attention to the dialectical relationships between social descriptions of the world (concreteness) and the political

[5] Compare with the remarks about sovereignty by Derrida, *The Beast and the Sovereign, vol 1* (n 2) 289.

[6] Timothy Mitchell, *Questions of Modernity* (University of Minnesota Press 2000) 17, 22.

[7] On the concept of practice see Andrea Bianchi, *International Law Theories: An Inquiry into Different Ways of Thinking* (OUP 2016) 7. See also Jean d'Aspremont, 'Theory and History: Ordering Through Distinctions' in Jean d'Aspremont (ed), *The History and Theory of International Law, vols I II* (Edward Elgar Publishing 2020).

[8] On the benefits and uses of structuralist tools of analysis in legal studies see David Kennedy, 'Critical Theory, Structuralism and Contemporary Legal Scholarship' (1985–1986) 21 *New England Law Review* 209. On the structuralist foundations of Martti Koskenniemi's account of international legal argumentation see Sahib Singh, 'International Legal Positivism and New Approaches to International Law' in J Kammerhofer and J d'Aspremont (eds), *International Legal Positivism in a Postmodern World* (Cambridge University Press 2014) 291–316. For a very insightful overview of the merits of structuralism for international legal thought see Justin Desautels-Stein, 'International legal structuralism: a primer' (2016) 8 *International Theory* 201.

[9] G Steiner, *After Babel: Aspects of Language and Translation* (Oxford University Press 1975).

[10] Robert Cover, 'The Supreme Court, 1982 Term – Foreword: Nomos and Narrative' (1983) 97 *Harvard Law Review* 4, 9.

prescriptions about the world (normativity) in international legal arguments.[11] Such works on the structure of international legal arguments were later continued and supplemented by examinations on the structural biases and special ethos that inform institutional legal practices and on the way in which situations are strategically defined and problematized.[12]

Interestingly, such critical inquiries about the dialectical structure of international legal arguments have not gone so far as to question the ontological dualism on which such dialectics are premised. Nor have they sought to emphasize the totality at work in these dialectical structures. It is true that they have sought to reveal the strategical universality of law for which such dialectics work. However, the disclosing of, or questioning of, the totality of international law and the world to which it applies has never been the aim, or part thereof, of such critical works. The dominant ontological dualism of international legal thought and practice, whereby international law is held as distinct from the world it applies to, has generally remained unquestioned.[13]

II The World Makes the Discourse

A first manifestation of the above-mentioned ontological dualism, whereby international law is held to be distinct from the world to which it applies, is found in the discursive necessity to ground international law in the actual world.[14] Grounding international law in the actual world is one of the most central discursive necessities of contemporary international legal discourses. In fact, a statement about international law can hardly be 'truth-claiming' if, in one way or another, it is not grounded in the actual world.[15] Although the need for this grounding is not unheard of in pre-classical international legal thought,[16] classical international legal thought—and especially in the work of Vattel and Martens—offered the first

[11] David Kennedy, *International Legal Structures* (Nomos 1987); Martti Koskenniemi, *From Apology to Utopia* (CUP 2005); Martti Koskenniemi, 'The Fate of International Law: Between Technique and Politics' (2007) 70 *Modern Law Review* 1.

[12] David Kennedy, *A World of Struggle: How Power, Law, and Expertise Shape Global Political Economy* (Princeton University Press 2016); Martti Koskenniemi, 'The Politics of International Law: 20 Years Later' (2009) 20 *European Journal of International Law* 7.

[13] On the idea that dialectical reasoning reinforces dualism see Latour (n 3) 77.

[14] This necessity to speak the real is what Martti Koskenniemi has referred to as the requirement of 'concreteness' of international legal argument. See Koskenniemi (n 11) 17–23.

[15] The invocation of 'nature' as the ultimate truth-claiming criteria is a common feature of technical discourses. See generally Bruno Latour, *Science in Action: How to Follow Scientists and Engineers Through Society* (Harvard University Press 1987).

[16] Indeed, authors from the 17th and 18th centuries, while prioritizing moral needs in international legal discourses, recognized that international law could partly be an emanation of the actual world. See S Pufendorf, *On the Law of Nature and of Nations* (CH Oldfather and WA Oldfather (trs, Clarendon Press 1934, originally 1672). See C Wolff, *Law of Nations Treated According to A Scientific Method* (JH Drake (tr), Clarendon Press 1934).

systematization of such discursive necessity.[17] For them, the actual world meant the will of states—which gained further currency in the first major treatises of the 19th century,[18] and in the following decades became one of the most central discursive necessities in international legal thought.[19] This need to ground international law in the actual world was continued in the 20th century and still governs international legal thought and practice today.[20]

Although the 20th century upheld the need to ground international law in the actual world, the way in which the actual world is understood underwent a significant development. Twentieth century international law took issue with the idea that the basis of international law is provided by the will of states,[21] consequently reinventing its understanding of the actual world, by ceasing to reduce it to the will of states, and including the deeds and sayings of a greater variety of actors.[22] It

[17] The 1758 work of Emmerich de Vattel, while perpetuating some of the assumptions of his predecessors regarding the necessity of natural law, made the need to ground international law in the actual world—which he reduced to the will of the states—the main cause of international law. Even more decisive was Georg Friedrich de Martens' radical move away from the moral necessities of natural law and the systematization of international law through treaty and custom *fondésur les traités et l'usage*. With Martens, the need to ground international law in the actual world became the exclusive cause of international law, the latter being turned into a discourse necessarily and exclusively articulated around the necessity to ground international law in the actual world. See E de Vattel, *The Law of Nations* (CG Frenwick (tr), Carnegie Institution of Washington 1916). See generally Georg Friedrich von Martens, *Précis du droit des gens moderne de l'Europe fondésur les traités et l'usage* (Dieterich 1789).

[18] See eg H Wheaton, *Elements of International Law* (1836); R Phillimore, *Commentaries upon International Law, 4 vols* (AG Benning 1854–1861); TD Woolsey, *Introduction to the Study of International Law* (4th edn, Scribnerm Amstrong & Co 1877). It should be noted that some of them, whilst making the need to ground international law in the actual world very central, continued to accommodate the idea that international legal discourses must respond to reason or natural law, or sometimes the will of God.

[19] It has been claimed that the necessity to ground international law in the actual world that arose in the 19th century was part of an overarching dialectical mode of argumentation that simultaneously required the espousal of some utopian principles. It was also said that, for 19th century authors, responding to the actual world was a strategy to avoid being utopian. This is the thesis defended by Koskenniemi (n 11) 71–157.

[20] Some 20th century authors claimed that departure from the 19th century's need to ground international law in the actual world ought to be the main project of the 20th century. This is very apparent in H Lauterpacht, *The Function of Law in the International Community* (2nd edn, OUP 2011) and H Lauterpacht, *Private Law Sources and Analogies of International Law (with Special Reference to International Arbitration)* (Lawbook Exchange 2002, originally published by Longmans 1927). Hans Kelsen's theorization of international law could also be read as countering this generalization of the need to ground international law in the actual world. Indeed, Kelsen's famous purification of international law was meant to make scholarly discourses autonomous from both crude facts and moral values. It must be acknowledged that Kelsen's charge against the need to ground international law in the actual world remained limited to scholarly discourses. Kelsen continued to construe international law as a product of factual—which he called political—phenomena, and thus as a set of rules grounded in the actual world. See eg Hans Kelsen, 'Law, State and Justice in the Pure Theory of Law' (1948) 57 *Yale Law Journal* 377, 383–84. For a similar reading J von Bernstorff, *The Public International Law Theory of Hans Kelsen: Believing in Universal Law* (CUP 2010) 2–3, 13, 44–48, 53.

[21] 20th century international lawyers came to develop a sophisticated doctrine of sources meant to mediate between the will of state and the legal forms by which a rule would be recognized as a legal rule. On the rise of the doctrine of sources see Jean d'Aspremont, *Formalism and the Sources of International Law* (OUP 2011) 38–82.

[22] For a contestation of the 19th century consensual basis of international obligations see L Brierly, 'The Basis of Obligation in International Law' in H Lauterpacht (ed), *The Basis of Obligation*

is this expanded and renewed notion of the actual world that 20th century international lawyers came to generalize as the idea of *practice* which any international legal claim or argument is now expected to respond to or draw on.

The need to ground international law in the actual world—now called 'practice'—was also extended in the 20th century to modes of study of international law and became almost a scholarly necessity. For instance, the New Haven School in the 1950s and in the 1960s can be read as an attempt to ensure that the study of international law was better grounded in the actual world.[23] Studies on the legitimacy of international law in the 1990s[24] similarly sought to finetune the focus of international legal studies on the actual world with a view to better understanding compliance dynamics.[25] In recent years, the need for studies of international law to be grounded in the actual world has continued to thrive unabated, be it through the rise of a new legal realism in international law,[26] or the vindication, under the banner of a 'new empirical turn', of a more organized and systematized use of empirical data to study the practical conditions under which international law is formed and has effects.[27]

Interestingly, it is only towards the end of the 20th century and at the beginning of the 21st century that international legal scholars, taking their cue from, for example, works in literary theory, linguistics, moral theory, critical sociology,[28] came to acknowledge that the actual world in which they ground international law

in International Law and Other Papers (Scientia Verlag Aalen 1977, originally published by Oxford University Press 1958) 1–67.

[23] See generally M Reisman, 'The View from the New Haven School of International Law' (1992) 86 *ASIL Proceedings* 118; W Michael Reisman, Siegfried Wiessner, and Andrew Willard, 'The New Haven School: A Brief Introduction' (2007) 32 *Yale Journal of International Law* 576. For a similar reading of the New Haven approach see Anne Orford, 'Scientific Reason and the Discipline of International Law' (2014) 25 *European Journal of International Law* 369, 381–82.

[24] See Thomas Franck, *Fairness in International Law and Institutions* (Clarendon Press 1995) 6.

[25] On this aspect of the turn to legitimacy see David Bederman, *The Spirit of International Law* (Georgia University Press 2002) 3. On the Manhattan School of international law and especially Tom Franck's school see the symposium in (2002) 13 *European Journal of International Law* 901. See also David Kennedy, 'Tom Franck and the Manhattan School' (2003) 35 *NYU Journal of International Law and Politics* 397.

[26] See generally G Shaffer, 'A New Legal Realism: Method in International Economic Law Scholarship' in CB Picker, I Bunn, and D Arner (eds), *International Economic Law: The State and Future of the Discipline* (Hart Publishing 2008) 29–42; H Erlanger and others,, 'New Legal Realism Symposium: Is it Time for a New Legal Realism?' (2005) 2 *Wisconsin Law Review* 335; S Macaulay, 'The New Versus the Old Legal Realism: Things Ain't What They Used to Be' (2005) 2 *Wisconsin Law Review* 365, 375; V Nourse and G Shaffer, 'Varieties of New Legal Realism: Can A New World Order Prompt A New Legal Theory' (2009) 95 *Cornell Law Review* 61.

[27] See Gregory and Ginsburg, Tom, 'The Empirical Turn in International Legal Scholarship' (2012) 106 *American Journal of International Law* 1. See also Jakob VH Holtermann and Mikael Rask Madsen, , 'Toleration, Synthesis or Replacement? The "Empirical Turn" and Its Consequences for the Science of International Law' (2016) 29 *Leiden Journal of International Law* 1001.

[28] Stanley Fish, *Doing What Comes Naturally* (Duke University Press 1989) 157; A MacIntyre, *Whose Justice? Which Rationality*? (Duckworth 1988) 352–53, 367; George Steiner, *Errata: An Examined Life* (Weidenfeld and Nicholson 1997) 86–87; Bourdieu, 'The Force of Law: Toward a Sociology of the juridical Field' (1987) 38 *Hastings Law Journal* 805; Goodman (n 1).

does not reveal itself to them, but is always mediated and constructed through a wide range of mental, social, and cultural pre-discursive categories and intelligibility frameworks,[29] which are themselves part of an ideological system of representation.[30] Since then, sophisticated examinations of the ways in which the actual world is constructed, cognized, captured, and perceived have started to populate the international legal literature.[31]

There is no need to explore further this central discursive necessity of contemporary international legal thought and practice to ground international law in the actual world. What matters for the argument made here is that this need is informed by a very strong ontological dualism by virtue of which international law is distinct from the world in which it must grounded. Indeed, whether for law-ascertainment or hermeneutic purposes, to provide theoretical foundations to international law, to evaluate international law's societal relevance, or to study the practical conditions under which international law is formed or bears effects, international law must always be grounded in a worldly actuality, historicity, and materiality which are distinct from international law itself.

III The Discourse Makes the World

Another manifestation of the ontological dualism, whereby international law is held as distinct from the world it applies to, can be witnessed in the sophisticated accounts of international law's world-making performances that populate international legal literature.[32] Indeed, it is now common for international lawyers to engage with the way in which international law shapes unitary spaces, experiences, and conflicts,[33] as well as with how it shapes the unequal

[29] This book can be understood as being part of such inquiry into the modes of capture of the actual world by international lawyers. See Bianchi and Hirsch, 'Introductory Insights' (n 1).

[30] On ideology as a system of representation see Louis Althusser, *For Marx* (Translated by Ben Brewster) (Verso 2006). For Paul de Man, the correspondence between linguistic categories and natural reality is what we should construe as the work of ideology. See Paul de Man, *The Resistance to Theory* (University of Minnesota Press 1986) 11.

[31] See eg Moshe Hirsch, *Invitation to the Sociology of International Law* (OUP 2016); Andrea Bianchi, 'Reflexive Butterfly Catching: Insights from a Situated Catcher' in Joost Pauwelyn and others (eds), *Informal International Lawmaking* (OUP 2012) 200–15; Andrea Bianchi, 'Epistemic Communities' in Jean d'Aspremont and Sahib Singh (eds), *Concepts for International Law: Contributions to Disciplinary Thought* (Edward Elgar Publishing 2019) 251–66; Bianchi (n 7) 7–9,17–18.

[32] This is an idea that I have myself extensively explored and defended in a series of essays published in Jean d'Aspremont, *Epistemic Forces in International Law. Foundational Doctrines and Techniques of International Legal Argumentation* (Edward Elgar Publishing 2015). For compilation of the concepts at work in world-making by international law see Jean d'Aspremont and Sahib Singh (eds), *Concepts for International Law. Contributions to Disciplinary Thought* (Edward Elgar Publishing 2019). See also the general observations of Bianchi (n 7) 16–19.

[33] See eg Monica Hakimi, 'The Work of International Law' 58 *Harvard International Law Journal* (2017) 1–46; See eg Kennedy (n 12); Koskenniemi (n 12) 7–19; Ingo Venzke, *How Interpretation Makes International Law: On Semantic Change and Normative Twists* (OUP 2012); Sundhya Pahuja,

character,[34] coloniality,[35] and masculinity[36] of the world constituted by international law.

Saying that international law makes the world to which it applies can possibly mean very different things. Three dimensions of the world-making capacity of international law are mentioned here as they illustrate not only what international lawyers have been looking into when examining the world-making performances of international law, but also other manifestations of the ontological dualism that dominates international legal thought and practice. First, saying that international law makes the world to which it applies means that international law paves the world with spatial, historical, and material continuities that pre-determine the phenomenality within that world.[37] Thus, from this perspective, anything that can be perceived, felt, or seen will be made within the repertoire of possible worlds and possible perceptions prescribed by international law's pre-discursive categories and intelligibility frameworks. In other words, there is little to perceive outside the pre-discursive categories and intelligibility frameworks of international law. Having been naturalized,[38] in advance by international law's pre-discursive categories and intelligibility frameworks, all pandemics, humanitarian disasters, cyber incidents, outer space discoveries, human-made environmental threats, terror in relation to which the international legal texts are invoked will all be experienced as natural.[39]

Secondly, that international law makes the world to which it applies means that there is no worldly phenomenality that is foreign to international law's

'Decolonization and the Eventness of International Law' in Fleur Johns, Richard Joyce, and Sundhya Pahuja (eds), *Events: The Force of International Law* (Routledge 2011) 91–105.

[34] See eg C Miéville, *Between Equal Rights: A Marxist Theory of International Law* (Haymarket Books, 2006); S Pahuja, 'The Postcoloniality of International Law' (2005) 46 *Harvard International Law Journal* 459; L Obregon, 'Empire, Racial Capitalism and International Law: The Case of Manumitted Haiti and the Recognition Debt'(2018) 31 *Leiden Journal of International Law* 597; E Jouannet, 'Universalism and Imperialism: The True-False Paradox of International Law?' (2007) 18 *European Journal of International Law* 379.

[35] See Antony Anghie, *Imperialism, Sovereignty and the Making of International Law* (CUP 2004) esp 197. M Mutua, 'What is TWAIL?' (2000) 94 *American Society of International Law Proceedings* 31; A Anghie, 'The Evolution of International Law: Colonial and Postcolonial Realities' (2006) 27 *Third World Quarterly* 740; BS Chimni, 'Third World Approaches to International Law: A Manifesto' (2006) 8 *International Community Law Review* 18; M Mutua, 'Savages, Victims and Saviors: The Metaphor of Human Rights' (2001) 42 *Harvard International Law Journal* 201; Sundhya Pahuja, 'The Postcoloniality of International Law' (2005) 46 *Harvard International Law Journal* 459, 461–62.

[36] C Chinkin, S Wright, and H Charlesworth, 'Feminist Approaches to International Law' (1991) 85 *American Journal of International Law* 613; Hilary Charlesworth and Christine Chinkin, *The Boundaries of International Law: A Feminist Analysis* (Manchester University Press 2000); H Charlesworth, 'Feminist Ambivalence about International Law' (2005) 11 *International Legal Theory* 1.

[37] Bruno Latour, *An Inquiry into Modes of Existence: An Anthropology of the Moderns* (Harvard University Press 2013) 370.

[38] On the ideas of naturalistic necessities and naturalized knowledge see Judith Butler, *Gender Trouble. Feminism and the Subversion of Identify* (2nd edn, Routledge 1990) 45. See also Judith Butler, *Notes Toward a Performative Theory of Assembly* (Harvard University Press 2018) 5, 40–41.

[39] For an illustration of such performativity in relation to the ideas and experiences of nation and nationalism see Benedict Anderson, *Imagined Communities: Reflections on the Origin and Spread of Nationalism* (Verso 2016).

pre-discursive categories and intelligibility frameworks. Having made the world it applies to, international law can be invoked in relation to basically anything in the world, with the consequence that the world is always perceived in a way that is intelligible for international lawyers.[40] As a result, there is, for example, no space, no phenomenon, no pandemic, no humanitarian disaster, no cyber incident, no outer space galaxy, no human-made environmental threat, or no terror that cannot be related back to international law's pre-discursive categories and intelligibility frameworks.[41] Although the world may sometimes seem to resist the pre-discursive categories and intelligibility frameworks of international law, such resistance is itself the expression of the world being squeezed in international law's pre-discursive categories and intelligibility frameworks.[42]

Thirdly, the world-making capacity of international law refers to its organization of conflicts and divergences in the experiences and perceptions of the world, as made by international law.[43] These conflicts (eg practice versus absence of practice; compliant behaviour versus non-compliant behaviour; effective control versus absence of effective control; endangered species versus non-endangered species; causation versus non-causation; contribution to injury versus absence of contribution to injury, impact versus no impact, influence versus no influence) are never accidental or fortuitous as they mechanically and neatly mirror international law's pre-discursive categories and intelligibility frameworks.[44] In other words, world-making also means that the conflicts about how the world, as made by international law, is experienced and perceived constitute organized dissonance within the pre-discursive categories and intelligibility frameworks of international law.[45]

What is also noteworthy for the argument made in this chapter is that all the above-mentioned world-making performances of international law studied by international lawyers, while being strategically administered by a whole range of self-declared experts pursuing specific or universal agendas,[46] primarily boil down to textual achievement.[47] Indeed, it only takes a few texts to host hugely powerful pre-discursive categories and intelligibility frameworks which define a certain type

[40] On the idea that concepts are deployed as identity checks see TW Adorno, *Negative Dialectics* (Continuum 2007) 5. See also Henri Bergson, *La pensée et le mouvant* (Flammarion 2014) 229, 240.

[41] What cannot be related back to international law is declared monstrous or ignored. On this question see generally Derrida, *De la Grammatologie* (n 2) 14.

[42] On the idea that theory cannot do its work on the phenomenal without resistance and that theory is itself this resistance see de Man (n 30) 12–19.

[43] On this idea see Jean-François Lyotard, *Le Différend* (Editions de Minuit 1983).

[44] See M Foucault, 'Politics and the study of discourse' in G Burchell, C Gordon, and P Miller (eds), *The Foucault Effect: Studies in Governmentality* (University of Chicago Press 1991) 58–59.

[45] Foucault (n 3) 66–69; Jean-François Lyotard, *La Condition Postmoderne* (Editions de Minuit 1979) 17.

[46] See n 12 above.

[47] This is not exclusive of the commitment to these texts by lawyers. See Michael Polanyi, *Personal Knowledge: Towards a Post-Critical Philosophy* (University of Chicago Press 1958) 311; Hans-Georg Gadamer, *Truth and Method, Bloomsbury*, 2013, 322; Lyotard (n 45) 71–72.

of phenomenality and prohibit others.[48] In the specific case of international law, defining the world is chiefly performed by the pre-discursive categories and intelligibility frameworks at work in texts such as the Statute of the International Court of Justice, the 2001 Articles on State Responsibility for Internationally Wrongful Act, the 1969 Vienna Convention on the Law of Treaties, in the key texts on the protection of human rights or the protection of the environment, etc. Defining the world is also performed by the pre-discursive categories and intelligibility frameworks at work in some of the canonical judgements of the International Court of Justice, and in key decisions of international organizations. Making the world along international law's pre-discursive categories and intelligibility frameworks always is a textual feat.

It would be of no relevance to further elucidate on the various dimensions of the world-making capacity of international law that can potentially be studied by international lawyers when engaging with world-making by international law. What matters is that, when international lawyers study the way in which international law, as a discourse, shapes the world in any of the dimensions mentioned in the previous paragraphs, they continue to postulate that the actuality, historicity, and materiality of the world to which international law applies is distinct from international law as well as from the pre-discursive categories and intelligibility frameworks that have engendered that world. All such rich scholarship thus remains committed to ontological dualism.

IV The Worldly Discourse in a Discoursed World

The previous sections have shed light on some common manifestations of the type of ontological dualism that informs international legal thought and practice. By virtue of such ontological dualism, international legal thought and practice constantly distinguishes between international law and the world to which international law applies. Whether it draws on the world or shapes it, the world and international law have distinct actuality, historicity, and materiality.

It is submitted in this section that such ontological dualism can be questioned and that an alternative reading of the relationship between international law and the world to which it applies can be advocated. It is, more specifically, argued here that international law and the world to which it applies cannot be distinguished as they form a totality. International law and the world to which it applies form a totality, not because they are constitutive of one another, but because the possibility

[48] It has long been shown that a few signs cobbled together can be the source of a huge plural process of signification. See Roland Barthes, *S/Z* (Seuil 1970) 9–20; Bruno Latour, *La fabrique du droit: Une ethnographie du Conseil d'Etat* (La Découverte 2004) 235. See the wonderful illustration provided by Jacques Rancière, *Le Maître Ignorant: Cinq Leçons sur l'Emancipation Intellectuelle* (Fayard 1987) 46.

of their respective existence is provided by the other.[49] In other words, they form a totality because international law exists nowhere else than in the world and the world exists nowhere else than in international law.[50] Such a totalizing take on the relationship between international law and the world to which it applies can be explained as follows.

On the one hand, *international law exists nowhere else than in the world to which it applies*. Indeed, one can speak of international law and the world precisely because both international law and the world inhabit the same world.[51] To be distinct from the world, international law must already be part of that world.[52] It is only because international law is part of the same world as the world to which it applies, that their distinctiveness is a possibility in the first place.[53] In ontological terms, this means that international law, as a discourse, is inevitably in the world it discusses. On the other hand, *the world exists nowhere else than in its representation by international law*.[54] In fact, the world to which international law applies has no existence outside its representation by international law and its definition through international law's pre-discursive categories and intelligibility frameworks.[55] The world is named by international law but is otherwise absent.[56] This means, in ontological terms, that the world is only in the discourse.

According to the foregoing, international law exists nowhere else than in the world to which it applies while that world exists nowhere else than in international

[49] See Lyotard (n 45) 25. Theodor Adorno made a similar claim about the voracity of any concept that he sees as creating a totality which draws everything into it, tolerates nothing outside its domain, and translates everything in its own terms, even contradictions to it. On the totalization of thought as a modern phenomenon see Theodor Adorno and Max Horkheimer, *Dialectic of Enlightenment* (Verso 1997) 24. See more generally TW Adorno, *Negative Dialectics* (EB Ashton (tr), Routledge 1973). See *contra* Raymond Williams, *Politics and Letters: Interviews with New Left Review* (New Left Books 1979) 252.

[50] What is meant by totality in this chapter has been theorized differently in the literature. For instance, This has been called the *dualism of the real* by Mitchell (n 6) 17, 22. For his part, John Law construes such totality as the work of an inscription device that deletes materiality, creates a certain class of reality and then deletes itself, thereby producing a world that is out-there. See John Law, *After Method: Mess in Social Science Research* (Routledge 2004) 32–37. Speaking of science Henri Bergson claims that science based itself on the light projected by the facts it has itself created. See Bergon (n 40) 251.

[51] Jacques Derrida, *The Beast and the Sovereign, vol 2* (University of Chicago Press 2011) 140.

[52] ibid 9.

[53] On this question in the context of modern thought see also Latour (n 3) 51–52. See also the observations of Michel Foucault, *L'archéologie du savoir* (Gallimard 1969) 203–304. See also Foucault (n 3) 64–70. On the possibility of otherness outside sameness see generally Emmanuel Levinas, *Totalitéet Infini* (Martinus Nijhoff, Kluwer Academic 1971).

[54] On the idea that the fact is never the result of an empirical observation but the result of an interpretive act see Stanley Fish, *Doing What comes Naturally* (Duke University Press 1989) 157.

[55] In Lacanian terms, this means that existence is a product of language. Language brings things into existence. This led Lacan to distinguish the real that precedes the language and is killed by it and the reality which is constituted by language, calling for an understanding of the real does not precede pre-language but exist alongside it. See generally Jacques Lacan, *Ecrits* (Seuil 1966) 848. On this aspect of Lacan see Bruce Fink, *The Lacanian Subject. Between Language and Jouissance* (Princeton University Press 1995) 24–25.

[56] Derrida, *The Beast and the Sovereign, vol 1* (n 2) 5.

law. Existing nowhere else than in one another, international law and the world to which it applies come to form a totality that does not distinguish between each of their respective actuality, historicity and materiality.[57]

This totality is not only an abstract construction. It helps reveal a formidable discursive effect which international law deploys and relies on. Indeed, deprived of their distinct actuality, historicity and materiality, international law and the world cannot be faulted. What international law says the world is can never be wrong because the world is nowhere else than in international law. In other words, international law always secures a confirmation of its own representation of the world in the world it applies to.[58] This formidable discursive effect corresponds to a mode of *self-confirming thinking*: the world to which international law applies confirms the world which international law's pre-discursive categories and intelligibility frameworks anticipate.[59]

As long as one upholds a form of ontological dualism, whereby international law and the world to which it applies are distinguished in their actuality, historicity, and materiality, international law's reliance on self-confirming thinking goes entirely unnoticed. In that sense, ontological dualism conveniently and efficiently hides the self-confirming thinking which international law resorts to. This is where the importance of a totalizing understanding of the relationship between international law and the world it applies to lies. It is argued here that only a totalizing understanding of the relationship between international law and the world it applies to—as has been suggested here—allows one to discern the self-confirming thinking that informs international legal thought and to appreciate that international law always secures a confirmation of its own representation of the world in the world it applies to.

V Concluding Remarks: Neither Visible nor Invisible

The previous sections have shown that although international lawyers are nowadays amenable to the pre-discursive categories and intelligibility frameworks through which the world to which international law applies is mediated, they have remained loyal to the dominant ontological dualism of discourses inherited from the Enlightenment period. This chapter has advocated a move away from ontological dualism and made the case for a totalizing understanding of the relationship

[57] This does not mean that such totality is total. On the idea that a totality can never be completed see Latour (n 37) 370. On the idea that Babel stands for the impossibility of the totality see Jacques Derrida, 'Des Tours de Babel' (Joseph F Graham (tr)) in Joseph F Graham (ed), *Difference in Translation* (Cornell University Press 1985) 165, 165–66.

[58] Timothy Mitchell, *Colonising Egypt* (Cambridge University Press 1991) xiii. Steiner (n 28) 88; Latour (n 48) 235.

[59] Self-confirming thinking is what Jacques Derrida has called the formidable 'simulacrum effect' of language. See Derrida, *The Beast and the Sovereign, vol 1* (n 2) 289.

between international law and the world it applies to. This chapter considers this move necessary to appreciate how international law always secures a confirmation of its own representation of the world in the world it applies to.

Two final considerations are in order. First, advocating a radical dispensation with ontological dualism and the consequent espousing of a totalizing understanding of the relationship between international law and the world to which it applies is only meant as a formative experiment. In fact, the purpose of this chapter is solely—and more modestly—to facilitate an appreciation of how international law does what it does and, in particular, to facilitate an appreciation of the centrality of self-confirming thinking in international legal thought and practice. The point is not to deprive international law of all its discursive stability,[60] let alone to support any kind of post-truth delinquency.[61]

A second observation pertains to the ambitious reflection attempted by the collection of essays assembled in this volume.[62] It is submitted at this final stage of discussion that, besides enhancing our ability to discern how international law does what it does, the totalizing understanding of the relationship between international law and the world to which it applies also bears important consequences as to the scope and limits of scholarly inquiries about the work of international law's pre-discursive categories and intelligibility frameworks. Indeed, according to the totalizing perspective that has been developed in the previous sections, the pre-discursive categories and intelligibility frameworks of international law are an indistinct part of the totality constituted by international law and the world to which international law applies, and find a confirmation of themselves in the very world they help constitute. In that sense, international law's pre-discursive categories and intelligibility frameworks have no more distinct actuality, historicity and materiality than international law and the world to which international law applies. Having no distinct actuality, historicity and materiality, international law's pre-discursive categories and intelligibility frameworks are indistinguishable from anything that international law is, does and applies to, including anything that can be said about what international law is, does, and applies to. Such pre-discursive categories and intelligibility can simply not be observed, captured, unveiled, fathomed, seen, or noticed.

That any engagement with the international law's pre-discursive categories and intelligibility frameworks are bound to be an indistinct part of the totality constituted by international law and the world to which it applies is not itself a problem,

[60] For an illustration of the simplistic association between poststructuralist thinking and nihilism see Niall Gildea, *The Cambridge Affair. Jacques Derrida's Cambridge Affair: Deconstruction, Philosophy and Institutionality* (Rowman & Littlefield Publishers 2019).

[61] See generally Bruno Latour, 'Why has Critique Run out of Steam? From Matters of Fact to Matters of Concern' (2004) 30 *Critical Inquiry* 225–48. See also Fuad Zarbiyev, 'International Law in an Age of Post-Shame' (2020) 9 *ESIL Reflections* 3.

[62] On the notion of frame see Bianchi and Hirsch, 'Introductory Insights' (n 1).

let alone an epistemological one. Only crude modernism entertains the illusion of the possibility of being above or outside discourse.[63] If anything, the totalizing understanding of the relationship between international law and the world advocated here can serve as a reminder that inquiries about international law's pre-discursive categories and intelligibility frameworks, that mimic scientific-like explorations, risk being quickly confronted with their inability to meet their own self-declared epistemological standards.[64]

[63] Such epistemological tautology is commonly met with the objection that it rests on a performative contradiction because it makes the enquiry as necessitarian as the discourses it observes and comes to posit what it claims to observe. See eg Jürgen Habermas, *The Philosophical Discourse of Modernity: Twelve Lectures* (Frederik Lawrence (tr), Polity Press 1987) 185–86, 279. See also Alasdair MacIntyre, *Three Rival Version of Moral Inquiry: Encyclopedia, Genealogy, and Tradition* (University of Notre Dame Press 1990) 55–56. This is also a charge that has surprisingly been raised against Michel Foucault's archeological work. See Hubert L Dreyfus and Paul Rabinow, *Michel Foucault: Beyond Structuralism and Hermeneutics* (2nd edn, University of Chicago Press 1983) 88, 99.

[64] See generally Lyotard (n 45) 51. Theodor Adorno and Max Horkheimer, *Dialectic of Enlightenment* (Verso 1997) 7–9. On the idea that scientific modes of inquiries have no distinct superiority over literary ones see generally Hayden White, *Tropics of Discourses: Essays in Cultural Criticism* (Johns Hopkins University Press 1986) 121–22, 142–43; Roland Barthes, *L'aventure sémiologique* (Seuil 1985) 14.

7

The Invisible Frames Affecting Wartime Investigations

Legal Epistemology, Metaphors, and Cognitive Biases

Shiri Krebs

I Introduction

On 3 October 2015, at 2:08 am, a United States Special Operations AC-130 gunship attacked a *Médecins Sans Frontières* hospital in Kunduz, Afghanistan, with heavy fire. Forty-two people were killed, mostly patients and hospital staff members. A US military investigation concluded that the attack resulted from several factors, ultimately attributed to the 'fog of war'.[1]

On the night of 4 May 2009, US forces attacked Taliban militants in Farah Province, Afghanistan, in three consecutive B-1 airstrikes. The US military concluded that 26 civilians were killed in the attack, but acknowledged that the number might have been much higher, citing the Afghan Independent Human Rights Commission, which reported that 86 civilians were killed. The US report concluded: '[N]o one will ever be able conclusively to determine the number of civilian casualties that occurred on May 4, 2009.'[2]

On 22 July 2002, the Israeli Air Force dropped a one-tonne bomb on Hamas' operative Salah Shehadeh's house in Gaza City, killing, in addition to Shehadeh and his assistant, 13 civilians, eight of them children.[3] An Israeli commission of inquiry found, in 2011, that this outcome was disproportionate, and yet determined that it was nonetheless lawful and that no individual should be held responsible for its outcomes. The Commission attributed the heavy number of casualties to an intelligence failure resulting from objective constraints

[1] US Central Command, Summary of the Airstrike on the MSF Trauma Center in Kunduz, Afghanistan on 3 October 2015: Investigation and Follow-on Actions, 2 (April 2016).

[2] US Central Command, US Central Command Investigations into Civilian Casualties in the Farah Province, Afghanistan, on 4 May 2009 (2009).

[3] For a detailed description of this operation and the work of the investigatory commission see Shiri Krebs, 'Reducing Uncertainty in Targeted Killing Decision-Making: Protecting Civilians from Both Terrorism and Counterterrorism' (2018) 44 *Florida State University Law Review* 943.

Shiri Krebs, *The Invisible Frames Affecting Wartime Investigations* In: *International Law's Invisible Frames*. Edited by: Andrea Bianchi and Moshe Hirsch, Oxford University Press. © Shiri Krebs 2021. DOI: 10.1093/oso/9780192847539.003.0008

relating to the urgency of the situation and the changing conditions on the ground.[4]

These examples demonstrate how an incomplete factual framework—justified and presented as inevitable through the 'fog of war' metaphor—renders otherwise unjustified killings as lawful and acceptable. Focusing on ex post legal investigations of military operations, this chapter unveils some of the normative, cognitive, and legal frames shaping the findings and outcomes of wartime investigations.[5] First, it sheds light on the *'fog of war'* metaphor, creating a reality where wartime facts are buried, forever, under eternal fog, justifying practices of unknowing, and frustrating ex post accountability measures. Secondly, it exposes the contingent nature of legal storytelling in this context. The commitment of investigatory bodies to a particular *legal ontology and epistemology* shapes the outcomes of the investigations. In particular, future-focused epistemological legal rules (such as the principle of proportionality, which focuses on anticipated, rather than actual, damage) give preference to facts which are particularly difficult to ascertain and are open to subjective interpretations (as opposed to, for example, the actual number of casualties). Thirdly, the chapter surveys *cognitive and motivational biases* influencing the collection and construction of facts during armed conflicts, both ex ante and ex post.

To demonstrate the operation of these legal frames, metaphors, and biases, the chapter analyses data from the Israeli investigation into the targeted killing of Hamas Leader Salah Shehadeh in Gaza in 2002. The data from this investigation suggests that the combination of future-focused legal epistemology, cognitive and motivational biases, and the fog of war metaphor generate *law-fulfilling prophecies*: a decision-making dynamic producing normative judgments that are consistent with the legal requirements and weaken the efficacy of review processes. The *fog of war* metaphor then serves to explain any inconsistencies between the expectations and the outcomes, and embraces uncertainty as a justification for gaps in the factual framework. The outcome is legitimization of otherwise unlawful actions, and perpetuation of faulty processes and human insecurity.

By shedding light on the legal frames, metaphors, and cognitive biases that shape the outcomes of wartime investigations, this chapter engages with and further advances a growing literature that adopts a behavioural approach to international law.[6] This approach is based on empirical observations and focuses on

[4] The Report of the Special Investigatory Commission on the targeted killing of Salah Shehadeh [in Hebrew] (27 February 2011) 99–101.

[5] By doing so, this chapter contributes to this book's inquiry into the invisible frames and processes shaping the social practice of international law. See Andrea Bianchi and Moshe Hirsch, 'International Law's Invisible Frames: Introductory Insights', 13 in this volume.

[6] See eg Tomer Broude, 'Behavioral International Law' (2015) 163(4) *University of Pennsylvania Law Review* 1099, 1152–53; Anne Van Aaken, 'Behavioral Aspects of the International Law of Global Public Goods and Common Pool Resources' (2018) 112(1) *American Journal of International Law* 67; G Sitaraman and D Zionts, 'Behavioral War Powers' (2015) 90 *New York University Law Review* 516.

actual rather than assumed behaviour.[7] Its central concept is the idea of bounded rationality, which recognizes that human cognitive capacities are not perfect but rather limited by a variety of cognitive, emotional, and social (or group-based) biases.[8] Accordingly, the main contribution of the behavioural approach to international law is to shed light on a variety of systemic biases in individual and group decision-making processes within various contexts of international law.[9] By unveiling the legal frames, metaphors, and biases affecting wartime investigations, as well as by suggesting methods to unlearn and reimagine some of these processes, this chapter contributes to, and engages with, this literature.

The chapter begins, in section II, with an exploration of the 'fog of war' metaphor and its effect on investigations of military operations. Section III provides an overview of the ontological and epistemological frames shaping such investigations, and section IV explores cognitive and motivational biases that further challenge the collection of facts during armed conflicts. Based on these normative legal frames and cognitive processes, section V develops the concept of law-fulfilling prophecies, using concrete examples form the Israeli investigation into the targeted killing of Hamas leader Salah Shehadeh in Gaza in 2002. Finally, section VI offers several recommendations designed to unlearn and reshape the invisible frames affecting fact-finding processes during armed conflicts, and to reimagine alternatives which are better suited to protect human lives.[10]

II The Fog of War Metaphor and the Defactualization of Wartime Investigations

The three investigations mentioned above concluded that it is impossible to ascertain significant facts relating to the investigated events. All three referred to—directly or indirectly—the physical and metaphoric 'fog of war', as a justification for their inevitable failure to discover the facts they were tasked to find.[11] Popular to this day, the 'fog of war' metaphor has a long history, dating back to the 19th century. In 1832, in his famous book *On War*, Prussian General Carl von Clausewitz had already employed the 'fog' metaphor as a representation of the uncertainty in

[7] Broude (n 6) 112–13.

[8] Daniel Kahneman, 'Maps of Bounded Rationality: Psychology for Behavioral Economics' (2003) 93(5) *American Economic Review* 1449.

[9] Sitaraman and Zionts (n 6) 520; Broude (n 6) 1150; Marko Milanovic, 'Establishing the Facts about Mass Atrocities: Accounting for the Failure of the ICTY to Persuade Target Audiences' (2015) 47 *Georgetown Journal of International Law* 1321.

[10] By doing so, the chapter engages with the process the editors of this book refer to as 'unlearning'; casting doubt on legal processes that for decades have been taken for granted, suggesting possible alternatives. Bianchi and Hirsch (n 5).

[11] For a comprehensive discussion of the various metaphors of international law see Harlan Grant Cohen, 'Metaphors of International Law', ch 12 in this volume.

war.[12] Clausewitz, however, used this term quite differently from the three investigations referred to above. Clausewitz did not use this metaphor to convey that truth is beyond our knowledge (certainly not in retrospect), but to describe the challenge, in real time, to ascertain battlefield information, and to make correct decisions based on imperfect data.[13] By using the term 'fog', Clausewitz referred to the obstacles military decision-makers face—in real time—when forced to act quickly and decisively based on partial information and unsubstantiated assumptions. Clausewitz concluded that to overcome this literal and figurative fog, as required by operational necessity, an individual must possess both intellect that leads to the truth and courage to face the danger in being mistaken.[14]

The investigation reports mentioned above did not use Clausewitz's famous fog metaphor to explain why operational errors occurred in *real time*, during battle, under the uncertainty conditions that applied in that situation. Instead, they employed it to justify their own failure to ascertain facts in *retrospect*. These ex post investigation reports used the fog of war metaphor to present gaps in their factual findings as natural and inevitable.[15] Elsewhere in this book, Cohen explains that metaphors 'allow international lawyers to create an alternative image of the world'.[16] Yet, he adds, they may, overtime, outlive their purpose, obscuring or bending findings that do not fit their structure.[17] In this sense, Clausewitz" original metaphor of temporal fog, illustrating the challenges faced by military commanders in real time, has been transformed into an image of eternal fog, creating an alternative image of military operations, in which the dust never settles on the relevant facts. This metaphoric fog continues to hover over battlefields for eternity, masking the facts—the building stones of 'what happened'—forever.

The result is a concrete risk of defactualization of wartime investigations, making legal determinations in the abstract, or based on a partial factual framework that is completed by convenient interpretations and assumptions. The recurring reference of the fog of war metaphor frames investigations of military operations as a futile exercise, inherently limited in what they can—and even aspire—to achieve. The acceptance of gaps in the factual framework as inevitable opens the door for other fact-shaping frames to affect the fact-finding process and fill in the gaps. These include epistemological legal choices that purport to be natural and objective, as well as cognitive and motivational biases affecting the construction and interpretation of facts.

[12] Carl von Clausewitz, *On War* (Princeton University Press 1989) 101.
[13] ibid.
[14] ibid 102.
[15] Similarly, in ch 12 in this volume, Harlan Grant Cohen demonstrates how reliance on natural phenomena metaphors gives customary international law rules an aura of inevitability. Cohen (n 11).
[16] ibid 13.
[17] ibid.

III The Contingent Nature of Legal Facts

Truth is a basic purpose of legal investigations of military operations. Two of the working assumptions of the practice of wartime legal investigations are (1) that accuracy in fact-finding constitutes a precondition for a just decision, and (2) that fact-finding is a neutral practice, aimed at ascertaining an objective 'truth'.[18] However, as I demonstrate in this section, the legal rules governing these fact-finding efforts are far from being neutral or natural, and produce a contingent version of reality. The legal rules frame the story, infuse it with meaning, and dictate how the relevant facts are construed.

Ontologically, the language of the law tells social stories and anchors social narratives through particular legal terms and categories.[19] When these labels are used to classify groups of people or to categorize real events and behaviours, complex social structures and ambiguous situations are inevitably simplified and reduced to fit a particular category.[20] Some labels require clear-cut categorization of facts into predetermined bins: legal or illegal, guilty or innocent, civilian or combatant. 'Grey area' situations are reinterpreted and redefined to fit one of the pre-existing legal categories. This process of interpreting facts to fit pre-existing legal categories creates a tension between the brute facts and their legal representation, thus losing information that could have otherwise been insightful.[21]

Moreover, the application of legal terms in itself constructs reality in a specific and contingent manner, creating a tension between the legal meaning of a particular term and its social, ethical, and political meanings.[22] Terms such as 'civilian', 'terrorist', 'torture', or even 'responsibility' have unique meanings as legal terms, and potentially other meanings outside the law, such as within political, ethical or moral discourses. When we adopt legal discourse to interpret reality and determine the truth, our findings relate to the legal reality, which may be very different from the moral, ethical, or political interpretation or construction of reality.[23] For

[18] see generally Théo Boutruche, 'Credible Fact-Finding and Allegations of International Humanitarian Law Violations: Challenges in Theory and Practice' (2011) 16 *Journal of Conflict & Security Law* 105; H Victor Condé, *A Handbook of International Human Rights Terminology* (2nd edn, University of Nebraska Press 2004) 88, 127; Bertrand G Ramcharan, 'Introduction' in *International Law and Fact-Finding in the Field of Human Rights* (Brill-Nijhoff 2013); see also GA Res. 46/49 Declaration on Fact-Finding by the United Nations in the Field of the Maintenance of International Peace and Security (9 December 1991).

[19] Bianchi and Hirsch (n 5).

[20] Yuval Shany, 'Binary Law Meets Complex Reality: The Occupation of Gaza Debate' (2008) 41 *Israel Law Review* 68, 69.

[21] Sherwin explores, more generally, the clash between law's demand for truth and justice and the modem mind's demand for closure and certainty, leading lawyers and adjudication processes to simplify reality, by leaving the 'messy things' out. Richard K Sherwin, 'Law Frames: Historical Truth and Narrative Necessity in a Criminal Case' (1994) 47 *Stanford Law Review* 39, 40–41.

[22] Michael S Moore, 'Legal Reality: A Naturalist Approach to Legal Ontology' (2002) 21 *Law and Philosophy* 619, 632; Jack M Balkin, 'The Proliferation of Legal Truth' (2003) 26 *Harvard Journal of Law and Public Policy* 5, 7.

[23] Balkin (n 22).

example, a legal finding that a government employee is not responsible for torturing a detainee depends on the legal interpretation and meanings of both 'torture' and 'responsibility'. However, were a moral interpretation to be applied, our findings concerning the existence of, or responsibility for, torture may be different from our findings following a legal interpretation of these terms.

Epistemologically, legal fact-finding determines questions of fact based on legal conventions, procedures, and rules of evidence that guide us in our decisions regarding what is considered 'true'. First, these rules carve the boundaries of the story itself, by limiting the universe of facts that are included in the legal account of 'what happened'. Only facts which are specifically relevant to establishing legal truth—such as causes of death or intent of the perpetrator—are included. Other facts—for example, relating to the roots of the conflict, social processes of dehumanization, or acts committed outside the temporal or geographical jurisdiction of the investigatory body—are excluded.

Secondly, legal epistemology further restructures the story by determining the weight, reliability, sufficiency, and admissibility of the relevant facts. Legal rules determine the value and strength of the information collected, preferring some facts over others. While many of these rules are designed to promote an accurate account of events, they nonetheless make a choice concerning how to construct reality. Moreover, some rules of evidence or procedure depart from the goal of ascertaining the truth, and favour other purposes, such as protecting national security. Concrete legal rules, such as the state secrets doctrine and matters of state or security privileges, limit fact-finding processes.[24] Either way, law requires us to determine 'what happened' while ignoring relevant facts that describe some aspects of the events in question. These epistemological choices serve, therefore, as invisible frames through which wartime actions are socially construed and evaluated.

IV Cognitive and Motivational Biases Affecting Military Decisions and Investigations

In addition to the unique effect of legal ontology and epistemology on the outcomes of wartime investigations, their findings are further affected by cognitive and motivational biases.[25] An extensive literature from several disciplines, including cognitive psychology and behavioural economics, details a number of such biases, and

[24] Daphne Barak-Erez and Matthew Waxman, 'Secret Evidence and the Due Process of Terrorist Detentions' (2009) 48 *Columbia Journal of Transnational Law* 3, 5; Sarah H Cleveland, 'Hamdi Meets Youngstown: Justice Jackson's Wartime Security Jurisprudence and the Detention of 'Enemy Combatants' (2005) 68 *Alabama Law Review* 1127, 1132–34.

[25] Bianchi and Hirsch survey some of these cognitive and social processes in their 'Introductory Insights' (n 5).

the way in which they affect decision-making preferences and risk perception.[26] While a significant portion of this literature focus on the effects of cognitive and motivational biases on individual decision-makers, some of these biases are alleviated or exacerbated at group level.[27] The following sub-sections elaborate on several cognitive and motivational biases that are prevalent in the context of military decision-making and risk assessment, both at the individual and group level.

These cognitive and motivational biases influence not only military decision-makers ex ante, but also shape ex post legal investigations. In the case of internal military investigations, these cognitive and organizational-level biases apply directly, as the investigating body is a part of the same organizational structure and culture. Some of these biases may also (become more pronounced at the ex post investigation level, as now that the decision was already made, an anchoring bias[28] is also at play). In the case of external investigations, commissions of inquiry, or judicial oversight, ex post fact-finders tend to defer to factual judgments made by the military decision-makers, thus reproducing decision-maker biases during the review process.[29] In other words, cognitive and organizational biases such as groupthink and overconfidence directly affect fact-finders during the ex ante decision-making process, and later on affect the ex post review process through deference to decision-makers' expertise, or through the legal doctrine requiring military decisions to be reasonable under the circumstances prevailing at the time (based on the information that was available to decision-makers).

A Cognitive Biases Affecting Military Risk Assessments

Cognitive biases refer to faulty mental processes that lead decision-makers to make sub-optimal decisions that deviate from normative principles.[30] In their influential studies of decision-making biases and heuristics, Kahneman, Slovic, and Tversky have grouped these biases under three broad categories: representativeness, availability, and anchoring.[31] Representativeness biases occur when people make judgments based on how closely an option resembled the problem scenario,

[26] For a compilation of individual-level biases affecting risk assessments see Gilberto Montibeller and Detlof Von Winterfeldt, 'Cognitive and Motivational Biases in Decision and Risk Analysis' (2015) 35(7) *Risk Analysis* 1230).

[27] NL Kerr, RJ MacCoun, and GP Kramer, 'Bias in Judgment: Comparing Individuals and Groups' (1996) 103(4) *Psychological Review* 687.

[28] Anchoring bias occurs when the estimation of a condition is based on an initial value (anchor) which is then insufficiently adjusted to provide the final true condition. Blair S Williams, 'Heuristics and Biases in Military Decision Making' (2010) 92(4) *Military Review* 40, 48).

[29] Robert M Chesney, 'National Security Fact Deference' (2009) 95 *Virginia Law Review* 1361.

[30] Montibeller and Winterfeldt (n 26) 1230.

[31] D Kahneman, P Slovic, and A Tversky (eds), *Judgement Under Uncertainty: Heuristics and Biases* (Cambridge University Press 1988).

in violation of rational laws of probability.[32] Availability biases occur when people overstate the likelihood that a certain event will occur because it is easily recalled, or because they can easily retrieve similar examples to mind.[33] In the context of military decision-making, availability biases make decision-makers less sensitive to alternative courses of action or information that runs contrary to their experience or worldview.[34] Anchoring biases occur when the estimation of a condition is based on an initial value (anchor), which is then insufficiently adjusted to provide the final true condition.[35] The starting point—the anchor—might result from intuition, the framing of the problem, or even a guess, and the problem is that decision-makers do not adjust sufficiently from this initial anchoring point.[36]

These cognitive biases are particularly prevalent in the context of military decision-making, as they affect experts precisely because of their experience and expertise. Slovic and others found that experts think they can estimate failure rates with much greater precision than is actually the case.[37] Some common ways in which experts misjudge factual information and associated risks are (i) failure to consider the ways in which human errors can influence technological systems; (ii) failure to anticipate human response to safety measures; and (iii) insensitivity to how technological systems function as a whole.[38] Analysing intelligence failures with regard to Iraqi weapons of mass destruction, Robert Jervis concluded that many of the intelligence community's judgments were stated with overconfidence, assumptions were insufficiently examined, and assessments were based on previous judgments without carrying forward the uncertainties.[39] Overconfidence becomes an even greater problem in the context of military decision-making, due to decision-makers' aversion of the associated risks considering the dire nature and potential consequences of attacks.[40] Analysing Israeli intelligence failures Kahana concluded that the Israeli intelligence community suffers from an inherent problem of overestimation of threats.[41]

[32] RJ Knighton, 'The Psychology of Risk and Its Role in Military Decision-Making' (2004) 4(3) *Defence Studies* 309, 320.

[33] Montibeller and Winterfeldt (n 26) 1233.

[34] Knighton (n 32) 322.

[35] Williams (n 28) 48.

[36] Knighton (n 32) 322.

[37] Paul Slovic, Baruch Fischhoff, and Sarah Lichtenstein, 'Facts and Fears: Understanding Perceived Risk' in Richard C Schwing and Walter A Albers (eds), *Societal Risk Assessment: How Safe is Safe Enough?* (Springer 1980) 181–216. See also Sitaraman and Zionts (n 6) 534–35.

[38] Slovic and others (n 37) 187.

[39] Robert Jervis, 'Reports, Politics, and Intelligence Failures: The Case of Iraq' (2006) 29 *Journal of Strategic Studies* 3, 14, 22.

[40] Mark G Stewart, Bruce R Ellingwood, and John Mueller, 'Homeland Security: A Case Study in Risk Aversion for Public Decision-Making' (2011) 15 *International Journal of Risk Assessment and Management* 367, 370.

[41] Ephraim Kahana, 'Analyzing Israel's Intelligence Failures' (2005) 18 *International Journal of Intelligence and CounterIntelligence* 262, 274. Jervis pointed out that states are prone to exaggerate the reasonableness of their own positions and the hostile intent of others. Robert Jervis, 'War and Misperception' (1988) *Journal of Interdisciplinary History* 675, 688.

As crucial military decisions are made within an organizational context, and with varying levels of group dynamics, several additional organizational factors exacerbate the operation of these biases.[42] These include group dynamics such as groupthink (or herding), deference to judgments made by others (including superiors), flawed information sharing processes, and lock-in effects stemming from an organizational culture.[43]

Groupthink is a mode of thinking that people engage in when they are deeply involved in a cohesive in-group, when their strivings for unanimity override their motivation to realistically appraise alternative courses of action.[44] Groupthink fosters excessive optimism, lack of vigilance, and stereotypical thinking about out-groups, while motivating members to ignore negative information.[45] Groupthink dynamics are particularly pronounced in organizational cultures where secrecy and information compartmentalization are core values, and where internal disagreements—where they occur—are buried at lower level discussions, and only the winning argument is brought forward to inform decision-makers.[46] Such flawed information sharing dynamics within and between intelligence and military organizations have been blamed for the intelligence failures concerning both 9/11 and Iraq.[47] Lock-in effects further constrain decision-makers in cohesive environments, where organizational culture negatively affect the organization's ability to respond to new challenges, or even prevent the organization from recognizing a change in the environment or the existing threats.[48]

B Motivated Cognition

Motivational biases refer to judgments and decisions that are influenced by self-interest, social pressures, or organizational context, and can be conscious or unconscious.[49] Motivated reasoning theories relate to a decision-maker's motivation to arrive at particular conclusions. Kunda finds that the motivation to reach a

[42] Dina Badie, 'Groupthink, Iraq, and the War on Terror: Explaining US Policy Shift Toward Iraq' (2010) 6 *Foreign Policy Analysis* 277, 280–81, 285.

[43] Luis Garicano and Richard A Posner, 'Intelligence Failures: An Organizational Economics Perspective' (2005) 19(4) *Journal of Economic Perspectives* 151.

[44] Irving L Janis, *Groupthink: Psychological Studies of Policy Decisions and Fiascoes* (2nd edn, Houghton Mifflin 1982) 9. See also Marleen A O'Connor, 'The Enron Board: The Perils of Groupthink' (2003) 71 *University of Cincinnati Law Review* 1233, 1258.

[45] O'Connor (n 44) 1258.

[46] AB Zegart, 'September 11 and the Adaptation Failure of US Intelligence Agencies' (2005) 29(4) *International Security* 78, 105–109.

[47] In the case of the Iraq war, for example, a number of CIA officers expressed doubts about the veracity of the intelligence information, but their superiors, who disagreed with this assessment, presented a filtered, unified point of view that failed to reveal the diversity of opinion at the lower levels. Garicano and Posner (n 43) 158–59.

[48] ibid.

[49] Montibeller and Winterfeldt (n 26) 1230.

particular conclusion or outcome affects reasoning through reliance on a biased set of cognitive processes (strategies for accessing, constructing, and evaluating beliefs) that are considered most likely to yield the desired conclusion.[50] There is considerable evidence that people are more likely to arrive at conclusions that they want to arrive at, but their ability to do so is constrained by their ability to construct seemingly reasonable justifications for these conclusions.[51] Montibeller and Winterfeldt identify a host of motivational biases that are relevant for risk assessments, and describe the way they distort analysis inputs. They further find that these motivational biases are particularly difficult to correct.[52]

A specific type of motivational bias that is particularly relevant for military decision-making and risk assessments is confirmation bias. Confirmation bias occurs when there is a desire to confirm one's belief, leading to unconscious selectivity in the acquisition and use of evidence.[53] Confirmation bias is a particular case of cognitive consistency bias, which connotes the seeking or interpreting of evidence in ways that are partial to existing beliefs, expectations, or hypothesis in hand.[54] Research has shown the prevalence of confirmation bias in the security risk assessment context, particularly with regard to assessing the credibility of intelligence information.[55]

V Law-fulfilling Prophecies

The concrete epistemological choices adopted to guide the collection of facts during legal investigations of wartime events, combined with the abovementioned individual and organizational-level biases, join in to produce a unique decision-making dynamic I term '*law-fulfilling prophecies*'.[56] The application of future-focused legal norms, which centre on *intentional* and *anticipated* rather than *actual* harm,[57] complicates the fact-finding process, and perpetuates the gap between

50 Ziva Kunda, 'The Case for Motivated Reasoning' (1990) 108 *Psychological Bulletin* 480.

51 ibid. See also Dan M Kahan, 'Ideology, Motivated Reasoning, and Cognitive Reflection: An Experimental Study' (2012) 8 *Judgment and Decision Making* 407.

52 Montibeller and Winterfeldt (n 26) 1235–36.

53 RS Nickerson, 'Confirmation Bias: A Ubiquitous Phenomenon in Many Guises' (1998) 2(2) *Review of General Psychology* 175.

54 ibid.

55 Martha Whitesmith, 'The Efficacy of ACH in Mitigating Serial Position Effects and Confirmation Bias in an Intelligence Analysis Scenario' (2019) 34(2) *Intelligence and National Security* 225.

56 For a discussion of the 'self-fulfilling prophecy' bias see Stephanie Madon, Lee Jussim, and Jacquelynne Eccles, 'In Search of the Powerful Self-Fulfilling Prophecy' (1997) 72(4) *Journal of Personality and Social Psychology* 791; Jeremy C Biesanz and others, 'When Accuracy-Motivated Perceivers Fail: Limited Attentional Resources and the Reemerging Self-Fulfilling Prophecy' (2001) 27(5) *Personality and Social Psychology Bulletin* 621.

57 For example, the principle of proportionality, which determines that disproportionate harm to protected individuals, is tolerated as long as this outcome was not *anticipated* (API, art 51(5)(b)); or the principle of precaution, determining that the selected course of action should be the one that is expected to cause the least danger to civilians' lives (API art 57(3)).

brute facts, which can easily be collected (such as number of casualties) and the legal facts, which are open for various interpretations and are more difficult to ascertain (such as the factual assumptions and intentions of decision-makers in real time, or the reasonableness of these assumptions).

At the decision-making level, legal standards that focus, for example, on anticipated damage, can more easily be affected by cognitive biases, including motivated cognition dynamics. This is because this type of facts requires interpretation of observed and available data, and this interpretation is the product of cognitive processes that can be affected by the motivation to approve or legitimize a military action. In other words, facts are being interpreted to be consistent with the legal requirement; and missing information and knowledge gaps are filled with assumptions that satisfy the legal rule. As ex post investigations focus on decision-makers' evaluation of the available facts at the time of the decision-making, future-focused legal rules motivate decision-makers in real time, consciously or unconsciously, to collect less facts about the presence of civilians, and to interpret the available facts in a way consistent with the legal standard.

At the ex post investigation level, these predictions—or prophecies—are fulfilled, as military actions are not being evaluated based on the actual damage they caused, but rather by the damage that was predicted—or prophesied—by decision-makers in real time. To demonstrate this dynamic, the next paragraphs analyse the report of the Israeli Investigatory Commission established to investigate the targeted killing of Salah Shehadeh in Gaza, which was completed and published in 2011.

Salah Shehadeh was head of the operational branch of Hamas in Gaza and was accused by Israel of having killed large numbers of Israeli military personnel and civilians. On 22 July 2002, the Israeli Air Force dropped a one-tonne bomb on Shehadeh's house in Gaza City, killing Shehadeh himself, his assistant, and 13 civilians, including Shehadeh's wife and daughter. Eight of the victims were children, and an additional 150 bystanders were injured.[58] Following this operation, the IDF conducted an internal investigation and decided not to initiate criminal proceedings. Several human rights organizations petitioned against this decision, and ultimately the Government agreed to establish an independent investigatory commission to investigate the operation. On 27 February 2011, the Commission published its final report,[59] concluding that Shehadeh was a legitimate target,[60] and considering the anticipated death of his wife as proportionate collateral damage. The Commission concluded, however, that the death of 12 other civilians was disproportionate and excessive.[61] Nevertheless, the Commission accepted the

[58] Krebs (n 3).
[59] Shehadeh Commission Report (n 4).
[60] ibid 55–60.
[61] ibid 66–67.

security agencies' claim that this disproportionate outcome was not anticipated, and that had such an outcome been anticipated, the operation would not have been carried out.[62] Consequently, the Commission concluded that neither international nor Israeli law was violated, and found no reason to suspect that a crime was committed by any of the persons involved in the planning, authorization, and implementation of the targeted killing operation.[63]

The Commission emphasized in its analysis that the legality of the operation should be considered on the basis of the available ex ante information, even if it turned out that the information was false.[64] The Commission determined that the disproportionate outcome of the operation resulted from severe intelligence failures (including misrepresentation of existing information). Yet these failures in the collection and interpretation of crucial facts were deemed irrelevant for the legal analysis. The Commission's final conclusion, therefore, was that the 'unfortunate harm' caused by the attack was unintentional and unpredictable, and that it resulted from an intelligence failure caused by 'incorrect assessments and mistaken judgments'.[65]

What were these inaccuracies and mistakes? The Commission did not identify concrete errors, yet it concluded that '*at some point, the missing information became positive information* that the garage house and tin shacks [where most of the victims were killed – S.K.] are uninhabited'.[66] This is an interesting finding, especially as a thorough examination of the available evidence suggests that this information was not missing at all. The documents inspected by the Commission included aerial photos that were available to decision-makers in real-time. These photos depicted water tanks and satellite dishes on the roofs of the tin shacks, signifying that civilians were living in the tin shacks adjunct to Shehadeh's residence. The Commission mentioned, in other parts of its report, the common knowledge that this area is densely populated. It also mentioned the air force estimations concerning severe collateral damage to the tin shacks and their inhabitants.[67] Additional evidence suggested that Shehadeh's daughter, Iman, was with him. *So how did it happen, that information about presence of civilians turned into information about their absence?*

A possible explanation is that this was an inevitable outcome of the legal frames through which the relevant facts were construed. The legal epistemology through which the legality of the plan was considered was the future-focused principle of proportionality, which takes into account (both ex ante and ex post) only anticipated damage. This focus on anticipated damage enabled decision-makers to see,

[62] ibid 67, 72.
[63] ibid 103–106.
[64] ibid 47, 97–98.
[65] Salah Shehadeh—Special Investigatory Commission, English summary prepared by the ministry of Foreign Affairs www.mfa.gov.il/MFA/Government/Law/Legal%20Issues%20and%20Rulings/Salah_Shehadeh-Special_Investigatory_Commission_27-Feb-2011.htm.
[66] ibid 79 (emphasis added).
[67] ibid 78.

in real time (and the investigatory commission to accept, ex post) empty buildings in the middle of a densely populated refugee camp. One example demonstrating this dynamic relates to the deliberations concerning the potential presence of Shehadeh's daughter, Iman, with him. On the night of the attack (22 July) the deputy head of the ISA estimated that Shehadeh's daughter, Iman, was at the house, or, at least, that based on the existing information her presence cannot be ruled out. He immediately called the head of the ISA and shared his concerns. The head of the ISA considered the information and concluded that it is highly unlikely that Iman is at the house (mainly, as there was no 'positive information' confirming her presence). As a result, he decided to continue with the operation as planned.[68]

Of course, there was also no 'positive information' about her absence, which seemed even less likely than her presence, given that the operation was cancelled twice during the preceding days (20 and 21 July) based on positive information about Iman's presence at the house.[69] This epistemological choice to require 'positive information' about the presence of civilians, shifted the burden of proof and embraced decision-making processes based on partial, uncertain, factual framework. Coupled with the future-focused proportionality standard, the positive information requirement enabled decision-makers to conclude that the anticipated collateral damage is expected to be low and lawful.

By accepting the ISA position that anticipated collateral damage should be based on certain, or positive, information about the presence of civilians, the Commission signalled to decision-makers that lethal operations can be approved based on a high degree of uncertainty or partial information (concerning the presence of civilians). It also embraced the 'fog of war' metaphor as an excuse and an explanation for any gaps between the anticipated damage and the actual one. This, in turn, generated an interpretive tool that transformed the absence of facts about the presence of civilians into existing facts about their absence. The result was that the prophecy that Iman Shehadeh (and the additional 11 civilian casualties) will not be harmed by the attack, fulfilled itself in the Commission's legal report. Iman's actual death was considered an unfortunate, causeless, tragedy, irrelevant for the outcome of the investigation. Her prophesied safety, however, was central to the determination that the attack was lawful.

In addition to the effects of the selected legal epistemology on the decision-making processes, the Commission's Report further demonstrates the effects of the cognitive and motivational biases described above on the decision to approve this targeted killing operation. In particular, groupthink and lock-in dynamics, the invisibility of internal disagreements, and a flawed stream of crucial information (partly resulting from the fragmentation within the security agencies), enabled ISA decision-makers selectively to choose intelligence information to fit with the

[68] ibid 69–70.
[69] ibid 68.

legal requirements. At the same time, motivated cognition dynamics were reflected through the growing frustration within the agency, as previous targeting plans were cancelled and they feared that Shehadeh would soon change his whereabouts. In particular, as evident from transcripts of crucial meetings at the ISA, the Head of ISA's decision to approve the operation as planned was based on the escalation in the number and severity of terror attacks, and on his concern that postponing the operation to collect more intelligence will thwart the efforts to kill Shehadeh and put a stop to his terror activities.[70]

Owing to space constraints, I shall focus here on a particular example that demonstrates several of the aforementioned biases.[71] On 19 July 2002, the deputy director of the ISA held a meeting of both ISA and Air Force personnel concerning the planned operation. In the meeting, the Air Force representatives estimated that the surroundings would suffer severe damage and indicated that there would be at least several wounded and dead in the tin shacks.[72] Several other sources of information also suggested that the tin shacks were inhabited, including visuals depicting water tanks and satellite dishes on their roofs.[73] Despite this assessment, and following an internal disagreement within the ISA, the head of ISA decided to approve the operation. His decision, which was relayed to the IDF chief of staff and later to the minister of defence and the prime minister, did not include any reference to the assessment that the tin shacks were inhabited, or to any anticipated casualties there.[74] The IDF chief of staff approved the operation based on the assumption that the tin shacks were not inhabited.[75] Following the IDF chief of staff's approval, the minister of defence was briefed by his military secretary and provided his authorization for the plan. The brief did not include any information on the danger to residents of the tin shacks, or any of the disagreements between senior officials of the ISA and IDF.[76]

This decision-making dynamic demonstrates the operation of cognitive biases at both the individual and organizational levels. First, this example demonstrates a fixation on the most salient risks (Shehadeh's future terror activities), at the expense of other, less salient ones (collateral damage resulting from the targeted killing operation). In addition to availability bias, this example also demonstrates how detailed planning can create a feeling of control which ultimately increases decision-makers' propensity to take risks. The detailed plan became an anchoring point, which caused decision-makers to view the existing conditions (of

[70] ibid 74–75.
[71] For additional examples see Krebs (n 3).
[72] Shehadeh Commission Report (n 65) 73.
[73] ibid 78.
[74] ibid 74–75.
[75] ibid 76.
[76] ibid 82–83. The operation was further approved by the Prime Minister, but due to his medical condition was unable to provide information to the Commission and it remained unclear whether he was informed about the expected presence of civilians in the tin shacks. ibid 84.

a densely populated refugee camp) in a way that fits the plan (the tin shacks were uninhabited). Overconfidence exacerbated these biases, reducing the sensitivity of decision-makers to potential weaknesses in the plan, or the existence of other feasible alternatives. At the organizational level, this example demonstrates problems arising from a culture of invisible disagreements and flawed information sharing processes.

VI Unlearning Legal Epistemology; Reinventing Legal Metaphors

What are the invisible frames affecting fact-finding processes during armed conflicts? This chapter *unveiled* three particular frames of international law affecting legal investigations of wartime events. These include the fog of war metaphor, the ontology and epistemology of legal fact-finding (including the anticipatory focus of the relevant legal rules), and cognitive and motivational biases affecting both ex ante decision-makers and ex post investigators.

The example of the Shehadeh Investigatory Commission was then used to *understand* the operation of these mechanisms and the way they shape the outcomes of fact-finding processes during armed conflicts. The number of civilian casualties depended on a legal definition, and the number of actual casualties became secondary to the number of anticipated casualties. Ultimately, the false prophecy that only Shehadeh and his wife would be killed was perpetuated in the legal reality. This prophecy was based on an insufficient, uncertain, factual framework, which was also preserved through the report's findings. The Commission concluded that had the death of the eight children and four adult civilians been anticipated, the operation would have been unlawful; but their deaths were not anticipated, and therefore no law was broken.

The detailed analysis of this concrete fact-finding process illustrates how the fog of war metaphor, combined with anticipatory legal rules (the proportionality principle) and cognitive and motivational biases, generate findings that legitimize erroneous military decisions that caused devastating outcomes. The invisibility of these frames presents contingent fact-finding practices as neutral and natural, masks subjective choices and choices made, and enables the reoccurrence of lethal mistakes. While intelligence and operational errors may be inescapable, investigators and ex post reviewers should be able to identify these errors in retrospect. Improving fact-finding requires, therefore, unveiling the frames through which facts are constructed, acknowledging the way they shape the outcomes of fact-finding processes during armed conflicts, *unlearning* these processes and dynamics, and reimagining popular metaphors and epistemological choices. In particular, the fog of war metaphor should return to its original temporal meaning, and ex post investigatory mechanisms should strive to disperse the fog of war rather than embracing it.

Indeed, in the era of drones, satellites, and cyber-surveillance, where battlefields and military operations are recorded by various devices and from many angles, investigations into military operations should not conveniently conclude that 'no one will ever be able conclusively to determine the number of civilian casualties that occurred on May 4, 2009'.[77] While the availability of information may be limited during some (but not all) military decisions, this should not discourage fact-finders from conducting a rigorous fact-finding process ex post, and continuing the investigation until all relevant facts are uncovered. While individual decision-makers may be judged based on the information available to them in real time, collecting information that may explain the gap between anticipated and actual outcomes should become central to ex post investigations.

In addition to reimagining the fog of war metaphor, factual uncertainties can be made visible through careful categorization of various types of facts related to military planning and actions. Some relevant facts describe physical phenomena, conveying information which is observable through human senses, such as the number of dead bodies at a certain location and time. Such physical, observable, facts are typically concerned with the past or the present. Other types of facts are concerned with the future: Will civilians be present? Will the targeted individual be involved in future attacks? These facts involve an additional layer of inferences and predictions from the observed data. Sometimes, these predictions about the future also involve value judgments, such as determinations concerning the excessiveness of the harm to civilians in comparison to the security gain. A different type of facts is legal facts; facts that describe not physical but rather legal reality, such as the classification of an individual as a civilian or a combatant for legal purposes, or evaluating individual legal responsibility for a concrete action. A physical or observational fact describing the number of casualties becomes a legal fact when describing a particular legal class of victims, such as the number of *civilian* casualties. Investigations into military operations rarely distinguish between these different types of facts, and fact-finders often disregard the unique empirical challenges raised by each type of facts.[78]

Additionally, despite the variety of epistemological standards and rules, investigations into wartime events typically adopt legal conventions that prefer assumptions about future casualties to actual numbers of casualties. These epistemological choices are applied with little or no scrutiny of the way they constitute the factual

[77] US Central Command, US Central Command Investigations into Civilian Casualties in the Farah Province, Afghanistan, on 4 May 2009 (2009).

[78] Michael D Risinger, 'Searching for Truth in the American Law of Evidence and Proof' (2013) 47 *Georgia Law Review* 801. See also Moore (n 22) 24–26 (distinguishing between propositions of fact, general law, interpretation, value, and logic).

reality they purport to objectively describe; and without considering possible alternatives. This is, of course, perfectly understandable, as it is the existing requirement of the applicable law. At the same time, adopting these legal conventions as the standard for fact-finding efforts influences the construction of available facts and hinders the identification of weaknesses in risk assessment and decision-making processes.

While moving away from anticipatory rules in this context would require major changes to the law of armed conflict, the consequences of such a change are not impossible to reimagine. In fact, adopting an alternative approach to the *jus in bello* principle of proportionality which focuses on actual—rather than anticipatory—outcomes, was already envisaged in 1977, with some delegates arguing that the focus on anticipatory outcomes sacrifices civilians' safety for real or assumed military advantages.[79] While calls for an outcomes-based approach to the principle of proportionality had ultimately been rejected during the negotiations concerning the protocols additional to the Geneva Conventions, it is not too late to revisit this legal structure and more meaningfully protect civilians during armed conflicts.

[79] During the negotiations that led to signing of the 1977 Additional Protocols of the Geneva Conventions, the codification of the proportionality principle was deeply contested. Some critics related to it as 'dangerous', and others pointed out that it opened the door to abuses. For example, the representative of Romania, who voted against this formulation of the proportionality rule, explained that the rule 'amounted to legal acceptance of the fact that one part of the civilian population was to be deliberately scarified to real or assumed military advantages'. *Official Records of the Diplomatic Conference on the Reaffirmation and Development of International Humanitarian Law Applicable in Armed Conflicts*, CDDH/III/SR.31 9 (Vol xiv, Geneva, 1974–1977) 305. See also David Traven, 'Moral Cognition and the Law and Ethics of Armed Conflict' (2015) 17(4) *International Studies Review* 556.

8

Labels as the *Visible* Part of International Law's *Invisible* Frames

The Case of the Framework Convention on Tobacco Control as an 'Evidence-based' Treaty

Margherita Melillo[*]

I Introduction

This chapter contributes to the investigation of the influence of socio-cognitive processes in international law by examining the use of labels as a tool to reinforce the framing of some specific issues. Framing alignment has famously been introduced in social movements theory by Snow et al, who described it as the use of ' "schemata of interpretation" that enable individuals "to locate, perceive, identify, and label" '.[1] This concept has had quite some success, being later criticized[2] and developed,[3] as well as assessed[4] by the same literature. From there, the concept of framing was borrowed by the international relations literature, where framing has come to be considered an important strategy in the hands of norm entrepreneurs and in norm creation.[5] Framing has been used to understand several developments

[*] I am indebted to Moshe Hirsch and Andrea Bianchi for very insightful comments that helped me shape the arguments in this chapter and enrich its theoretical framework. I also thank my PhD supervisor, Joanne Scott, for her constant support, feedback, and inspiring discussions.

[1] This definition is given by David A Snow and others, 'Frame Alignment Processes, Micromobilization, and Movement Participation' (1986) 51(4) *American Sociological Review* 464. It builds on the earlier work and definition by Erving Goffman, *Frame Analysis: An Essay on the Organization of Experience* (Harvard University Press 1974).

[2] Rodger A Payne, 'Persuasion, Frames and Norm Construction' (2001) 7 *European Journal of International Relations* 37.

[3] David A Snow and Robert D Benford, 'Ideology, Frame Resonance, and Participant Mobilization' (1988) 1 *International Social Movement Research* 197; David A Snow and Robert D Benford, 'Master Frames and Cycles of Protest' (1992) 133 *Frontiers in Social Movement Theory* 155; Hank Johnston and John A Noakes, *Frames of Protest: Social Movements and the Framing Perspective* (Rowman & Littlefield Publishers 2005).

[4] Robert D Benford and David A Snow, 'Framing Processes and Social Movements: An Overview and Assessment' (2000) 26 *Annual Review of Sociology* 611; David Snow and others, 'The Emergence, Development, and Future of the Framing Perspective: 25+ Years Since" Frame Alignment" ' (2014) 19 *Mobilization: An International Quarterly* 23.

[5] Martha Finnemore and Kathryn Sikkink, 'International Norm Dynamics and Political Change' (1998) 52 *International Organization* 887, 897; Margaret E Keck and Kathryn Sikkink, *Activists Beyond Borders: Advocacy Networks in International Politics* (Cornell University Press 1998) 2–3; Michele

Margherita Melillo, *Labels as the* Visible *Part of International Law's* Invisible *Frames* In: *International Law's Invisible Frames*. Edited by: Andrea Bianchi and Moshe Hirsch, Oxford University Press. © Margherita Melillo 2021.
DOI: 10.1093/oso/9780192847539.003.0009

in international law, including the campaign against landmines,[6] the making of the ozone treaty,[7] and the international moratorium on whaling.[8] The role of frames has also been acknowledged to shape several issues pertaining to what is nowadays called 'global health governance',[9] which is the topic of this chapter.

Against that background, the chapter explores how labels contribute to the formation and reinforcement of frames. In the definition used here, labels are words or phrases used in discourses to attach some attributes to a specific object, person, or concept.[10] Labels can accordingly reinforce cognitive associations between an object, person, or a concept, and its attributes. For this reason, the scholarship on social movements theory has recognized that labelling can help framing issues.[11]

Labels are even more important in the context of law-making. Since words are the constitutive fractions of law, when negotiating a treaty or any other legal instrument, labels can help framing issues and can also ultimately shape the final legal text. Sociological and anthropological scholarship have underlined the significance of analysing legal language as part of social practices.[12] Accordingly, identifying the labels and understanding their origin can shed light on the historical and sociocultural factors underpinning international norms. For this reason, I argue that studying labels can help us reveal the invisible frames of international law. Labels can be considered a representative element of the 'cycle of knowledge' described in the introduction of this book. Labels are the outcome of knowledge production processes, and, once they become widespread, they influence social cognition, which in turn can influence subsequent knowledge production processes.

The history of the World Health Organization (WHO) Framework Convention on Tobacco Control (FCTC)[13] is used here to provide some examples of the uses of labels and of the associated frames. The FCTC represents an interesting case-study for at least two reasons. First, although it is often hailed as a very successful

Merrill Betsill and Elisabeth Corell, *NGO Diplomacy: The Influence of Nongovernmental Organizations in International Environmental Negotiations* (MIT Press 2008) 33.

[6] Richard Price, 'Reversing the Gun Sights: Transnational Civil Society Targets Land Mines' (1998) 52 *International Organization* 613.

[7] Karen T Litfin, 'Framing Science: Precautionary Discourse and the Ozone Treaties' (1995) 24 *Millennium* 251.

[8] Charlotte Epstein, *The Power of Words in International Relations: Birth of an Anti-Whaling Discourse* (MIT Press 2008).

[9] Colin McInnes and Kelley Lee, *Framing Global Health Governance* (Routledge 2016).

[10] This definition is further discussed in section 2.

[11] Snow and others (n 2) 464.

[12] Pierre Bourdieu, 'The Force of Law: Toward a Sociology of the Juridical Field' (1986) 38 *Hastings Law Journal* 805, 819–20; Sally Engle Merry, 'The Discourses of Mediation and the Power of Naming' (1990) 2 *Yale Journal of Law & the Humanities* 1; Elizabeth Mertz, 'Legal Language: Pragmatics, Poetics, and Social Power' (1994) 23 *Annual Review of Anthropology* 435; John M Conley, William M O'Barr, and Robin Conley Riner, *Just Words: Law, Language, and Power*, (3rd edn, University of Chicago Press 2019).

[13] WHO Framework Convention on Tobacco Control (signed on 21 May 2003, entered into force on 27 February 2005) 2303 UNTS 166.

treaty, the FCTC is relatively underappreciated by international law scholarship.[14] Secondly, a great number of primary sources on the FCTC history are available and easily accessible, including the *travaux préparatoires*,[15] and accounts of the history of the FCTC negotiations.[16] These documents make it possible to carry out an in-depth investigation of the FCTC negotiations and to unearth many of the underlying views and tensions.

The chapter proceeds as follows. The next section defines the notion of labels and explains the relevance of studying them. The third section presents an empirical case-study on the use of frames and labels in the history of the FCTC negotiations. Finally, the fourth section reflects on how analysing labels can enhance our understanding of international law.

II Labels as the Visible Part of International Law's Invisible Frames

Labels (in French, *étiquettes*) can be commonly found on bottles and packages as slips of paper indicating their contents; however, they also have a more abstract meaning. The *Cambridge Dictionary* defines a label as 'a word or a phrase that is used to describe the characteristics or qualities of people, activities, or things.'[17] Adopting this definition of labels, the chapter posits that *labels* are more than simple *names* given to things. Labelling implies attaching a specific meaning to a person or a thing (eg a bottle of Chianti wine). Names, conversely, have no

[14] Gian Luca Burci and Claude-Henri Vignes, *World Health Organization* (Kluwer Law International 2004) 126–31; Alan Boyle and Christine Chinkin, *The Making of International Law* (OUP 2007) 146–48; José E Alvarez, *The Impact of International Organizations on International Law* (BRILL 2016) 233–43.

[15] Documentation in all official language of the Conference of the Parties, http://apps.who.int/gb/fctc/E/E_process.html (accessed 19 August 2020).

[16] Allyn L Taylor and Douglas W Bettcher, 'WHO Framework Convention on Tobacco Control: A Global Good for Public Health' (2000) 78 *Bulletin of the World Health Organization* 920; Gregory F Jacob, 'Without Reservation' (2004) 5 *Chicago Journal of International Law* 287; Ruth Roemer, Allyn Taylor, and Jean Lariviere, 'Origins of the WHO Framework Convention on Tobacco Control' (2005) 95 *American Journal of Public Health* 936; Vera Luiza da Costa e Silva and Douglas Bettcher, 'Origins and Status of the WHO Framework Convention on Tobacco Control" in Peter Boyle and others (eds), *Tobacco: Science, Policy and Public Health* (Oxford University Press 2010); L A Reynolds, E M Tansey and Witness Seminar, WHO Framework Convention on Tobacco Control (London, 26 February 2010): *WHO Framework Convention on Tobacco Control: The Transcript of a Witness Seminar Organized by the Wellcome Trust Centre for the History of Medicine at UCL, in Collaboration with the Department of Knowledge Management and Sharing, WHO. Held in Geneva, on 26 February 2010* (London: The History of Modern Biomedicine Research Group at UCL 2012) http://archive.org/details/whoframeworkconv00reyn (accessed 19 August 2020); Derek Yach, 'The Origins, Development, Effects, and Future of the WHO Framework Convention on Tobacco Control: A Personal Perspective' (2014) 383 *The Lancet* 1771; Katherine DeLand, Gemma Lien, and Heather Wipfli, 'The WHO Framework Convention on Tobacco Control and the Tobacco Free Initiative' in Andrew D Mitchell and Tania Voon (eds), *The Global Tobacco Epidemic and the Law* (Edward Elgar Publishing 2014); Heather Wipfli, *The Global War on Tobacco: Mapping the World's First Public Health Treaty* (JHU Press 2015).

[17] 'LABEL | Entry in the Cambridge English Dictionary' https://dictionary.cambridge.org/dictionary/english/label (accessed 14 October 2019).

particular attached meaning (eg wine from Castello di Verrazzano). Naming a concept or a thing can reify it, signalling its existence as a separate object (eg Castello di Verrazzano and Castello di Vicchiomaggio each produce different but equally good varieties of Chianti). Labelling a concept or a thing, however, has another role, insofar as it contributes to defining its features (eg if I offer you a glass of Chianti, you would expect a dark-coloured liquid containing ethanol, with a rich and full-bodied taste).

It is in this respect that the power of labels emerges. By attaching some attributes to a concept, a person, or an object, labels reinforce cognitive associations, making them easy to identify, immediately and almost automatically. Ffor instance, when offered a glass of wine, what makes us anticipate its rich and full-bodied taste? Is it its appearance, or the fact we are told it is a glass of Chianti?

Existing scholarship has already recognized the power of *names* in international law. Finnemore and Sikkink contend that the use of language to 'name' issues is an important strategy in norm creation.[18] Naming and translating are also core concepts of the vernacularization process which Merry analysed.[19] Far less attention, however, has been devoted to analysing the specific function of labels.

One needs to look at different strands of scholarship to find a theory of labelling. Sociological theory, in particular, has underlined the importance of labels in understanding criminal deviance. Labelling theory holds that once an individual is labelled as 'deviant', the label can 'reinforce or stabilize' such deviant behaviour.[20] Similarly, research on the social construction of mental illness holds that applying the label 'mentally ill' to an individual can lead to stigma, and hence to the protraction or recurrence of the mental illness.[21]

In this context, some authors have underlined that criminal labels are particularly 'salient' when they are *formalized*, for example, through a trial or an arrest.[22] *Formal* labelling, in turn, leads to *informal* labelling, and thus to social exclusion. Another way of looking at this is that labels are particularly powerful when they are embedded in a (formal) legal norm, and that a (formal) legal label can influence (informal) social relations and practices. Theorists of law would find this statement unsurprising. Although they may adopt different approaches, most theories of law start from the assumption that there is something special about the authoritative power of law and of legal language.[23] It follows that, although labels are per se

[18] Finnemore and Sikkink (n 6) 897.

[19] Sally Engle Merry, *Human Rights and Gender Violence: Translating International Law into Local Justice* (University of Chicago Press 2009).

[20] Jón Gunnar Bernburg, 'Labeling Theory' in Marvin D Krohn and others (eds), *Handbook on Crime and Deviance* (Springer International Publishing 2019) 179.

[21] Bruce G Link and Jo C Phelan, 'Labeling and Stigma' in Carol S Aneshensel and Jo C Phelan (eds), *Handbook of the Sociology of Mental Health* (Springer US 1999); Bruce G Link and Jo C Phelan, 'Conceptualizing Stigma' (2001) 27 *Annual Review of Sociology* 363.

[22] Bernburg (n 21) 181.

[23] Lawrence M Solan and Peter M Tiersma, 'Introduction' in Lawrence M Solan and Peter M Tiersma (eds), *The Oxford Handbook of Language and Law* (OUP 2012) 1–9.

valuable objects of inquiry, they are even more relevant when used in international law-making. Being embedded in a legal text, in fact, confers on labels a particularly authoritative force which contributes to reinforcing and perpetuating the underlying frames.

III Supporting the Negotiations of the WHO Framework Convention on Tobacco Control: Strategies, Frames, and Labels

Against the theoretical backdrop developed here, this section presents an empirical case-study on the use of framing and labels in the history of the FCTC. The first sub-section presents a brief history of how the negotiations of the FCTC were conceived and carried out. The second and third sub-sections analyse two labels used in the FCTC negotiations: the tobacco industry as a 'vector' of the tobacco epidemic, and the FCTC as an 'evidence-based' treaty.

A The FCTC Negotiations as a Strategic Enterprise

Tobacco has been used for centuries. The first solid evidence on the hazardous effects of tobacco smoking emerged in the 1950s and 1960s.[24] The solution was ostensibly self-evident: tobacco products ought to be strictly regulated with a view to limiting their consumption. However, tobacco control measures did not follow with the promptness the medical profession might have expected.[25] Speculating about the delay in regulating tobacco products, it appeared evident that one major obstacle was causing this: the resistance of the tobacco industry.[26] Between 1994 and 1998, a series of legal actions in the United States led to the publication of millions of the tobacco industry's internal documents.[27] They allowed researchers to draw a full picture of the so-called 'tobacco tactics'.[28] What researchers discovered was shocking: for decades, the tobacco industry had thrived by adopting

[24] Ruth Roemer, *Legislative Action to Combat the World Tobacco Epidemic, Second Edition* (WHO 1993); Richard Doll, 'Tobacco: A Medical History' (1999) 76 *Journal of Urban Health* 289, 304; David Reubi and Virginia Berridge, 'The Internationalisation of Tobacco Control, 1950–2010' (2016) 60 *Medical History* 453, 456.

[25] Doll (n 25) 309.

[26] Roemer (n 25) 165.

[27] WHO, 'The Tobacco Industry Documents, a Practical Manual' 1 http://www.who.int/tobacco/communications/TI_manual_content.pdf.

[28] Lisa Bero, 'Implications of the Tobacco Industry Documents for Public Health and Policy' (2003) 24 *Annual Review of Public Health* 267; Allan Brandt, *The Cigarette Century: The Rise, Fall, and Deadly Persistence of the Product that Defined America* (Basic Books 2009); Robert N Proctor, *Golden Holocaust: Origins of the Cigarette Catastrophe and the Case for Abolition* (University of California Press 2012).

tactics such as altering cigarettes' content, relentless lobbying, corruption, and manufacturing of false evidence.[29]

In parallel, and as an attempt to strengthen tobacco control efforts world-wide, some academics proposed the elaboration of a treaty on tobacco control.[30] A proposal started materializing in 1998, when Gro Harlem Brundtland was nominated Director-General of the WHO.[31] The groundwork for the FCTC negotiations started immediately.[32] In 1999, the World Health Assembly finally requested the WHO Secretariat to convene an International Negotiating Body (INB) to launch negotiations over a framework convention on tobacco control.[33] From there, progress was relatively swift, leading to the conclusion and adoption of the FCTC in 2003.[34]

That the FCTC negotiations would be a successful endeavour was not a given. Up to that time, the WHO's law-making activities had been very limited.[35] Some members of the WHO Secretariat had initially opposed the idea of negotiating a treaty on tobacco control, claiming it would stray from the WHO's way of doing things, and would take too long.[36] And yet, after only three years of negotiations, the 170+ participants to the INB managed to reach consensus on a common text.[37] One year after it was opened for signature, 168 states had signed it, making it 'one of the most widely embraced treaties in the United Nations history'.[38]

How did the WHO, with little prior experience, succeed in having the FCTC negotiated in only three years, and on such a contentious matter as tobacco control? This chapter argues that one of the key factors in the treaty's success treaty was the highly strategic planning that the WHO Secretariat undertook. In particular, WHO officials acted as 'norm entrepreneurs',[39] organizing the critical pre-negotiations phase (1998–2000), and continuing to oversee the process during the subsequent intergovernmental phase (2000–2003). Mindful of the public health community's previous failures to regulate tobacco, and the tireless lobbying efforts

[29] Naomi Oreskes and Erik M Conway, *Merchants of Doubt: How a Handful of Scientists Obscured the Truth on Issues from Tobacco Smoke to Global Warming* (A&C Black 2011).

[30] Roemer, Taylor, and Lariviere (n 17) 936.

[31] ibid 938; Reynolds, Tansey, and Witness Seminar (n 17) xxv.

[32] 'Report of the WHO Meeting of Public Health Experts, Hosted by the Government of British Columbia (Canada)' (1998) WHO/NCD/TFI/99 7.

[33] 'World Health Assembly, Resolution "Towards a WHO Framework Convention on Tobacco Control"' (1999) WHA52.18 para 1(1).

[34] 'WHO, Intergovernmental Negotiating Body on the WHO Framework Convention on Tobacco Control, Sixth Session, Summary Records' (2003) A/FCTC/INB6/ SR.

[35] Allyn L Taylor, 'Making the World Health Organization Work: A Legal Framework for Universal Access to the Conditions for Health' (1992) 18 American Journal of Law & Medicine 301, 326–29; David P Fidler, 'International Law and Global Public Health' (1999) 48 *University of Kansas Law Review* 1.

[36] Roemer, Taylor, and Lariviere (n 17) 937–38.

[37] 'WHO, Intergovernmental Negotiating Body on the WHO Framework Convention on Tobacco Control, Sixth Session, List of Participants' (2003) A/FCFC/INB6/DIV/2 Rev. 2.

[38] 'FCTC Secretariat, History of the WHO Convention on Tobacco Control' (2009) 26.

[39] Finnemore and Sikkink (n 6) 899.

of the tobacco industry, a strategic plan may have been considered the best way to counter the industry's aggressive lobbying.

Some of the strategies used by the WHO Secretariat to build up the FCTC negotiations have already been illustrated by former participants in the negotiations and by WHO officials.[40] As described in the next sub-sections, a few of these strategies were actually framing strategies, and were supported by the use of labels.

B Labelling the Tobacco Industry as a 'Vector'

The depiction of the tobacco industry as the direct cause of the tobacco epidemic is the first framing strategy employed during the FCTC negotiations (and precisely diagnostic framing, or the 'identification of a problem and the attribution of blame or causality'[41]). As described in the previous sub-section, in the 1990s the public health community had been shocked by the publication of tobacco industry documents revealing the extent and nature of that industry's tactics. Brundtland reinforced that sense of shock. In 1999, she established an expert group tasked with examining whether the tobacco documents contained indications on activities that the tobacco industry carried out at the WHO. The report, published in 2000 (immediately before the beginning of the FCTC negotiations), contained several equally alarming findings on how the tobacco industry had unduly influenced WHO efforts to promote tobacco control.[42]

A former WHO official, Derek Yach, has noted how unveiling these tactics helped 'refram[e] the tobacco control debate in terms of corporate accountability rather than human frailty'.[43] Countless sources confirm that the willingness to isolate and hold the tobacco industry liable was (and remains) one of the driving forces behind the FCTC.[44] Careful use of language by WHO officials supported that framing, as well as the use of a specific medical-sounding label—'vector'. In a speech, Brundtland referred to the tobacco industry (and not simply to tobacco) as the 'vector of the tobacco epidemic'[45]—thus referring to the industry as

[40] Yach (n 17) 2–5; Wipfli (n 17)36–38.

[41] Snow and Benford, 'Ideology, Frame Resonance, and Participant Mobilization' (n 4) 200.

[42] 'Report of the Committee of Experts on Tobacco Industry Documents, "Tobacco Companies Strategies to Undermine Tobacco Control Activities at the World Health Organization" ' (2000).

[43] Yach (n 17) 2.

[44] Derek Yach and Douglas Bettcher, 'Globalisation of Tobacco Industry Influence and New Global Responses' (2000) 9 *Tobacco Control* 206; Derek Yach, ' "In Their Own Words …" Using Tobacco Industry Documents to Advance Truth' (31 January 2001) https://www.who.int/tobacco/dy_speeches1/en/ (accessed 19 August 2020); 'WHO. The WHO FCTC Secretariat's Knowledge Hubs and the Tobacco Industry Monitoring Centres (Observatories)' (*WHO*) http://www.who.int/fctc/implementation/knowledge-management/en/ (accessed 13 March 2019); 'WHO FCTC, Conference of the Parties, Decision "Guidelines for Implementation of Article 5.3 of the WHO Framework Convention on Tobacco Control on the Protection of Public Health Policies with Respect to Tobacco Control from Commercial and Other Vested Interests of the Tobacco Industry" ' FCTC/COP3(7) 3.

[45] 'WHO, Intergovernmental Negotiating Body on the WHO Framework Convention on Tobacco Control, Fifth Session, Statement by the Director-General' (2002) A/FCTC/INB5/DIV/7 2.

the carrier of a disease. Derek Yach appears to have used the same 'vector' label.[46] While 'vector' label did not outlive the FCTC negotiations, some traces of the underlying frame are still discernible in the text of the treaty. One of the general obligations under the FCTC foresees that states should 'act to protect the[ir] policies from commercial and other vested interests of the tobacco industry' (Article 5.3).[47]

C Labelling the FCTC an 'Evidence-based' Treaty

The most powerful strategy applied in the FCTC negotiations was arguably using evidence to push for stronger and stricter tobacco control measures to be embedded into the treaty text and framing it as a solid body of scientific certainty that provided clear solutions (prognostic framing, or 'to suggest solutions to the problem'[48]).

As a scientific organization, the WHO has an obvious penchant for evidence; respect for science, evidence, and expertise is inscribed in its organizational culture. The WHO's penchant for evidence, however, reflects only part of the story of why evidence was so cardinal in the negotiations. The other part of the story is found in the context within which the treaty was conceived. Derek Yach felt that the FCTC provided an opportunity to make the tobacco industry's 'scientific strategy ineffective'.[49] In a statement released immediately before the beginning of the FCTC negotiations, Brundtland highlighted how the arguments that the tobacco industry advanced had no 'evidence base', while the WHO's position was 'based on available evidence'.[50] By disseminating evidence, and embedding its main findings in the FCTC, the WHO could once and for all debunk the myths and false truths created by the tobacco industry.

The evidence on the effectiveness of tobacco control measures is, by its own nature, naturally uncertain and incomplete.[51] However, during the FCTC negotiations the evidence was not simply offered but was framed as a solid body of

[46] Yach and Bettcher (n 45) 207; Yach (n 45).

[47] FCTC, art 5.3.

[48] Snow and Benford, 'Ideology, Frame Resonance, and Participant Mobilization' (n 4) 201.

[49] Derek Yach and Stella Aguinaga Bialous, 'Junking Science to Promote Tobacco' (2001) 91 *American Journal of Public Health* 1745, 1747.

[50] 'WHO Director General's Response to the Tobacco Hearings, Statement WHO/6' (13 October 2000) https://www.who.int/tobacco/framework/public_hearings/dghearings_en.pdf?ua=1 (accessed 19 August 2020).

[51] By 'evidence on tobacco control' I refer to a category that comprises not only the evidence on the harmful effects of tobacco (the risk assessment dimension), but also on the effectiveness of tobacco control measures (the risk management dimension). On this point see Margherita Melillo, 'Evidentiary Issues in Philip Morris v Uruguay: Complex Challenges, the Relevance of the Framework Convention for Tobacco Control, and Lessons for NCD Prevention' (2020) 21 *Journal of World Investment & Trade* 724.

knowledge providing ready-made solutions for policy-makers. As Brundtland explained in a speech:

> [T]he good news is that we can buck and reverse the global tobacco trend. We know what works and how. Taxes work and the young are especially susceptible to increased prices. Advertising and sponsorship bans work. Smoke-free policies work. Such policy interventions could, in sum, bring unprecedented health and economic benefits. WHO's message is that there is a political solution to tobacco and it is routed through policy interventions and political vision.[52]

To support that framing, the FCTC began to be labelled as an 'evidence-based' treaty by WHO officials, including Derek Yach,[53] as well as by civil society organizations.[54] I maintain that this labelling was part of the strategic actions that the WHO Secretariat, as a norm entrepreneur, imprinted on the FCTC negotiations. By labelling the treaty 'evidence-based', the norm entrepreneurs wanted to convey the message that evidence provided all the answers to the tobacco epidemic. 'Evidence-based' is not a common concept in international law, but is, however, a fundamental concept of modern medicine.[55] Using this label in the context of the tobacco treaty may have triggered a comforting sense of familiarity among the medical professionals attending the INB.[56] More generally, the 'evidence-based' label is considered an effective tool because it 'reif[ies] and reinforce[s] rationalist thinking while simultaneously categorising and condemning other forms of reasoning as inferior'.[57]

Unlike the 'vector' label, the 'evidence-based' label outlived the FCTC negotiations. When discussing the FCTC, the 'evidence-based' label is ubiquitous, used in scientific articles, reports, judgments, and newspaper articles.[58] The use of this

[52] Gro Harlem Brundtland, 'WHO's International Conference on Global Tobacco Control Law: Towards a WHO Framework Convention on Tobacco Control' (7 January 2000) https://web.archive.org/web/20070709052826/http://www.who.int/director-general/speeches/2000/english/20000107_new_delhi.html.

[53] 'Report of the WHO Meeting of Public Health Experts, Hosted by the Government of British Columbia (Canada)' (n 33) 15; Taylor and Bettcher (n 17) 925; Douglas W Bettcher, Derek Yach, and G Emmanuel Guindon, 'Global Trade and Health: Key Linkages and Future Challenges' (2000) 78 *Bulletin of the World Health Organization* 521, 524.

[54] 'WHO, Intergovernmental Negotiating Body on the WHO Framework Convention on Tobacco Control, First Session, Summary Records' (2000) A/FCTC/INB1/SR 45; 'WHO, Intergovernmental Negotiating Body on the WHO Framework Convention on Tobacco Control, Sixth Session, Summary Records' (n 35) 33.

[55] Gordon H Guyatt, 'Evidence-Based Medicine' (1991) 114 *ACP Journal Club* A16.

[56] C Whan Park and V Parker Lessig, 'Familiarity and Its Impact on Consumer Decision Biases and Heuristics' (1981) 8 *Journal of Consumer Research* 223.

[57] McInnes and Lee (n 10) 7.

[58] Kenji Shibuya and others, 'WHO Framework Convention on Tobacco Control: Development of an Evidence Based Global Public Health Treaty' (2003) 327 *British Medical Journal* 154; Kenneth E Warner, 'The Framework Convention on Tobacco Control: Opportunities and Issues' (2008) 50 *Salud Pública de México* 283, s287; Melanie Wakefield and Jonathan Liberman, 'Back to the Future: Tobacco Industry Interference, Evidence and the Framework Convention on Tobacco Control' (2008) 17 *Tobacco Control* 145.

label has spilled over into the post-conclusion life of the FCTC. The guidelines adopted by the FCTC Conference of the Parties (COP) to give guidance to the Parties on how to implement FCTC provisions are indeed often described as being 'evidence-based.'[59] Finally, the label has slowly become official. A formal decision of the COP adopted in 2014 used the 'evidence-based' label to refer to the measures recommended by the FCTC.[60] Hence, pursuant to Article 31(3)(a) of the Vienna Convention on the Law of the Treaties,[61] it can be argued that the parties to the FCTC recognized the 'evidence-based' label and the nature of the FCTC.

IV Labels in International Law

The history of the FCTC negotiations described above provides an interesting case study of how investigating labels can bring into view the invisible frames used in international law-making, and thus enhance our understanding of those processes.

The 'evidence-based' label, furthermore, provides some additional insights on the importance of labels. In fact, the label 'evidence-based' has not only become a common and formal descriptor of the treaty and of its associated instruments, but is also used to interpret its provisions. Different adjudicators (panels of the World Trade Organization, an investment tribunal, and the Court of Justice of the European Union) have relied on the provisions and recommendations of the FCTC and its guidelines to affirm that the challenged tobacco control measures were supported by scientific evidence.[62] What is even more noteworthy for our purposes, is that none of those adjudicators felt the need to explain *why* they would rely on a treaty and on some guidelines as evidence in a case.

[59] Wakefield and Liberman (n 59) 145; Gian Luca Burci, 'Health: Practitioner Comment' in Simon Chesterman David Malone, and Santiago Villalpando (eds), *The Oxford Handbook of United Nations Treaties* (Oxford University Press 2019) 360.

[60] 'WHO FCTC, Conference of the Parties, Decision "Policy Options and Recommendations on Economically Sustainable Alternatives to Tobacco Growing (in Relation to Articles 17 and 18)"' (2014) FCTC/COP6(11) para 1.

[61] Vienna Convention on the Law of Treaties, 1155 UNTS 331 (VCLT).

[62] WTO, *United States—Measures Affecting the Production and Sale of Clove Cigarettes*, Panel Report, WT/DS406/R (2 September 2011) 7.412-7.415; Case C-358/14 *Republic of Poland v European Parliament and Council of the European Union* ECLI:EU:C:2016:323 (4 May 2014) 46; Case C-547/14 *Philip Morris Brands SARL and Others* ECLI:EU:C:2016:325 (4 May 2016) 112, 207; *Philip Morris Brands Sàrl, Philip Morris Products SA and Abal Hermanos SA v Oriental Republic of Uruguay*, ICSID Case No ARB/10/7, Award (8 July 2016) 391, 401; *Australia—Certain Measures Concerning Trademarks, Geographical Indications and Other Plain Packaging Requirements Applicable to Tobacco Products and Packaging*, Panel Reports, WT/DS435/R, WT/DS441/R, WT/DS458/R, and WT/DS467/R (28 June 2018) 7.412, 7.664–7.665, 7.798, 7.800, 7.803–7.804, 7.807. See Margherita Melillo, 'The Legal and Evidential Value of the Guidelines for Implementation of the Framework Convention on Tobacco Control: Recent Developments and Critical Views' (2017) 8 *European Journal of Risk Regulation* 186; Lukasz Gruszczynski and Margherita Melillo, 'The FCTC and Its Role in WTO Law: Some Remarks on the WTO Plain Packaging Report' (2018) 9 *European Journal of Risk Regulation* 564.

The history of the FCTC and its label is possibly unique. However, the scholarship reports other instances in which names that could be considered labels (according to the definition laid out in section 1) have been used in international law-making. An interesting case, for example, is given by the recent literature on indicators. The editors of the book *Governance by Indicators* have noted how the act of naming certain data indicators of concepts like 'transparency' or 'human development' is substantially arbitrary; however, once the data is named it is assumed that it can give a faithful representation of these complex concepts.[63] This act of labelling substantially reduces the complexity of the issues, framing them in a way that is both simpler to understand and easily quantifiable.

Other examples of labelling can be found in international environmental law.[64] Even a well-known concept like the precautionary principle could potentially be considered a label. Although the precautionary principle emerged in international discourses in the 1980s, it has not yet been univocally defined.[65] Sunstein has famously criticized the precautionary principle for being an ambiguous blanket that offers no real guidance, and notes that it is invoked as a cure-all to justify any type of regulatory action.[66] Specifically, Sunstein sees the use of the precautionary principle 'as a way of emphasizing the importance of attending to issues, especially environmental issues, which may otherwise be neglected'.[67] If one accepts Sunstein's critique, the precautionary principle would not be so much of a principle, because it offers no real guidance for action. Conversely, the precautionary principle would be a label used to define a regulatory action as the *most sensible and rational* way to respond to a particular risk or situation. Rather than suggesting the *actual* most rational response, however, the precautionary principle would be used as a label to reinforce the framing of a discourse that prioritizes the importance of protecting the environment over other concerns.

V Conclusions

Labels are powerful tools for norm entrepreneurs, and accordingly scholars should consider them as valuable tools. I have argued here that analysing the use of labels

[63] Kevin Davis and others, *Governance by Indicators: Global Power Through Classification and Rankings* (OUP Oxford 2012) 8.

[64] Steffen Bauer, 'Does Bureaucracy Really Matter? The Authority of Intergovernmental Treaty Secretariats in Global Environmental Politics' (2006) 6 *Global Environmental Politics* 23, 40; Ronald Bruce Mitchell and others, *Global Environmental Assessments: Information and Influence* (MIT Press 2006) 178–80.

[65] Joanne Scott, 'Legal Aspects of the Precautionary Principle' (The British Academy 2018) https://www.thebritishacademy.ac.uk/publications/europe-british-academy-brexit-briefing-legal-aspects-precautionary-principle.

[66] Cass R Sunstein, 'Beyond the Precautionary Principle' (2003) 151 *University of Pennsylvania Law Review* 1003.

[67] ibid 1030.

(the visible part of frames) in international law instruments can enhance our understanding of the underpinning discourses and strategies, as well as the historical and sociological context in which those instruments were formed (the *invisible frames*).

This chapter has explored the use of labels in international law, presenting an empirical case-study based on the history of the FCTC. It has introduced two instances in which the frames backing its negotiations were supported by labels: the tobacco industry as a 'vector' of the tobacco epidemic, and the evidence validating the making of the FCTC an 'evidence-based' treaty. The last part of the chapter reflects on how understanding the origins and use of labels can enhance our understanding of international law. To this end, it shows that the 'evidence-based' label of the FCTC has influenced the interpretative process which international adjudicators conducted. Moreover, it has provided some additional examples of uses of names or concepts in international law that could be considered instances of labelling. International law is probably full of many other similar examples. Far from being able to draw up a complete list, this chapter can only express the wish that future research will unearth them.

SECTION II

MAKING KNOWLEDGE PRODUCTION VISIBLE: STRUCTURES, ACTORS, AND PROCESSES

9
Knowledge Production in International Law: Forces and Processes

Andrea Bianchi

I Knowledge production processes: a heuristic approach

If until recently the prevailing conception was that international law was some sort of objective social practice that could be apprehended as such by unbiased scholars, nowadays there is widespread awareness that what we know as international law is produced by knowledge-production mechanisms of a different nature. Social practices and intellectual processes that are influenced by theories and theoretical discourses shape the social phenomenon we qualify as international law. Prevailing 'discursive policies' grounded in power structures and shaped by epistemic forces determine what is deemed to be an acceptable and competent thing to say about international law. The same structures and forces determine the contours of the policies that control the discipline, and that are reflected in accepted social practices.

In this dynamic process, eventually leading to the production of knowledge, different actors interact. Just by way of example, some international organizations produce such instruments as benchmarks and indicators to measure and appraise certain phenomena, which then shape the culture by which problems are addressed and strategies are developed.[1] Likewise, other epistemic forces may be at play in different domains. By epistemic forces one refers to the ensemble of actors and institutions that create the episteme of any given field. How norms come into being has little to do with a natural and objective process. Which norms emerge and in what circumstances often result from norm entrepreneurs having specific goals and using certain advocacy strategies to attain their desired normative outcomes.

Sometimes it is difficult to disentangle the role of the theoretical discourse on, and the social practice of international law in, the creation of knowledge. This is why their interaction ought to be studied accurately. Knowledge once produced

[1] See Jan Klabbers, 'Reflections on the International Telecommunication Union: International Organizations as Epistemic Structures', ch 11 in this volume.

Andrea Bianchi, *Knowledge Production in International Law: Forces and Processes* In: *International Law's Invisible Frames*. Edited by: Andrea Bianchi and Moshe Hirsch, Oxford University Press. © Andrea Bianchi 2021.
DOI: 10.1093/oso/9780192847539.003.0010

can be used in a variety of ways. It can be embedded in a narrative,[2] circulated, and used as a means of socialization. Or, it can be challenged and contested.[3] In this case, whether a certain type of knowledge will prevail over another is largely a matter of how the communities favouring one over the others will be able to impose their views through control of the disciplinary discourse.

When I tell students that the pursuit of disciplinary knowledge is a violent struggle among individuals and social groups within a community, I reach two distinct goals, both undesirable. On the one hand, I cause my popularity rating to drop dramatically. On the other hand, I get the feeling that I have committed a terrible crime; I have killed innocence for which there cannot be atonement. Stunning as this may seem, lawyers are not known for asking certain questions; nor are they trained to do so. As Pierre Schlag once put it, lawyers are often characterized by a 'stunningly selective sense of curiosity'.[4] Be that as it may, it does remain a mystery to me how people interested in the study of international law cannot take an interest in better understanding how we come to apprehend what international law is, what is it for, how it works, and by whom it is made.

All these things are hardly a given, something to be taken for granted or that goes without saying. They are the result of complex processes, different forces being at play, and various actors interacting with one another in specific contexts. Unfortunately, the idea of knowledge as a tangible good that can be purchased at institutions of higher learning, or, alternatively, the idea of knowledge as an incontrovertible truth to be revealed by disciplinary priests are still the most widespread and popular views on what the production of knowledge is about. Certainly, these views demand less of an effort by those who say to be interested in the pursuit of knowledge. It is much easier than wondering what particular processes are at play in any given community to produce knowledge and to inquire who is in charge of them.

The production of knowledge is admittedly an exotic object of inquiry for (international) lawyers,[5] but it seems to me compelling to start unfolding the varied processes that like for all other disciplines lead to the production of what can be termed 'disciplinary knowledge'. In the abstract, the modalities for the acquisition of

[2] See Matthew Windsor, 'Counterstorytelling in International Economic Law', ch 13 in this volume; and Eyal Benvenisti and Doreen Lustig, 'Revisiting the Memory of Solferino: Knowledge Production and the Laws of War', ch 14 in this volume.

[3] See Akbar Rasulov, 'The Discipline as a Field of Struggle: The Politics and Economy of Knowledge Production in International Law, ch 10 in this volume.

[4] Pierre Schlag, *The Enchantment of Reason* (Duke University Press 1998) 140.

[5] A most interesting exception is Elisabeth Schweiger, 'Listen Closely: What Silence Can Tell Us about Legal Knowledge Production' (2018) 6 *London Review of International Law* 391, investigating the role of silence and acquiescence in the area of the use of force, and widely acknowledging the political character of knowledge production processes. Also of relevance, albeit marginally, is Samuel Moyn, 'Knowledge and Politics in International Law' (2016)129 *Harvard Law Review* 2164, a review essay on David Kennedy, *A World of Struggle: How Power, Law and Expertise Shape Global Political Economy* (Princeton University Press 2016).

knowledge could be thought to be the same for the different disciplines. In fact, the set of beliefs and protocols that preside over disciplinary knowledge are remarkably different, and, although the debates and disagreements within the various scientific communities tend to be similar, it would be almost utopian to try and sketch out a general theory of knowledge protection that be valid across the board.

In 1918, Kenneth Mees devoted an essay to the production of scientific knowledge in the still highly prestigious scientific review *Nature*.[6] In a somewhat linear fashion, the production of new knowledge would occur by publishing the results obtained in scientific laboratories in scientific reviews, thus allowing critical comparison with other knowledge and, eventually, new knowledge to come about. Mees analogized this process to the formation of thought, where perceptions acquired from the sensory world are stored in memory and then compared with other perceptions to form, eventually, a conception.[7] At the time, the utilization of scientific knowledge was encouraged through the publication of monographs and handbooks the circulation of which would promote its use and practical application.[8]

Nowadays, the debate on the production of knowledge in the hard sciences rests on dramatically different premises. One of the main issues is how to reconcile academic knowledge and the increasing commodification of science and scientific outputs.[9] Recent studies flag the concern that academic knowledge production processes 'generated in response to problems defined and solved in relation to cognitive and social norms'[10] are increasingly constrained by commercial and market considerations that tend to favour the emerging of a form of knowledge which is 'transformed into a commodity owned and controlled by those paying for it and seeking to exploit it'.[11] The transition from academic to 'useful' science would be signalled by an increasing 'bureaucratization' of knowledge production processes, consistently with contemporary cultural trends.[12] In social sciences, the focus is rather on how to develop and use solid and robust methodologies by which to acquire knowledge about the world that is essentially human and social.[13]

Whether one conceives of international law as social practice or scholarly representation, hardly anyone calls into question the inherently human and social

[6] CE Kenneth Mees, 'The Production of Scientific Knowledge' (1928) *Nature* 355.
[7] ibid.
[8] ibid 358.
[9] Rebecca Boden, Deborah Cox, Maria Nedeva, and Katharine Barker, *Scrutinizing Science. The Changing UK Government of Science* (Palgrave Macmillan 2004).
[10] ibid 137.
[11] ibid 140.
[12] John Ziman, *Real Science: What It Is and What It Means* (Cambridge University Press 2000) 82: 'The transition from academic to post-academic science [commodified] is signalled by the appearance of words such as management, contract, regulation, accountability, training, employment etc. which previously had no place in scientific life. This vocabulary did not originate inside science, but was imported from the more 'modern' culture which emerged over several centuries in Western societies—a culture characterised by Weber as essentially "bureaucratic".'
[13] William H Starbuck, *The Production of Knowledge: The Challenge of Social Science Research* (Oxford University Press 2006) 4, 142–43.

character of international legal processes. What we experience as *the* practice of or *the* scholarly discourse about international law is, in fact, the product of a set of knowledge production processes. Such processes remain invisible to most international lawyers and they are generally thought to be outside the scope of legal inquiries. To bring them into focus in light of insights drawn from other disciplines, and to invite reflection upon some of these mechanisms should contribute to a better understanding of the discipline of international law. This chapter aims to emphasize the dynamic and collective character of some of the intellectual and social processes whereby the discipline structures itself in order to produce knowledge, accepted as such by its members.[14]

II Discourse and Discursive Practices

In order to understand how knowledge is produced I have always found useful to resort to Michel Foucault's notion of discourse.[15] One of the most often used and, yet, highly heterogeneous concepts ever used by the French philosopher, 'discourse'—unlike its English semantic connotation—is more taken up with such notions as institutions, practices, and, ultimately, power. Discourse is what makes certain statements, practices and procedures to stay in circulation and others to be excluded. It is about unwritten rules and structures that produce particular utterances and statements that, in turn, generate patterns of practice.[16] Likewise, one could say that discourse and discursive policies, elaborated by social groups of professionals and grounded on power structures, shape what we mean by international law and set the boundaries of what is or is not a permissible argument within the field, be it the discipline or the social practice of international law.

Famously introduced in his inaugural lecture at the Collège de France in 1970: '[I]n every society the production of discourse is at once controlled, selected, organised and redistributed by a certain number of procedures',[17] and one of the

[14] This approximate definition of knowledge production processes echoes the one used recently in Boden and others (n 9) 136: 'Knowledge production processes are defined here as how the vision and the organization of science combine together to actually produce scientific knowledge through socio-economic processes.'

[15] See in particular Michel Foucault, 'The Order of Discourse' in Robert Young (ed), *Untying the Text: A Post-Structuralist Reader* (Routledge 1981) 48–78; Michel Foucault, *The Archaeology of Knowledge* (AM Sheridan Smith tr, Routledge 2002). More generally, on the notion and use of discourse in other contexts see Sara Mills, *Discourse* (2nd edn, Routledge 2004).

[16] See Sara Mills, *Michel Foucault* (Routledge 2003) 65: '[d]iscourses should be seen as groups of statements which are associated with institutions, which are authorised in some sense and which have some unity of function at a fundamental level.' Foucault gave also a multi-layered definition of the meaning of discourse: 'Instead of gradually reducing the rather fluctuating meaning of the word "discourse", I believe I have in fact added to its meanings: treating it sometimes as the general domain of all statements, sometimes as an individualizable group of statements, and sometimes as a regulated practice that accounts for a number of statements.' See Foucault, *The Archaeology of Knowledge* (n 15) 80.

[17] Foucault, 'The Order of Discourse' (n 15) 52.

'procedures for controlling and delimiting discourse' is precisely the culture of discipline', the notion of discourse is examined in *The Archaeology of Knowledge* where discourse formation processes are analysed.[18] The idea is that, over time, positivities or regularities are formed, together with rules for the formation of objects and concepts, modalities of statement, and theoretical choices. All these different elements then emerge through and are shaped by a discursive practice. This practice is specified by its form and rigour, by the objects with which it deals, the type of enunciations that it uses, the concepts that it manipulates. and the strategies it employs. 'Discursive practices' were defined by Foucault as 'characterised by the delimitation of a field of objects, the definition of a legitimate perspective for the agent of knowledge, and the fixing of norms for the elaboration of concepts and theories. Thus each discursive practice implies a play of prescriptions that designate its exclusions and choices'.[19]

In many ways, the concept of discourse could be debated in the context of social cognition, as discourse is 'a system which structures the way that we perceive reality' and as such it 'should be seen as something which constrains our perceptions'.[20] Foucault would not deny the existence of the physical world, but he would say that 'we can only think about and experience material objects and the world as a whole through discourse and the structures it imposes on our thinking'.[21] Its relevance to our purposes, however, resides in its capability of explaining by analogy how certain intellectual processes and social practices are constitutive of how our knowledge about international law is formed. Of particular interest is the regulatory function performed by discourse, as well as the procedures that constrain it in different contexts.

In examining a first set of procedures constraining discourse by way of exclusion, Foucault makes reference to three practices, the most relevant of which is the distinction between true and false.[22] Truth is no absolute, and the will to truth that has shaped our understanding of it is rather 'a system of exclusion, a historical, modifiable, and institutionally constraining system'.[23] The will to truth like any

[18] 'We shall call discourse a group of statements in so far as they belong to the same discursive formation; it does not form a rhetorical or formal unity, endlessly repeatable, whose appearance or use in history might be indicated (and, if necessary, explained); it is made up of a limited number of statements for which a group of conditions of existence can be defined.' See Foucault, *The Archaeology of Knowledge* (n 15) 131 (compare this definition with the one given in the same book by Foucault (n 16)).

[19] Michel Foucault, *Language, Counter-memory, Practice: Selected Essays and Interviews* (Donald F Bouchard (ed), Cornell University Press 1977) 199. The historically contingent character of a discursive practice had been emphasized by Foucault in *The Archaeology of Knowledge* (n 15) 131, when he referred to it as 'a body of anonymous, historical rules, always determined in the time and space that have defined a given period, and for a given social, economic, geographical, or linguistic area, the conditions of operation of the enunciative function'.

[20] Mills (n 16) 55.

[21] ibid 56.

[22] Foucault, 'The Order of Discourse' (n 15) 52 ff. The other two exclusionary procedures are prohibition, and the juxtaposition between reason and madness.

[23] ibid 54.

other system of exclusion 'rests on an institutional support: it is both reinforced and renewed by whole strata of practices, such as pedagogy, of course; and the system of books, publishing, libraries; learned societies and laboratories now'.[24] But also 'the way in which knowledge is put to work, valorised, distributed, and in a sense attributed, in a society' contributes to shaping the will to truth.[25] While 'all that appears to our eyes is a truth conceived as a richness, a fecundity, a gentle and insidious universal force... we are unaware of the will to truth, that prodigious machinery designed to exclude'.[26]

This powerful insight on truth being about exclusion becomes even more compelling when considered hand in hand with another principle of limitation of discourse: discipline.[27] Designated as an internal procedure delimiting and controlling discourse, together with 'commentary' and 'author', discipline is described as 'a set of methods, a corpus of propositions considered to be true, a play of rules and definitions, of techniques and instruments: all this constitutes a sort of anonymous system at the disposal of anyone who wants to or is able to use it'.[28] Discipline is a powerful means to control discourse, *inter alia*, by distinguishing between true and false propositions, and pushing back 'a whole teratology of knowledge beyond its margins'.[29] Before being able of being associated with or integrated into a discipline, a proposition 'must fulfil complex and heavy requirements... before it can be called true or false, it must be "in the true"'.[30] And one can only be 'in the true' by 'obeying the rules of a discursive "policing"' which one has to reactivate in each of one's discourses'.[31] Once again, Foucault's insight is powerful, as it shows how disciplines can mark their own boundaries, by determining what can be considered as admissible knowledge and what can be excluded from their scope of inquiry. Also, the idea that there is a 'discursive policing' makes one realize that the process

[24] ibid 55.
[25] ibid.
[26] ibid 56.
[27] Foucault, 'The Order of Discourse' (n 15) 59. Discipline remains a somewhat ambivalent and ever-evolving notion in Foucault's work. Most commonly associated with a form of power and with the modalities of its exercise (Michel Foucault, *Discipline and Punish: the Birth of the Prison* (Sheridan Smith (tr), Penguin 1977)), here 'discipline', in a different connotation, is seen primarily as an internal constraint to discourse. For an interesting read on the historical and etymological origins of such terms as 'discipline' and 'doctrine' see David R Shumway and Ellen Messer-Davidow, 'Disciplinarity: An Introduction' (1991) 12 *Poetics Today* 201. For the idea that this ambiguity on discipline being 'a branch of knowledge' and a 'system of correction and control' might be intended see Michael Walzer, 'The Politics of Michel Foucault' in David Couzens Hoy (ed), *Foucault: A Critical Reader* (Basil Blackwell 1986) 64.
[28] Foucault, 'The Order of Discourse' (n 15) 56. See also Mills (n 16) 44: 'For Foucault, discipline is a set of strategies, procedures and ways of behaving which are associated with certain institutional contexts and which then permeate ways of thinking and behaving in general. Developed within the setting of the prison, disciplinary regimes now permeate the workplace, the army, the school, the university.'
[29] Foucault, 'The Order of Discourse' (n 15) 60.
[30] ibid.
[31] ibid 61.

of control is a knowingly and deliberate one which relies on power structure and knowledge production control mechanisms.

The third category of procedures constraining discourse has to do with the conditions of its applicability and the rules that determine who may say what and who may have access to the discourse itself. Foucault speaks of the 'rarefaction of the speaking subject', as 'none shall enter the order of discourse if he does not satisfy certain requirements or if he is not, from the outset, qualified to do so'.[32] In this context too, where the focus is primarily on who is authorized to speak authoritatively, on how rituals may define the qualification which must be possessed by individuals who speak, a particular importance is attributed to 'doctrine', that is social groups the allegiance of whose members is determined 'by the holding in common of one and the same discursive ensemble.'[33] Doctrine 'brings about a double subjection: of the speaking subjects to discourses, and of discourses to the (at least virtual) group of speaking individuals'.[34]

It is hard at this point to deny the similarity of the concept of 'doctrine' to academic disciplines and to social practices characterized by fairly rigid structures and common mechanisms of exclusion. Nothing better than an educational or training system can assure the social appropriation of discourse and the power that comes with it, including the power to determine what knowledge is admissible and what is not. The political nature of any educational system or vocational training is attested by its capacity to maintain or alter the appropriation of discourses, by determining what true knowledge is and by allocating social power to specific individuals or groups.[35]

A final observation that may be relevant to our inquiry is that discourse, related as it is to power relationships, can be both an instrument to exercise power and preserve the status quo and a tool for resistance and contestation. As aptly observed by Sara Mills, Foucault made express reference to the ambivalent character of discourse in his *History of Sexuality*, where he wrote that 'discourse can be both an instrument and an effect of power, but also a hindrance, a stumbling block, a point of resistance and a starting point for an opposing strategy. Discourse transmits and produces power; it reinforces it, but also undermines it and exposes it, renders it fragile and makes it possible to thwart it'.[36]

[32] ibid 61–62.
[33] ibid 63.
[34] ibid 64.
[35] Foucault, 'The Order of Discourse' (n 15) 64: 'Any system of education is a political way of maintaining or modifying the appropriation of discourses, along with the knowledges and powers which they carry… What, after all, is an education system, other than a ritualisation of speech, a qualification and a fixing of the roles for speaking subjects, the constitution of a doctrinal group, however diffuse, a distribution and an appropriation of discourse with its power and knowledges?'
[36] Michel Foucault, *History of Sexuality, Vol I: An Introduction* (Robert Hurley (tr), Penguin 1978) 100–101, cited in Mills (n 16) 54–55.

Foucault's insights may not always be germane, his distinctions are not always neat and tidy, and sometimes their real value gets lost in translation (into English). It seems to me, however, that Foucault's analysis contains pretty much everything that is important to understand when assessing how a 'discourse' is shaped, and knowledge produced, particularly within a discipline: the societal element and the dynamic process whereby a plurality of actors interact in a given context and within ever-shifting power structures. The regularities that are formed, the objects of investigations that are defined, the concepts that are elaborated and the theoretical choices that are made all are reminiscent of the Foucauldean categories of discourse and discipline. Likewise, the attention paid to what obtains and what is excluded, to that which is not obvious or immediately visible, as well as the sensibility for the inherent role played by power, ambition, and desire at the individual and collective levels in what is otherwise regarded as a scientific and objective process are all analytical tools of investigation that one can borrow directly from Foucault.

Similar considerations apply also to social and intellectual practices that originate and develop in discursive form. Discursive practices are turned into discursive policies when used strategically by the prevailing social forces—little matters if in society generally or within a discipline more specifically. And these discursive policies become the Subject (with the capital letter), as discourse is shaped by power and desire, and it almost inevitably aims at exerting control over what can be said authoritatively and by whom. To use the ancient Greece imagery of skeptron-holders, the fight is among those who have the authority to hold the skeptron and are entitled to speak authoritatively to the audience and to mark the boundaries of the discipline by saying what's inside and what's outside; what's the core and what lies on the fringes.[37]

Be that as it may, I trust that Foucault would approve of this piecemeal approach to his work. He appears to have said in an interview that: 'All my books . . . are little tool boxes . . . if people want to open them, to use this sentence or that idea as a screwdriver or spanner to short-circuit, discredit or smash systems of power, including eventually those from which my books have emerged . . . so much the better.'[38] This is precisely the spirit by which I have extensively drawn on Foucault's work. Not so much to transfer lock, stock, and barrel his various insights into another context, pretending that they have the same explanatory force there than in their original setting, but rather to adjust them to and use them heuristically in my own field of inquiry.

[37] See Andrea Bianchi, 'On the Skeptron: Visions of Authority in International Law' Paper submitted at the Conference: Constructing Authority in International Law, Durham Law School, 25–26 April 2017 (on file with the author). See also Fuad Zarbiyev, 'Saying Credibly What the Law Is: On Marks of Authority in International Law' (2018) 9 *Journal of International Dispute Settlement* 291.

[38] Michel Foucault, *Power, Truth, Strategy* (Meaghan Morris and Paul Patton (eds), Feral Publications 1979) 199.

III Epistemic Forces at Play: Epistemic Communities and the Shapers of Discourse

The other thing that I have found particularly useful to play with in understanding how the discourse is produced and by what forces, is the concept of 'epistemic communities'.[39] I should point out at the outset that I do not take 'epistemic communities' to mean what is usually meant by Peter Haas, who is generally credited for having used and explained the concept better than others in political science.[40] According to Haas, epistemic communities are networks made of professionals who provide scientific expertise to decision-makers in complex and highly technical contexts.[41] The fact that members of epistemic communities share causal beliefs and normative commitments and constitute a cohesive social group distinguishes them from other actors and groups that try to influence policy-making. Whereas epistemic communities operate in the realm of brute and hybrid facts, where science 'reigns', norm entrepreneurs operate in the field of social facts.[42] Ultimately, the function of epistemic communities would lie in achieving consensual knowledge in any given domain of expertise that, later, other actors diffuse and use in policy contexts. A paradigmatic example of an 'epistemic community' in the field of environmental protection would be the Intergovernmental Panel on Climate Change (IPCC) that has been a decisive factor in shaping the international legal and political regime of climate change.

A Shapers

I take the concept of epistemic communities to mean something quite different from Haas' definition. In particular, I take epistemic communities to mean the *ensemble* of the actors involved in the dynamic processes whereby our knowledge of

[39] I have dealt with this topic in two recent essays: 'Epistemic Communities' in Jean d'Aspremont and Sahib Singh (eds), *Concepts for International Law—Contributions to Disciplinary Thoughts* (Edward Elgar Publishing 2019) 251; and 'Epistemic Communities in International Arbitration' in Federico Ortino and Thomas Schultz (eds), *Oxford Handbook of International Arbitration* (Oxford University Press 2020) 569. The considerations that follow are largely drawn from these two essays.

[40] See Peter M Haas, 'Introduction: Epistemic Communities and International Policy Coordination' (1992) 46 *International Organization* 1; Peter M Haas, 'Epistemic Communities' in Daniel Bodansky, Jutta Brunnée, and Ellen Hey (eds), *The Oxford Handbook of International Environmental Law* (Oxford University Press 2012) 792; Peter M Haas, 'Ideas, Experts and Governance' in Monika Ambrus, Karin Arts, Ellen Hey, and Helena Raulus (eds), *The Role of 'Experts' in International and European Decision-Making Processes: Advisors, Decision Makers or Irrelevant Actors?* (Cambridge University Press 2014) 19.

[41] A more detailed definition of the concept can be found in Haas, 'Epistemic Communities' (n 40) 792–94; Haas, 'Introduction' (n 40) 3; Haas, 'Ideas, Experts and Governance' (n 40) 29–30.

[42] Haas, 'Ideas, Experts, and Governance' (n 40) 26; see also Andy Olson, 'An Empire of the Scholars: Transnational Lawyers and the Rule of Opinio Juris' (2000) 29 *Perspectives on Political Science* 23: 'In many respects, the community of international lawyers provides a model example of Haas's definition of an epistemic community of elites. This community views itself as a guild of accredited specialists engaged in the formation of society's rules and uniquely qualified to interpret international law.'

international law—ie the understanding of what international law is and how it works—is formed and shaped. The 'knowledge' we have of a given field, the way in which we come to apprehend it theoretically, to use it practically and to explain its operation is the production of processes shaped by epistemic communities. The latter, in turn, are held together by a common set of collective shared beliefs and presuppositions that inform, in our case, the field of international law, understood both as a scientific field of theoretical inquiry and as a social practice.

My definition seems to be oblivious to the philosophical debate underlying the distinctions (to name just a few) between episteme on the one hand, and *doxa* or *techne* on the other.[43] While traditionally, episteme is contrasted to *doxa*—understood as opinion or common belief—and to *techne*—referred to as craft or practice—to me the very notion of episteme tends to include also aspects of the latter terms. I personally do not attribute to the term episteme the connotation of some sort of scientific knowledge or truth claim as opposed to some inferior social beliefs or collective representation of reality that would not be founded on any reliable theoretical framework. I tend to look at episteme as a set of beliefs and presuppositions collectively shared that inform the way in which we understand reality. In some sense, therefore, the dialectics between episteme and *doxa* does not allow representing the two as juxtaposed concepts.

Along similar lines, I believe that *techne*—which I take to mean craft or the practical capacity to do things—is also based on some episteme of sorts, as the 'how to do' part of any craft necessarily presupposes a form of acquisition of knowledge and the interiorization of intellectual schemata. In many ways, the latter distinction is reminiscent of the distinction between theory and practice that characterizes many debates in practically all disciplines and branches of knowledge. Be that as it may, I believe that both the theoretical discourse on and the social practice of international law presuppose an episteme and, therefore, an epistemic community that shapes the discourse and sets the boundaries for what is accepted and/or acceptable in the scientific discipline and in the practice of international law.[44]

Another important aspect to be highlighted is that the concept of epistemic community is a modular one and allows for different degrees of generality. One may think of the complex and broad epistemic community that shapes up international law *tout court*. In turn, one can also think of distinct epistemic communities that constitute the episteme of international law as an academic discipline or a social practice. Moreover, several epistemic communities can be thought to exist

[43] For a cursory and yet accurate overview of the debate see Richard D Parry, 'Episteme and Techne' in Edward N Zalta (ed), *The Stanford Encyclopedia of Philosophy* (Fall 2014 edn) http://plato.stanford.edu/archives/fall2014/entries/episteme-techne/; see also Anthony Preus, *Historical Dictionary of Ancient Greek Philosophy* (2nd edn, Rowman & Littlefield 2015).

[44] On the distinction between law as theoretical discourse and as a social phenomenon see my 'Reflexive Butterfly Catching: Insights from a Situated Catcher' in Joost Pauwelyn, Ramses A Wessel, and Jan Wouters (eds), *Informal International Law-Making* (Oxford University Press 2012) 200.

that exercise an influence in the various areas of international law and that are subject matter specific. One can have an epistemic trade law or human rights community.[45] Just as well the other domains of international law could all have a distinct epistemic community. Several epistemic communities can be at work at the same time. I am using the concept of modularity precisely in this sense.[46]

Although the aesthetics of (international) law tends to favour 'impersonal *personae*' such as the state, the court, the judge, the law-maker, and the likes of them, the concept of epistemic communities should help us think of all those immaterial entities in terms of individual human beings and social groups. These are communities of individuals that tend to behave as collectives. The interplay between the individual and the collective dimensions is fundamental to understanding the dynamics of epistemic communities. Even if some individual members may come to acquire a prominent position, it is by way of interaction amongst the members of the group that the episteme of the field is produced. The vision of the world propounded by an epistemic community is invariably an 'inter-subjective enterprise'.[47]

B The Functions of Epistemic Communities

At this juncture it might be worth asking what are exactly the functions that epistemic communities perform and what interest there is for us to understand whom they are made of and how they work. First and foremost, epistemic communities fix the terms of the discourse and shape the way in which we look at international law. A good illustration is provided by the widely held view that the sources of international law are listed in Article 38 of the Statute of the International Court of Justice.[48] It suffices to look at the majority of international law textbooks' chapters on the sources of international law or—even better—to ask any international law student, to realize how the conviction that Article 38 lists the sources of international law has become entrenched. This is what most of us in legal education first, and, later, in the practice of international law have been trained to believe. The proviso being just a determination of what law the International Court of Justice must apply when deciding cases within its jurisdiction, there is hardly anything

[45] See, as an example, G Shaffer and J Trachtman, 'Interpretation and Institutional Choice at the WTO' (2011–2012) 52 *Virginia Journal of International Law* 103.

[46] Just to provide an example in different areas of knowledge see Gerhard Schlosser and Günter P Wagner (eds), *Modularity in Development and Evolution* (University of Chicago Press 2004); Peter Carruthers and Andrew T Chamberlain (eds), *Evolution and the Human Mind: Modularity, Language and Meta-Cognition* (Cambridge University Press 2000); Jerry Alan Fodor, *The Modularity of Mind* (MIT Press 1983).

[47] In the same sense, although in relation to 'interpretive communities' see Ian Johnstone, 'The Power of Interpretive Communities' in Michael Barnett and Raymond Duvall (eds), *Power in Global Governance* (Cambridge University Press 2004) 185, 186.

[48] See, as an apt illustration, Hugh Thirlway, *The Sources of International Law* (Oxford University Press 2014).

logical about portraying Article 38 as such. And yet no one would even dream of penalizing a student for saying that Article 38 lists the sources of international law! Article 38 is indeed a good illustration of the general epistemic community of international law producing an intellectual construct that is now part and parcel of the collective imagery of international lawyers.

Along similar considerations, one may think at how epistemic communities over time have moulded the concept of soft law or shaped the perception of what is and what is not international law. To see how strategically the epistemic communities at play started using the notion of soft law to redistribute power within the international community to the benefit of newly independent states,[49] and to see how the very same concept of soft law later became a locus for political struggle about what is and what is not international law, is quite telling about their power to shape the contours of international law-making.[50]

Epistemic communities produce a worldview that determines the visual parameters by which we relate to that particular world. They tend to be insular if not completely self-referential, and they often ignore what is going on in other areas, as they tend to believe 'that the only meaningful practice or the very core business of international law is their own specialisation'.[51] They are carriers of 'distinct normative visions' that they advocate more or less overtly in order to gain or consolidate control of any given field,[52] be it the whole of international law or one of the substantive areas in which they operate. The divide between arbitrators who come from different legal backgrounds (commercial law, trade law, public law, and public international law) could be put forward as an example of contending epistemic communities.[53] Just as well, the competing visions of the 'three tribes'—criminal lawyers, human rights lawyers, and international lawyers—engaged in the shaping of the discourse in international criminal law may be seen as instances of a fragmented episteme leading to a different perception of the very same legal issues.[54]

To focus on epistemic communities, that is social groups of professionals and academics that shape the discursive policies of international law, should not be taken as merely an exercise in some sort of sociological enquiry about membership in the group. Although the latter is a good starting point to understand the nature of the enterprise, what matters most is to analyse the processes whereby such

[49] See eg Oscar M Garibaldi, 'The Legal Status of General Assembly Resolutions: Some Conceptual Observations' (1979) 73 *American Society of International Law Proceedings* 324.

[50] See in this latter respect Pauwelyn, Wessel, and Wouters (n 44).

[51] Andrea Bianchi, 'Gazing at the Crystal Ball (Again): State Immunity and Jus Cogens Beyond Germany v Italy' (2013) 4 *Journal of International Dispute Settlement* 457, 464.

[52] The expression is used with reference to 'interpretive communities' by Michael Waibel, 'Interpretive Communities in International Law' in Andrea Bianchi, Daniel Peat, and Matthew Windsor (eds), *Interpretation in International Law* (Oxford University Press 2015) 147, 160.

[53] Anthea Roberts, 'Clash of Paradigms: Actors and Analogies Shaping the Investment Treaty System' (2013) 107 *American Journal of International Law* 45.

[54] Andrew Clapham, 'Concluding Remarks: Three Tribes in the Future of International Criminal Law' (2011) 9 *Journal of International Criminal Justice* 689.

policies are produced, the strategies are deployed, and, more generally, how these communities are structured and how they function. Opening up the social life of these communities makes it possible to better understand how law as a social field or as a 'form of life' operates.[55] Knowledge is produced and put to use in practice by epistemic communities. This process could be the object of a multifaceted inquiry that aims to unveil what theoretical and intellectual frameworks, what techniques, methodological tools, and both express and unsaid presuppositions are used within the field, and the way in which these are represented to the outside world. The way in which international law is thought of and practiced is pretty much the making of epistemic communities that shape our knowledge of international law at the theoretical and practical level.

Ultimately, epistemic communities are also in charge of the social identity of the discipline and the profession.[56] They discharge important communal functions in so far as they represent shared beliefs and interests. By putting forward a common vision of the world, epistemic communities shape the perception of social agents and determine the fundamental tenets of the discourse. If, nowadays, there seems to be different views about international law, this is due to the increasing fragmentation of the episteme that no longer allows representing the discipline and the practice of international law as a unitary phenomenon. This plurality of visions quite obviously entails a struggle between different social groups that attempt to impose their own view as the most authoritative and legitimate one.[57] To determine who is entitled to speak authoritatively about international law is certainly a stake that most members of the different epistemic communities at play in international law would consider to be worth fighting for.

The increasing awareness of the mechanisms and processes whereby knowledge is being formed and used will most likely lead to the development of more sophisticated strategies to acquire control of the field. As I have argued in another context '[t]hose who create and shape knowledge at all possible levels possess power', and discursive strategies elaborated by knowledge-wielding bodies or groups are controlling.[58] Fixing the boundaries of what international law is and setting the parameters for what is or is not an acceptable argument is no less than making the law.

[55] Law is also a form of social knowledge in the sense expounded by Charles Camic, Neil Gross, and Michèle Lamont (eds), *Social Knowledge in the Making* (University of Chicago Press 2011): see their definition of social knowledge at 3.

[56] See Jean d'Aspremont, 'Wording in International Law' (2012) 25 *Leiden Journal of International Law* 577.

[57] I have dealt with this aspect in my 'Reflexive Butterfly Catching' (n 44).

[58] Andrea Bianchi, 'On Power and Illusion: The Concept of Transparency in International Law' in Andrea Bianchi and Anne Peters (eds), *Transparency in International Law* (Cambridge University Press 2013) 1, 18.

IV The Invisible 'Gatekeepers'

Epistemology and its rather difficult intellectual implications can be understood also at a much more down-to-earth level. As Foucault aptly said in an interview about his intellectual work, which is applicable to epistemology and many other areas of intellectual inquiry, sometimes the work of an intellectual consists not so much in unearthing hidden relations that are kept secret, but rather in drawing people's attention to what is already on the surface of things. In other words, he took his work to be about making visible what seems to be invisible even if it is conspicuously within our sight.[59]

If one applies this relatively intuitive insight to try and imagine what's going on at the epistemological level which is perfectly visible even though hardly anybody notices it or speaks about it, at least in terms of knowledge production, I would mention the following actors and processes: major publishing companies and academic commissioning editors; law journal/review editors-in-chief and editorial boards; peer-reviewers and peer-review mechanisms; and the strategies whereby different actors and social groups create fields or sub-fields in any given discipline. To some extent the actors overlap with what I earlier referred to as shapers of knowledge and members of epistemic communities. I would surmise, however, that the actors and processes I am talking about in this section have the distinct feature of being 'gatekeepers', in the sense that they possess the power of regulating access to knowledge-production-wielding bodies or processes. Let us have a quick look at them.

To begin with major international publishers, it is well known that they do—by act—and undo—by omission—academic careers. Whether one publishes with one publisher rather than another can make the author eligible or not eligible for appointment in prestigious academic institutions. Publishers are ranked either officially or informally and, in a world increasingly subject to metrics, and measurements more generally, the prospects of having a brilliant academic career may depend on who publishes your work. Publishers also shape the disciplines' discursive policies by deciding what to publish or not to publish.[60] The role of commissioning editors is incredibly important. It would be good to know more about who they are, what they want to foster; whether they are more conservative or progressive in the intellectual attitudes towards the discipline; whether they are dull or imaginative; what corporate constraints they act under, and so on. Regrettably, hardly

[59] 'What I look for are not secrets, hidden relations that are more silent or more profound than the consciousness of people. I try rather to define relations that are on the surface of discourse; I try to make visible what is invisible only because it's too much on the surface of things!' See Michel Foucault, *The Punitive Society: Lectures at the Collège de France, 1972-1973* (Palgrave Macmillan 2015) 289.

[60] See also the interesting essay by Ana Luísa Bernardino, 'Going by the Book: What International Law TextbooksTeach Us Not to Learn', ch 16 in this volume.

anybody speaks about such matters in an overt manner, out of fear of antagonizing powerful players in the academic arena.[61]

Analogous considerations apply to law journals and reviews and their editors-in-chief and editorial boards. Besides shaping the contours of the disciplinary discourse by setting disciplinary protocols and, occasionally, even by standardizing language, they too act as gatekeepers. Although quantitatively significant competition may at times trigger more virtuous processes of knowledge production than in the book publishing business, law journals are also rated, ranked and measured in terms of output and prestige. In certain disciplines not to have published in certain reviews may remain a life-long stigma. Conversely, publishing in them at an early stage of your career may open the door to academic recognition and success.

It is of note that the whole business of academic publication relies on the so-called 'peer-review mechanism'. There are slight variations to the model. Peer review can be blind or double blind, but the fundamental idea remains that publication is in the hands of your peers who judge your work, give praise and approval, or make suggestions on how to ameliorate it, or simply trash it. Peer review these days is hardly peer ... It is difficult to secure the services of those who are regarded in the profession in different circles and for different reasons as the 'big shots'. Even if they are good citizens, they would do a handful of reviews per year. Sometimes their anonymity is dubious or non-existent. In the past few years, the editor-in-chief of the *European Journal of International Law* has taken up the habit of publishing online the names of the peer reviewers used by the journal during the year in order to thank them. With a little time and patience, if one would want to do this, it would have been perfectly possible to make reasonable speculations about who revised what.

Most importantly, however, reviewers frequently do not know how to do their job: there is no school or vocational training for that and common sense can hardly be expected of academics. Personal acrimonies and academic rivalries can often be vindicated when the peer review is not double blind. Rather than making sure that the reviewed piece meets some basic standards of academic quality and conforms to some acceptable disciplinary protocols, the reviewer often wants to make the point that the book on that topic ought to be written in an entirely different manner and often even tells you how!

Finally, strategies are deployed and means of a different nature are used to create fields and disciplines or sub-disciplines. The emergence of fields within the discipline of international law such as trade, investment, international criminal

[61] On the role of academic commissioning editors in contemporary academia see Francis Dodds, 'Changes in the Role of the Commissioning Editor in Academic Book Publishing' (2015) 28 *Learned Publishing* 35–42; and the report by Katharine Reeve, *The Role of the Editor: Publisher Perspectives* https://ucldigitalpress.co.uk/BOOC/Article/1/60/.

law and international humanitarian law can often be explained on mundane grounds. They all have emerged out of idealism, fear, and/or greed for money. Very often they have been founded by certain individuals or groups of academics in order either to carve out a space or enhance their reputation in the academic space they occupy; or to become the beneficiaries of celebrity-building mechanisms. The fact that one might be credited with founding a new school or for becoming an expert of a previously neglected or inexistent area often times provide more than an adequate incentive to be proactive. Indeed, this might turn out to be an interesting epistemological query, and I am sure that the findings will cast more than a doubt on the hypothesis that fields emerge out of an authentic need to pursue knowledge.[62]

V The Contemporary Episteme: General Trends

Another important question to ask is where all these epistemic forces are leading us. Once again, Foucault's categories come in handy. I am thinking in particular of the notion of episteme. Discussing the different types of history of the sciences, Foucault in the *Archaeology of Knowledge*, speaks of episteme as 'suspected of being something like a world-view, a slice of history common to all branches of knowledge, which imposes on each one the same norms and postulates, a general stage of reason, a certain structure of thought that the men of a particular period cannot escape'.[63] The idea that it might be possible to identify a set of often conflicting discursive frameworks that 'condition how people think, know and write' paves the way for a further reflection.[64]

Can one spot some general trends that shape the episteme of international law at present? Epistemic communities constantly shape and redefine the episteme of the discipline and the profession in a dynamic and ever-evolving process. So, it is not easy to spot with great accuracy at any given moment in time what the prevailing trends are and what are the big ideas or projects shaping up and informing the episteme. But let me have a chance at it and focus on a few discursive frameworks or ways of thinking that are currently used to produce knowledge in international legal scholarship.

[62] Interesting readings in this area would include: Andrew Abbott, *The Chaos of Disciplines* (University of Chicago Press 2001); and Yves Dezalay and Bryant Garth, *Dealing in Virtue: International Commercial Arbitration and the Construction of a Transnational Legal Order* (University of Chicago Press 1996).

[63] Foucault, *The Archaeology of Knowledge* (n 15) 211. This episteme would be like 'a great legislation written once and for all by some anonymous hand', and would refer to 'the total set of relations that unite, at a given period, the discursive practices that give rise to epistemological figures, sciences, and possibly formalized systems' (ibid).

[64] Mills (n 16) 63.

A The Fragmentation of Theory and Armchair Theorising

The idea, still entertained by many in the profession, that international law is a *lingua franca* through which we communicate and do things together at the international level is inaccurate and somewhat naive. As I have argued elsewhere, international law is not a truly universal language anymore, if it ever was; rather, it comprises a traditional way of thinking that goes hand in hand with multiple diverse approaches.[65] At times, the same dialect appears to be spoken; at others, it is as if entirely different languages were involved. Hence, in order to be a competent practitioner or a learned scholar it is important to be familiar with the different dialects and languages in which international law is spoken nowadays.[66]

The mainstream doctrinal approach that for a long time has dominated the international law discourse has come under sustained criticism. Just to mention a few grounds of critique, the mainstream is increasingly looked down upon for its extreme intellectual poverty, for its worshipping of empty and irrelevant institutions, for its fetishizing of rituals and practices that have lost their original social meaning, and for its refusal to engage with a changed society. It may still be the 'twin sister' of the 'official discourse' of international law,[67] but more and more it is challenged by alternative visions and intellectual accounts.

Inevitably, the proliferation of theoretical frameworks and methodologies, at least as compared to the past, creates a sense of instability, particularly in the intellectual representation of international law. This is presumably one of the reasons why more and more international law theories tend to present themselves as fully fledged, comprehensive, and coherent accounts of the discipline. In the 1950s, the American sociologist C. Wright Mills had spotted what he qualified as 'grand theory' as a general trend in the contemporary social sciences.[68] The same holds true for international law nowadays.

The fundamental tenets of any grand theory is to start from a level of thinking so general and abstract that it has lost touch with the social and historically contingent processes it aims to explain.[69] On a grand theory, it is impossible to get down

[65] Andrea Bianchi, 'Looking Ahead: International Law's Main Challenges' in David Armstrong (ed), *Routledge Handbook of International Law* (Routledge 2009) 392, 407.

[66] See Andrea Bianchi, *International Law Theories: Different Ways of Thinking about International Law* (Oxford University Press 2016).

[67] ibid 33 ff, 35–36: 'I rather tend to see the two as twin sisters, inextricably linked by an indissoluble bond of reciprocal need. The official discourse and traditional approaches draw strength and legitimacy from each other. They both produce and provide justifications for choices that are continuously made in practice and constantly rationalized and re-affirmed in the scholarly discourse. As is often the case with twins, one is the image of the other, even though at closer scrutiny a trained eye could probably trace imperceptible differences. But the overall impression is that of oneness, made of two parts' (footnote omitted).

[68] Charles Wright Mills, *The Sociological Imagination* (Oxford University Press 1959, 40th anniversary edn 2000) 25 ff.

[69] ibid 33.

to the level of particularity that the analysis of social processes like law inevitably requires in order to be credible. The author is enchanted with and possessed by the one model of legal order they have created and that they believe to be universal, simply because they have 'fetishized' the concepts and theoretical presuppositions that they have themselves constructed.[70] This often goes hand in hand with a cryptic style, as if the theoretical discourse were to be reserved to a handful of initiates.

Indeed, academics often have the bad habit of indulging in what I call 'armchair theorizing'.[71] By this expression, I mean the disturbing tendency of some academics to elaborate theoretical constructs that are far removed from the reality they purport to explain. This is often accompanied by a certain degree of self-assertiveness and intolerance towards other ways of looking at the same phenomenon. In many ways, this attitude is reminiscent of the one described and criticized by Bourdieu, who considered it a serious epistemological mistake 'to put a scholar inside the machine'.[72] Armchair theorizing contributes to the vilification of theory more generally, and to the denigration of theorists for allegedly deflecting attention from the real problems that practice faces.

'Grand theory' remains attractive for its capacity to mobilize consensus on universal explanations. In law, this takes often the guise of prioritizing the need for unity and coherence over the fragmented and the contradictory. The quest for systematic and logically compelling models for the sake of pursuing intellectual consistency often end up building castles in the sand. The attitude of scholars is often to blame: the narcissism with which some look at themselves and their work or the fact that they may be taken up in the social game of reputation building. The goal consists of becoming a celebrity. Prisoners of concepts projected into reality regardless of their fitting the phenomenology they are supposed to order and explain, scholars no longer consider giving intellectual accounts of and explanations for actual legal processes occurring in real life as a compelling professional need.

B Obsession with Method and Empiricism

In a much-celebrated article in the *American Journal of International Law* published in 2012, Gregory Shaffer and Tom Ginsburg emphasized the turn to empirical

[70] ibid 48, 49. According to Wright Mills '[t]he ideological meaning of grand theory tends strongly to legitimate stable forms of domination.'

[71] Andrea Bianchi, 'The International Regulation of the Use of Force: The Politics of Interpretive Method' (2009) 22 *Leiden Journal of International Law* 651, 653.

[72] According to Bourdieu, this has the undesirable effect of 'picturing all social agents in the image of the scientist, or, more precisely, to place the models that the scientist must construct to account for practices into the consciousness of agents, to operate as if the constructions that the scientist must produce to understand practices, to account for them, were the main determinants, the actual cause of the practices': Pierre Bourdieu, 'The Scholastic Point of View' (1990) 5 *Cultural Anthropology* 380, 384.

studies in international legal scholarship.[73] The authors assertively affirmed the turn to empirical studies in international legal scholarship at the outset and presented it as a given, something that the authors took for granted, an inevitability of sorts. Shaffer and Ginsburg stated that what needed to be studied were the conditions under which international law is 'formed and has effects'.[74] This so-called 'conditional' international law theory stemmed from the new generation of social science approaches to international law, which, according to its proponents, calls for more empirical work. 'Empirical work' here means the use of both qualitative and quantitative research methods.[75] In this theory, law is regarded as 'a form of technology that can promote certainty and predictability, provide normative guidance, allocate institutional responsibility, enlist reasoning and resolve disputes'.[76] The article stirred considerable debate and contributed to the discussion on the role that social science methodologies should play in international law.

Indeed, the applicability to international law of a certain sensibility to methodologies borrowed from social sciences is very much in keeping with the spirit of the time.[77] Methodology is increasingly perceived to be key to production of knowledge. Method becomes the specialization and one loses sight of the issues or problems to be tackled. It determines the issues, the questions to be asked. The 'what to investigate' question has been replaced by the 'how to investigate', and method gets centre-stage. Since familiarity with epistemology (the study of the grounds for and limits of knowledge production) is difficult to acquire, more and more scholars tend to become dogmatic about the method they know and master.[78]

The only studies that seem to be valued nowadays are those that have the appearance of having been empirically tested, according to established protocols and disciplinary practices. A few years ago in Copenhagen, at the Centre of Excellence *iCourts*, when presenting a paper on international law and emotions I was asked

[73] Gregory Shaffer and Tom Ginsburg, 'The Empirical Turn in International Legal Scholarship' (2012) 106 *American Journal of International Law* 1.

[74] ibid 1.

[75] Henry Brady and David Collier (eds), *Rethinking Social Inquiry: Diverse Tools, Sacred Standards* (2nd edn, Rowman & Littlefield 2010). Quantitative studies provide the means of testing empirically research hypotheses, by relying on large quantities of data processed with statistical techniques and control variables. While it is sometimes difficult to measure social realities and to establish causal inferences, quantitative studies remain a widely used methodology in social sciences and law as well. Qualitative studies, by contrast, are more evaluative and often rely on field interviews. Techniques have been developed to control for the bias and presuppositions of both the researcher and the interviewees. Researchers can decide whether they want to use quantitative or qualitative methodology and much will depend on the research questions they set out to investigate.

[76] ibid 202.

[77] See Willem H van Boom, Pieter Desmet, and Peter Mascini (eds), *Empirical Legal Research in Action—Reflections on Methods and their Applications* (Edward Elgar Publishing 2018); Terry Hutchinson, 'Empirical methodologies knowledge and expertise: a 'necessary' skill for lawyers?' in Bart van Klink and Ubaldus de Vries (eds), *Academic Learning in Law: Theoretical Positions, Teaching Experiments and Learning Experiences* (Edward Elgar Publishing2016) 142–59; Jan Smits, *The Mind and Method of the Legal Academic* (Edward Elgar Publishing 2012).

[78] Wright Mills (n 68) 74.

how I would go about measuring emotions.[79] I simply replied that I do not do measurements, and that I only try to make people think. The audience looked deeply unimpressed by my answer.

The intellectual pressure can be strong, and the discourse on method tends to absorb other more important intellectual concerns. Again, in Charles Wright Mills' words: 'To have mastered method … is to have become a self-conscious thinker, a man at work and aware of the assumptions and the implications of whatever he is about. To be mastered by … method is to be kept from working, from trying, that is, to find out about something that is going on in the world.'[80] Scholars and intellectuals tend to be replaced by experts in academic institutions and think tanks that look like and act like bureaucratic machines, fully committed to abstract empiricism and pretentious scientism. These professional profiles are no longer able and willing to engage with the big questions of power and authority, distributive justice and the likes. They overlook the structured social realities, which they should explain. 'What' to look for, what to verify, what hypothesis to test are the real issues … not just 'how' to do it.

C National Approaches

Another distinct feature of the contemporary episteme of international law is the opposition between the universal and progressive narrative of the mainstream and an increasing trend to look at international law from nationalist and/or regional perspectives. Although the attempt to connote geographical approaches has always been present in international law, the idea that international law might be strongly influenced by national approaches to its definition, interpretation, and application is a relatively recent one. I would identify two different strands of scholarship that promote this way of thinking.

The first strand is the so-called 'foreign relations law' school of thought.[81] Distinctly US in its origins and cultural roots, this approach has been promoted primarily by constitutional and international law-sceptic scholars who look at and focus on the way in which the US legal system deals with all things foreign, or with the rest of the world if you like.[82] The domestic law concerned could be

[79] The paper is now published: see Andrea Bianchi and Anne Saab, 'Fear and International Law-Making: An Exploratory Inquiry' (2019) 32 *Leiden Journal of International Law* 351.

[80] Wright Mills (n 68) 121.

[81] I am thinking, in particular, about Alejandro Álvarez's view on American international law (for a succinct account of Álvarez's ideas see Jorge L Esquirol, 'Latin America' in Anne Orford and Bardo Fassbender (eds), *The Oxford Handbook of the History of International Law* (Oxford University Press 2016) 553; and, more recently, about Laurii Mälksoo's study on *Russian Approaches to International Law* (Oxford University Press 2015).

[82] Curtis Bradley, 'What is Foreign Relations Law' in Curtis Bradley (ed), *The Oxford Handbook of Comparative Foreign Relations Law* (Oxford University Press 2019) 3.

constitutional or statutory law, administrative regulations and judicial decisions. According to Bradley, foreign relations law is not meant to encompass pure questions of international law (defined as a nation's obligations under treaties and customary international law). While international law governs in part how a nation conducts its foreign relations, it is too vast and 'in many respects too undifferentiated in its application to each nation' to be included in a working definition of foreign relations law.[83] Although, recently, an effort has been made to expand the reach of the US foreign relations law approach to any other domestic legal system in the world,[84] the cultural sensibility of the movement as well its analytical tools appear to be strongly rooted in the US domestic legal system.

The other attempt to promote national approaches to international law is the recent launch, and branding of the idea of 'comparative international law'. Despite earlier inchoate attempts to get the idea off the ground,[85] the need to create a new field of comparative international law was strategically anticipated by an article in the *American Journal of International Law* in 2015, followed by a monograph and an edited volume published by two prestigious university presses.[86]

Broadly defined as concerned with 'identifying, analysing, and explaining similarities and differences in how actors in different legal systems understand, interpret, apply and approach international law',[87] comparative international law sets out to spot where the system (international rules and doctrines) is successful. This approach would allegedly help give better solutions to legal problems by providing more creative answers to these problems, based on comparative experiences with similar issues. The local adaptability of international rules and doctrines might also favour compliance with international law or explain non-compliance. Furthermore, comparative international law could, in the view of its proponents, enhance institutional design. Treaties and international institutions could be more effective if they were to be designed on the basis of a comparative analysis. Comparative analysis might also make these treaties and institutions more responsive to and reflective of diversity within the international legal system.[88]

To study the similarities and differences in interpreting and applying international law and the factors that might explain them; to explore different national

[83] ibid 4.

[84] Bradley (n 82).

[85] See Boris Mamlyuk and Ugo Mattei, 'Comparative International Law' (2011) 36 *Brooklyn Journal of International Law* 385. Most likely, the little traction the article had on international legal scholarship was probably due to the fact that the two authors are comparative lawyers.

[86] See respectively: Anthea Roberts, Paul Stephan, Pierre-Hughes Verdier, and Mila Versteeg, 'Comparative International Law: Framing the Field' (2015) 109 *American Journal of International Law* 467; Anthea Roberts, *Is International Law International?* (Oxford University Press 2017); and Anthea Roberts, Paul B Stephan, Pierre-Hugues Verdier, and Mila Versteeg (eds), *Comparative International Law* (Oxford University Press 2018).

[87] Roberts, Stephan, Verdier, and Versteeg (eds), *Comparative International Law* (n 86) 6.

[88] Roberts, Stephan, Verdier and Versteeg, 'Comparative International Law: Framing the Field' (n 86) 473–74.

and regional approaches, asking how many states to include (horizontal dimension) or how deeply one can delve into the details of each and every legal system (vertical dimension); or to group states on the basis of their belonging to categories of legal families and traditions are the main tasks for the international law comparatist. Indeed, some of the methodological challenges faced by comparative international law are shared with traditional comparative legal studies.[89] These include: (i) whether one should focus on formal or functional equivalence across legal systems (the functionalist method consists of comparing seemingly different legal rules and doctrines that may have similar functions and produce similar outcomes); (ii) whether to compare systems' approaches at a high level of generality or focus on specific rules; or (iii) whether to analyse formal legal rules only (so-called thin comparativism) or rather actual practices (so-called thick comparativism); and (iv) whether empirical studies can be reconciled with case studies and all other sorts of methodological challenges that are known to the social sciences.[90]

Overall, the tendency to underline the 'local' character of international law's interpretation and application and to foster comparison among different ways of interpreting it and using it stands in juxtaposition with traditional (and declining) universal representations of the system.[91] These conflicting discursive frameworks currently co-exist in the scholarly representation and the social practice of international law, and their constant interaction shapes the contemporary episteme of international law. It is undeniable, however, that the centripetal epistemic forces are increasingly pushing international law to pull out of its universalist claim, and to disperse or diffuse itself into its multiple national and regional dimensions.

VI Antidotes against Invisibility of Knowledge Production Processes and Their Underlying Power Structures

The coat of invisibility that masks some of the most important knowledge production processes in international law is not easily removed. The surreptitious character of mechanisms that we take for granted, as they are ingrained into an unwavering tradition that prevents us from calling its postulates into question, makes

[89] Mathias Reimann and Reinhard Zimmermann (eds), *The Oxford Handbook of Comparative Law* (2nd edn, Oxford University Press 2019).

[90] Roberts, Stephan, Verdier, and Versteeg, 'Comparative International Law: Framing the Field' (n 86) 471–72.

[91] Consider, for example, the following extract from Mathias Forteau's article in the *American Journal of International Law*: 'If one admits that there are different approaches to international law (i.e., a real comparative international law), is there still room for an "*international* law"? It is one thing for international law to tolerate, as it does, multiculturalism in the domestic sphere and quite a different thing for multiculturalism to have an impact on the international plane through the manifestation of different conceptions of international law.' See Mathias Forteau, 'Comparative International Law Within, Not Against, International Law: Lessons from the International Law Commission' (2015) 109 *American Journal of International Law* 498, 499.

us overlook how knowledge is formed and what its underlying power structures are. But are there antidotes against this system of knowledge production? How can one fight against sectarian and inequitable practices, vested interests, and deeply rooted disciplinary processes? How can one contribute individually to the shaping of a disciplinary and professional episteme without having the impression of automatically yielding to the power of the prevailing epistemic forces at play?

I suppose that a bit of critical thinking might help, particularly to liberate us from the shackles of the many false necessities that inhabit our world and our collective imagery. Only critical thinking can make one aware that 'false consciousness' is a way to make reality appear as normal and inevitable, while at the same time concealing the deeper structures of social and legal relations. Think also of Roberto Unger's notion of 'false necessity', where Unger, in a typical critical legal studies posture, maintains that things do not have to be as they are: 'The illusions of false necessity arise because we surrender to the social world and then begin to mistake present society for possible humanity, giving in to the ideas and attitudes that make the established order seem natural, necessary, or authoritative'.[92] Our international lawyerly world is populated by false necessities that we take for uncontroversial and universal truths.

One does not need the Frankfurt School to exercise critical thinking.[93] One might start with 'disturbing oneself' as Starbuck's used to say.[94] How? By changing vocabulary and grammar to test and call into question one's way of thinking;[95] by looking at something using a plurality of perspectives, as the object of investigation may dramatically change when one changes perspective; and by using dialectics, binaries, and juxtapositions to test the plausibility of one's hypothesis against opposite terms.[96]

To be critical is a way of thinking and requires a particular mindset. It has to do, among other things, with the capacity to identify issues and to frame them in an analytical and intellectually critical way, to analyse the increasing alienation and reification of modern societies 'in terms of how they imperilled the exercise of subjectivity, robbed the world of meaning and purpose, and turned the individual into a cog in the machine'.[97] To clarify 'the values and interests that existing ideologies and institutions tend to hide' is the mission of critical inquiry.[98]

[92] Roberto M Unger, *False Necessity: Anti-Necessitarian Social Theory in the Service of Radical Democracy, from Politics: A Work in Constructive Social Theory* (Verso 2001), 'Introduction to the New Edition', xx.
[93] Bianchi (n 66) 138 ff.
[94] Starbuck (n 13) 143 ff.
[95] I, for instance, should ask myself whether I am being 'normative' or 'descriptive' when I say what I say in this chapter, as I am notoriously averse to this distinction that seems to have huge traction in contemporary scholarship.
[96] Starbuck (n 13), 145 ff.
[97] Stephen Eric Bronner, *Critical Theory: A Very Short Introduction* (Oxford University Press 2011) 4–5.
[98] ibid 115.

Finally, I believe that we should rely more often on the power of... imagination. Entire fields have been shaken by powerful calls to use imagination. I have quoted several times Charles Wright Mills, author of *The Sociological Imagination*, and one could add James Boyd White and his *The Legal Imagination*.[99] Creative imagination helps 'raise new questions, new possibilities, to regard old problems from a new angle' and this is what makes science advance. And these are not my words, but Albert Einstein's.[100] It is imagination and a certain 'playfulness of mind' that distinguishes the scientist and the intellectual from the technician. The former have something that the latter lacks: the quality of combining ideas 'that no one expected to be combinable' and 'a truly fierce drive to make sense of the world'.[101] The technician usually lacks these qualities as '[p]erhaps he is too well trained, too precisely trained. Since one can be *trained* only in what is already known, training sometimes incapacitates one from learning new ways'.[102]

Imagination also helps widening the range of options, keeping a sense of possibility, as Robert Musil so aptly put it in *The Man without Qualities*:[103]

> Whoever has a sense of possibility does not say, for instance, here this or that happened, will happen, must happen. If he is told that something is the way it is, he will think: Well it could probably just as well be otherwise. So, the sense of possibility could be defined outright as the ability to conceive of everything that might be just as well, and to attach no more importance to what is... than to what is not.[104]

Likewise, there is plenty of room for exploring the blurred boundaries of what is and what is not. Imagination serves to see, and not just to dream. Imagination can help think the unthought, shift perspective, and combine things no one would think or dare putting together. A certain 'playfulness of mind', the use of metaphors and analogies are indispensable tools of a creative intellect and a substantial aid to uncovering the hidden structures of knowledge production.

Scholarship construed around intellectual good faith, critical thinking, style and imagination may produce results that are infinitely better than those produced by the worship of method, whatever the method. One does not need to go as far as Feyerabend's *Against Method* to claim that the advancement of science hardly follows a pattern and that methodological anarchy has to be encouraged.[105] My claim

[99] James Boyd White, *The Legal Imagination* (University of Chicago Press 1973).

[100] Albert Einstein and Leopold Infeld, *The Evolution of Physics: The Growth of Ideas from Early Concepts to Relativity and Quanta* (Cambridge University Press 1938) 92.

[101] Wright Mills (n 68) 211.

[102] ibid 211–12 (emphasis in the original).

[103] R Musil, *The Man Without Qualities* (S Wilkins and B Pike (trs), Picador 2011).

[104] ibid 11. See also Milan Kundera, 'Our Dreams Prove that to Imagine – to Dream about Things that Have Not Happened – Is Among Mankind's Deepest Needs' in Milan Kundera, *The Unbearable Lightness of Being* (Harper 2009) 29.

[105] Paul Feyerabend, *Against Method* (1975, 3rd edn, Verso 1993).

is rather more limited. It consists of acknowledging the potential of being imaginative. To be imaginative is not tantamount to say that one is not rigorous, unless you equate rigour with the *rigor mortis* either of method for its own sake or of conformity with the official discourse.[106]

The real stakes of research consist of finding out and accounting for what goes on in any given disciplinary field. This exercise demands intellectual honesty and a craft, it requires clarity of purpose and object of inquiry, respect for materials, the mastery of one's own field of intellectual inquiry as well as mastery of the traditional knowledge about it. But the mastery of technique in and of itself does not generate knowledge. Intellectual curiosity, a firm grasp on history and culture, imagination and a wide-enough, if not Renaissance-like, set of varied skills are the tools that can be put to good use when doing scholarly work.[107] Rigorous scholarship has an ethics of its own, for the absence of which no method and no technique can make up.[108]

Can the above consideration be of any use to the individual scholar and to the epistemic communities that shape the terms of the discourse in international law? I do not know—which is quite a conclusion for an essay on the production of knowledge—but even if I do not know I wish it could be so.

[106] On the notion of 'scientific rigour' see also Bianchi (n 66) 36.

[107] See Todd Gitlin's *Afterword* to Wright Mills (n 68) 232.

[108] 'Classic social science, it may be said in tribute, is, among other things, an attempt to improve the chances that our guesses about important matters may be right ... Verification consists of rationally convincing others, as well as ourselves. But to do that we must follow the accepted rules, above all the rule that work be presented in such a way that it is open at every step to the checking up of others. There is no One Way to do this; but it does always require a developed carefulness and attention to detail, a habit of being clear, a sceptical perusal of alleged facts, and a tireless curiosity about their possible meanings, their bearings on other facts and notions. It requires orderliness and system. In a word, it requires the firm and consistent practice of the ethics of scholarship. If that is not present, no technique, no method, will serve.' See Wright Mills (n 68) 126–27.

10

The Discipline as a Field of Struggle

The Politics and the Economy of Knowledge Production in International Law

Akbar Rasulov

I Introduction: Aim and Method

This chapter forms part of a broader research project aimed at developing a sociological account of international law as a system of knowledge production. It has two essential purposes. The first is to explain international law's basic character as a field of theoretical practice: what is it that actually stands behind this 'thing' we call the *discipline of international law*? The second is to provide a relatively systematized account of the discipline of international law as a social phenomenon.

The argument proposed in these pages is a product of two theoretical traditions. The first is historical materialism broadly so understood.[1] The second is Karl Mannheim's theory of ideology.[2]

The materialist component is relatively short. Every discipline constitutes a discursive formation. Every discursive formation is the product of a certain 'world-vision' or 'collective consciousness'. Every collective consciousness 'is a tendency which is developed as a result of a particular social and economic situation'.[3] Seen in these terms, the discipline of international law can be provisionally defined as *a particular kind of discursive formation* that has developed as the result of a *particular socio-economic situation* established among the *community of international lawyers*. Note the last detail: the socio-economic context that this version of the materialist approach invites us to focus on covers only the immediate social field of the international law profession *lato sensu*, not anything broader, more 'global', or more abstract. The argument that I outline in these pages is not, in other words, an argument about the general reasons for the existence of the discipline of international law, ie about that aspect of macro-level collective consciousness as a result of which the general expectation that there should be such a 'thing' as international

[1] For a general overview of the historical materialist tradition see Perry Anderson, *In the Tracks of Historical Materialism* (Verso 1983). See also Karl Marx and Frederick Engels, *The German Ideology: Part One* (Lawrence & Wishart 1999).

[2] Karl Mannheim, *Ideology and Utopia* (Routledge & Kegan Paul 1979).

[3] Lucien Goldmann, *The Hidden God* (Verso 2016) 18.

Akbar Rasulov, *The Discipline as a Field of Struggle* In: *International Law's Invisible Frames*. Edited by: Andrea Bianchi and Moshe Hirsch, Oxford University Press. © Akbar Rasulov 2021. DOI: 10.1093/oso/9780192847539.003.0011

law, and that this thing deserves to be studied, can emerge and persist. The inquiry proposed in this chapter has no such universal ambitions. Its scope is much more local and its aim is only to expose the *internal logic* of the discipline of international law as a field of theoretical practice and a social form.

A different way of stating the same point would be to propose that since the discipline of international law is essentially what international lawyers do,[4] it is what they actually do—rather than what they talk about or how they speak—that we ought to study and record. What gives the discipline of international law its essential theoretical identity, thus, has far less to do with its *central operative ideas and typical narrative structures*—its grammar of legal argument, its specialist vocabularies, standard reasoning protocols, typical subjects of discussion, and so on—than the *ground-level material realities* that are shared by the respective community of disciplinary practitioners. The first and the most important of these realities, from the historical-materialist perspective, is structured around the question of the *intra-disciplinary division of labour*: who are the main participants in the discipline's constituent labour processes, what sort of 'material' do these labour processes 'work' on, how centralized or decentralized are they in terms of their setup, what kind of added value is created as a result of this kind of labour, and how and by whom is this value appropriated?

This is not to suggest, of course, that ideas and discursive structures do not generally matter. The point rather is that we will not be able to understand how or why the history of international law as a disciplinary formation has unfolded the way that it has if we only studied its discursive and ideational elements. Theories—narratives and ideas—are symptoms. It is never a good idea to ignore one's symptoms, to be sure. But one must also not forget the difference between symptoms and causes. A systematic examination of symptoms will be indispensable if we want to make sense of the immediate experience as it is lived by the respective subjects. But to explain why and how that experience came to form in the first place, what factors enabled it, how common or prevalent it is, and how it can be improved or changed, we have to start looking at the underlying root causes.

Whatever may be the intellectual experiences that take place within the discursive plane of international law, their root causes lie outside it. The materialist part of the argument proposed in these pages suggests that these causes ought to be sought in the *basic material conditions* of international law's disciplinary community's day-to-day collective existence, that is to say, the *general conditions of the labour process* under which the different segments of the international law profession exist and are organized vis-à-vis one another.

The Mannheimian part of the argument builds directly on the materialist part. International law is an enterprise of theoretical labour that is aimed at the

4 Martti Koskenniemi, *The Gentle Civilizer of Nations* (Cambridge University Press 2002) 7.

production of knowledge. By deploying a certain type of 'theoretical tools' the discipline enables us to generate various sets of knowledge-products that did not exist before and would not have come into existence without it. In the final analysis, the political economy of this labour process determines the overall shape and form of the discipline's collective consciousness and, through that, the general form and content of its discursive self-realization. The immediate structure and the main defining features of the actual disciplinary imaginary that arises in the course of this process, however, are not just a direct reflection of this background system of labour practices. They are also, in large part, a consequence of the specific character of that basic medium in which this labour is carried out and the institutional context in which the products it produces circulate and are consumed. The primary medium in which international law's theoretical labour is carried out is a system of normative concepts and argument templates (as opposed to, say, economic statistics, lab results, or divine revelations). The institutional context that grounds the circulation and consumption of international law's disciplinary products is a combination of *academicism*, *technocratic professionalism*, and the idea of international law as a form of *governance expertise*.[5]

A large part of what determines the specific structure of the international legal discipline as a discursive formation today comes down to the fact that, firstly, international law is a field in which the basic transmission of knowledge—education, training, research—is carried out mostly in an academic institutional context, ie by means of university degrees, scholarly journals, academic conferences, etc. Secondly, international lawyers are constituted as a learned profession whose members are meant to possess and exercise a certain kind of specialist expertise. Thirdly, this expertise is essentially technical in nature and, as commonly understood, relates somehow to the conduct and performance of global governance.[6]

Not least because of the general role assigned within the non-academic segment of the profession to the acquisition of formal academic credentials—such as, eg, specialist graduate degrees and, higher up the scale, scholarly publications in reputable sources—from the standpoint of determining the overall shape and structure of international law's disciplinary consciousness, *the dominant role in the discipline of international law today is assumed, on the whole, by its academic component*. It is the academic segment of the international law profession that primarily controls the production and transmission of the disciplinary imaginary and drives forward the discipline's theoretical labour process. Every tension and

[5] For further background see chapters by Rene Uruena, Sara and Yves Dezalays, and Martti Koskenniemi in Jean d'Aspremont and others (eds), *International Law as a Profession* (Cambridge University Press 2017).

[6] On international law's status as a learned profession and an expertise in the conduct and performance of global governance see David Kennedy, *A World of Struggle* (Princeton University Press 2016). See also chapters by Jean d'Aspremont, Martti Koskenniemi, and Richard Collins and Alexandra Bohm in Jean d'Aspremont and others (eds), *International Law as a Profession* (Cambridge University Press 2017).

contradiction that defines the character of international law's disciplinary process of labour, thus, can be traced more or less directly to the *principal institutional features and social characteristics* of this sub-community.

For our purposes, the most important among these institutional features today is the principle of *structural decentralization*—the pattern whereby the structure of international law's academic field continues to remain relatively horizontal and the relations of power established within it relatively open and in flux. At the ideational and discursive level, this principle finds its clearest expression in what can be termed a *culture of liberal agnosticism*:[7] the commonly shared assumption that there is not really one right answer or one right approach to 'doing' international legal theory; that theories and approaches exist in something like an open marketplace, so we should just let everyone choose and pick whatever theory they like and let the best theories, thus, be determined, ultimately, by forces of supply and demand (free market competition). In recent decades, the dominance of this basic liberal sensibility has been reinforced by the rise of various species of *anti-theoreticist relativism* and the general ethos of postmodern libertarianism.[8] How widespread this new pattern may be outside the Anglo-American international law scene remains unclear. But the basic effect of its infusion into the discipline's traditional culture of liberal agnosticism has been an even deeper entrenchment at the level of the discipline's general ideological climate of a deeply Darwinist motif: let a hundred voices sing; the more perspectives, the better; those with the best ideas will ultimately prevail, others will wither away.

Although the parallels are never direct, what happens at the level of ideational expression often tends to reflect what takes shape at the level of the underlying socio-economic realities. In the socio-material context, the discipline's tendency towards structural decentralization finds its expression in what often comes across as the process of the *continuing disintegration of the traditional structures of disciplinary authority and hierarchy*. Even in England, the academic segment of the discipline no longer looks up to Oxford and Cambridge as its 'natural centres', access to academic appointments is no longer conditioned on getting anointed by these institutions, and the research agendas set there no longer dictate the research agendas taken up elsewhere in the country.

One aspect of this disintegration of hierarchy and authority can be seen in the *gradual loosening of the previously fixed territorial circuits of academic circulation*. Whether in the context of annual conference attendance or the typical geographies of graduate training trajectories, the territorial dynamic within the discipline is gradually losing its once clearly pronounced core-periphery character. Another

[7] One of the first notable attempts to grapple with this culture and its implications for the discipline's internal politico-economic space was Martti Koskenniemi, 'Letter to the Editors of the Symposium' (1999) 93 *American Journal of International Law* 351.

[8] I discuss some aspects of this process in greater detail in Akbar Rasulov, '*From Apology to Utopia* and the Inner Life of International Law' (2016) 29 *Leiden Journal of International Law* 641, 651–54.

aspect of the same process can be detected in the steady proliferation of countless new 'perspectives', 'theoretical projects', and 'research agendas', a trend that is reinforced both by the steady lowering of the relative entry costs into the discipline's discursive marketplace and the pressing need to distinguish one's position therein from those of one's competitors.

In political economy terms, this pattern of project proliferation, of course, constitutes only a symptom. New projects and agendas do not appear of their own accord. What stands behind the steady multiplication of new theoretical brands, movements, and projects is a growing *intensification of the general process of intra-disciplinary contestation.*

The traditional distribution of social power and economic resources within the profession are increasingly coming into question. Groups that previously might have been satisfied with their place in the hierarchy no longer seem to be willing to accept their prospects. Power struggles in a disciplinary context, of course, can only be waged in a more or less coded manner. As the conflict between the competing groups intensifies, an increasing part of it assumes the form of 'theoretical' clashes between the respective methods and projects. Different groups put forward competing theoretical positions encoded in the form of variously abstracted arguments about matters of legal method, policy, doctrine, or history. What each of these positions channels, ultimately, is *a particular vision of intra-disciplinary organization* and, through that, a proposal for *a corresponding (re-)distribution of the appropriate resources*: an argument about how the disciplinary labour process should be organized, the surplus value it produces allocated, and the corresponding social hierarchies arranged and transformed.

The formal content of the ideational materials employed in the course of these theoretical contestations can sometimes be helpful in explaining the basic dynamics of conflict and opposition between the respective groups. This in turn can shed light on some of the less obvious tensions and possibilities inscribed within the disciplinary labour process. But to work our way through this sort of multi-level analysis in a rigorous fashion, descending from the plane of ideational expression to the plane of the material organization of labour, requires not just a general notion of symptomatic interpretation, but a full-fledged model of *theory as sublimated ideological conflicts.* Mannheim's concept of ideology as a process of struggle among highly particularized social groups advocating competing world-views (ideological intelligentsias) offers an important starting point for constructing this model.[9]

[9] It is not the only clue that we would need in order to develop a full account of this model. Other elements include a narrative semiotics of the international legal discourse, a critical ideologematics of these narrative structures, and a reflexive sociology of the principal institutional sites, apparatuses, and forms used in the contemporary international legal academia—but also the international civil service, international adjudication sector, the juridical dimension of the global civil society, and other segments of what can broadly be considered today the 'invisible college' of the international law profession.

A brief summary of what the rest of this chapter is going to cover: in Section II, I provide a general overview of the standard accounts, theories, and models of international law's disciplinary character currently available in the literature. The object of my critique in this section is to contextualize the basic theoretical background against which the present exercise is meant to take place. The context having been thus set out, in Section III, I then flesh out the historical-materialist-Mannheimian account in greater detail. The aim of that section is to outline *a general model of international law as a system of theoretical labour*. The argument that I put forward there is built around a concept of knowledge as both a process and a product of a certain type of collective labour and the idea of disciplinary economy as a field of sublimated political struggles refracted through the particular structure of international law's internal labour conditions and the particular specificities of its 'productive material'. In the concluding section, I summarize the main themes of this argument and offer a brief restatement.[10]

II The State of Play: Traditional Theories of International Law's Disciplinary Character

It is said that the word 'discipline' comes originally from the Latin word for pupil (*discipulus*) and is meant, in that regard, to convey the general notion of training, instruction, and education.[11] A less abstract, but perhaps more to-the-point, account of the contemporary meaning of the term, as it is applied in relation to academic settings, is offered by the American constitutional law scholar Jack Balkin:

> A discipline organizes and empowers thought. It makes having certain kinds of thought possible. [A]n undisciplined mind would be unable to proceed very far ... Disciplines offer the academic forms of cultural know-how, or what I like to call 'cultural software'. [They] provide their members with tools of understanding [and] push [them] towards asking the kinds of questions with which these tools are best equipped to deal and treating all other questions as variants of these ... They are also ongoing, self-regenerating enterprises. They instil cultural

On the concept of ideologematic analysis see MM Bakhtin and PN Medvedev, *The Formal Method in Literary Scholarship* (Johns Hopkins University Press 1978) 8–9, 13–15, 21–23.

[10] A note on influences and theoretical genealogies: the account of international law that is outlined draws its greatest inspiration from David Kennedy, 'When Renewal Repeats Itself: Thinking against the Box' (2000) 32 *New York University Journal of International Law and. Politics* 335. My thinking about the politics of legal-theoretical contestation has also been influenced by Duncan Kennedy, *A Critique of Adjudication (fin de siècle)* (Harvard University Press 1997) and Pierre Schlag, 'The Brilliant, the Curious, and the Wrong' (1987) 39 *Stanford Law Review* 917.

[11] JM Balkin, 'Interdisciplinarity as Colonization' (1996) 53 *Washington and Lee Law Review* 949, 953.

software in their members so that their members can instil software in their successors.[12]

As far as what legal scholars usually have to say on the subject, one could hardly find a better starting point. Clear and concise, Balkin's summary simultaneously highlights the chicken-and-egg relationship between disciplines and cultural capital, the self-reproduction dynamics that undergirds every disciplinary formation, the Procrustean effects of disciplinary training on reason and imagination, and the enormous amount of labour that goes into preserving and reproducing this training across time. But what exactly is this *process of labour* actually a process of?

Labour, as every Marxist knows, is an inherently social process that is supposed to be permeated with all kinds of internal structural tensions and contradictions. What is the actual social structure behind that specific form of theoretical labour which corresponds to the discipline of international law? What sort of tensions and contradictions characterize this structure? What is the basic object towards which this labour is directed? What does this labour actually produce? What does it labour on? And what does its human dimension look like? Taken as a distinct social form, what exactly is the discipline of international law today a social form of? What is that basic content which is contained within this form? What are its principal defining characteristics? The answers most commonly given to this sort of questions over the last one hundred years, for the most part, seem today quaint and misguided.

Whatever might be the proper object and province of *moral theory*, as any textbook on the law of treaties or international monetary regulation can quickly show, the discipline of international law is not just a branch of it.[13] Nor is it really *a species of science*,[14] *a form of applied rhetoric*,[15] or *a remedial service enterprise* established in order to meet the research needs of some broader community of international practitioners and decision-makers.[16] Even the briefest look at the kind of activities typically performed by most international lawyers today will be enough to put to rest all of these naïve arguments. Between managing grant projects, applying for postdoc scholarships, and jostling to place articles with appropriately ranked

[12] ibid 955.

[13] The tradition of equating the study of international law with the study of moral theory goes back to the English jurisprude John Austin but also EH Carr and Hans Morgenthau. Austin's views on the subject are helpfully summarized in James B Scott, 'The Legal Nature of International Law' (1905) 5 *Columbia Law Review* 124, 128–30. For an overview of Carr and Morgenthau's approaches see Sean Molloy, *The Hidden History of Realism* (Palgrave 2006).

[14] For a classical illustration that puts this view into practice see L Oppenheim, 'The Science of International Law: Its Task and Method' (1908) 2 *American Journal of International Law* 313.

[15] For a classical illustration that puts this view into practice see Friedrich Kratochwil, *Rules, Norms, and Decisions* (Cambridge University Press 1989) 12–19.

[16] For a classical illustration that puts this view into practice see Myres McDougal and others, 'Theories about International Law: Prologue to a Configurative Jurisprudence' (1968) 8 *Virginia Journal of International Law* 188, 195–96.

publications, it seems abundantly clear that most international law academics these days do not toil in the pursuit of transcendent moral progress, objective scientific truth, or the opportunity to perform uncompensated research assistance for the benefit of some nebulous group of international practitioners. Nor, by the same token, do most international practitioners today actually seem to care so much for the vast majority of the research output produced by international legal scholars. However simple or complex may be the relationship between these two communities, it certainly seems to be very different from the traditional model of academia-as-the-servant-of-practice.

If none of the standard accounts offered by the mainstream tradition seem helpful, could one find perhaps something better among the so-called heterodox legal traditions? Alas, here, too, the usual offerings do not seem particularly inspiring.

Take, for example, the first wave of the so-called New Approaches to International Law (NAIL) scholarship. The process of learning to 'think like an international lawyer', argued NAIL scholars, is essentially equivalent to that of mastering a new language.[17] What separates international lawyers from everyone else, on this view of things, is their ability to reformulate whatever problems and matters of international concern are presented to them by processing them through a relatively esoteric system of classificatory categories, tropes, and argument templates, without any concern for the actual details of the particular problems in question – a practice that both allows them constantly to defer the final moment of normative closure and to avoid at the same time the twin pressures of nihilism and contextual equity.[18] Now, as a matter of basic practical observation, most of this account seems to ring true. But while it certainly helps emphasize the essentially strategic character of international law as a discursive process, it does not really tell us very much about the underlying social relations and processes that underpin that system. Beyond some brief references to the idea that most international lawyers aspire to safeguard the discursive independence of international law from international politics[19] and the apparent unavoidability of inter-generational cycles,[20] first-wave NAIL scholarship does not, in this sense, offer any far-reaching insights on this front.

The same finding, albeit for a different set of reasons, applies also to feminist international law scholarship[21] and the so-called Third World Approaches to

[17] See eg Martti Koskenniemi, *From Apology to Utopia* (Cambridge University Press 2006); David Kennedy, *International Legal Structures* (Nomos 1987).

[18] On constant deferral see Kennedy (n 17) 196–97. On nihilism and contextual equity see Koskenniemi (n 17) 533–61.

[19] Koskenniemi (n 17) 17–23.

[20] David Kennedy, 'A New World Order: Yesterday, Today, and Tomorrow' (1994) 4 *Transnational Law & Contemporary Problems* 329.

[21] See eg Anne Orford, 'Feminism, Imperialism and the Mission of International Law' (2002) 71 *Nordic Journal of International Law* 275; Hilary Charlesworth and Christine Chinkin, *The Boundaries of International Law: A Feminist Analysis* (Manchester University Press 2000).

International Law (TWAIL) movement.[22] Though each of these traditions has succeeded in making major inroads into the study of international law's broader political function as a site and a mechanism of global governance, neither of them to date has managed to explain the actual organization of the international legal discipline as a field of theoretical labour. Apart from some general observations about the discipline's structural complicity in the reproduction of racialized and gendered forms of oppression, injustice, and inequality, no actual attention has yet been paid to the broader question of the discipline's internal social logics.[23] Not that such observations have little critical value. Exposing the discipline's contribution to the enablement of imperialism, colonial exploitation, and patriarchy is an extremely powerful move. But the research programme it usually gives rise to cannot explain how and why, in the process of 'choosing' among all the different configurations on the basis of which this enabling function could be carried out, the discipline of international law has ended up choosing the ones that it ultimately did.

Nor, for that matter, do things look very different if one turned instead to the various self-declaredly Marxist, Marxo-Hegelian, and Hegelo-Kantian traditions. Uncovering the discipline's predisposition to mimic the exact same cultural shifts which brought about the aesthetics of modernist experimentalism in classical music[24] or recognizing, Clausewitz-style, that international law really is just an extension of some broader process of power politics—be it the politics of post-modern warfare[25] or bourgeois commodity fetishism[26]—does not explain much about how international law, in fact, differs from commercial law or constitutional law, or what exactly is that actual labour which international law scholars contribute to executing these cultural shifts and political games.

Whichever way one turns, the same structure of blind spots and omissions persists. What may be the causes behind it, is not immediately clear. One possible explanation might be that this is probably a function of historical habits: international law scholars are generally unaccustomed to thinking of themselves as intellectual labourers and thus to discussing their work in terms of production planning, consumption needs, surplus value, and so on. Alternatively, one may approach this problem as a reflection of the basic economy of academic research activities that

[22] See eg Antony Anghie, *Imperialism, Sovereignty and the Making of International Law* (Cambridge University Press 2005); Makau Mutua, 'What is TWAIL?' (2000) 94 *Proceedings of the American Society of International Law* 31.

[23] A partial but important exception is Anne Orford, 'Embodying Internationalism: The Making of International Lawyers' (1998) 19 *Australian Yearbook of International Law* 1.

[24] See Nathaniel Berman, 'Modernism, Nationalism, and the Rhetoric of Reconstruction' (1992) 4 *Yale Journal of Law & the Humanities* 351.

[25] See David Kennedy, *Of War and Law* (Princeton University Press 2006).

[26] See China Miéville, *Between Equal Rights* (Brill 2005).

has emerged as a result of what typically gets rewarded in terms of career promotion and professional recognition opportunities.

What angle one goes for, in the end, does not probably matter. The essential problem still remains: none of the standard answers historically proposed within the discipline actually addresses the question of international law's disciplinary reality in terms of its underlying social processes and forms of disciplinary labour.

And yet it seems beyond doubt that there does, in fact, exist such a 'thing' as the discipline of international law, and that most of us seem to have a relatively strong understanding that not only is it different from, say, other legal disciplines, philosophy, or social sciences, but that those of us who are a part of it are also engaged in some kind of common labour – that we all, in this sense, are working together with one another, that a great many disagreements exist among us about how this work ought to be done, and that most of these disagreements have nothing to do with what political, national, or ideological backgrounds we come from but everything to do with how our relations with one another—as participants of this common productive undertaking—are set up.

III International Law as a System of Knowledge Production

A Main Thesis

The theory which I am going to outline in these pages is not going to be very complimentary to the average scholarly ego, especially one steeped in the traditional mythologies of legal science[27] or legal thought as the vehicle for political emancipation.[28] The argument I present here is grounded in a decidedly less exalted vision. One could say its roots lie in Marxism, though it probably needs to be noted that it has much less in common with what typically passes under this rubric today in international law[29] than such a comment might otherwise imply.

Here is what this argument says, in a nutshell:

The ontology of any disciplinary formation is a field of social practices. A field of social practices is a system of relatively fixed, in the context of that field, *subject positions*, *relations of difference (opposition) and exchange (connection)* between them, a commonly shared *sense of stakes*, and the corresponding *mode of collective consciousness* that brings all of these elements together.

[27] See Roberto Ago, 'Science Juridique et Droit International' (1956–II) 90 *Recueil des Cours de l'Académie de Droit International* 849.

[28] See Mohammed Bedjaoui, *Towards a New International Economic Order* (UNESCO 1979).

[29] See Akbar Rasulov, 'A Marxism for International Law: A New Agenda' (2018) 29 *European Journal of International Law* 631.

The mode of collective consciousness that defines the contemporary discipline of international law is that of a productive system. A system of production is any system in which a group of people labour together, in conflict and in co-operation with one another, with a view to producing something that would not otherwise exist. That something in the case of international law can be defined cumulatively as 'international legal knowledge'. Taken as a disciplinary formation, international law can thus be defined *as a system of specialized knowledge production.*[30]

More specifically, what this means is that the discipline of international law constitutes a system that

(1) consists of four basic components:
  (a) *the process of the conceptual appropriation of the 'actually existing' international legal system and its history*—by which one should understand the discursive production of collectively shared mental representations (collective consciousness) of the 'external reality' of international legal relations ('international law as it exists outside our heads');
  (b) *the foundational problematic*—by which one should understand all the constituent theoretical conflicts on the basis of which the above-mentioned process of conceptual appropriation is organized;
  (c) *a series of discursively sublimated inter-group conflicts*—by which one should understand all the various ideological contestations among the rival schools, traditions, and movements that are conducted within the parameters of (b) and ostensibly on the pretext of changing the end-product of (a) and, if possible, also the structure of (b), but that are in practice motivated primarily by reasons of (d);
  (d) *a struggle over the distribution of institutionally inscribed economic resources of the kind typically valorized within Western-style legal-academic settings*—by which one should understand all the various types of social capital and the accompanying institutional forms that historically first emerged within the institutional context of Western legal academia and, due to the continuing prevalence of core-periphery patterns, have spread across other parts of the world;
  and

(2) is almost entirely propelled, in terms of its historical development, by its *internal contradictions*, that is to say, by the tensions created by the above-mentioned struggle over institutionally inscribed resources (1.d) as refracted through the respective inter-scholar contestations (1.c) and constrained by the terms of the foundational problematic (1.b).

[30] See Andrea Bianchi and Moshe Hirsch, 'International Law's Invisible Frames: Introductory Insights' in this volume.

B Commentary

The argument set out in the previous sub-section is not the easiest piece of text to wade through. Let me unpack it in a little more detail:

(i) Every serious inquiry into the ontology of knowledge, notes the French philosopher Pierre Macherey, has to contend with the fact that knowledge is, essentially, an *active process*:

> thought is not the passive perception of a general disposition ... The act of knowing is not like listening to a discourse already constituted ... which we have simply to translate. It is rather the elaboration of a new discourse, the articulation of a silence.
>
> Knowledge is not the discovery or reconstruction of a latent meaning, forgotten or concealed. It is something newly raised up, an addition to the reality from which it begins.[31]

What we know about the world is not simply given to us. Facts, concepts, and categories around which the discourse of international law is built—constructs like extraterritorial jurisdiction, international armed conflict, or crimes against humanity—do not arise spontaneously from the 'objective reality' of international relations. They are produced, rather, by the discipline of international law, that is to say, they are brought into existence through the transformative work carried out by its practitioners. Everything we know about the international legal system, its history, its structure, and its potential, we know because of this transformative work. There is nothing self-evident or natural about international legal knowledge. All of it is artificial. All of it is a *product*.

(ii) Every system of production is determined as much by its underlying economic structure as by the corresponding political conditions within which this structure exists and which it presupposes. That is to say, international law's essential character and defining features as a discipline, in the last instance, are determined not only by which types of *raw materials* and *productive technologies* are involved in the production of its *final product*, but also by what *broader patterns and forms of social conflict* are engendered by the corresponding *division of labour* that enables and is necessitated by this productive process.

(iii) Presuming that the final product in the present case can be defined provisionally as 'international legal knowledge', the next two questions that need to be clarified are, first, how many different types of knowledge products it is possible to distinguish within the total body of output generated by international law's

[31] Pierre Macherey, *A Theory of Literary Production* (Routledge & Kegan Paul 1978) 6.

knowledge production; and, second, since production always involves transformation, what is the actual process of transformation by means of which these knowledge products are generated?

The answer that I propose to give to these questions here may seem somewhat schematic. In its main contours it builds on the broader argument developed by the French philosopher Louis Althusser.[32] Reduced to its most basic form, it states that, in the first instance, we should distinguish between three analytically separate components:

- the *'raw data'* which enters the knowledge process from outside—acts of state practice, statements of international bodies, 'empirical givens', 'historical record', 'interdisciplinary insights', 'facts' about the 'objective reality' of international legal relations, etc.;
- the *theoretical apparatuses* and *analytical procedures* that are applied to this data in order to generate a piece of specialist knowledge about international law—those specialist lexicons that NAIL scholars so persistently drew our attention to and the archetypal argument-bites (micro-level master narratives) through the lens of which international lawyers approach and try to make sense of the surrounding realities they're engaging with;[33]
- the *various kinds of specialist knowledge-products* which international lawyers as a community are generally known to 'have' and to 'trade' in—diagnostic summaries of the law in force, overviews of 'main legal issues', 'answers to legal problems', general policy prescriptions, normative proposals, etc.

In the second instance, the argument continues, we should also aim to distinguish between those specialist knowledge-products which in principle are intended for mostly *external* consumption (even if they are never so consumed)—answers to legal problems, summaries of the applicable law, programmatic normative prescriptions—and those which, by their very design, are intended for almost exclusively *internal* consumption—abstract systematizing categories and second-order legal constructs, ie those knowledge-products out of which the abovementioned theoretical apparatuses and analytical procedures are eventually assembled—what one might otherwise call *properly operative legal-theoretical concepts*. The most important and enduring conflicts that are fought within the discipline of international law are fought precisely over this last category. The reasons for that are essentially twofold. In the first place, for the actual participants of the knowledge-production process, these second-order concepts carry extremely high

[32] See, in particular, Louis Althusser, *For Marx* (Verso 2005) 182–6.

[33] The phenomenon of argument-bites has not yet been given any attention in the international law literature. Outside international law, to my mind, it has been covered most productively in Duncan Kennedy, 'A Semiotics of Legal Argument' (1991) 42 *Syracuse Law Review* 75.

stakes: who wants to end up having to operate a theoretical machinery one has no familiarity with? In the second place, together with the human component of the discipline and its institutional landscape, these theoretical apparatuses and analytical procedures constitute the discipline's basic *productive forces*. As every Marxist knows, whoever controls the forces of production essentially controls the rest of the productive system and the broader economy established around it.

(iv) To understand the reality of any productive system developed under the conditions of the general dominance of the capitalist mode of production, requires the recognition not only of the very high likelihood of replication within that system of the *objective structural contradiction* between the element of labour (ie the immediately productive part of the system) and the element of capital (ie that part of it where the surplus-value produced by the labour gets extracted, removed, reinvested, and profited from by somebody other than the actual producers that produced it), but also of the essential inevitability of the continuous *subjective conflicts and struggles* within each of these elements, ie the competition and rivalry among the different groups of labouring producers as well as among the different appropriators of the surplus value.

What all of this means in the present context is that to grasp the essential logic of international law's knowledge-production process requires us, in addition to everything else, to study the tensions and contradictions not only between the *various communities of producers and appropriators* of specific international law knowledge-products (eg the objective structural contradiction between those international lawyers who, say, produce practitioner-oriented summaries of the applicable legal regimes or write their histories and those who produce studies of these summaries and histories, say, from a Marxo-Hegelian or a TWAILian perspective), but also between the *different schools, scholarly movements, and theoretical traditions* that are vying to secure a more dominant role within the disciplinary productive process, eg by changing the terms of the discipline's foundational problematic or its taxonomy of admissible reasoning protocols and output genres.[34]

(v) These conflicts and struggles, though they are never conducted in a pure, unmediated form, focus, ultimately, on the distribution of, and access to, different categories of *disciplinary resources*—both those that are considered valuable because they constitute a factor of production and those that are valorized in the discipline's internal social arena for whatever other reasons.

[34] The question, 'what makes something a school of thought or a scholarly movement?', has also not been given much attention in the international law literature to date. The most insightful discussion of the problem can be found in Kennedy, 'Thinking against the Box' (n 10) 373–75. An important limitation of Kennedy's approach, however, comes from the fact that he essentially tackles this question by pointing to the idea of a shared epistemic orientation—commonly practised analytical protocols and 'argumentative default positions'—which from the perspective proposed here is, if not exactly a confusion of cause and effect, then at the very least a conflation of causes and attributes. More generally, Kennedy's model also appears to sidestep the issue of the subjective element, ie the question: how much does 'being a school' depend on having consciously shared ideological goals and aspirations?

How does the structure of these resources influence the course of these conflicts and struggles? I have discussed this subject in greater detail elsewhere.[35] For the present purposes, let me recall two main points. The first point is the *principle of general resource convertibility*. Any given type of disciplinary resource, under the right circumstances, can be converted into another type of resource. Even those forms of disciplinary capital that at first glance appear to be productively 'useless' can be leveraged to help increase access to those resources which are of direct productive value: eg scholarly prizes, honorary appointments, and other career achievement indicators can be used to improve one's chances in the competition for grants or to attract more industrious junior colleagues to one's research project.[36]

The second point is the importance of *institutional control*. All economic processes are institutionally embedded and mediated. Whoever controls the discipline's principal institutional sites—graduate training programmes, funding councils, editorial boards, book commissioning committees, etc.—controls not only what theoretical apparatuses and analytical procedures dominate within the disciplinary knowledge-production process, but also the basic terms of the above-mentioned process of resource convertibility.[37]

(vi) If it does not take the form of an open direct conflict, what form does the intra-disciplinary struggle over resources usually assume? The answer to this question, in a nutshell, goes as follows. The single most important formal constraint on the conduct of intra-disciplinary struggles in modern international law comes from the fact that the general structure of the discipline's discursive output process is consistently overdetermined by its purported function as a body of *technical expertise* relating to the *conduct and performance of global governance*. Form influences substance. The medium influences the message. Whatever struggles and contestations take place within the discipline's internal social space, by necessity, tend to assume the form of conflicts over the ways in which the theoretical labour process leading to the production of specialist expert knowledge relating to the conduct and performance of global governance is set up and operated.

What sort of knowledge-products should qualify as disciplinarily valuable given that, at the end of the day, the discipline's theoretical labour should yield a body of expert knowledge relating to global governance? What kind of surplus value can the discipline of international law add in the course of its conceptual appropriation of whatever external realities it proposes to study? Should the initial processing of these realities be done on the basis of quantitative empirical methods, traditional positivist analysis, or some form of interdisciplinary methodology?

[35] See Akbar Rasulov, 'What Is Critique? Towards a Sociology of Disciplinary Heterodoxy in Contemporary International Law' in Jean d'Aspremont and others (eds), *International Law as a Profession* (Cambridge University Press 2017) 189.

[36] ibid 199–204.

[37] ibid 220.

Once these initial products are produced, how can the surplus value (theoretical insights) added by the respective scholars be best extracted, distributed, and reinvested into further knowledge production? Should those scholars who build on other scholars' work be treated with suspicion because their own produce thereby is shown to be 'derivative' and 'secondary'? Or does subscribing to this view actually betray a naive artisanal sensibility that really ought to have no place in modern (late-capitalist) academia? More generally, how should the know-how relating to the processes of generating, accumulating, and reinvesting the surplus value added by the discipline usually be transmitted? Should it be taught in a more or less systematic fashion, passed on through mentor-mentee networks, or left to be picked up through some kind of osmosis?

Given the standard understanding of the term politics, none of these questions would typically strike one as openly political. And yet it is here that the most important form of politics that animates the discipline's internal social space comes out to the surface most clearly: the politics that is truly indigenous to the discipline as a distinct social form. Other political forces and dynamics—colonialism, patriarchal domination, great power rivalries—can impact the course of the discipline's theoretical evolution, and leave an imprint on the knowledge-products it generates and the basic productive forces it relies on. But each of them, ultimately, has what one might call an *effectivity limit*. The discipline is not a fully transparent medium: the shockwaves produced by global and external political impulses do not just 'go through' it. The politics that is generated by the scholarly struggles over the set-up of the discipline's labour processes, however, is neither global nor external to the discipline's ideational and discursive materials. There is no part of the discipline's knowledge-production process—no theoretical apparatus, no publishing convention, no abstract epistemic assumption—that falls outside the reach of this kind of politics, just like there is no part of its social space—no theoretical tradition, no professional sub-community, no circuit of career trajectories—that remains uninvolved in the kind of power struggles and contestations which it generates.

C Foundational Problematic

As a subject of research, the idea of international law's foundational problematic has not yet generally received much attention. Drawing on the work of first-wave NAIL and TWAIL scholars, it seems possible to hypothesize that some of those foundational problems that underpin the theoretical structure of modern international law probably include questions such as: how can international legal knowledge be both descriptively accurate (concrete) and politically programmatic (normative)? can binding law exist among sovereigns? how can the pursuit of violence (war) and greed (trade) be ordered and regularized in the absence of both natural justice and a world government? how can a common legal order be established between societies representing radically different cultural formations? how can process replace substance and sources replace process?[38]

In its basic contours, the concept of the foundational problematic that I propose to draw on in this context comes from the work of Althusser and Macherey. Every given body of discourse, notes Macherey, tends to present itself to the untrained eye as a relatively systematized series of inter-related ideas, narratives, and conversations. What should be resisted, however, is the lazy assumption that the textual formation that is thus manifested can somehow be considered fully identical with itself, that it is not, in other words, a product of something other than that which is visible on its surface. No discourse ever emerges spontaneously, of its own accord, nor unfolds perfectly smoothly, without any cleavages or contestations. To grasp the operative logic of any given discursive formation, writes Macherey, it is important that, instead of viewing it merely as a body of inter-connected ideas, statements, or conversations, we try to uncover behind it that *initial set of disagreements* an enduring preoccupation with which has produced the *need* for these ideas, statements, and conversations to connect with one another.[39] We must retrieve, in other words, that basic set of concerns which not only justified initiating these conversations in the first place but also required that they be conducted together, alongside one another, within the same shared intellectual space.

What sort of problems, concerns, and preoccupations are we talking about in this case? In general, the *operative logic* of any actually existing discursive formation can be best uncovered through a close narratological analysis of the respective textual outputs. What exactly should we understand by the idea of 'close narratological analysis'? What kind of analytical tools, methods, and procedures are we talking about? A number of different answers suggest themselves, ranging from Foucauldian archaeology[40] and Jungian psychoanalysis,[41] to Mieke Bal's narrative semiotics[42] and Fredric Jameson's Marxian ideologematics.[43] The field of possibilities is wide open, and it is difficult at this point to predict which of the different methods or approaches will prove more effective. Whatever method one chooses, however, it is important to remember that every foundational problematic basically functions as a *mythopoetic device*. Every myth, at its core, is an attempt to work out an imaginary figurative resolution to a real social contradiction.[44] The ultimate objective of international law's foundational problematic—seen in these terms—is to provide the discourse of international law with a sufficiently stable sense of

[38] See generally Koskenniemi (n 17); Kennedy (n 17); Anghie (n 22).

[39] See Macherey (n 31) 8–9.

[40] Michel Foucault, *The Archaeology of Knowledge* (Pantheon Books 1972).

[41] Christopher Booker, *The Seven Basic Plots* (Continuum 2004).

[42] Mieke Bal, *Narratology: Introduction to the Theory of Narrative* (2nd edn, University of Toronto Press 1997).

[43] Fredric Jameson, *The Political Unconscious* (Routledge 2002) 69–81.

[44] See Claude Levi-Strauss, *Structural Anthropology* (Basic Books 1963) 229.

coherence and logical consistency to enable the thought processes constituted on its basis to rationalize and mediate whatever political, economic, and cultural contradictions the community of international lawyers typically encounters in its day-to-day existence.[45]

IV Conclusion

The argument that I put forward in this chapter can be summarized s follows: the discipline of international law is a system of knowledge production. The knowledge-products that it produces have the form of abstract mental objects: insights, hypotheses, policy prescriptions, and explanatory narratives. Taken as a whole, the totality of these knowledge-products is intended to constitute, or to help improve the constitution of, a certain body of technical expertise. The object of this expertise concerns the conduct and performance (know-how) of global governance. The discipline of international law, seen in these terms, is basically a system for the production of abstract mental objects that, put together, constitute a body of technical expertise relating to the exercise of global governance. Conceptualizing the discipline of international law in this manner carries an important critical connotation. In the first place, it allows us to reinsert the question of phenomenology (subjective intention) into the broader question of objective socio-economic conditions (production of mental objects). In the second place — and no less significantly— it allows us also to flag up the essential instability of any inter-disciplinary boundaries between *international law*, *international relations*, and *international political economy*. Based on what we know about the 'external' ambitions of each of these disciplinary formations – the immediate contents of their respective foundational problematics and internal institutional landscapes aside – each of them, by and large, appears to *want* to occupy the same basic theoretical field. This both signals the fundamental economic threat these three formations present towards one another (hostile takeover, competitive undercutting) and predicts that the incidence of inter-disciplinary linkages (merger, cross-breeding) among these particular formations is generally going to be much higher than between them and other disciplinary formations.

At the root of the particular theoretical labour that goes into the production of international law's knowledge-products lies the process of conceptual appropriation—mental transformation of externally obtained data—in the context of which the practitioners of the discipline, by employing the various theoretical

[45] The aim here, as Jameson notes, is not to 'abandon ... the formal level [of the foundational problematic] for something extrinsic to it—such as some inertly social "content"—but [to grasp its] formal patterns as a symbolic enactment of the social within the formal ...whereby real social contradictions, insurmountable in their own terms, find a purely formal resolution in the [theoretical] realm'. Jameson (n 44) 63–64.

apparatuses and analytical protocols approved within the disciplinary economy, process the objective reality of the international legal system and its history with a view to converting it into the above-mentioned totality of insights, hypotheses, policy prescriptions, etc. The process of this conceptual appropriation is socially embedded within the institutional landscape of the international law profession, the central role in which is played by the profession's academic segment. It is also structured, thematically and narratologically, by the discipline's foundational problematic, ie that basic set of unresolvable disagreements and interminable contestations an enduring preoccupation with which keeps the academic discourse of international law going and ensures its relative coherence across space and time.

Inasmuch as the discipline's foundational problematic remains relatively general—and the implications of each of its constituent contestations therefore remains indeterminate—this enables the emergence of second-order theoretical contestations aimed at rearranging the general taxonomy of the discipline's theoretical apparatuses, analytical protocols, research agendas, etc. As different schools, traditions, and movements struggle to impose their respective visions in the process of this second-order theoretical struggle, the conflict between these visions turn into the motor of intra-disciplinary politics.

Because of the institutional significance of the profession's academic segment, the course of this second-order theoretical struggle not only reflects the broader institutional landscape of modern legal academia, but is also fundamentally overdetermined by its standard social forms and socialization protocols: research-led teaching, standardized educational curricula, graduate training programmes, specialist publications, academic conferences, etc. As a field of intellectual inquiry, the discipline of international law, thus, constitutes (i) a hypostasized sublimation of the *collective struggle* over the basic terms of the discipline's general agenda, apparatuses, protocols, and, ultimately, foundational problematic; (ii) that is structured, enabled, and embedded within the broader *institutional landscape* of modern legal academia and realized through self-propelling *second-order theoretical skirmishes* between distinct *scholarly groups and collectivities* that are (iii) dressed in the garb of *first-order theoretical interventions*, scholarly writings, substantive legal debates, etc.

At the most abstract level, the ultimate prize of all intra-disciplinary politics thus defined, can be described as the *power of localized world-making*: the ability to determine the general parameters of disciplinary imagination, ie to shape what after the Indian-American anthropologist Arjun Appadurai we may call the basic *ideoscape*[46] of the international law profession—the structure of values, beliefs, and expectations about how the international law profession should imagine and experience itself and the world around it, how it can self-organize as a community,

[46] Arjun Appadurai, *Modernity at Large* (University of Minnesota Press 1996) 33–36.

what terms of social contract it can offer to its different members, what labour divisions it can recognize, what identitarian categories it can make available to its different members, etc.

Note the reference to the idea of sublimation invoked earlier: since the 'economic' and 'political' realities of the discipline's internal collective life are refracted through multiple layers of Feuerbachian alienation, very few international law scholars have any reason to experience their day-to-day professional existence in precisely these terms. Even at their most self-reflective, what they will usually recognize as the ultimate goal of their disciplinary work will be the competition for the various *localized congealments of this abstract power*—or what in Marxian terms one would call fetishes—such as the membership of hiring committees, editorial control over leading publications, the disbursement of research grants, or the examination of doctoral theses. Each of these fetishes can be ultimately understood as a certain kind of *political resource* that can be used in the struggle for intra-disciplinary theoretical supremacy, or, which is essentially the same thing, as a form of *social capital* that is valorized within the discipline's internal economy. The important thing to bear in mind, however, is that the conquest or accumulation of each of these resources, in the final analysis, only constitutes a means to an end.

11

Reflections on the International Telecommunication Union: International Organizations as Epistemic Structures

Jan Klabbers

I Introduction

The law of international organizations is in a state of confusion, and has been so for quite some time.[1] This can most likely be traced back to a fundamental ambivalence inherent in the very concept of international organization: part vehicle for member states (or agent for a collective principal), and part independent and autonomous actor. Or, put differently, part platform for political debate and negotiations between states, and part managerial authority. The diagnosis as such is far from novel;[2] nor is the observation that the concept of international organization may slowly be moving away from a conception of international organizations as vehicles towards a conception emphasizing the relative autonomy of international organizations—autonomy from their members, at any rate.[3]

If the diagnosis has been around for some time, remedies have remained out of reach: discussions on such topics as the accountability of international organizations[4] suggest that the discipline still needs to develop an appropriate theoretical framework. The framework that has been in place for about a century, developed by scholars such as Paul Reinsch,[5] is inadequate, as accountability for the better

[1] Jan Klabbers, 'The EJIL Foreword: The Transformation of International Organizations Law' (2015) 26 *European Journal of International Law* 9.

[2] Jan Klabbers, 'Two Concepts of International Organization' (2005) 2 *International Organizations Law Review* 277; Catherine M Brölmann, *The Institutional Veil in Public International Law* (Hart Publishing 2007).

[3] Richard Collins and Nigel White (eds), *International Organizations and the Idea of Autonomy: Institutional Independence in the International Legal Order* (Routledge 2011); Jan Klabbers and Panos Koutrakos (eds), *An Anatomy of Autonomy* (2019) 88 *Nordic Journal of International Law* 1.

[4] A recent example is Carla Ferstman, *International Organizations and the Fight for Accountability: The Remedies and Reparations Gap* (Oxford University Press 2017).

[5] Paul S Reinsch, *Public International Unions, Their Work and Organization: A Study in International Administrative Law* (McGinn 1911); for discussion see Jan Klabbers, 'The Emergence of Functionalism in International Institutional Law: Colonial Inspirations' (2014) 25 *European Journal of International Law* 645.

Jan Klabbers, *Reflections on the International Telecommunication Union: International Organizations as Epistemic Structures* In: *International Law's Invisible Frames.* Edited by: Andrea Bianchi and Moshe Hirsch, Oxford University Press. © Jan Klabbers 2021. DOI: 10.1093/oso/9780192847539.003.0012

part remains firmly outside the relations between the organization and its member states. As a result, the accountability of those member states becomes an issue, while relegating the accountability of the organization itself to the background—the latter remains out of reach.[6] And the law, owing to this structural and inadequate concentration on relations with member states, has little to say about the increasing encounter with the private sector (which can take on a variety of forms),[7] or the largely novel development of relations among and between international organizations.[8]

This chapter proposes a different perspective on international organizations, viewing them as political actors and sites of political struggle between states as well as others. And it hopes to do this by zooming in on knowledge production by international organizations, as such a perspective, more than traditional perspectives on 'law-making', can lay bare gaps in our current knowledge and understanding, while simultaneously shedding some light on what has hitherto remained largely in the shade.

One delimitation and one caveat are in order. My interest resides primarily not with the knowledge that is being produced, nor with the way it is produced (not primarily, at any rate), but rather with the production and work of the *machinery* of knowledge production[9] and, as an international lawyer, with the role played in that process by the law: how does international law (including, for present purposes, the internal rules of organizations[10]) help to structure the knowledge production machinery of international organizations, and how does the work of international organizations feed back into legal thinking about international organizations? These are mainly, it must be pointed out, ideational developments, active on the level of ideas about the law rather than immediately visible as part of the law itself, but for that no less forceful.

[6] This applies, in different ways, to early studies, such as Matthias Hartwig, *Die Haftung der Mitgliedstaaten für internationale Organisationen* (Springer 1993); Moshe Hirsch, *The Responsibility of International Organizations Toward Third Parties: Some Basic Principles* (Martinus Nijhoff 1995); and more recent work such as Ana Sofia Barros, *Governance as Responsibility: Member States as Human Rights Protectors in International Financial Institutions* (Cambridge University Press 2019).

[7] But see Gian Luca Burci, 'Public/Private Partnerships in the Public Health Sector' (2009) 6 *International Organizations Law Review* 359; Jan Klabbers, 'Notes on the Ideology of International Organizations Law: The International Organization for Migration, State-making, and the Market for Migration' (2019) 32 *Leiden Journal of International Law* 383; a useful political science study is Liliana Andonova, *Governance Entrepeneurs: International Organizations and the Rise of Global Public-Private Partnerships* (Cambridge University Press 2017).

[8] Laurence Boisson de Chazournes, *Interactions between Regional and Universal Organizations: A Legal Perspective* (Martinus Nijhoff 2017); Evelyne Lagrange, 'Les relations entre les organisations internationales' in Michele Vellamo (ed), *Il futuro delle organizzazioni internazionali: prospettive giuridiche* (Editoriale Scientifica 2015); Jan Klabbers, 'Transforming Institutions: Autonomous International Organisations in Institutional Theory' (2017) 6 *Cambridge International Law Journal* 105.

[9] This draws on Karin Knorr-Cetina, *Epistemic Cultures: How the Sciences Make Knowledge* (Harvard University Press 1999) 11.

[10] On this distinction see Lorenzo Gasbarri, 'The Dual Legality of the Rules of International Organizations' (2017) 14 *International Organizations Law Review* 87.

The caveat is this: while I draw to some extent on sociological theorizing as far as knowledge production goes, I am not aiming either to demonstrate the utility or veracity of one approach over another, nor am I particularly keen on textual exegesis of the great sociologists or philosophers. My microscope, to put it bluntly, is trained on international organizations, not on the writings of Michel Foucault, or Pierre Bourdieu, or Antonio Gramsci, or Bruno Latour, although the attentive reader will probably recognize traces here and there. I am not interested, for present purposes, in establishing whether Latour is more useful than Foucault, or whether Bourdieu was right.[11] Moreover, when such authorities are invoked in legal work they end up doing fairly little work, and are used mostly by way of quasi-intellectual veneer. I have little interest, for present purposes, in adding to that particular practice, although a sociologist of science might have a field day with the uses and abuses of Foucault and Bourdieu in legal studies. Instead, I wish to find out what international organizations do, and will use an eclectic mix of ideas and insights to help me make sense thereof.

This chapter is structured as follows. In section II, I will lay down some primers regarding knowledge production in bureaucracies, followed in section III by a cursory look at the work of one specific international organization, the International Telecommunication Union (ITU). On the basis thereof, I will develop in section IV the outline of a different approach to international organizations law which, for ease of reference, I will refer to as supra-functionalism.[12] Section V concludes the chapter.

II Constructing Knowledge

Almost a century ago, the well-known historian Carl L. Becker gave a lecture on the seemingly mundane topic of historical facts, pointing out that facts rarely, if ever, speak for themselves. By invoking the incontrovertible example of Julius Caesar crossing the Rubicon in 49 BC, Becker demonstrated three things of great importance. First, facts rarely come alone. Caesar crossed the Rubicon together with a number of soldiers and footmen; to say only that Caesar crossed, while not inaccurate, is rather limited. Secondly, historical facts, when they play out, are facts, not historical. They become historical facts only with hindsight, to be distinguished from all other historical facts, many of which are bound to have been

[11] This follows (perhaps paradoxically) an affinity with Valverde's approach, suggesting that other scholars' analytical tools 'have a dangerous tendency to turn into cookie-cutters', and may become 'short-circuits to thinking'. Mariana Valverde, *Chronotopes of Law: Jurisdiction, Scale and Governance* (Routledge 2015) 87.

[12] This builds on Jan Klabbers, 'International Organizations and the Problem of Privity: Towards a Supra-Functionalist Approach' in George Politakis, Tomi Kohiyama, and Thomas Lieby (eds), *ILO 100: Law for Social Justice* (ILO 2019) 629.

forgotten and thus, while these are facts that have occurred in history, they do not come to be seen as historical facts. Thirdly (and relatedly), as Becker pointed out, facts acquire their meaning over time. Caesar must have crossed other rivers; he may even have crossed the Rubicon on other occasions, but the one that has come to matter is his crossing in the year 49 BC.[13] The point, as Becker emphasized, is that historical facts largely work as symbols of some bigger event, considered to be important. Had today's vocabulary been available a century ago (itself a point worth reflecting on), he would not have hesitated to claim that historical facts are socially constructed.

What applies to historical facts, it may be suggested, applies to knowledge more broadly. Regardless of the attempts by research funding agencies and others engaged in the knowledge industry to insist that there is such a thing as pure science, with facts waiting to be discovered and speaking for themselves if only we look hard and deep enough and generate a paradigm shift or two,[14] reality is somewhat more resilient: philosophers, economists, historians, and sociologists alike[15] have long agreed that reality is, by and large, socially constructed, often through processes that escape direct scrutiny, let alone control.

If this is even remotely accurate, two implications immediately seem to follow with respect to international organizations. First, there can be no objection to international organizations aiming to play a role per se in the construction of social reality, for example, through gathering statistics, measuring performances, suggesting authoritative interpretations, and so on. They have much the same 'right' to engage in such activities as the rest of us, even if the rest of us (unless active as scientists or scholars) tend to construct knowledge inadvertently, often merely just by doing.

Secondly, though, it also follows that the knowledge produced by international organizations is as much suspect as knowledge produced by others, and perhaps even more, precisely because it is often produced on purpose. While our everyday knowledge production is usually fairly random and dispersed, the result of many interactions involving journalists, critics, advertisers, ordinary folk, and even so-called 'influencers' (what's in a name …), not systematically in pursuit of a political agenda, the knowledge production of international organizations, like that of states, will often follow an agenda, in support of someone's political project. With international organizations this involves typically the main function for which the organization was set up (and has to follow; its main *telos*[16]), but this too

[13] Carl L Becker, 'What are Historical Facts?' (1955) 8 *Western Political Quarterly* 327. While not published until 1955, the paper was first presented at a meeting of the American Historical Association in 1926.

[14] The risks of the latter are already sharply outlined by Albert O. Hirschman, 'The Search for Paradigms as Hindrance to Understanding' (1970) 22 *World Politics* 329.

[15] See, for example, John R Searle, *The Construction of Social Reality* (London: Penguin, 1995); Friedrich Kratochwil, *Praxis: On Acting and Knowing* (Cambridge University Press 2018).

[16] Seamas Miller, *The Moral Foundations of Social Institutions* (Cambridge University Press 2010).

is susceptible to varying interpretations and can often accommodate various different approaches. Refugee protection as practised by UNHCR, for instance, has been said to concentrate on *non-refoulement* and immediate relief and assistance, rather than (and perhaps at the expense of) more lasting asylum procedures.[17]

Such literature as exists on how exactly international organizations—or bureaucracies generally—produce knowledge, suggests two relevant concerns, sometimes pulling in opposite directions. On the one hand, bureaucracies are portrayed as sites of political struggle, where 'stakeholders' fight over what gets measured (and what is deemed legally relevant or irrelevant[18]), how it gets measured, whether measurement is a good idea to begin with, and what should happen with measurements. And in the context of international organizations, the relevant stakeholders will include not just representatives from member states, but also the organization's secretariat, outside experts such as academics brought in as advisers, experts from organizations working in related fields or on related topics, and non-governmental organizations. And from within the organization's own setting, the staff involved will be a mixture of substantive experts and those with an understanding of research techniques or data collection methods: statisticians for instance, or economists.[19]

In some organizations, specific substantive expertise is 'built-in' in the organization's architecture: Interpol started life as an organization of police officers; the World Meteorological Organization (WMO) consists by and large of meteorologists as member states' delegates, whereas the International Labour Organization (ILO)'s tripartite structure guarantees that the experiences of labour and capital will somehow be involved. In other organizations, substantive expertise is generally expected on the part of the staff, with the World Health Organization (WHO) employing many doctors and nurses and the World Bank employing many economists.[20]

On the other hand, and perhaps pulling in the opposite direction, bureaucracies (and international organizations are no exception) also are known to work in, well, bureaucratic fashion, meaning broadly speaking that reports will beget further reports. Often the language of reports is mimetic (ie copy-pasted from earlier reports), as mimetic language reduces the chances of 'rocking the boat' or 'waking up sleeping dogs'. Those who write reports might be reluctant to take a position; their

[17] Ingo Venzke, *How Interpretation Makes International Law: On Semantic Change and Normative Twists* (Oxford University Press 2012).

[18] Fleur Johns, *Non-Legality in International Law: Unruly Law* (Cambridge University Press 2013).

[19] Kevin Davis and others (eds), *Governance by Indicators* (Oxford University Press 2012); Sally Engle Merry, *The Seduction of Quantification* (University of Chicago Press 2016); Ole Jacob Sending, *The Politics of Expertise: Competing for Authority in Global Governance* (University of Michigan Press 2017); Annabelle Littoz-Monnet (ed), *The Politics of Expertise in International Organizations: How International Bureaucracies Produce and Mobilize Knowledge* (Routledge 2017).

[20] This is by no means always the case, however: one will find few labourers in the ILO Secretariat; few refugees in UNHCR, and migrants working at the International Organization for Migration (IOM) will for the better part be highly educated expats.

bosses most likely are reluctant too, up to and including the political leadership. And such change as is anticipated tends to be mostly verbal and, ultimately, somewhat marginal, a disposition well-recorded in the (fictional) dialogue recorded by Shirley Hazzard. When asked whether she was busy, an official at an imaginary international organization answered in the affirmative, and proceeded: 'We're finishing up the report on Methods of Enforcement.' 'How is it this year?' 'A much stronger preamble than the last issue. And some pretty tough recommendations in Appendix III.'[21]

This picture is confirmed in the work of International Relations scholar cum anthropologist Iver Neumann. Having spent a considerable amount of time working for Norway's Foreign Ministry, Neumann observes that, when left to their own devices, 'administrations are wont to continue doing what they have always done.'[22] Perhaps in part as a result, he suggests that cooperation with other ministries should be seen to be someone else's initiative, allowing the bureaucracy to position itself as being responsive to a demand but without assuming responsibility for any activism. Beyond this, official positions must be untraceable to individuals (individual voices must be drowned out), and repeated rather than questioned or interrogated or deepened, something Neumann is mildly sympathetic (or ironic, perhaps?) towards: 'Making the world seem stable when it is in fact in constant flux means that wielding power involves the ability to freeze meaning.'[23]

International organizations not only produce knowledge by gathering and collecting information. They also create a loop by informing their member states about what constitute 'best practices', by setting 'benchmarks', by distilling their knowledge into codes of conduct or guidelines, and asking those member states to report back. In some respects, this is a classic technique, aimed at getting the member states to follow a particular course of behaviour without exercising formal law-making powers. Some of the classic international organizations already deploy variations on the technique: for example, in the ILO member states are under an obligation to report on the steps they have taken to secure ratification of conventions adopted under ILO auspices,[24] and how they respond to recommendations adopted by the ILO plenary.[25] As we shall shortly see, the ITU has opened up categories of membership for companies and academic institutions.[26]

[21] Shirley Hazzard, *People in Glass Houses* (Picador 1964) 38. In Hazzard's collection of stories, the organization concerned is never identified, other than (in Orwellian terms) as The Organization. However, it is widely believed to be modelled after the United Nations.

[22] Iver B Neumann, *At Home with the Diplomats: Inside a European Foreign Ministry* (Cornell University Press 2012) 46.

[23] ibid 78–80.

[24] ILO Constitution, art 19(5)(c).

[25] ibid art 19(6)(c).

[26] There is no claim here that the ITU is in any way representative for the genus of international organizations. My interest is piqued, instead, by a combination of factors: it is one of the oldest organizations around; it deals with a sector at the vanguard of technological development; and it has been subjected to little legal discussion. Hence, in part this is a self-indulgent exercise: I wanted to look at the ITU because I wanted to learn about it.

III An Excursion: A Bird's Eye View of the ITU

The ITU was set up as early as 1865, as one of the first of the public unions. Once it transpired that trade and commerce were opening up in the 1850s and 1860s,[27] and once it became clear that communication was a vital element, the ITU was created to regulate and manage telegraphic communications. It standardized the use of a version of Morse code, making communications across the globe possible, and played a vital role in what has been dubbed the first telecommunications revolution: companies rallied around the ITU, and its existence prompted governments to harmonize their telegraph systems and harmonize their policies. The ITU helped governments to complete the public works necessary for global commerce, as Murphy puts it.[28] This was all the more useful as governments were concerned about security (telegraphs could communicate in real time), and initially reluctant to invest in telegraph networks, let alone to spread the technology. While the cables spread across the globe, the knowledge and equipment stayed within largely British hands.[29]

With telegraphs becoming outdated, the ITU 'came to allocate radio spectrum and devise procedures for international phone calls',[30] and following the absorption of the younger International Radio Telegraph Union (IRU), the ITU changed its name into International Telecommunication Union in 1937.[31] For many years the United States (US) officially stayed outside; its telecommunications operators, including telegraph lines, tended to be privately owned, while those in Europe tended to be public entities, giving rise to divergent philosophies. Nonetheless, it often participated as observer, and eventually joined the ITU in 1932. The ITU currently boasts 193 member states—exactly as many as the United Nations, of which it is a specialized agency. Until 1947, the ITU was effectively run by Switzerland with Swiss directors, almost invariably trained as engineers or natural scientists. This scientific orientation continued after the Second World War. The post of director-general (which had replaced the earlier 'director') was no longer a Swiss prerogative, but most of the directors-general have been trained as engineers or natural scientists, with two exceptions in the form of Argentina's Marco Aurelio Andrade and Japan's Yoshio Utsumi, both trained as lawyers who ran the ITU for a combined period of a little over a decade.

[27] Ben Wilson, *Heyday: The 1850s and the Dawn of the Global Age* (Weidenfeld & Nicolson 2016).

[28] Craig Murphy, *International Organization and Industrial Change: Global Governance since 1850* (Polity 1994) 85.

[29] Daniel R Headrick, *The Invisible Weapon: Telecommunications and International Politics 1851-1845* (Oxford University Press 1991) 46.

[30] Emily S Rosenberg, *Transnational Currents in a Shrinking World 1870-1945* (Harvard University Press 2012) 15.

[31] Bob Reinalda, *Routledge History of International Organizations: From 1815 to the Present Day* (Routledge 2009) 88; Reinalda notes that the IRU allowed for much stronger private sector representation than the ITU.

The scientific orientation is reflected in the ITU's practice and its composition. Its practice has been, since the start in 1865, to have member state delegations include technical experts, in addition to diplomatic representatives.[32] Next to its 193 member states, it has embraced representatives of industry and academia as well. Its platinum sector members are a number of companies including Microsoft, Intel, Orange, and Verizon, as well as public sector entities (the EU, for one). Another group of companies, including Apple, Nokia, Viasat, and Facebook are listed as gold sector members, as is the Bill and Melinda Gates Foundation. The difference is one of participation: the ITU has three broad departments ('sectors'), and while gold sector members participate in two of these three, platinum sector members participate in all three; it is also possible to participate in one sector only. In addition to member states and sector members, there is also a category of 'associate members' (again possibly in one, two, or all three sectors), whereas academic institutions (universities, research institutes) can be members in their own right. The result is a huge network of states, research institutions, and private entities (193 states, some 700 others). Since 1994, sector members (ie private industry, for the better part) may formally participate in ITU decision-making, a position solidified in the ITU Constitution in 1998.[33]

The ITU has a complicated legal structure, not only in terms of membership but also in terms of governance. At the apex stands the Constitution of the ITU, with further relevant instruments being the Convention on the ITU and Administrative Regulations, in this hierarchical order.[34] Membership, as noted, comprises both states and sector members, and the three sectors effectively function as distinct pillars with their own organs, which in turn entails the need also to have common organs. Moreover, within each sector, there are two plenaries envisaged: the regular assembly, and the more incidental world conference, with both typically having overlapping competences, in that (in the radio communications sector, by way of example) both the assembly and the conference can decide on amendment of the Radio Regulations; their meetings can also overlap or coincide, or be kept separate. The one main difference is that conferences can only be attended, as a formal matter, by member state delegates; assemblies are also open to observers defined in the Constitution.[35] And that sounds stricter than it is, in that committee meetings at conferences can (with some exceptions) also be attended by observers.[36]

The Constitution of the ITU oozes a technical, professional atmosphere. Not only have most of the directors and directors-general been trained in engineering

[32] Reinsch (n 5) 16.

[33] Ian Walden, 'International Telecommunications Law, the Internet and the Regulation of Cyberspace' in Katharina Ziolkowski (ed), *Peacetime Regime for State Activities in Cyberspace; International Law, International Relations and Diplomacy* (NATO CCD COE 2013) 268–69.

[34] ITU Constitution, art 4. From the very beginning, a distinction was made between the overarching document and a more technical *règlement*; the vocabulary has changed, but the idea has remained.

[35] ITU Convention, art 25.

[36] See General Rules of Conferences, Assemblies and Meetings of the Union, rule 13.

or the natural sciences, it is also the case that arguably the main standard-setting organ of the ITU, the Radio Regulation Board, needs to be composed of individuals with the relevant professional backgrounds. The Constitution insists, for example, that while members of the Radio Regulation board are elected, these elected members—at most two handfuls—are 'thoroughly qualified in the field of radiocommunications and possessing practical experience in the assignment and utilization of frequencies'.[37] Those members, moreover, are supposed to be as apolitical as humanly possible; they shall not take instructions from any government or any organization, and shall serve 'as custodians of an international public trust'.[38] This aligns with the general idea that the public has a right to use telecommunications, and that services, charges, and safeguards shall be provided without discrimination: they 'shall be the same for all users in each category of correspondence without any priority or preference'.[39] While formal decision-making powers rest with the plenaries, the Board nonetheless does the preparatory work, and as such exercises considerable influence, also given that it functions as an appeals board to appeal frequency assignments done by the Radiocommunication Bureau. Like all Administrative Regulations in the ITU, once adopted, the Radio Regulations are binding on the organization's entire membership.

In addition to the Radio Regulation board (there is no equivalent in the two other sectors), in the Radiocommunication sector there are also active so-called study groups, an advisory group, and a bureau.[40] Their functions, as spelled out in the Convention (the second-level instrument, following the Constitution) are of a technical nature, so much so that members of these study groups who lack a technical background will mostly feel lost, even though some of the work also is of a public administration nature.

The most open-ended of the three, by its very nature, is the Development sector, and it should come as no surprise that here the ITU is at its most adventurous, or most proactive perhaps. In this sector, the ITU works hard to come to terms with in particular cyber-related issues, occupying itself with, for example, cybersecurity, e-waste, digital inclusion, digital broadcasting, and network development. Naturally, this shades into questions of internet governance, formally the province of other actors, most obviously perhaps the private not-for-profit Internet Corporation for Assigned Names and Numbers (ICANN). Indeed, in the corridors some grumblings can occasionally be heard about the ITU taking on more than it should and stepping on the toes of other relevant actors.[41]

If the global business world and its captains of industry meet annually in Davos, Switzerland, to discuss the state of the global economy, the ITU organizes its own

[37] ITU Constitution, art 14(1).
[38] ibid art 14(3).
[39] ibid art 33; at this point, it might help to remember that the ITU is a specialized agency of the UN.
[40] The other two pillars are similarly structured.
[41] See also Walden (n 33).

equivalent, ITU Telecom World, in a different location every year, the 2020 event having been scheduled to take place in Hanoi.[42] The event brings member states together with industry people, including many small and medium-sized enterprises, government ministers, representatives of other international organizations, and so on. The meeting's agenda is filled not just with substantive panel discussions, but also with many so-called 'networking events', typically hosted by a company or a government, and typically billed as opportunities to relax, make new connections, and exchange views. The official programme of ITU Telecom World 2019, which took place in Budapest, showed some five to eight networking events (sometimes overlapping) for every full day of the meeting, and this of course does not take into account the informal meetings in corridors, over drinks, and over dinner, that take place outside the formal programme. In essence, therefore, ITU Telecom World offers broad opportunities for epistemic cultures to manifest themselves.

All in all, a picture emerges of the ITU as an organization which has long said goodbye to top-down management and public authority asserting power over everyone else; instead, authority is manufactured in the ITU through its bringing together of member states, sectoral members, and academia, and through the events, including the networking events, taking place every year at ITU Telecom World. This is not the international organization as a steering group; instead, the ITU carefully sustains an image as facilitator, bringing various 'stakeholders' (technical experts in addition to politicians and business leaders, or perhaps technical experts *as* politicians and business leaders) together and involving them in planning, decision-making, and dissemination.

The ITU has certain law-making powers, in that its Administrative Regulations, including the Radio Regulations, are binding on all members, and all members should make sure also that non-government entities within their jurisdiction respect them.[43] The use of these powers is, however, relatively sparse, it seems. The idea behind radio regulations goes back a long time, and used to be part of the *raison d'être* of the ITU, no doubt, so it is no surprise that such regulations are currently in force. This also follows from their functional logic: these are practical, concrete instruments concerning the allocation of costs and benefits; it would be impossible to promulgate them in any other form than as 'distribution imperatives'.[44]

However, this is not where the lawyer's interest should stop. Many of the ITU's standard-setting activities are made available in the form of handbooks and the like. Over the years, the ITU has published a large number of handbooks on topics as diverse as spectrum monitoring, radiowave propagation, digital sound broadcasting, mobile-satellite services, digital radio-relay systems, wireless access,

[42] It was rescheduled in light of the Covid-19 crisis, and should take place in 2021.

[43] ITU Constitution arts 4(3), 6(2).

[44] I adapt the term from Roberts, who speaks of commands of the type 'Do X' as 'action imperatives': see Robert C Roberts, 'Virtues and Rules' (1991) 51 *Philosophy and Phenomenological Research* 325.

digital terrestrial television broadcasting, mobile systems, marinized terrestrial cables, telecommunications and network security, emergency telecommunications, internet-protocol based technologies, and much, much else besides.

The conclusion is nigh-on inescapable: the ITU works much like a domestic regulatory agency would, gathering information and interest from a number of stakeholders considered relevant, digesting these into some kind of outcome, and promulgating them under the same stakeholders, whose participation almost guarantees that they feel they have a commitment to implement. The use of regulatory legal instruments in such circumstances is almost superfluous, and to the extent that the ITU wants to formalize things, it can utilize the still fairly informal instrument of the recommendation.

While some of these recommendations are short and to the point, especially when dealing with a specific and limited topic (for instance, internet access for Palestinian refugees), many are long and winding, with their preambles making up the lion's share of the text. Such befits, of course, the non-legally binding instrument to some extent, but there is more to it, or so it seems. The long and meandering preambles again make it possible to give a voice to the most wide-ranging opinions and interests, culminating eventually, after all things have been 'considered', the meeting has 'noted' the relevant circumstances, and is 'mindful' of all concerns, in a limited *dispositif* (if that is the right word to use in a non-legally binding context), often consisting of a few instructions or requests to the relevant ITU organs.

It is abundantly clear, in other words, that the ITU does not rely on the classic instrument of 'hard law', a term not characterized by much precision but often used, since the 1970s, as the opposite of 'soft law'. Yet, soft law has not proven to be a very useful term either, for the good reason that it redescribes a poorly understood phenomenon by using a poorly understood term, therewith at best shifting the discussion but not adding to understanding. Instead, it might be more illuminating to suggest the ITU is using epistemic authority, in both the passive and active senses of the term.[45]

Passively, much of the authority of the ITU stems from the circumstance that it gathers, collects, and produces knowledge through its sectoral and academic members, through its ITU Telecom World events, and through is openness to voices and opinions from industry, regulators, and scientists. The ITU is highly unlikely to adopt or voice opinions which do not have a proper scientific basis, even on a conceptually pluralist notion of science. To put it graphically, the chances of the ITU adopting the sort of politicized nonsense that sometimes prevails at politicized bodies such as the UN General Assembly (think of the infamous 'zionism is racism' resolution) are slender to non-existent; cooler heads will prevail, because the system is geared towards involving cooler heads. That is not to say the ITU

[45] This builds on the framework developed in Jan Klabbers, 'The Normative Gap in International Organizations Law: The Case of the WHO' (2019) 16 *International Organizations Law Review* 272.

is apolitical: quite the opposite. As noted, some are disgruntled by its forays into cyber-related issues, and scientists and engineers are not always known for their political or social sensibilities. Politics can also be spotted in the fact that the plight of the Palestinians is a recurring agenda item, in various forms, and the organization is dedicated to such things as gender equality, and development.

As far as active epistemic authority goes, the ITU also promulgates much of its opinions through epistemic mechanisms, exercising epistemic authority. As noted, the standard legal form is rarely used by the ITU; much authority takes the form of handbooks and similar tools, and is then disseminated at ITU Telecom World events; and those forms can be as effective as, or even more effective than, the standard legal form. An indication, moreover, is that the dispute settlement mechanism of the ITU is sketched in the briefest of terms.[46] Where with other international organizations dispute settlement is a lengthy and detailed affair, this is not the case in the ITU—a clear sign that few serious legal problems are expected.

In short, like so many international organizations, the ITU receives knowledge, builds knowledge, and promulgates knowledge. That knowledge is, like all knowledge, inherently contestable, and reflects a view on the world, in this case a view developed together by states, industry, and the academy. Many are involved in the process, with the result that few will object to specific emanations. Thus, the irony is that the ITU stands for both apolitical, scientific knowledge, and simultaneously stands for highly politicized knowledge, the sort of knowledge produced by deliberative procedure. Yet, the old adage 'a camel is a horse designed by a committee' does not seem to apply: most of the committee members seem to sing from the same hymn sheet. And this, as Foucault and Gramsci might emphasize, only means that authority (or power) is very effectively exercised—so effectively as to generate little dissent.

IV The Law: Towards Supra-functionalism

Throughout its history, the ITU's work has had important distributive ramifications. In the late 19th century, it made sure that telegraph cables would spread across the globe, but that knowledge remained in the hands of a small, largely British, elite. In the first decades of the 20th century, it distributed radio frequencies, followed later by creating a regime for the distribution of slots in the geostationary satellite orbit. While the US and the United Kingdom (UK), with the support of a few other Western states, favoured a first-come, first-served approach, secure in the knowledge that their technological supremacy would give them pole

[46] Article 56 sketches a general obligation to settle disputes peacefully. Article 41 of the ITU Convention provides a procedure, which is amplified a little for parties to an optional protocol on dispute settlement.

position, the developing countries (and quite a few developed ones) opted for distribution on a more rational, central-planning basis. And later still, the ITU addressed demands from the developing nations for technical assistance and similar initiatives.[47]

Another truly remarkable aspect of the ITU is the configuration of private sector representation. If the WHO is known for its participation in 'public-private partnerships' and the ILO for its 'tripartite structure', the ITU stands out by the private sector representation in the form of sectoral members, be it (like airline loyalty schemes) platinum, gold, or otherwise. It turns out the ITU and its members can be characterized as a large epistemic community, and in this epistemic community the voices of the private sector can make certain they will be heard.[48] Put differently, the chances of the ITU these days adopting a strongly managerial, central planning type of attitude towards the regulation of telecommunications seem slender; the private sector representation would make clear that such a change would meet with strong resistance—if it would survive initial debate to begin with.

And a third remarkable aspect is that while its formal law-making powers are limited, it nonetheless seems to exercise great authority, through the publication of handbooks and similar instruments, and by organizing the annual telecommunication jamboree in the form of ITU Telecom World. In so doing, the ITU also displays the active variant of epistemic authority, promulgating behaviour deemed desirable through techniques other than formal legal instruments.

None of this makes any sense in terms of the traditional categories and concepts of international organizations law, such as it is.[49] If international organizations are understood as agents exercising delegated powers, powers delegated by their member states—as in the traditional, functionalist conception—then strictly speaking, there is no knowledge production taking place in or by international organizations, except to the extent that those organizations are empowered (have been endowed with the competence) to conduct studies, collect information, and related activities. On this conception, international organizations are little else but collective data clearing houses, gathering information on behalf of their collective member states.

Such a conception assumes rather too much. It assumes, amongst other things, that knowledge is a single product, which can be gathered or not: the idea that the same objects may look differently to different observers, with all of them looking in good faith through their own spectacles, has no place in this traditional conception.

[47] For a relatively early discussion see George A Codding Jr, 'The International Telecommunication Union' in Paul Taylor and AJR Groom (eds), *International Institutions at Work* (Pinter 1988).

[48] On epistemic communities see Andrea Bianchi, 'Epistemic Communities' in Jean d'Aspremont and Sahib Singh (eds), *Concepts for International Law: Contributions to Disciplinary Thought* (Edward Elgar Publishing 2019) 251.

[49] Jan Klabbers, 'The Paradox of International Institutional Law' (2008) 5 *International Organizations Law Review* 151.

And it has no place because, as data clearing house, the international organization's task here is to help inform policy-making, the policy-making of those member states. Conceptual pluralism, as philosophers sometimes refer to the same object being seen in different, and equally valid, ways, is far removed from such a conception.[50] And what applies to objects applies even more strongly to data, which, by their very nature, require interpretation: economic figures, migration statistics, or environmental projections.

The traditional picture also assumes that international organizations do little with their knowledge themselves, other than producing and storing it. And yet, international organizations are also often chided for telling member states what to do, for exercising normative authority over their member states, despite having only limited formalized law-making powers. In other words, there is something of a serious normative gap inherent in the traditional conception of international organizations.[51]

A third key assumption underlying the traditional conception relates to acceptance of the authority of international organizations. With international organizations being depicted as exercising delegated powers, it logically follows that their authority need only be accepted on a consensual basis, when law-making authority has been explicitly granted. The organization, on this idea, cannot make law except when empowered to do so, and its authority can only derive from acts of consent, typically expressed in the form of joining an organization: by joining, its law-making powers are consented to.

In short, international organizations do far more, both in terms of collecting knowledge and spreading knowledge, than the traditional conception would allow for. Put like this, the traditional conception sounds rather inadequate; yet, despite this, it is still immensely popular, acting much like international ideology.[52] Most international lawyers are socialized into thinking about international organizations along these lines, with the leading treatises reproducing this conception.[53] And much the same applies to writings in international relations, where so-called 'realists' only see institutions providing 'false promises',[54] if they think of them at all, while 'institutionalists' view international organizations predominantly as

[50] Hilary Putnam, *Ethics without Ontology* (Harvard University Press 2004).

[51] For further exploration see Klabbers (n 45).

[52] Jan Klabbers, 'What Role for International Organizations in the Promotion of Community Interests? Reflections on the Ideology of Functionalism' in Eyal Benvenisti and Georg Nolte (eds), *Community Interests Across International Law* (Oxford University Press 2018).

[53] HG Schermers and Niels M Blokker, *International Institutional Law: Unity Within Diversity* (6th edn, Martinus Nijhoff 2018); CF Amerasinghe, *Principles of the Institutional Law of International Organizations* (2nd edn, Cambridge University Press 2005).

[54] Seminal is John J Mearsheimer, 'The False Promise of International Institutions' (1994) 19 *International Security* 5.

vehicles for their member states,[55] thus again reproducing and fortifying the traditional conception.

A more accurate legal understanding of international organizations can only be gained by adopting a different conception and formulating a different theory about their functioning on the basis thereof, as the excursion into the work of the ITU suggests. Functionalism, the traditional theory governing the legal existence and operations of international organizations, is inadequate on a number of key points.[56] First formulated in the late 19th and early 20th centuries, it has served international organizations well, and continues to do so—as ideology.[57] But as an explanatory theory it needs at the very least to be updated.

A more accurate theory of international organizations should pay far more attention to the 'organization' element in the term international organization. Usually, what is emphasized is the 'international', but that is insufficient: it leaves unanswered why the particular organizational form was chosen (and thus preferred over alternative modes of cooperation), and asking this question suggests that there is some appeal to that particular form. This is no surprise: humanity has since time immemorial created institutions, and as institutional economists (who themselves rarely look at international organizations) teach us, these typically perform three generic tasks: they regulate, they manage, and they allocate costs and benefits.[58]

This applies at all levels, and regardless of whether institutions are public or private in nature—although emphases may differ. The local welfare office will regulate, manage, and allocate; the local chess club regulates, manages, and allocates; Harvard University regulates, manages, and allocates, and so do the Catholic Church, the League of European Research Universities (LERU), the Union of European Football Associations (UEFA), the International Olympic Committee (IOC), and the United Nations (UN). Many of these larger ones are composed of smaller organizations, and thus constitute so-called 'meta-organizations'. International organizations are institutions and, as such, they play an autonomous political role, independent from their member states. These may retain the formal power to dissolve the organization, but this is a power that is historically used only in rare circumstances.

[55] It says a great deal about this approach that a recent study could portray a departure from the traditional conception as revolutionary: Tana Johnson, *Organizational Progeny* (Oxford University Press 2014).

[56] Jan Klabbers, 'Theorising International Organisations' in Anne Orford and Florian Hoffmann (eds), *The Oxford Handbook of the Theory of International Law* (Oxford University Press 2016).

[57] To paraphrase Neufeld, functionalism 'has validated its truth-claims by demonstrating its ability to guide … policy-making … [it] is 'true' because it has met the needs of the policy-makers'; see Mark Neufeld, *The Restructuring of International Relations Theory* (Cambridge University Press 1995) 55.

[58] Douglass C North, *Institutions, Institutional Change and Economic Performance* (Cambridge University Press 1990); Elinor Ostrom, *Governing the Commons: The Evolution of Institutions for Collective Action* (Cambridge University Press 1990); Jon Elster, *Local Justice* (Russell Sage Foundation 1992).

The costs and benefits at issue can be material or financial in nature, as discussions over 'net contributions' to the EU over past decades have made clear. But often enough, they can also be more in the nature of values, including recognition. The reason why North Macedonia and Albania are keen to join the same EU is not only because they expect direct financial gain—although it is that too, probably—but mainly also that membership of the EU would mean recognition as legitimate states in Europe, legitimate members of the political community constituted by the EU. And Brexit signifies the United Kingdom's conviction (fallacious though it may be) that it does not need such continued recognition, and that the United Kingdom is no longer interested in being part of that particular political community. It is for much the same reason (recognition) that Kosovo in recent years was keen to join the Permanent Court of Arbitration (PCA) and the World Customs Organization (WCO); and why Palestine wanted to become a member of the PCA and United Nations Educational, Scientific and Cultural Organization (UNESCO), and made an unsuccessful bid to join the UN. Among the benefits international organizations can provide is that of according political legitimacy, and that can be of far greater interest than direct material concerns.

A useful accompanying step entails expanding the circle of 'subjects' of the output of international organizations. It is customary, going back to the late 19th century,[59] to think of international organizations as affecting only their member states, but this too is no longer tenable—if it ever was. Historically, it transpires that many organizations owe their existence to private initiatives, perhaps none more famously so than the World Intellectual Property Organization (WIPO), whose predecessors owed much to the zealous advocacy of writers interested in international protection of their own work, among them Victor Hugo and Louisa May Alcott. It is also well documented that the newly created World Trade Organization (WTO), set up in 1995 and covering dispute settlement on intellectual property, owed much to lobbying by the US pharmaceutical industry and Hollywood.[60] Intriguingly, moreover, the Universal Postal Union (UPU), while owing much to the frustrations of US postmaster general Montgomery Blair, vented in 1862, illustrates the connection between organizations and the private sector in exemplary fashion.[61] In 2018, President Trump announced US withdrawal from the UPU, inspired mainly by the circumstance that postal rates within the UPU (so-called terminal dues) worked to the disadvantage of US companies. This resulted in an emergency meeting of the UPU's governing body, which in 2019 reached a compromise: more attractive rates for US companies, and thus Trump revoked his

[59] Emblematic is Louis Renault, 'Les unions internationales: leurs avantages at leurs inconvénients' (1896) 3 *Revue Générale de Droit International Public* 14.

[60] Susan K Sell, *Private Power, Public Law: The Globalization of Intellectual Property Rights* (Cambridge University Press 2003).

[61] See John F Sly, 'The Genesis of the Universal Postal Union' (1927) 233 *International Reconciliation* 393.

withdrawal. The point, which should be obvious, is that none of this would make any sense without including the private sector and private forces into the analysis.

A further step would be to subject the epistemic authority of international organizations to legal analysis. It is through authority that costs and benefits are often allocated, and circumventing recognizably legal forms ('decisions', 'resolutions') makes it all the more imperative that lawyers do not look away. This kind of authority often replaces the law, and with it also the sort of guarantees associated with the rule of law, and challenges the creativity and alertness of international lawyers. The very nature of authority has changed—our categories and assumptions should not lag behind.[62]

Organizations are not, contrary to all theoretical assumptions, based solely on impulses from states, and do not, contrary to all theoretical assumptions, work solely at the behest of member states. States are the formal founding fathers, concluding the constituent documents of international organizations, but an analysis which stops there remains limited—to put it charitably. That claim would be akin to suggesting that Hollywood movies are created by their producers to serve the interests of those producers; such a claim is not exactly untrue, but it does omit the roles that directors, writers, actors, and the audience have to play.

In short, the reality of international organizations, embedded as they are in legal structures, can be captured with greater accuracy by a model that allows the observer to look at relations between organizations and their member states, but also beyond,[63] and that views international organizations for the political actors they are, engaged not so much in guaranteeing that 'swords' can turn into 'plowshares' (which is perhaps a tall order for the WMO or the International Olive Council to begin with) but also, and of greater everyday relevance, in regulating and managing behaviour, and allocating costs and benefits.[64]

V By Way of Conclusion

The way knowledge is produced (and disseminated) within the ITU suggests that the existing legal framework governing the existence and operations of

[62] For a brief discussion see Jan Klabbers, 'The Cheshire Cat that is International Law' (2020) 31 *European Journal of International Law* 269.

[63] Organizational sociologists and anthropologists do this to some extent by concentrating on the role of secretariats, organizational culture, and the like, but this often misses the distributive role of international organizations. Insightful works in sociological or anthropological vein include Michael Barnett and Martha Finnemore, *Rules for the World: International Organizations in Global Politics* (Cornell University Press 2004); Richard Harper, 'The Social Organizations of the IMF's Mission Work' in Marilyn Strathern (ed), *Audit Cultures: Anthropological Studies in Accountability, Ethics and the Academy* (Routledge 2000); and Galit A Sarfaty, *Values in Translation: Human Rights and the Culture of the World Bank* (Stanford University Press 2012).

[64] The point refers to the classic by Inis L Claude Jr, *Swords into Plowshares: The Problems and Progress of International Organization* (2nd edn, Random House 1959).

international organizations, as recounted in textbooks and the pages of learned journals, is inadequate. It may (or may not) have been accurate enough in earlier periods—and there is reason to assume that when international organizations were thought only to address states, perhaps the theory was reasonably adequate[65]—but the example of the ITU suggests that the prevailing theory is no longer capable of doing much of the explanatory and conceptual heavy lifting that one might legitimately expect from any academic theory.

It is not the case that the ITU, in the detail of its governance structures and its organizational set-up, can be deemed representative. While other organizations have forms of stakeholder representation, few are as exuberant as the ITU. While other international organizations promulgate standards through epistemic means rather than formal legal instruments, few organize annual events to do so. And while some have made sure to encompass technical expertise, few have done so in the way the ITU does it.

But if the ITU is somehow sui generis, so are most other international organizations, and it is a curious methodological issue in the law of international organizations that somehow commonalities must be found amongst entities that have very little in common other than the basic idea that they are usually set up by public authorities to perform a seemingly public task.

This contribution has tried to formulate the beginnings of a different way of thinking about international organizations, one that takes them seriously as 'organizations' and has an eye for their institutional functions: regulation, management, and most of all the authoritative allocation of values. As the ITU example suggests (and its core findings could be multiplied by similar studies of many other international organizations), there is far more to international organizations than their sheer existence, and perhaps this is a point where counterfactual analysis might play a role—the world of telecommunications would be a dramatically different place if there were no ITU, in much the same way as global migration would look radically different without the International Organization for Migration (IOM), and global public health might even be a contradiction in terms without the WHO, as the Covid-19 crisis illustrates.

In this light, it is disconcerting that studies of regimes (used here in its generic sense) tend to ignore the institutional component.[66] International relations scholars and international lawyers alike, including international organizations lawyers, are by and large stuck in a state-centric paradigm. Viewing international organizations as sites for the articulation and promotion of state preferences, as international relations scholars often do, or viewing law-making by international

[65] This is further developed in Jan Klabbers, 'The European Union in the Law of International Organizations: Misfit or Model?' in Ramses Wessel and Jed Odermatt (eds), *Research Handbook on the European Union and International Organizations* (Edward Elgar, 2019).

[66] An exception is Jill Hills, *Telecommunications and Empire* (University of Illinois Press 2007).

organizations solely through the perspective of formal law-making based on state consent, as international lawyers are wont to do, misses the point that international organizations actually or potentially, directly or indirectly, exercise an enormous influence. Focusing on knowledge production by international organizations has the heuristic benefit of making their influence visible, and forces the observer to step outside the prevailing state-centric paradigm.

12

Metaphors of International Law

Harlan Grant Cohen[*]

I Introduction

In 1837, following his famous trip to the Galapagos islands, Charles Darwin sketched in his notebook[1] a rough tree to describe how different species might be related to one another.[2] This 'tree of life' was not the first metaphor Darwin played with—he first played with the image of coral, growing over time as new polyps grew on the remains of old ones. Nor did he pull it out of thin air—the tree of life was an already well-known image from the Bible and Aristotle, sometimes used to describe a 'ladder of nature' or 'great chain of being' linking inanimate objects like rocks through insects to higher-level beings and sometimes, to angels and God. But Darwin's 'tree of life' metaphor, eventually published between pages 116 and 117 of his 1859 *On the Origin of Species*, was the one that stuck, in no small part because, repurposed, it evocatively described the process of evolution through natural selection that he had discovered. For the past century and a half, that metaphor became the structure guiding work in evolutionary sciences. Placing species on the tree, first through careful anatomical analysis and then through DNA evidence, was a core intellectual endeavour—until the discovery of horizontal gene transfer. The increasing recognition that DNA often jumped from bacteria and viruses into other species, including humans, and that the boundaries between species and even kingdoms are far more permeable than understood, hacked away at the idea that life had evolved in an ever-branching upward direction. But the tree of life metaphor did not go away, as researchers sought to reconcile their findings to it, drawing different root structures, tangling branches, or bushes. The metaphor that had helped push science forward for so long had begun to get in its way.

Metaphors are part of international law's scaffolding.[3] They provide a language to describe and convey the law's operation, they help international lawyers identify

* Thank you to Connor Harbin, Ashley Henson, and Joshua Jones.

1 Known now as 'Transmutation Notebook B'.

2 The discussion in this paragraph is derived from David Quammen, *The Tangled Tree: A Radical New History of Life* (Simon & Schuster 2018).

3 Writing about metaphors in international law, one is faced with a choice: (1) to try as best as possible to use a spare, clinical language, avoiding metaphors in the discussion to better highlight the

Harlan Grant Cohen, *Metaphors of International Law* In: *International Law's Invisible Frames*. Edited by: Andrea Bianchi and Moshe Hirsch, Oxford University Press. © Harlan Grant Cohen 2021. DOI: 10.1093/oso/9780192847539.003.0013

legal subjects and categorize situations in doctrinal categories, and they provide normative justifications for the law. Part of their shared cognitive system, metaphors allow international lawyers to build a shared, tangible universe of legal meaning. In so doing, however, metaphors also help hide international law's dark side, blind international lawyers to alternative ways of organizing the world, and prejudge legal outcomes.

Sometimes obvious, sometimes obscured, metaphor's role as architecture remains largely invisible.[4] This chapter seeks to unveil[5] the hidden structures metaphors support. Section II thus explores three levels at which metaphor operates—(1) Law as Metaphor, (2) Law's Metaphors, and (3) Metaphor as Narrative—through specific examples—naturalistic metaphors for customary international law, international 'personality', the contested nature of the internet, and liberalized trade's role in 'raising all boats' or 'growing the pie'. As will become obvious, these three levels, while distinguishable, are not hermetically sealed. A single metaphor may operate at multiple of these levels at the same time, explaining, categorizing, and/or justifying legal phenomena. Section III revisits the role metaphors play in each and across these examples, describing how metaphors reify international law and its community of practitioners, both as an imagined utopia and a dark and forbidding fortress.[6]

That metaphors are important to law will surprise no one. Metaphors are first and foremost thought of as figures of speech, rhetorical tools suggesting an implicit analogy between one object and another.[7] Webster's dictionary, for example, defines a metaphor as a 'figure of speech containing an implied comparison, in which a word or phrase ordinarily and primarily used of one thing is applied to another'.[8] For lawyers, focused on how words are used to persuade, to rationalize, or to justify, the power of such tools is obvious. Metaphors are, as will be discussed more below, arguments in miniature—ways of describing why a particular actor, object,

specific roles metaphors play [Ha! Couldn't even do it there. Now you're picturing sterile white rooms and lab coats.], or (2) to turn into the skid, embracing the metaphors at every turn, highlighting their ubiquity and variety, success and failure. The latter, at least, seems more fun.

[4] See Andrea Bianchi and Moshe Hirsch, 'International Law's Invisible Frames: Introductory Insights' in this volume 7–12 (discussing the invisibility of these cognitive frames and its consequences). As they explain, one 'noticeable feature that social cognition and knowledge production share is that they are often invisible processes that take place without us being fully aware that they are at play'. ibid 6–7.

[5] See ibid 13.

[6] In their introductory chapter, Bianchi and Hirsch explain that their goal for the volume is to 'unveil', 'understand', and 'unlearn' the cognitive biases that currently frame and structure international law. ibid. Section II of this chapter is primarily concerned with the first two; section III begins to tackle the third.

[7] The Merriam-Webster dictionary defines 'metaphor' as 'a figure of speech in which a word or phrase literally denoting one kind of object or idea is used in place of another to suggest a likeness or analogy between them (as in drowning in money)'. See 'metaphor, n' (Merriam-Webster Online) https://www.merriam-webster.com/dictionary/metaphor (accessed 2 December 2020).

[8] *Webster's New World Dictionary* (3rd College edn, 1988) 852.

or situation deserves to be treated a certain way.[9] It is thus unsurprising that judicial opinions, briefs, and scholarly articles are replete with metaphors, some hackneyed and clichéd, others fresh and interesting, and still others disastrous failures.[10]

But metaphors' *impact reach far deeper* than mere rhetoric, as the three linked metaphors in this sentence demonstrate. They are deeply woven into our language as a means for describing real and abstract ideas. They 'help decipher what might be difficult to understand otherwise'.[11] And while some of these metaphors may have lost their full imaginative bite—we rarely think about what it means to 'grasp' an idea (and as such may be thought of as a 'dead' metaphor), others continue to have force, bringing with them chains of associations that shape how we talk about and conceive of a particular thing, person, or idea. As Thomas Ross observed, lawyers 'live in a magical world of law where liens float, corporations reside, minds hold meetings, and promises run with the land. The constitutional landscape is dotted with streams, walls, and poisonous trees. And these wonderful things are cradled in the seamless web of law'.[12] At some level, this is unsurprising. Legal rules are abstract ideas. They have no physical form. While legal rules may inspire or motivate physical actions, they do not take them themselves. Metaphors are necessary in order to describe their operation and application. Entirely mental processes of determining proportionality are described and shared as 'balancing' or 'weighing'.[13]

And deeper still we go. Some have suggested that all language, perhaps even all cognition is metaphorical.[14] In fact, following up on the seminal[15] work of George

[9] Macmillan's dictionary, for example, defines a 'metaphor' as 'a word or phrase that means one thing and is used for referring to another thing in order to emphasize their similar qualities'. See 'metaphor, n' (Macmillan dictionary) https://www.macmillandictionary.com/us/dictionary/american/metaphor (accessed 2 December 2020). See also Jonathan H Blavin and I Glenn Cohen, 'Gore, Gibson, and Goldsmith: The Evolution of Internet Metaphors in Law and Commentary' (2002) 16 *Harvard Journal of Law & Technology* 265, 266.

[10] What perhaps is more surprising is how little legal literature there is on the role of metaphors. Certainly, there are pieces looking at the role of particularly prominent metaphors in, for example, US constitutional law see eg Haig Bosmajian, *Metaphor and Reason in Judicial Opinions* (Southern Illinois University Press 1992) 37, and some of the most prominent legal scholars, among others, have dabbled with the issue. See eg Cass R Sunstein, 'On Analogical Reasoning' (1993) 106 *Harvard Law Review* 741; Richard Posner, *Law and Literature* (Harvard University Press 1988). But deep theorizing about the role of metaphor remains on the fringe of legal discourse. Perhaps digging too deeply reveals uncomfortable truths about the work metaphors do standing in for reasoned arguments and holding a legal community together.

[11] Bianchi and Hirsch (n 4) 6.

[12] Thomas Ross, 'Metaphor and Paradox' (1989) 23 *Georgia Law Review* 1053, 1053.

[13] See eg Michael R Smith, 'Levels of Metaphor in Persuasive Legal Writing' (2007) 58 *Mercer Law Review* 919, 928. For an explanation of the cognitive origins of such legal metaphors, including the ways human physical experience is transposed to legal analysis see Jacob Livingston Slosser and Mikael Rask Madsen, 'Institutionally Embodied Law: Cognitive Linguistics and the Making of International Law' in this volume.

[14] David E Leary, 'Psyche's Muse: The Role of Metaphor in the History of Psychology' in David E Leary (ed), *Metaphors in the History of Psychology* (CUP 1990) ('All knowledge is ultimately rooted in metaphorical (or analogical) modes of perception and thought').

[15] A metaphor perhaps better left dead?

Lakoff and Mark Johnson,[16] metaphors have widely been reconceived not merely as figures of speech but as figures of thought.[17] '[M]etaphor is not merely a figure of speech, but is a specific mental mapping that influences a good deal of how people think, reason, and imagine in everyday life.'[18] And work in the cognitive sciences has built on these insights to develop models to describe how a 'source domain' (the object of the comparison) is linked to a more familiar 'target' domain through specific mental pathways.[19]

This makes the task of writing about metaphors in international law quite daunting. Metaphors suffuse the language of international law, operating (1) at the level of language and cognition itself, (2) as general descriptions of law's operation, (3) as more specific descriptions of international law's development, (4) as doctrinal frames and cues, and (5) as normative narratives underpinning the law's desirability or morality. Perhaps the most difficult aspect of writing about metaphors in international law is thus deciding the level at which to situate the investigation. Lost in the mysteries of the deep, directions back to the surface become difficult to discern.

For this chapter, I have chosen to focus on the third, fourth, and fifth levels.[20] At these levels, the role of *international law*, both as an object of metaphors and in choosing metaphors becomes more distinct. As such, it is also at these levels that metaphors' roles in creating a community of practice become more apparent—creating shared languages of the law, shaping legal categories, defining orthodox and unorthodox views. It also allows us to explore how metaphors can be both useful and dangerous in their operation within international law.[21]

[16] George Lakoff, 'The Contemporary Theory of Metaphor' in Andrew Ortony (ed), *Metaphor and Thought* (CUP 1993) 202–203; George Lakoff and Mark Johnson, *Metaphors We Live By* (1st edn, University of Chicago Press 1980) 3.

[17] Steven L Winter, 'What is the "Color" of Law?' in Raymond W Gibbs Jr (ed), *The Cambridge Handbook of Metaphor and Thought* (CUP 2008) 368; George Lakoff and Mark Turner, *More Than Cool Reason: A Field Guide To Poetic Metaphor* (University of Chicago Press 1989) xi.

[18] Raymond W Gibbs Jr, 'Taking Metaphor Out of Our Heads and Putting it into the Cultural World' in Raymond W Gibbs Jr. and Gerard J Steen (eds), *Metaphor in Cognitive Linguistics* (John Benjamin Publishing Company 1997) 145.

[19] See eg discussion in Stephanie A Gore, 'A Rose by any other Name: Judicial Use of Metaphors for New Technologies' (2003) 2 *University of Illinois Journal of Law, Technology & Policy* 403.

[20] Drawing on the cognitive sciences, Jacob Livingston Slosser has done pathbreaking work at the nexus between the first two levels, exploring how the framing of rights impacts decisions regarding their potential violation. Jacob Livingston Slosser, 'Interpreting the "Quality of Law" at the European Court of Human Rights: Metaphorical Framing and Evaluative Judgment' (2018) iCourts Working Paper Series, No 143 https://ssrn.com/abstract=3251277 (accessed 7 May 2020). Slosser continues that work in his chapter here with Mikael Rask Madsen. Together, they explore the lessons of cognitive linguistics for international law generally and the European Court of Human Rights' articulation of the margin of appreciation doctrine specifically. See Slosser and Madsen (n 13).

[21] Although some work on the cognitive science of metaphors distinguishes between the mental processes (and meaning) of metaphors and similes, much like the posters in an elementary school classroom see eg Sam Glucksberg, 'How Metaphors Create Categories: Quickly' in Raymond W Gibbs Jr (ed), *The Cambridge Handbook of Metaphor and Thought* (CUP 2008) 74–76, international law's common, shared imagery take varied linguistic form depending on context, and I purposely use a more inclusive definition.

II International Law's Metaphors

A Law as Metaphor

1 *'Natural' laws*

What is customary international law, and how does it develop? This is, of course, one of the thorniest questions in international law. International lawyers have little difficulty identifying a sort-of international conventional wisdom on acceptable or unacceptable behaviour. But the contestable instincts of international lawyers are hardly a solid base for legal obligations. Visible, describable instances of state practice thus become key to grounding any argument for customary international law. But those too are merely snapshots of practice, incapable of proving in-and-of themselves the presence of a generalizable rule. When a practice evidences a legal obligation as opposed to something else remains as elusive as the rule itself. The jurisgenerative process remains more a theory than an observable phenomenon.

Enter metaphors. In order to explain and justify this unseen process, international lawyers have often turned to natural phenomena.[22] Sometimes these metaphors are organic. Customary international law rules grow, ripen,[23] or evolve.[24] Other times, they sound in geology. Rules crystallize[25]; practices accrete[26]; norms are slowly deposited into a sediment[27] of international law. The metaphors are logical and evocative, providing simple and persuasive visuals of how a seed of an

[22] For a deeper dive into metaphors of ripening and crystallizing and customary international law see Maks Del Mar, 'Metaphor in International Law: Language, Imagination and Normative Inquiry' (2017) 86 *Nordic Journal of International Law* 170, 186–95.

[23] See eg *Fisheries Case (UK v Norway)* (Judgment) [1951] ICJ Rep 116; Fisheries Jurisdiction (*UK and Northern Ireland v Iceland*) (Judgment) [1974] ICJ Rep 3; *The Paquete Habana*, 175 US 677, 686 (1900) ('By an ancient usage among civilized nations, beginning centuries ago and gradually ripening into a rule of international law').

[24] See eg *Jurisdictional Immunities of the State (Germany v Italy: Greece Intervening)* (Judgment) [2012] ICJ Rep 99, 292.

[25] See eg *North Sea Continental Shelf (Federal Republic of Germany/Denmark; Federal Republic of Germany/Netherlands)* (Judgment) [1969] ICJ Rep 3 [69]; *Fisheries Jurisdiction (Federal Republic of Germany v Iceland)* (Judgment) [1974] ICJ Rep 175; *Case concerning the Continental Shelf (Libyan Arab Jamahiriya/Malta)* (Declaration) [1985] ICJ Rep 13; *Case concerning Military and Paramilitary Activities in and Against Nicaragua (Nicaragua v US)* (Judgment) [1986] ICJ Rep 14, 95; *Jurisdictional Immunities of the State (Germany v Italy: Greece Intervening)* (Judgment) [2012] ICJ Rep 99, 292.

[26] See eg *Nuclear Tests (Australia v France)* (Judgment) [1974] ICJ Rep 253, 435, Dissenting Opinion of Judge Sir Garfield Barwick ('It cannot be doubted that customary law is subject to growth and to accretion as international opinion changes and hardens into law').

[27] See eg *Obligations Concerning Negotiations Relating to Cessation of the Nuclear Arms Race and to Nuclear Disarmament (Marshall Islands v UK)* (Judgment) [2016] ICJ Rep 834, 991 (Dissenting Opinion of Judge Cançado Trindade) ('There is an *opinio juris communis* to this effect, sedimented during recent decades, and evidenced in the successive establishment, in distinct continents, of nuclear-weapon-free zones, and nowadays in the Conferences on the Humanitarian Impact of Nuclear Weapons'); Philip Allott, 'The Concept of International Law' (1999) 10 *European Journal of International Law* 31, 342 ('Customary international law is the legal form of the sedimentary self-ordering of a self-evolving international society').

idea might grow into full-fledged rule. It is no surprise that they have had such staying force in international legal discourse and decisions.

But as obvious as those metaphors may seem, they are far from neutral. For one thing, they are used in ways that portray customary international law in largely positive and progressive terms. Rules are fruits or gems. Adaptations help rules survive and match their environments.[28] Rarely are the metaphors turned on their heads to reveal the dark sides of these processes. We seldom speak of rules spoiling or growing rotten,[29] metastasizing or collecting barnacles, producing eruptions or earthquakes.

More importantly, these metaphors obscure the agency behind these developments. Relying on natural phenomena gives customary international law rules an aura of inevitability. Missing are the states and other actors whose concerted actions and reactions over time helped push the rule in one direction or another. Missing, in others words, is power.

Custom could easily be described as a battlefield. Customary international law is a contest in which particular international rules confer specific benefits to particular actors.[30] Combatants make moves and countermoves aimed at protecting, shoring up, and conquering territory and position within a field of rules. Consensus over customary international law is less recognition than acquiescence. Rules about territory and obligation favour older powers over newly liberated ones. Rules of armed conflict often favour the weaponry and tactics of powerful states. Rules regarding nationalization protect wealthy state investors rather than developing state publics. To the extent those rules have shifted, it has been the result of sustained opposition.

Self-defence against non-state actors is a current battleground for custom. While one group of states asserts a customary international law rule supporting their military efforts in states 'unwilling or unable' to counter non-state actor threats emanating from within their borders, another group of states, many of them more likely to face such unwilling or unable claims, rails against it.[31] The first set of states asserts their interpretation through military actions and justifications; the latter

[28] As Antony Anghie explains of the 'natural selection' metaphor: 'Species evolved over time; but whatever the nature of the changes, they took place in accordance with the fundamental laws that had been identified by Darwin. Ideas of progress and evolution were embodied in international law thinking, and biological metaphors were often used by international lawyers.' Antony Anghie, 'Finding the Peripheries: Sovereignty and Colonialism in Nineteenth-Century International Law' (1999) 40 *Harvard International Law Journal* 1, 20 n 6.

[29] See eg Maurice H Mendelson, *The Formation of Customary International Law* (Martinus Nijhoff 1998) 176 (explaining of custom that 'we are more interested in knowing, when we bite it, if it is now ripe or still too hard or sour').

[30] See eg Timothy Meyer, 'Codifying Custom' (2012) 160 *Pennsylvania Law Review* 995 (for such an account).

[31] See eg Kevin Jon Heller, 'Specially-Affected States and the Formation of Custom' (2018) 112 *American Journal of International Law* 191.

through protests and votes. While the first asserts crystallization of a permissive rule,[32] the second focuses on state 'acts' in violation of existing rules.[33]

These blind spots, while perhaps easy to ignore, are likely not accidental. For international lawyers as whole, the naturalistic metaphors provide a shared club language that reinforces their self-perception as disinterested scientists.[34] It also serves to immunize their techniques from external critiques that custom is nothing more than power-politics reified. But these blind spots are also ways to obscure the role of power within the club, to reify status, and defend the mainstream against its critics.

2 *Person-ality*

The ur-metaphor[35] of international law is the equation of states with persons. The metaphor stands at the centre of international law doctrine, explaining and justifying a suite of basic rules and assumptions about how the system operates. States, like persons, are the natural holders of international legal *person*ality. States have rights, duties, and immunities, and can make contracts and claims. Others may have such powers, but only because states, the natural persons of international law, bestow or delegate them. Sovereign equality recognizes that states, like persons, are equal before the law.

Although the analogy goes back at least as far as Hobbes, who imagined states living in the state of nature that individuals had succeeded in transcending,[36] the analogy takes on particular force in the shift from the 'law of nations' to 'international law', creating frameworks that filtered out the variety of legal actors and legal forms that characterized the former, distilling the system down into its state- and consent-focused form.

But the metaphor is far more pervasive. When we talk about global affairs, we speak of states (rather than their leaders) acting, thinking, and believing.[37] We talk about states' bodies—they act through an 'arm' of the state and sub-state units are described as 'organs'. Most of all, the analogy between states and persons has reified the state as a 'natural' unit of international relations. Like persons, we perceive

[32] See eg Michael P Scharf, 'How the War Against ISIS Changed International Law' (2016) 48 *Case Western Reserve Journal of International Law* 15, 65–66 (identifying when a rule permitting self-defence against non-state actors 'crystallized').

[33] Heller (n 31) 211–12.

[34] The effect is particularly pronounced when these metaphors are translated into other languages.

[35] The prefix 'ur-', meaning primitive, primordial, original, has its origins in German, but nonetheless seems to metaphorically invoke the image of the ancient city of Ur and, with it, an imagined origin of civilization. An interesting false metaphor, perhaps.

[36] See eg Thomas Hobbes, *Leviathan* (Richard Tuck ed, first published 1651, CUP 1991) 244 ('[T]he Law of Nations, and the Law of Nature, is the same thing. And every Soveraign hath the same Right, in procuring the safety of his People, that any particular man can have, in procuring his own safety').

[37] Game theoretic models of international relations provide an interesting corollary, imagining states a rational 'actors'. In the 'prisoner's dilemma', states are reduced to petty criminals, eager to stay out of jail.

states' bodies to be inviolable,[38] condemning violations of state boundaries, and indivisible, recoiling at attempts at amputations[39] or at their vivisection. The metaphor has both internal and external facing implications. Internally, the state was made up of the 'body politic'.[40] Externally, the state could be part of an international society or a 'family' of nations. There is a dark side to this metaphor, however. As Antony Anghie observes, the analogy of states and persons, while perhaps now a source for notions of sovereign equality, was once used to deny access to non-Europeans.[41] Characterizations of persons as barbaric or civilized were transposed to groups; such civilized groups—states—were defined by their 'family' resemblance to European states, and only such civilized groups were worthy of membership in the family of nations of international society.[42]

The state-personhood metaphor thus obscures the messy mix of dissonant voices within states, the range of transnational actors for whom state boundaries have little meaning, the plural, overlapping legal communities in which people live, and the contingent, contested nature of current state borders. It valorizes and empowers those who gain control of the state's mouthpiece over all other groups, regardless of their on-the-ground authority.

When non-state actors do need to be conceptualized, the personification of the state creates a metaphorical baseline. As Natasha Wheatley explains: 'Metaphors can function as a mental tunnel between the known and the unknown.'[43] International organizations, for example, are described as living creatures birthed or created by states.[44] Andrew Guzman's invocation of Frankenstein's monster as a metaphor for international organizations is notable in this regard for its description of international organizations not only as artificial persons, but as imperfect

[38] See eg Declaration on Principles of International Law concerning Friendly Relations and Co-operation among States, UNGA Res 2625 (XXV) (24 October 1970) ('The territorial integrity and political independence of the State are inviolable').

[39] Dissenting from the ICJ's *Kosovo* Advisory opinion, for example, Judge Koroma condemns the unilateral declaration of independence as an attempt to 'dismember or amputate part of the territory of a State Kosovo' in violation of international law. *Accordance with International Law of the Unilateral Declaration of Independence in Respect of Kosovo* (Advisory Opinion) [2010] ICJ Rep 404, 475, Dissenting Opinion of Judge Koroma. See also *Western Sahara* (Advisory Opinion) [1975] ICJ Rep 12, Separate Opinion of Judge Dillard; *Case concerning the Territorial Dispute (Libyan Arab Jamahiriya/ Chad)* (Judgment) [1994] ICJ Rep 6; *Case concerning Maritime Delimitation and Territorial Questions Between Qatar And Bahrain (Qatar v Bahrain)* (Judgment) [2001] ICJ Rep 40, 149, Joint Dissenting Opinion of Judges Bedjaoui, Ranjeva, and Koroma.

[40] See eg Note, 'Organic and Mechanical Metaphors in late Eighteenth-Century American Political Thought' (1997) 110 *Harvard Law Review* 1832, 1841–42.

[41] See generally Anghie (n 28).

[42] ibid 28–29.

[43] Natasha Wheatley, 'Spectral Legal Personality in Interwar International Law: On New Ways of Not Being a State' (2017) 35 *Law and History Review* 753, 764.

[44] See eg Guy Fiti Sinclair, *To Reform the World: International Organizations and the Making of Modern States* (OUP 2017) (describing International Organizations as 'organic' or 'living' creatures); David J Bederman, 'The Souls of International Organizations: Legal Personality and the Lighthouse at Cape Spartel' (1996) 36 *Virginia Journal of International Law* 275 (international organizations described as 'organisms', 'creatures', 'living', and 'evolving').

simulacrums and dangerous experiments.[45] Not quite persons, international organizations become different creatures, divergent forms of life. Other non-state actors are described as a veritable menagerie of pseudo-persons. Natasha Wheatley brilliantly disinters the varied beings conjured during the interwar period as metaphors for minorities, League of Nations Mandates, and other holders of partial personality.[46] Embryos, slaves, and specters—'familiar genres of incomplete or deficient personhood'—suddenly populated a diversifying imaginary.[47] The creativity of interwar international lawyers though actually underlines their conservatism. All new developments had to be understood through the ur-metaphor of states as persons.

B Law's Metaphors

At a second level, metaphors help define legal categories. Categorization is a key first step in applying the law to a situation. Real-world situations are messy; facts need to be sifted to determine whether an issue sounds in contract or tort, nuisance or crime. That categorization process is itself metaphorical. A messy real-world situation is described in terms of its similarity to a legal-world ideal type. Does the story most resemble that of a spurned business partner, a car accident, a loud party, or a burglarized home? Is a treaty a contract, legislation, or a constitution? In common-law systems, this type of legal reasoning is not only obvious, but valued. Civil law systems might disavow the most robust versions of this reasoning in favour of the code's greater precision (though the code itself may exhibit such reasoning), but some version of this reasoning is the inevitable product of fitting life's infinite variety into the law's more finite cognition. And to the extent that lawyers share a normative commitment to treating like cases alike, comparisons with categorized cases are unavoidable.

The force of such doctrinal metaphors is particularly pronounced in international law, where a smaller group of subspecialities has long dominated the field. Categorizing an issue as one of trade or investment, environment or human rights, armed conflict or resource management, brings a whole suite of special assumptions and rules.[48] Categorizing an issue tells us which codebook to take down from

[45] Andrew Guzman, 'International Organizations and the Frankenstein Problem' (2013) 24 *European Journal of International Law* 999.

[46] Wheatley (n 43).

[47] As Wheatley recounts, Hersch Lauterpacht appealed to international law's rogues gallery for analogies: 'When we wish to refute the orthodox view of States only being the subjects of international law, we have to fall back upon such exotic examples as pirates, blockade runners, carriers of contraband, recognized belligerents, and so on.' Wheatley (n 43) 756 (quoting Lauterpacht).

[48] Affordable medicines might be a question of human rights or of trade. See Andreas Fischer-Lescano and Gunther Teubner, 'Regime-Collisions: The Vain Search for Legal Unity in the Fragmentation of Global Law' (2004) 5 *Michigan Journal of International Law* 999, 1024–32. Tuna might be framed as a food resource or as an endangered species. See Margaret A Young, 'Protecting Endangered Marine

our mental shelf. Necessity and proportionality, for example, have defined meanings special to *jus ad bellum* and *jus in bello*, human rights, or investment.

1 *Contesting cyberspace*

Making activity on the internet legally cognizable exemplifies the need for and power of such doctrinal metaphors.[49] As Molly Sauter has observed:

> The use of conceptual metaphors in the construction and implementation of internet policy is extremely attractive, given the black-boxed, complex nature of technological systems up to this point. Many people have no way of speaking about network communications technologies at the high level needed for policy development without the use of metaphors.[50]

As such, internet metaphors abound: 'the "information super highway", a "series of tubes", "the cloud", the "global village", an "agora", or even just the "space" of "cyberspace" '.[51]

Since the internet's popularization, we have struggled to plug the behaviours taking place on it into existing legal categories.[52] 'Hacking' provides a good example. We have variously described hacking as involving identity 'theft', the 'pirating' of intellectual property,[53] the release of 'viruses' that 'infect' computers and servers, or as 'cyberattacks' auguring 'cyberwars' or 'cyberconflict'. The underlying conduct involved isn't obviously distinguishable, but the labels tell very different legal stories invoking very different legal regimes and tools: ordinary criminals arrested by local police, public health crises requiring coordinated technical responses, or military threats and responses governed by the laws of armed conflict.

A search of articles over the last five years is revealing. When 'cyberwar' is used in the title of an article, that article invariably applies law of armed conflict

Species: Collaboration Between Food and Agriculture Organization and the Cities Regime' (2010) 11 *Melbourne Journal of International Law* 441.

[49] The example is particularly pointed because it doubly requires metaphors—to describe the 0s and 1s transmitted through cables and to describe the operation of law upon them. See also Gore (n 19); Blavin and Cohen (n 9) 267.

[50] Molly Sauter, 'Show Me on the Map Where They Hacked You: Cyberwar and the Geospatial Internet Doctrine' (2015) 47 *Case Western Reserve Journal of International Law* 63, 66.

[51] ibid 64. On conceiving the internet as a physical 'space' see also Gore (n 149).

[52] At the domestic level, questions abound about privacy, freedom of expression, and government surveillance, among others, with fraught metaphors in tow—filing cabinets and desk drawers, books and magazines, mail, telephone lines, public squares, etc.

[53] Piracy is a particularly problematic metaphor in international law, whose meaning may shift with shifting views of pirates. Pirates are common characters in popular culture and their image may invoke cut-throat menace or a romantic outlawry. International law, built around the security of *state* authority, has painted the pirate as the ultimate stateless threat—*hosti humani generis*. But the popular imagination may see something different, complicating the term's use. The romantic image of the outlaw may explain why to some, labelling file-sharing programmes like Napster as piracy may backfire.

principles to its analysis. Articles using a 'cyberattack' in the title are more varied, applying law of armed conflict principles about half of the time. In a similar vein, Molly Sauter, found that the conceptual metaphor, 'the Internet has real-world geography' dominated various official documents, including the Tallinn Manual, and that with that metaphor came normative conclusions about nation-state control, competition, and contestation.[54] 'In the geographic metaphor, existing states of conflict and interstate aggression can be seamlessly transferred into the online space, along with existing state-determined structures of *enemies* and *bad actors*'[55] and 'In this interpretation of the metaphor the internet is quickly converted into an additional operational zone of warfare, complete with familiar enemies and allies.'[56]

Such case-studies highlight the stakes of these metaphors. The metaphors we use to describe activity on the internet will dictate how we seek to regulate it. Whether we see it as an 'agora', a space for protecting freedom of expression; a 'marketplace' in need of consumer protection; a 'highway' or 'commons' requiring regulatory co-operation;[57] or an extension of national spaces threatened by external attacks, will invariably dictate legal frameworks, the regulatory goals and responses, and the responsible governing agencies. Perhaps proving the point, in attempting to argue that it is the internet companies themselves that are the real threat, Shoshana Zuboff proffers a range of new, alternative metaphors—surveillance, extractive mining operations, conquistadors, telemetry and herds of animals, among others.[58]

C Metaphors as Narrative

The contest over legal frames suggests a third level at which metaphors operate within international law. Each of the different metaphors in play in the cyber context—agorae, marketplaces, surveillance, pirates, viruses, cyberattacks—brings not only an off-the-shelf rulebook, but a set of normative commitments as well. Each embodies a narrative of why regulation, and why specific types and forms of regulation are warranted, valuable, and good. Metaphor acts as normative justification, a normative narrative undergirding the area of law.[59]

Such justificatory narratives may be embedded in legal categories. They may also be implicit in the metaphors we used to describe the law itself. Describing states as

[54] Sauter (n 50).
[55] ibid 74.
[56] ibid.
[57] See Blavin and Cohen (n 9) 269–74 (discussing judicial decisions invoking the highway metaphor).
[58] Shoshana Zuboff, *The Age of Surveillance Capitalism: The Fight for a Human Future at the New Frontier of Power* (PublicAffairs 2019).
[59] For an example see Shiri Krebs' thoughtful and incisive discussion of the role played by the 'fog of war' metaphor in this volume: Shiri Krebs, 'The Invisible Frames Affecting Wartime Investigations: Legal Epistemology, Metaphors, and Cognitive Biases' in this volume.

persons may justify, explicitly or implicitly, rules that exclude other voices from negotiation or making claims or that disincentivize secession, like *uti possidetis juris*. Describing custom in naturalistic terms may justify applying its rules to new, post-colonial states that not only had no say in developing them, but may have been their direct victims. But those justificatory metaphors can also exist outside the four corners of the legal doctrine. These narratives help shape doctrines that might otherwise be normatively neutral or contested, a collective justification for reading the rules one way or another.

Policies and legal regimes depend on normative narratives.[60] Shared narrative principles guide practitioners in their interpretation of that regime's rules, suggesting answers that better fit the goals or values that those rules are meant to achieve.[61] As such, shared normative narratives also support the coherence of the rules in a particular regime,[62] stringing them together as part of a logical whole.[63] By providing coherence and distinguishing rules from arbitrary exercises of sovereign authority, these narratives also contribute to the perceived legitimacy of the regime.[64] Put another way, normative narratives present a type of political-moral conventional wisdom. These narratives capture the basic, shared understanding of why a policy is worthwhile. Alternatively, these narratives can help describe problems that need to be solved, challenges that must be met, to improve the law or achieve the law's goals.[65]

1 Marketplace of ideas

One such metaphor is the well-known 'marketplace of ideas'. Originating in the work of John Milton and John Stuart Mill,[66] the metaphor provides a potent, vivid justification for freedom of expression. Picked up by courts,[67] commentators, and the public, the metaphor suggests an efficient idea market, in which ideas are in competition and in which the best ideas and the truth will eventually win more adherents. When applied to legal questions, the metaphor acts as an argument against

[60] See Robert M Cover, 'The Supreme Court, 1982 Term—Foreword: Nomos and Narrative' (1983) 97 *Harvard Law Review* 4.

[61] See Ronald Dworkin, *Law's Empire* (Harvard University Press 1986) 254–58.

[62] See Thomas M Franck, 'Legitimacy in the International System' (1988) 82 *American Journal of International Law* 705, 712.

[63] See Dworkin (n 61) 176–224.

[64] See Lon L Fuller, *The Morality of Law* (Yale University Press 1964).

[65] Anthea Roberts and Taylor St John have done an extraordinary job exploring such narratives regarding reform of investor–state dispute settlement. See Anthea Roberts and Taylor St John, 'UNCITRAL and ISDS Reform: In Sickness and In Health' *EJIL:Talk!* (23 October 2019) https://www.ejiltalk.org/uncitral-and-isds-reform-in-sickness-and-in-health/ (accessed 7 May 2020). See also Nicolas Lamp, 'How Should We Think about the Winners and Losers from Globalization? Three Narratives and Their Implications for the Redesign of International Economic Agreements' (2019) 30 *European Journal of International Law* 1359.

[66] See Stanley Ingber, 'The Marketplace of Ideas: A Legitimizing Myth' (1984) 33 *Duke Law Journal* 1, 3.

[67] See eg *Mouvement Raëlien Suisse v Switzerland*, App no 16354/06 (13 July 2012) (Dissenting Opinion of Judge Pinto de Albuquerque).

limitations of speech.[68] More speakers, more ideas, will produce a better market and a more informed public. Government censorship of speakers, no matter how heinous, is likely to backfire. Of course, public speech does not look like an efficient market; it is not, as the metaphor might suggest, entirely free. Structural considerations like wealth and power give some greater access, a louder voice, or perhaps even control. And revealing truth is only one justification for freedom of expression. Protection of individual conscience and promotion of democratic participation serve as alternative justifications. Invocation of the marketplace of ideas and everything associated with the metaphor can though crowd those other ideas out and, in so doing, dictate specific legal answers over others.

2 Raising all boats/growing the pie

Ideas that free trade is a 'rising tide that raises all boats' or 'grows the pie' provide another such set of justificatory narrative metaphors.[69] Both of these metaphors carry the accepted wisdom within economics that free trade makes all parties better off. Protectionism, the narrative argues, is usually misguided. It may be aimed at helping domestic workers, but it actually has the opposite effect, raising prices, stifling growth, and shrinking the domestic economy.[70] Trade liberalization, on the other hand, while perhaps causing transitional pain to domestic industries and workers, encourages growth and, through the magic of comparative advantage, increases the overall welfare of all states, giving each more wealth to allocate among its population.[71] In this sense, free-er trade grows the global and national pie and can make everyone better off. Free-er trade is a rising tide, raising all national boats and all individuals in them.

These metaphors do not suggest that trade liberalization will in-and-of itself better the lives or fortunes of everyone. But they do suggest that questions about the redistribution of trade's welfare gains are best and most efficiently answered through domestic, rather than international, policy-making.[72] Questions about how to slice the pie should be secondary to questions about how to grow it.

These metaphors thus justify policies of trade liberalization and legal rules that give them effect. But they go further, justifying a division of international trade from

[68] See ibid. See also Observations of the United States of America on the Committee for the Elimination of Racial Discrimination's Thematic Discussion on 'Racist Hate Speech' https://www.ohchr.org/Documents/HRBodies/CERD/Discussions/Racisthatespeech/USA.pdf (accessed 26 May 2020) ('The better course is to ensure that avenues of expression remain open—in order to expose, contradict, and drown out hateful speech in a marketplace of ideas').

[69] See Harlan Grant Cohen, 'What is International Trade Law For?' (2019) 113 *American Journal of International Law* 326.

[70] See Robert Z Lawrence and Robert E Litan, 'Why Protectionism Doesn't Pay' (1987) *Harvard Business Review* 60, 61.

[71] See Joost Pauwelyn, Andrew Guzman, and Jennifer Hillman (eds), *International Trade Law* (3rd edn, Wolters Kluwer 2016) 11–19.

[72] See Paul Krugman and Maurice Obstfeld, *International Economics: Theory & Policy* (7th edn, Addison Wesley 2005) 214–17.

other policy areas and a focus on liberalization over other potential negotiating goals. They set up liberalization as the rule, and other policies—protection of health, the environment, labour protections, for example—as exceptions, forcing the latter to meet standards of necessity and non-discrimination. In blunt terms, the metaphors explain why the current trade regime is good and what sorts of policies and rules would make it better.

But the metaphors are just metaphors. Trade agreements move forward at a variable pace, liberalizing some areas more or faster. Not all agreements do raise all boats. Some boats may rise much faster, while others stagnate. Moreover, the division of trade from other areas of policy is entirely artificial. Once other interests are considered alongside trade, the question of what goods are being maximized, what pie is being grown, become much more questionable, much more fraught. In this sense, these metaphors aren't just justifications, animating the system, they are silencers or blinders, obscuring the real policy tradeoffs involved in any negotiation behind poorly scrutinized 'truths' and aphorisms.

III Paradise or/and Prison

Metaphors are particularly important in describing law and its operation. Law is a concept. It describes standards of behaviour accepted within and demanded by a particular community of actors. It exists and exerts its force primarily in and upon the minds of community members. It has no physical or tangible form until it is applied or described. The words on the page of the law book, the court decision, the foreign ministry statement, or the military manual are not the law, but mere manifestations, interpretations. Nor are the arrests, the punishments, or the ordered compensation the law; they are merely reactions to it. This makes law and its processes very difficult to describe. Operating upon our collective minds, metaphors—analogies to tangible, visible things—become a necessity. And given law's collective character, setting expectations within some community, description and communication are necessary. The law must be transmitted from one mind to others in order to operate.

We are always in the cave, and international law is always experienced as mere shadows on its walls.[73] But we are not merely passive observers. Seeking to understand the world outside, we develop more and more tools, lenses, to refract and bend the light into visible forms. As we do so, we gain greater insight into how international law works. The ever more refined lenses give us confidence that we

[73] As Bianchi and Hirsch explain in their Introduction to this volume: 'The point of departure is that we do not directly sense information, as cognitive processes mediate between sensory input from the environment and behaviour.' Bianchi and Hirsch (n 4) 1: 'The overarching idea is that there is no unmediated access to knowledge and that knowledge is mentally and socially constructed.' ibid 6.

are getting closer to describing the true international law. But we also lose sight of how our perceptions are framed by our chosen lens—the world is not the light refracted through the prism or the color-coded chart of microwave emissions, but something far more massive and complex.

This is a well-known problem in the sciences.[74] Metaphors developed to describe and organize complex processes are at first liberating—sparking creativity, facilitating organized thinking, and suggesting routes of investigation. Darwin's metaphor of the tree of life, itself borrowed from other corners of the culture, became an intellectual superstructure guiding investigations of evolution and the cataloguing of life-forms.[75] But those metaphors can, over time, outlive their purpose, obscuring or bending findings that don't fit the metaphors structure. As mentioned above, the late 20th century discovery of horizontal gene transfer—the inheritance of important DNA strands from bacteria and viruses—struggled to reconcile itself with the tree metaphor.[76] Scientists attempted to rethink the way branches or roots were drawn, alluded to bushes rather than trees, all in an attempt to uphold the metaphor in the face of conflicting evidence. The tree metaphor, once such a potent tool for scientific progress, had become a hindrance, a confounding distraction.

This gets at the complex duality inherent in metaphor's role in international law. Metaphor is creative, not only in the traditional, figurative sense, but in its literal sense. Metaphors allow international lawyers to create an alternative image of the world, one in which the chaos of everyday life is transformed into a more orderly model suitable for description, study, and organization. States are rendered as persons, living in communities or society, sometimes trading with each other, sometimes engaged in gladiatorial combat. Pirates, rogues, savages, and outlaws threaten from the peripheries. International organizations—monsters, chimera, and spirits—are conjured to help solve problems. Laws are mined or grown for sustenance, picked when ripe.

In this shared imaginary, metaphors can allow for creative leaps, opening up ways of seeing the world previously obscured. They can also be a font of utopian dreaming, allowing international lawyers to imagine a better world in which all the pieces fit together in harmony.[77]

Over time, however, these metaphors can ossify. The stories they invoke become old, predictable, and clichéd. No longer novel, the stories become canon. We

[74] See Thomas S Kuhn, *The Structure of Scientific Revolutions* (2nd edn, University of Chicago Press 1970) 43–46.

[75] See Quammen (n 2).

[76] ibid. Cf Anthea Roberts, 'Clash of Paradigms: Actors and Analogies Shaping the Investment Treaty System' (2013) 107 *American Journal of International Law* 45 (using the difficulty taxonomizing the platypus to highlight the difficulty categorizing investment treaties).

[77] See also Wheatley (n 43) 764–65.

become dull to the feats of imagination they involve, taking their metaphorical nature for granted. As Thomas Ross has observed:

> Every individual is at once the beneficiary and the victim of the linguistic tradition into which he has been born—the beneficiary inasmuch as language gives access to the accumulated records of other people's experience, the victim insofar as it ... bedevils his sense of reality, so that he is all too apt to take his concepts for data, his words for actual things.[78]

In other words, metaphors can be new and surprising, inspiring flights of imagination and a torrent of new ideas.[79] But, they can, over time, become clichéd—still evocative, but more numbing than exciting, suggesting images that are worn, boring, taken for granted. When this happens, metaphors may actually work against both imagination and logic, trapping us in a series of unthinking stories and lulling us into believing their truth.[80] The state is someone we know (isn't it?); the marketplace of ideas is a place we have visited (right?); we have ridden the rising boats and enjoyed the growing pie (haven't we?). As then Chief Judge of the New York Court of Appeals Benjamin Cardozo observed: 'Metaphors in law are to be narrowly watched, for starting as devices to liberate thought, they end often by enslaving it.'[81]

This is accentuated by the way in which metaphors help group communication. As explained above, metaphors are potent ways to convey abstract ideas to others. In a community setting, where sharing common ideas is important for establishing group norms and solidarity, shared metaphors are essential. A shared repository of metaphors allows quick and easy communication; good metaphors will create a type of shared shorthand, conveying normative ideas and logical extensions far faster than long-form discussions. They also help community members identify one another in their use of a shared language, one that might not be obvious to outsiders. International lawyers recognize each other in their invocation of legal 'personality' or 'crystallizing' rules. Given the transnational, trans-linguistic nature

[78] Ross (n 12) 1053.

[79] This imaginative power of metaphor is a particular focus of Del Mar (n 17) 173–82. Intriguingly, using metaphors involves a whiff of danger. In invoking non-obvious images to describe something, the author hopes that the listener will recognize the qualities in the metaphor they hope to convey. It is entirely possible though that the listener will recognize it, but be unimpressed, not recognize the reference at all, or most dangerous, recognize the reference, but bring to it an entirely different set of emotions and narratives. Successful metaphors build off deep wells of shared culture and, in that sense, both are the product of and help construct international law's communities of practice.

[80] Eventually, some metaphors may die, their original meaning lost as they are repeated over and over again. Language is full of such metaphors. When we 'grasp' an idea, we rarely imagine ourselves holding it in our hands. Sports metaphors are emblematic of this process. 'Arguing balls and strikes' still evokes baseball; 'striking out' in some endeavor may not; an 'out of left field' idea almost certainly does not. 'Stepping into the ring' may invoke boxing or wrestling; 'standing in one's corner' or 'throwing in the towel' or 'going to the mat' likely no longer does.

[81] *Berkey v Third Ave Ry Co*, 155 NE 58, 61 (NY 1926).

of international practice, this shared repertoire of images can be extraordinarily important.

The shared metaphors also create a sense of mystique in belonging to a secret society replete with its own code words and secret handshakes.[82] In that sense, these shared metaphors act a bit like international law's vestigial (or invented[83]) Latin and French phrases—*opinio juris*, *pacta sunt servanda*, *rebus sic stantibus*, *travaux préparatoires*. They imbue the practice, and skilled practitioners, with special forms of social capital. But in fostering that group solidarity, these metaphors also separate practitioners from others. International law practitioners in non-English or non-French speaking countries may find themselves repeating metaphors with little to no meaning in their native cultures.[84] And those metaphors may create barriers to entry. Mere obscurity to outsiders may keep others out; but in some cases, the barriers may be actively defended by international lawyers unwilling to give up their mystical tools.[85] As Molly Sauter observes:

> The existence of these discourse communities, essentially defined by their ability to effectively speak to each other, makes effective discussion and consensus possible, while at the same time these groups are hampered, by their very nature, from ever moving beyond the conceptual metaphors that tie them together.[86]

Ironically, then, focusing on international law's metaphors reminds us of the very human activity at the centre of the international law project. It reminds us of the power of international lawyers to translate their imagination into power, to create new physical realities through words—Abra Kadabrah. But it also reminds us of the human frailty and weakness that keeps old ideas alive through groupthink, even as they have outlived their purpose or come to cause real harm.

[82] One of the most venerable metaphors in international law is the 'invisible college of international lawyers', the self-serving self-description of international law professionals as benevolent scientists brought together across time and space to protect and propagate special world wisdom. See Oscar Schacter, 'The Invisible College of International Lawyers' (1977) 72 *Northwestern University Law Review* 217, 217. For a comparison of international lawyers to rabbis see Harlan Grant Cohen, 'The Primitive Lawyer Speaks! Thoughts on the Concepts of International and Rabbinic Laws' (2020) 64 *Villanova Law Review* 665.

[83] See Robert Kolb, 'Origin of the twin terms *jus ad bellum/jus in bello*' (1997) 37 *International Review of the Red Cross* 553.

[84] As Maiko Meguro describes, 'crystallization' is used by international lawyers in Japan, but the term otherwise only has scientific meaning. 'Cyberattack' is transliterated rather than translated. Situations like these may put non-English, non-French speaking international lawyers in the complicated position of being both insiders and outsiders within international law's metaphorical community, as various metaphors may be difficult to translate into their languages at all. Alonso Gurmendi mentions terms like 'Catch-22', fighter, executing contracts, or treaties entering into force, as phrases with only imperfect Spanish counterparts.

[85] See Bianchi and Hirsch (n 4) 4 ('Power structures, epistemic forces and discursive policies—influenced as they are by theories and theoretical discourse—determine what is deemed to be an acceptable and competent thing to say about international law').

[86] See eg Sauter (n 50) 66.

It also recentres efforts at critique and reform. International law is reified through its metaphors; shared metaphors are the ingredients from which international lawyers' imaginary is conjured, the code on which their virtual world is played. Critiquing doctrines may shift power within international law, but doing so leaves its alternate reality intact. We might challenge and refine what constitutes an 'armed attack' in cyberspace, but as long as we invoke cyberwarfare as our frame, our imagination and options will be limited by its terms. International law has shed many of the explicitly colonial implications of state personality, but the distortive effects of the basic metaphor remain. A return to the real world—a reset of the code—must ultimately scrutinize the international law's world-building metaphors. The world of international law is brought into being through the ritual incantations of metaphors by its lawyer-priests. Changing those incantations remakes that world.

13
Counterstorytelling in International Economic Law

*Matthew Windsor**

> The greater part of the stories current today we shall have to reject.
>
> Plato[1]

I Once upon a Time

Let me tell you a story. In my first job after law school, I clerked for a judge at the Court of Appeal of New Zealand. A case that I worked on haunted me then and now. In the proceedings, almost 300 claims concerning historic claims of abuse in mental health institutions were struck out on procedural grounds. At the conclusion of his dissenting opinion, I persuaded the judge to include a passage from Janet Frame's autobiographical novel ***Faces in the Water***, which concerned similar events.[2] The inclusion of this literary extract in an appellate judgment was an effort at counterstorytelling—an attempt to render the lived experience of the litigants legible in the law reports, despite the jurispathic resolution of the dispute.[3]

This chapter investigates the existence and efficacy of counterstorytelling in the field of international economic law. International law is saturated with storytelling, shaping our knowledge of the discipline as well as what sits outside orthodox professional parameters. International economic law's rules and normative preferences are embedded deeply in narratives and myths that construct our understanding of

* I am grateful for the excellent comments provided by friends and colleagues at the book workshop at the Hebrew University of Jerusalem and the International Economic Law Collective conference at the University of Warwick.

[1] Plato, *The Republic* (Penguin Books 1955) 115.

[2] *Crown Health Financing Agency v P* [2009] 2 NZLR 149, 276 (citing Janet Frame, *Faces in the Water* (Pegasus Press 1961): 'Every morning I woke in dread, waiting for the day nurse to go on her rounds and announce from the list of names in her hand whether or not I was for shock treatment . . . Waiting in the early morning, in the black-capped frosted hours, was like waiting for the pronouncement of a death sentence').

[3] Robert M Cover, 'The Supreme Court 1982 Term Foreword: *Nomos* and Narrative' (1983) 97 *Harvard Law Review* 4, 40–44.

Matthew Windsor, *Counterstorytelling in International Economic Law* In: *International Law's Invisible Frames*. Edited by: Andrea Bianchi and Moshe Hirsch, Oxford University Press. © Matthew Windsor 2021.
DOI: 10.1093/oso/9780192847539.003.0014

their meaning and operation in specific contexts. In a very tangible sense, international law is both defused by and infused with narrative, its stories operating as mechanisms of 'blindness and insight'.[4]

This double movement is explored in what follows. Section II surveys the intellectual origins and conceptual assumptions of the narrative turn in legal thought. Section III critically appraises the shortcomings and strengths of counterstorytelling, a style of narrative jurisprudence that emerged primarily in the context of critical race theory, and whose power inheres in its mythbusting potential. Section IV illustrates the force of counterstorytelling in the context of the past, present, and future of international economic law, focusing respectively on Adom Getachew's historical account of the New International Economic Order (NIEO) in *Worldmaking after Empire*,[5] the diagnostic of the current backlash against economic globalization in Lynn Nottage's play *Sweat*,[6] and efforts to forecast the trajectories of neoliberal capitalism. If international law constitutes a 'bridge between the social past and the social future through the social present',[7] we must be reflective about the stories that propel us forward, as well as the ones that hold us back.

II Law and Narrative

Narrative is ubiquitous in life and law, offering an indispensable means of understanding our world and ourselves.[8] Facts are not comprehensible in a vacuum, but always require a 'socially acceptable narrative to absorb, sustain and circulate them'.[9] Indeed, in a world without stories, Walter Benjamin cautioned that it would be as if something 'inalienable to us, the securest among our possessions, were taken from us: the ability to exchange experiences'.[10]

Narrative has an overt affinity with both social cognition and knowledge production, the animating themes of this volume. In relation to social cognition, narrative operates as an 'instrument of mind in the construction of reality'.[11]

[4] Paul de Man, *Blindness and Insight: Essays in the Rhetoric of Contemporary Criticism* (University of Minnesota Press 1983).

[5] Adom Getachew, *Worldmaking after Empire: The Rise and Fall of Self-Determination* (Princeton University Press 2019).

[6] Lynn Nottage, *Sweat* (Nick Hern Books 2018).

[7] Philip Allott, *The Health of Nations: Society and Law beyond the State* (Cambridge University Press 2002) 317.

[8] François Ost, 'Towards a Critique of Narrative Reason' (2013) 7(1) *Law and Humanities* 55, 55 ('Of all the characteristics ascribed to the human entity … it is this fictioning faculty which strikes me as the most fundamental one').

[9] Edward Said, 'Permission to Narrate' (1984) 13 *Journal of Palestine Studies* 27, 34.

[10] Walter Benjamin, 'The Storyteller' in Walter Benjamin, *Illuminations: Essays and Reflections* (Schoken Books 2007) 83.

[11] Jerome Bruner, 'The Narrative Construction of Reality' (1991) 18(1) *Critical Inquiry* 1, 6.

Cognitive narratologists have long illuminated the 'storied nature of perception, sense-making, memory, and identity formation',[12] maintaining that stories frequently exist in the mind independently of concrete representations in a particular medium.[13] As far as knowledge production is concerned, Hannah Arendt famously posited the individual *qua* storyteller at the centre of her account of action, claiming that '[w]ith word and deed, we insert ourselves into the human world'.[14] For Arendt, it is through storytelling that the meaning of action is retrospectively enunciated; in the absence of stories, the memory of past actions would not be preserved.

Narrative is not only in the business of recollection but also construction, with storytellers assiduously giving 'shape and significance to life'.[15] The historian Hayden White observed that narration is more than a chronological collection of events, but a process where events are given an 'order of meaning' that they do not convey as 'mere sequence'.[16] White further claimed that every historical narrative is produced from a larger assemblage of events, which could have been incorporated but were not.[17] Notwithstanding view from nowhere posturing to the contrary,[18] the implication is that storytellers are never neutral: 'they investigate, but also suggest, create and legislate meanings'.[19]

That narrative knowledge production always already involves a knowledge reduction reveals something significant about the explanatory nature of stories.[20] Rather than subscribing to scientific metrics of causality or probability,[21] stories achieve their explanatory effect through appealing to the affective—completing an 'emotional cadence'[22]—and by producing an account that is broadly verisimilar.[23] The epistemological challenge this engenders is how an instrument as unreliable as

[12] Manfred Jahn, 'Cognitive Narratology' in David Herman, Manfred Jahn, and Marie-Laure Ryan (eds), *Routledge Encyclopaedia of Narrative Theory* (Routledge 2005) 67. See also David Herman, *Storytelling and the Sciences of Mind* (MIT Press 2013).

[13] Steven L Winter, 'The Cognitive Dimension of the *Agon* Between Legal Power and Narrative Meaning' (1989) 87 *Michigan Law Review* 2225.

[14] Hannah Arendt, *The Human Condition* (University of Chicago Press 1958) 176.

[15] Peter Brooks, 'Narrative Transactions: Does the Law Need a Narratology?' (2006) 18(1) *Yale Journal of Law and the Humanities* 1, 24.

[16] Hayden White, 'The Value of Narrativity in the Representation of Reality' (1980) 7 *Critical Inquiry* 5, 9. For his classic account of emplotment, see Hayden White, *Metahistory: The Historical Imagination in 19th Century Europe* (Johns Hopkins University Press 1973).

[17] White, 'The Value of Narrativity in the Representation of Reality' (n 16) 14.

[18] Thomas Nagel, *The View from Nowhere* (Oxford University Press 1986).

[19] Maria Aristodemou, *Law & Literature: Journeys From Her to Eternity* (Oxford University Press 2000) 3.

[20] Paul Kahn, *Finding Ourselves at the Movies: Philosophy for a New Generation* (Columbia University Press 2013) 71 ('Creating the narrative . . . I cut the world one way rather than another').

[21] Donald Polkinghorne, *Narrative Knowing and the Human Sciences* (State University of New York Press 1988).

[22] James David Velleman, 'Narrative Explanation' (2003) 112(1) *The Philosophical Review* 1, 6.

[23] John Ruggie, 'Epistemology, ontology, and the study of international regimes' in John Ruggie, *Constructing the World Polity: Essays on International Institutionalisation* (Routledge 1998) 85, 94.

narrative can be permitted to participate in creating a social consensus regarding truth.[24]

Perhaps for that reason, many lawyers adamantly avoid acknowledging the law's narrative nature.[25] For such detractors, admitting that law may produce results other than those derived directly from legitimate authority risks provoking a 'massive housewrecking of judicial-rhetoric-as-usual'.[26] Yet storytelling is unquestionably a pervasive feature of legal practice. In a canonical contribution, Robert Cover observed that '[n]o set of legal institutions or prescriptions exists apart from the narratives that locate it and give it meaning'.[27] In the context of the courtroom, storytellers regularly 'give comfort, inspire, provide insight; they forewarn, betray, reveal, legitimise [and] convince'.[28]

The insight that law is 'awash in storytelling'[29] is a testament to the intellectual contribution of the law and literature movement in American legal scholarship, which classically distinguished between law *in* literature, and law *as* literature.[30] As an interdisciplinary project, law and literature broadly drew on three intellectual strands:[31] (1) humanism, offering literature as a corrective to the technocratic vision of law and economics;[32] (2) hermeneutics, drawing on literary theory to destabilize orthodox modes of textual interpretation;[33] and (3) narrative, joining the humanist preoccupation with individual agency and a hermeneutic recognition of the multiplicity of meaning.[34] Notwithstanding this taxonomy, storytelling was at the centre of the law and literature project from its inception. In its foundational text *The Legal Imagination*, James Boyd White opined that:

> [T]he central act of the legal mind, of judge and lawyer alike, is this conversion of the raw material of life—of the actual experiences of people and the thousands of

[24] Albrecht Koschorke, *Fact and Fiction: Elements of a General Theory of Narrative* (De Gruyter 2018).

[25] Peter Brooks, 'Narrative in and of the Law' in James Phelan and Peter J Rabinowitz (eds), *A Companion to Narrative Theory* (Blackwell 2008) 415 ('one searches in vain for any recognition within legal doctrine that narrative is one of law's categories for making sense of its affairs').

[26] Peter Brooks, 'Policing Stories' in Austin Sarat, Lawrence Douglas, and Martha Merrill Umphrey (eds), *Law's Madness* (University of Michigan Press 2003) 29, 43.

[27] Cover (n 3) 4.

[28] Anthony G Amsterdam and Jerome Bruner, *Minding the Law* (Harvard University Press 2000) 115.

[29] ibid 110.

[30] Simon Stern, 'Literary Analysis of Law: Reorienting the Connections Between Law and Literature' (2018) 5(2) *Critical Analysis of Law* 1 (dispensing with this choice to inquire how legal and literary forms and methods can be explored in tandem).

[31] Jane Baron, 'Law, Literature, and the Problems of Interdisciplinarity' (1999) 108 *Yale Law Journal* 1059; Julie Stone Peters, 'Law, Literature, and the Vanishing Real: On the Future of an Interdisciplinary Illusion' (2005) 120(2) *Publications of the Modern Language Association* 442.

[32] James Boyd White, *The Legal Imagination* (University of Chicago Press 1973); Martha C Nussbaum, *Poetic Justice: The Literary Imagination and Public Life* (Beacon Press 1995).

[33] Stanley Fish, *Is There A Text in This Class? The Authority of Interpretive Communities* (Harvard University Press 1980); Sanford Levinson and Steven Mailloux (eds), *Interpreting Law and Literature: A Hermeneutic Reader* (Northwestern University Press 1988).

[34] Peter Brooks and Paul Gewirtz (eds), *Law's Stories: Narrative and Rhetoric in the Law* (Yale University Press 1998).

ways they can be talked about—into a story that will claim to tell the truth in legal terms.[35]

Although law and literature have only made modest inroads in international law scholarship,[36] proficiency in storytelling is a crucial attribute for success in the discipline.[37] This is because stories either help safeguard or erode the authority of a given international legal interpretation.[38] Compelling examples of international legal scholarship exist which broadly correspond to the aforementioned taxonomy of humanism,[39] hermeneutics,[40] and narrative.[41] The advent of fragmentation in the international law discourse exposed how different narratives are advanced to support different projects at different times by differently situated actors.[42] Such narratives greatly influence what international lawyers identify both as problems and solutions.[43]

Instead of regarding narrative as a Trojan horse engineered to stress-test and destabilize legal argumentation, the relationship between legal and literary modes of production is better understood as a recursive exchange.[44] Despite a general disciplinary shift to more expansive analyses of the relationship between law and cultural production, the lingering legacy of the encounter between law and literature is to 'unsettle whatever boundaries and confines may unwittingly restrain us'.[45] A focus on storytelling in international legal practice and process continues to be of intellectual assistance in 'examining, critiquing and revising

[35] White, *The Legal Imagination* (n 32) 243.

[36] Andrea Bianchi, *International Law Theories* (Oxford University Press 2017) 287–310.

[37] Andrea Bianchi, 'International Adjudication, Rhetoric and Storytelling' (2018) 9(1) *Journal of International Dispute Settlement* 28.

[38] Julia Otten, 'Narratives in International Law' (2016) 99(3) *KritV* 187.

[39] Joseph R Slaughter, *Human Rights Inc: The World Novel, Narrative Form and International Law* (Fordham University Press 2007); Christopher Warren, *Literature and the Law of Nations 1580-1680* (Oxford University Press 2015).

[40] Ed Morgan, *The Aesthetics of International Law* (University of Toronto Press 2007); Daniel Peat and Matthew Windsor, 'Playing the Game of Interpretation in International Law' in Andrea Bianchi, Daniel Peat, and Matthew Windsor (eds), *Interpretation in International Law* (Oxford University Press 2015) 3–33.

[41] Matthew Windsor, 'Narrative Kill or Capture: Unreliable Narration in International Law' (2015) 28 *Leiden Journal of International Law* 743; Anne Orford, *Reading Humanitarian Intervention: Human Rights and the Use of Force in International Law* (Cambridge University Press 2008); Ana Luísa Bernardino, 'The Discursive Construction of Facts in International Adjudication' (2020) 11 *Journal of International Dispute Settlement* 175, 188–91.

[42] Surabhi Ranganathan, 'The Value of Narratives: The India–USA Nuclear Deal in Terms of Fragmentation, Pluralism, Constitutionalisation and Global Administrative Law' (2013) 6(1) *Erasmus Law Review* 17.

[43] Anne Saab, *Narratives of Hunger in International Law: Feeding the World in Times of Climate Change* (Cambridge University Press 2019) 56.

[44] Robin Wharton and Derek Miller, 'New Directions in Law and Narrative' (2019) 15(2) *Law, Culture and the Humanities* 294, 299.

[45] Elizabeth S Anker and Bernadette Meyler (eds), *New Directions in Law and Literature* (Oxford University Press 2017) 25.

the particular narratives embedded in law, and the identities and institutions these narratives enable'.[46]

III Counterstorytelling as Mythbusting

Who speaks and which stories get told? This section focuses on a specific strand of narrative jurisprudence, explicitly motivated by a desire to make the point of view of outsiders audible.[47] A specific methodological intervention in critical race theory was to use storytelling as a 'window onto ignored or alternate realities'.[48] In a 'plea for narrative', Richard Delgado asserted that stories are 'powerful means for destroying mindset—the bundle of presuppositions, received wisdoms, and shared understandings against a background of which legal and political discourse takes place'.[49] For critical race theorists, such shared understandings privilege the pale, male, and stale, and pay short shrift to the 'experiences of people of colour, of the poor, of women, of those who cannot describe their experiences in the language of the law'.[50] To transpose the aesthetic credo of novelist Toni Morrison, the ambition was to 'free up the language from its sometimes sinister, frequently lazy, almost always predictable employment of racially informed and determined chains'.[51]

As a key critical race theory tactic, counterstorytelling offered alternative stories that could be deployed to call dominant narratives into question, and pave the way for new ones. Such stories set out to disrupt institutional logics, often revealing an underbelly of 'pain, exclusion, and both petty and major tyranny'.[52] In an emblematic example, Patricia Williams recounted her experience of being denied entry to the Benetton's store on racial grounds, and the challenges she faced in publishing about the experience in a law journal symposium.[53] The editors of the symposium on 'Excluded Voices' first replaced Williams' 'active personal' with the 'passive

[46] Guyora Binder and Robert Weisberg, *Literary Criticisms of Law* (Princeton University Press 2000) 23.

[47] Kim Lane Scheppele, 'Foreword: Telling Stories' (1989) 87 *Michigan Law Review* 2073, 2077 (defining outsiders as 'those whose perspectives had been excluded in the law's construction of an official story for the particular case'); Mari Matsuda, 'Looking to the Bottom: Critical Legal Studies and Reparations' (1987) 22 *Harvard Civil Rights–Civil Liberties Law Review* 323, 324 (advocating 'looking to the bottom' as 'adopting the perspective of those who have seen and felt the falsity of the liberal promise').

[48] Richard Delgado and Jean Stefancic, *Critical Race Theory: An Introduction* (3rd edn, New York University Press 2017) 46; Derrick Bell, *And We Are Not Saved: The Elusive Quest for Racial Justice* (Basic Books 1987). See also Sandra Harding (ed), *The Feminist Standpoint Theory Reader: Intellectual and Political Controversies* (Routledge 2004).

[49] Richard Delgado, 'Storytelling for Oppositionists and Others: A Plea for Narrative' (1989) 87 *Michigan Law Review* 2411, 2413.

[50] Scheppele (n 47) 2084.

[51] Toni Morrison, *Playing in the Dark: Whiteness and the Literary Imagination* (Vintage Books 1992) xi.

[52] Delgado, 'Storytelling for Oppositionists and Others' (n 49) 2439.

[53] Patricia J Williams, *The Alchemy of Race and Rights* (Harvard University Press 1991) 44–51.

impersonal',[54] and subsequently omitted all references to Benetton's and her race. For Williams, this resulted in an 'aesthetic of uniformity' that eliminated her experience from the realm of the legally cognizable.[55] Williams was subsequently excoriated for 'privileging a racial perspective' and failing to include the 'salesman's side of the story'.[56] Yet subject position is everything in Williams' oeuvre, which to this day rejects any 'linguistic effacement of agency' that 'tells us where to look and where not to'.[57]

With popularity came controversy for counterstorytelling in the American legal academy. For adherents, standpoint epistemologies offered a promising terrain for the pursuit of identity politics.[58] Less sanguine commentators impugned critical race theorists for presupposing the inherent truth of stories,[59] privileging the emotive impact of stories over reasoned analysis,[60] and producing scholarship that eluded orthodox modes of evaluation.[61] Critics of counterstorytelling, understood as methodological gatekeepers, clearly feared the subversive implication that 'stories if well told can become part of the narrative base and so change the way we understand the world'.[62]

Persuasive rejoinders to the truth, emotion, and evaluation critiques can readily be advanced. Regarding the truth critique, the whole point of counterstorytelling was to resist narrative banalization,[63] recasting dominant narratives as 'stories' rather than 'reality'.[64] Outsider storytelling helped to reveal the 'unstated reference points of ostensible universals',[65] and offered a safe discursive terrain for the formation of subjects with different truths to convey.[66] Through sustained narrative denaturalization, the reader is forced to reckon with the following questions:[67]

[54] ibid 47.
[55] ibid 48.
[56] ibid 51.
[57] Patricia Williams, 'Language is part of the machinery of oppression: just look at how black deaths are described' *The Guardian* (10 June 2020).
[58] Francesca Polletta, *It Was Like a Fever: Storytelling in Protest and Politics* (University of Chicago Press 2006).
[59] Daniel Farber and Suzanna Sherry, *Beyond All Reason: The Radical Assault on Truth in American Law* (Oxford University Press 1997).
[60] Mark Tushnet, 'The Degradation of Constitutional Discourse' (1991) 81 *Georgetown Law Journal* 251.
[61] Edward L Rubin, 'On Beyond Truth: A Theory for Evaluating Legal Scholarship' (1992) 80(4) *California Law Review* 889.
[62] Richard Delgado, 'Rodrigo's Final Chronicle: Cultural Power, the Law Reviews, and the Attack on Narrative Jurisprudence' (1995) 68 *Southern California Law Review* 545, 565.
[63] Bruner (n 11) 9 (the idea that a narrative is 'so socially conventional, so well known, so in keeping with the canon, that we can assign it to some well-rehearsed and virtually automatic interpretive routine').
[64] Catharine MacKinnon, 'Law's Stories as Reality and Politics' in Peter Brooks and Paul Gewirtz (eds), *Law's Stories: Narrative and Rhetoric in the Law* (Yale University Press 1998) 235.
[65] Francesca Polletta et al, 'The Sociology of Storytelling' (2011) 37 *Annual Review of Sociology* 109, 113.
[66] Maki Kimura, 'Narrative as a Site of Subject Construction: The 'Comfort Women' Debate' (2008) 9(1) *Feminist Theory* 5, 13.
[67] Delgado, 'Storytelling for Oppositionists and Others' (n 49) 2435.

> Can my world still stand? What parts of it remain valid? What parts of the story seem true? How can I reconcile the two worlds, and will the resulting world be a better one than the one with which I began?

An eloquent response to the emotion critique is offered by Amia Srinviasan, who defends the 'aptness of anger' in some circumstances.[68] For Srinivasan, the invidious choice between acting prudentially and getting angry gives rise to a situation of affective injustice for the oppressed.[69] Affective injustice might be alleviated by taking steps to dissolve the perceived dichotomy between 'reason' and 'emotion': 'Since it is oppressed people who have greatest reason to be angry, excluding anger from the public sphere is an efficient rationalisation for excluding those who most threaten the reigning social order.'[70]

In relation to the evaluation critique, counterstorytelling studiously avoided capitulation to conventional modes of assessment. Indeed, the purpose was to provide a space in which dominant cultural myths might be disrupted.[71] To the extent that myths make 'contingency appear eternal',[72] they were regarded as susceptible to contestation and rupture. As a style of mythbusting, counterstorytelling did not necessarily purport to be 'epistemologically more complete than the knowledges that were their base', but was instead targeted towards the 'metacognitive task of strengthening the struggles against oppression'.[73]

Acknowledging the narrativity of international law enables us to 'open up our usual stories', making the 'space for new ones to be told'.[74] Although they do not directly employ the language of counterstorytelling from critical race theory, a number of approaches in international legal scholarship foreground the dynamics of power and perspective at work in conventional narratives,[75] including feminist approaches to international law,[76] the New Haven School's sensitivity to 'observational standpoint',[77] David Kennedy's sensitivity to 'blind spots and biases' in

[68] Amia Srinivasan, 'The Aptness of Anger' (2018) 26(2) *Journal of Political Philosophy* 123.

[69] ibid 127.

[70] ibid 142. See also Miranda Fricker, *Epistemic Injustice: Power and the Ethics of Knowing* (Oxford University Press 2009).

[71] See generally Peter Fitzpatrick, *The Mythology of Modern Law* (Routledge 1992). In the pedagogical context see Ahmed Raza Memon and Suhraiya Jivraj, 'Trust, Courage and Silence: Carving Out Decolonial Spaces in Higher Education Through Student–Staff Partnerships' (2020) 54(4) *The Law Teacher* 475.

[72] Roland Barthes, *Mythologies* (Paladin 1973) 155.

[73] Boaventura de Sousa Santos, *The End of the Cognitive Empire: The Coming of Age of Epistemologies of the South* (Duke University Press 2018) 147.

[74] Saab (n 43) 171.

[75] Windsor (n 41) 766 ('The struggle for control of the narrative is ultimately a struggle for interpretive power, with the resulting ability to "kill or capture" conflicting narrative visions').

[76] Hilary Charlesworth, Christine Chinkin, and Shelley Wright, 'Feminist Approaches to International Law' (1991) 85(4) *American Journal of International Law* 613; Loveday Hodson and Troy Lavers (eds), *Feminist Judgments in International Law* (Hart 2019).

[77] Myres S McDougal and Harold Lasswell, 'Trends in Theory About Law: Maintaining Observational Standpoint and Delimiting the Focus of Inquiry' (1976) 8(1) *Toledo Law Review* 1.

the operation of international legal expertise,[78] and revisionist historiography.[79] As far as the emotion critique is concerned, the affectedness of a scholarly idiom that styles itself as an affect-free zone has not escaped comment.[80] Regarding the evaluation critique, third world approaches to international law share an anti-subordinating mandate with critical race theory,[81] given that they seek to 'disrupt and hopefully dismantle the racial hierarchies on which unequal production about the knowledge of international law is practiced'.[82] The next section transposes the practice of counterstorytelling from critical race theory to an economic modality of domination: neoliberal capitalism, and its expression in international economic law.[83]

IV Narrating the Neoliberal

A *'This Little State Went to Market . . .'*

Economic life is motored by storytelling.[84] There is no convincing way to determine a priori what belongs in the domain of the market and the domain of politics,[85] outside the realm of ideological preference—and narrative is integral to the production of ideological effects.[86] In 1944, two highly influential stories were told about the relationship between the state and the market. Friedrich Hayek's *The Road to Serfdom* famously cautioned that the suppression of market competition through state planning would lead to the destruction of freedom.[87] Meanwhile,

[78] David Kennedy, 'The Disciplines of International Law and Policy' (1999) 12 *Leiden Journal of International Law* 9. The work of international legal scholarship that arguably bears the greatest aesthetic resemblance to counterstorytelling in critical race theory is David Kennedy, *The Rights of Spring* (Princeton University Press 2009).

[79] Immi Tallgren and Thomas Skouteris (eds), *The New Histories of International Criminal Law: Retrials* (Oxford University Press 2019) 11 (understood as efforts to write 'beyond, against, or in the shadow of the master narrative').

[80] Gerry Simpson, 'The Sentimental Life of International Law' (2015) 3(1) *London Review of International Law* 3, 11; Naz K Modirzadeh, 'Cut These Words: Passion and International Law of War Scholarship' (2020) 61(1) *Harvard International Law Journal* 1.

[81] Makau Mutua, 'Critical Race Theory and International Law: The View of an Insider–Outsider' (2000) 45 *Villanova Law Review* 841; James Thuo Gathii, 'Writing Race and Identity in a Global Context: What CRT and TWAIL Can Learn From Each Other' (2021) 67 *UCLA Law Review* 1610.

[82] James Thuo Gathii, 'The Promise of International Law: A Third World View' (2021) *Proceedings of the American Society of International Law* (forthcoming).

[83] Richard Delgado, 'Rodrigo's Reconsideration: Intersectionality and the Future of Critical Race Theory' (2011) 96 *Iowa Law Review* 1247, 1287–88 (urging the 'race-crits' to move 'beyond their original perimeters'). For linkages between racial and economic modalities of domination in international law see Robert Knox, 'Valuing Race? Stretched Marxism and the Logic of Imperialism' (2016) 4(1) *London Review of International Law* 81; Ntina Tzouvala, *Capitalism as Civilization: A History of International Law* (Cambridge University Press 2020).

[84] Jens Beckert and Richard Bronk (eds), *Uncertain Futures: Imaginaries, Narratives, and Calculation in the Economy* (Oxford University Press 2018).

[85] Ha-Joon Chang, *Economics: The User's Guide* (Pelican 2014) 378.

[86] Jack Balkin, *Cultural Software: A Theory of Ideology* (Yale University Press 1998) 188–215.

[87] Friedrich von Hayek, *The Road to Serfdom* (Routledge 1962).

Karl Polanyi's *The Great Transformation* observed that the establishment and maintenance of 'free' markets required ongoing state intervention, with regulation helping to achieve freedom for all.[88]

The latter half of the 20th century was dominated by the neoliberal narrative.[89] Rejecting Keynesianism and democratic socialism, neoliberalism foregrounded free market mechanisms through the liberalization of trade, investment, and finance policies, and favoured the dismantling of the welfare state through an ensemble of privatization, deregulation, and austerity reforms. International economic law was deeply implicated in the neoliberal enterprise as a project that sought to 'transform all states into liberal states, entrench market principles as the basis of government both domestically and internationally, and organise itself around the idea of freedom'.[90]

Repeated invocation of the invisible hand of market competition myth masks the state's active role in facilitating neoliberal policy.[91] Neoliberal policy always required a strengthening of the state to implement the rules necessary for market competition and to develop the subjectivities required for a neoliberal social order.[92] A significant recent intervention is Quinn Slobodian's intellectual history of neoliberal globalism. In a 'narrative [that] corrects this storyline', Slobodian insists that neoliberalism is 'less a discipline of economics than a discipline of statecraft and law'.[93] For Slobodian, neoliberals consciously deployed the regulatory state in their project of protecting capitalism on a global scale.

To eschew the 'stories we like to tell' regarding the bifurcation of the economic and non-economic realms in our discipline,[94] how might the project of counterstorytelling as mythbusting be advanced in international economic law?[95] We must start by recognizing the general distinction between 'hegemonic tales'

[88] Karl Polanyi, *The Great Transformation* (Octagon Books 1975).

[89] Adam Tooze, 'Neoliberalism's World Order' *Dissent* (Summer 2018) ('Milton Friedman, the Chicago School, Pinochet, Thatcher and Reagan's market revolution, IMF structural adjustment, and shock-therapy transition programs from the post-Communist states are all fixtures in the narrative of the neoliberal turn').

[90] Anne Orford, 'Food Security, Free Trade, and the Battle for the State' (2015) 11(2) *Journal of International Law and International Relations* 1, 26.

[91] Andrew Lang, 'Market Anti-Naturalisms' in Justin Desautels-Stein and Christopher Tomlins (eds), *Searching for Contemporary Legal Thought* (Cambridge University Press 2017) 312.

[92] Loïc Wacquant, 'Three steps to a historical anthropology of actually existing neoliberalism' (2012) 20(1) *Social Anthropology* 66; Honor Brabazon (ed), *Neoliberal Legality: Understanding the Role of Law in the Neoliberal Project* Routledge 2016).

[93] Quinn Slobodian, *Globalists: The End of Empire and the Birth of Neoliberalism* (Harvard University Press 2018) 2, 11.

[94] John Linarelli, Margot E Salomon, and M Sornarajah, *The Misery of International Law* (Oxford University Press 2018) 30, 33 (rejecting the 'fictitious neoliberal construction that pits the state against the market').

[95] Daniel Tarullo, 'Logic, Myth, and the International Economic Order' (1985) 26 *Harvard International Law Journal* 533, 552 (advising to 'take seriously experiences that do not fit the "normal" world, to see how the history that was not written might have looked'). Two notable initiatives are the AfronomicsLaw blog (www.afronomicslaw.org/) and the IEL Collective (https://warwick.ac.uk/fac/soc/law/research/centres/globe/ielcollective/).

which 'reproduce existing relations of power and inequity', and 'subversive stories' that help make 'explicit the connections between particular lives and social organisation'.[96] More specifically, we must recognize that neoliberalism has long been in the business of suppressing 'narratives that promoted more egalitarian distributive measures'.[97] Given that the phenomenon of accumulation by dispossession occurs both materially *and* narratively, how can the economic subaltern speak?

B Potential of the Past: The New International Economic Order

One of international law's most frequently recited progress narratives goes something like this:[98] the project of building nation states in the era of decolonization inaugurated true universality in the field of public international law. Characterized by 'discipline optimism',[99] the self-determination story zeroed in on formal sovereign equality. However, this narrative focalization paid short shrift to continuing inequalities of political power and relations of economic dependence after empire.[100]

A powerful exemplar of counterstorytelling has been offered recently by political scientist Adom Getachew.[101] Rejecting '[n]arratives that equate decolonisation with the transition from empire to nation-state',[102] Getachew recast anticolonial nationalism as 'worldmaking'—a project that sought institutions in the international domain to ensure non-domination.[103] A site of 'conceptual and political innovation',[104] worldmaking was sensitive to the persistence of racial hierarchy in a statist international order, and motivated by a desire for equality of integration in a post-imperial world.

The project of economic world-making was conducted under the banner of the NIEO.[105] The objective of the NIEO was to transform the governance of the global

96 Patricia Ewick and Susan S Silbey, 'Subversive Stories and Hegemonic Tales: Toward a Sociology of Narrative' (1995) 29(2) *Law & Society Review* 197.

97 David Harvey, 'Neoliberalism as Creative Destruction' (2007) 610 *Annals of the American Academy of Political and Social Science* 22. See generally Wendy Brown, *Undoing the Demos: Neoliberalism's Stealth Revolution* (Zone Books 2015).

98 Thomas Skouteris, *The Notion of Progress in International Law Discourse* (Asser Press 2009).

99 Oliver Diggelmann, 'The Periodisation of the History of International Law' in Bardo Fassbender and Anne Peters (eds), *The Oxford Handbook of the History of International Law* (Oxford University Press 2012) 997, 1008.

100 Walter Rech, 'International Law, Empire, and the Relative Indeterminacy of Narrative' in Martti Koskenniemi, Walter Rech, and Manuel Jiménez Fonseca (eds), *International Law and Empire: Historical Explorations* (Oxford University Press 2017) 57.

101 Getachew (n 5).

102 ibid 9.

103 ibid 15. See also Partha Chatterjee, *Nationalist Thought and the Colonial World: A Derivative Discourse?* (University of Minnesota Press 1986).

104 Getachew (n 5) 75.

105 Besides the demand for a NIEO, Getachew also focuses on the institutionalization of a right to self-determination at the United Nations, and efforts to realize regional federation in Africa and the Caribbean.

economy by directing more of the economic benefits of integration towards developing countries. Its egalitarian demands included permanent sovereignty over natural resources, increased regulation of multinational corporations, and colonial reparations. For Getachew, the NIEO envisaged a 'welfare world' that aimed to 'enhance the bargaining power of postcolonial states, democratize decision-making, and achieve international redistribution'.[106]

According to Getachew's historical narration, the world-making prefigured by the NIEO was swiftly displaced by a neoliberal counter-revolution.[107] The fall of self-determination paved the way for Washington Consensus prescriptions of structural adjustment and policy conditionality, and the juridification of international economic law under conditions of formal state equality in a reformed GATT.[108] Yet, for Getachew, it remains vitally important to re-tell the story of the NIEO. Although she does not seek to directly transpose the NIEO's 'welfare world' to the present, she regards it as a 'mistake to collapse the partiality and eventual decline of a set of languages and strategies for making a world after empire with the demise of the moral and political vision that looked forward to an egalitarian and domination-free world'.[109] On this account, the fall of self-determination 'marks not only a dead end but also a staging ground for reimagining [the] future'.[110]

Getachew's counterstorytelling of anti-colonial world-making chimes with recent analyses of historical contingency in international legal scholarship.[111] Although a consideration of how international law might have been otherwise can be challenging to convey in narrative form,[112] a promising counterstorytelling strategy is to focus on unrealized 'potentials' rather than concrete 'possibilities'.[113] In a corrective to orthodox disciplinary teleology, Getachew's narrative retrieval of

[106] Getachew (n 5) 12.

[107] ibid 174. See also Slobodian (n 93) 220 ('The scaling up of the democracy principle to the international level after the end of decolonisation threatened the doubled world of global capitalism envisaged by neoliberals').

[108] Slobodian (n 93) 218–62.

[109] Getachew (n 5) 181.

[110] ibid.

[111] Ingo Venzke and Kevin Jon Heller (eds), *Contingency in International Law: On the Possibility of Different Legal Histories* (Oxford University Press 2021). See Robert Gordon, 'The Arrival of Critical Historicism' (1997) 49 *Stanford Law Review* 1023, 1024 (calling for 'rival perspectives (such as those of the losers rather than the winners) for surveying developments, or that posit[] alternative trajectories that might have produced a very different present').

[112] On this phenomenon see Kahn (n 20) 194 ('Contingency is banished; reasons replace causes; and narrative organises our world').

[113] Ingo Venzke, 'Possibilities of the Past: Histories of the NIEO and the Travails of Critique' (2018) 20 *Journal of the History of International Law* 263–65 (claiming that a return to the NIEO is not an 'expression of nostalgia' but 'evidence of its normative surplus'); Nils Gilman, 'The New International Economic Order: A Reintroduction' (2015) 6(1) *Humanity* 1, 10 (classifying the NIEO as an 'unfailure'—'the paradox that many seemingly failed political and social movements ... often live on as prophetic visions, available as an idiom for future generations to articulate their own hopes and dreams').

the NIEO catalyses a reckoning with the fact that the real 'progress' may have been in the past.[114]

Getachew's counterstorytelling also offers the salutary lesson that our capacity to transcend our present knowledge horizons is undermined if we rely exclusively on Western narratives that disregard other traditions. We must resist the tenacious mythology that posits the Global North as the site of epistemic production, and the Global South solely as a site of reception.[115] In this regard, *Worldmaking after Empire* contributes to the counter-archive,[116] signifying an effort to assert some control over the 'construction of our common histories and narratives'.[117]

C Problems of the Present: On *Sweat* and *Sacrifice*

The current geopolitical conjuncture is characterized by a backlash against economic globalization.[118] The 'rising tide lifts all boats' mantra has repeatedly been exposed as myth, given that the form of globalization prescribed by neoliberal policy was inattentive to issues of inequality between and within states.[119] Recent international economic law scholarship has responded by appealing to a different 'normative narrative' that is more attuned to questions of distribution.[120]

Lynn Nottage's play *Sweat* tells a powerful story about the shuttering of industrial factories in the American rustbelt, the impact of technological change on the conditions of labour, and the limits of class mobility.[121] When *Sweat* received the Pulitzer Prize for Drama in 2017, Nottage was commended for 'remind[ing] audiences of the stacked deck still facing workers searching for the American Dream'.[122]

[114] See David Scott's recommendation of tragic—rather than romantic—narrative emplotment in narrating the history of anticolonial struggle, recognizing that the past, present, and future do not 'line up neatly as though history were heading somewhere': *Conscripts of Modernity: The Tragedy of Colonial Enlightenment* (Duke University Press 2004) 166. See also Adil Hasan Khan, 'Ghostly Visitations: "Questioning Heirs" and the Tragic Tasks of Narrating Bandung Futures' in Luis Eslava, Michael Fakhri, and Vasuki Nesiah (eds), *Bandung, Global History, and International Law: Critical Pasts and Pending Futures* (Cambridge University Press 2017) 108.

[115] Priyamvada Gopal, *Insurgent Empire: Anticolonial Resistance and British Dissent* (Verso 2019) 8–9.

[116] Stewart Motha and Honni van Rijswijk (eds), *Law, Memory, Violence: Uncovering the Counter-Archive* (Routledge 2016).

[117] Gabriel Rockhill, *Counter-History of the Present: Untimely Interrogations into Globalisation, Technology, Democracy* (Duke University Press 2017) 9.

[118] Martti Koskenniemi, 'International Law and the Far Right: Reflections on Law and Cynicism' (Asser Press 2019).

[119] Matthew C Klein and Michael Pettis, *Trade Wars are Class Wars: How Rising Inequality Distorts the Global Economy and Threatens International Peace* (Yale University Press 2020).

[120] Harlan Grant Cohen, 'What is International Trade Law For?' (2019) 113 *American Journal of International Law* 328; Gregory Shaffer, 'Retooling Trade Agreements for Social Inclusion' (2019) 2019 *Illinois Law Review* 1.

[121] Nottage (n 6).

[122] https://www.pulitzer.org/winners/lynn-nottage-0 (accessed on 6 July 2020).

The play also offers an effective theatrical distillation of neoliberal capitalism and its contradictions.[123]

Commissioned as part of an artistic programme on American Revolutions, Nottage chose to focus on the American 'De-Industrial Revolution', where people who were 'invested in using their hands as a means of living no longer [had] a place in the economic food chain'.[124] The play was based on two-and-a-half years of ethnographic work in the town of Reading in Pennsylvania, which—at the time of the play's writing—was the poorest city of its size in America. During her interviews, Nottage found that her subjects repeatedly spoke of their city in the past tense, leading her to conclude that a 'city that couldn't imagine itself in the present or in the future was a city that had lost its narrative'.[125]

A chief reason for Reading's industrial decline was likely the passage of the North American Free Trade Agreement (NAFTA) and its effects upon the American manufacturing industry and the unions upon which its workers relied.[126] Yet NAFTA only makes the most fleeting of appearances in *Sweat*. Early in the play, in a local bar where steel workers congregate, the barman quips: 'You could wake up tomorrow and all your jobs are in Mexico, whatever, it's this NAFTA bullshit'. One of the steel workers responds: 'What the fuck is NAFTA? Sounds like a laxative'.[127] Although the play's central characters are not well-versed in the detail of international trade policy, its distributional effects are their lived reality, compounding their economic precarity.[128]

According to the neoliberal logic of labour market flexibility, the shuttered factory is not a 'tombstone to a lost way of life, but a monument to the forward march of the market'.[129] But the story that focuses on net gain through outsourcing, pursuant to comparative advantage, distracts from the job losses that inevitably ensue. The disempowerment experienced by the steel workers in *Sweat* is not an 'unfortunate side of a largely benevolent and successful model—it is part of the sacrificial logic of its functioning'.[130] However, repeated patterns of sacrifice by the same citizens, with no prospect of redistribution of the burdens,

[123] Charles Isherwood, '*Sweat* Examines Lives Unraveling by Industry's Demise' *New York Times* (17 August 2015) (describing the play as examining the 'mechanics of 21st century American capitalism bearing down on these characters with the brutal power of a jackhammer smashing through concrete').

[124] Jocelyn L Buckner, 'On Creativity and Collaboration' in Jocelyn L Buckner (ed), *A Critical Companion to Lynn Nottage* (Routledge 2016) 180, 186.

[125] Nottage (n 6) 6.

[126] Courtney Elkin Mohler, 'Three Readings of Reading, Pennsylvania: Approaching Lynn Nottage's *Sweat* and Douglas Carter Beane's *Shows for Days*' (2016) 68 *Theatre Journal* 79.

[127] Nottage (n 6) 32.

[128] Susan Silbey, 'Let Them Eat Cake: Globalisation, Postmodern Colonialism, and the Possibilities of Justice' (1997) 31(2) *Law & Society Review* 207.

[129] Slobodian (n 93) 51.

[130] Susan Marks, 'Exploitation as an International Legal Concept' in *International Law on the Left* (Cambridge University Press 2008) 281, 301–302; Wendy Brown, 'Sacrificial Citizenship: Neoliberalism, Human Capital, and Austerity Politics' (2016) 23(1) *Constellations* 3.

give rise to disappointment and resentment, and contributes to the erosion of democratic life.[131]

Although set in the years 2000 and 2008, *Sweat* vividly anticipated the election of Donald Trump and the current agonistic political moment.[132] When asked in an interview about her apparent prophetic voice, Nottage's response was simple: 'I showed up and listened.'[133] *Sweat* helps its audience to confront their 'empathy walls' in relation to Trump's blue-collar electoral base by conveying the 'deep story' of sacrificial citizenship.[134] One need not engage in romanticizing the rustbelt to acknowledge the 'important agenda of democratic reform disrupting elite democratic politics', and concede that anti-populism is not the only response.[135]

While some might balk at a critical race theory method being deployed to better understand those who seek to 'make America great again',[136] *Sweat* engages in counterstorytelling to the extent it highlights the impact of multilateral trade regulation on local communities,[137] rather than parroting the neoliberal narratives preferred by those in positions of power.[138] Lynn Nottage's play is perhaps best understood as inhabiting a liminal space prior to Trump's inauguration,[139] offering a jeremiad for the afflictions of those who later felt compelled to seek solace in economic nationalism.

D Forecasting the Future

The future has long been a political and scientific project.[140] Yet for some time, neoliberal capitalism has been the only game in town, exerting a stranglehold on

[131] Danielle Allen, *Talking to Strangers: Anxieties of Citizenship Since Brown v Board of Education* (University of Chicago Press 2004).

[132] Michael Billington, '*Sweat* review: breathtaking drama about life in the American rustbelt' *The Guardian* (20 December 2018) ('I can't think of any recent play that tells us so much, and so vividly, about the state of the union').

[133] Nottage (n 6) 7.

[134] Arlie Russell Hochschild, *Strangers in Their Own Land: Anger and Mourning on the American Right* (New Press 2016) 5, ix.

[135] Robert Howse, 'Epilogue: In Defense of Disruptive Democracy: A Critique of Anti-Populism' (2019) 17(2) *International Journal of Constitutional Law* 641, 641.

[136] Frank B Wilderson III, *Afropessimism* (Liveright 2020) 229 (rejecting the equivalence framing of 'Blackness' and 'oppressed worker[s]').

[137] Joseph Singer, 'Persuasion' (1989) 87 *Michigan Law Review* 2442 (discussing stories of plant closings and job losses as a pedagogical tool). In the context of international investment law see Nicolás M Perrone, 'Making Local Communities Visible: A Way to Prevent the Potentially Tragic Consequences of Foreign Investment?' in Alvaro Santos, Chantal Thomas, and David Trubek (eds), *World Trade and Investment Law Reimagined: A Progressive Agenda for Inclusive Globalisation* (Anthem Press 2019) 171.

[138] Nicolas Lamp, 'How Should We Think About the Winners and Losers from Economic Globalisation? Three Narratives and their Implications for the Redesign of International Economic Agreements' (2020) 30(4) *European Journal of International Law* 1359 (juxtaposing 'Trump' and 'establishment' narratives).

[139] I am grateful to David Schneiderman and Ruth Buchanan for this point.

[140] Jenny Andersson, *The Future of the World: Futurology, Futurists, and the Struggle for the Post-Cold War Imagination* (OUP 2018).

the imagination.[141] However, a generative line of economic inquiry has recently maintained that narratives not only come about as a result of economic realities, but may also drive them.[142] Recent efforts to think economics after neoliberalism demand to be understood as stories in this vein.[143] Mariana Mazzucato, for instance, has decried the 'biased storyline' of the inefficiency of the public sector vis-à-vis the private sector.[144] For Mazzucato, this 'mythmaking' has given rise to an 'immense amount of value extraction', necessitating the need for 'new stories' about wealth creation in the contemporary economy.[145] Storytelling emerging from the law and political economy camp involve similar efforts to displace the *protagonismo* of the market and reclaim the state,[146] often using Polanyi to trump Hayek.

The COVID-19 pandemic—ongoing at the time of this chapter's writing—also gave rise to a narrative outbreak regarding future political economies.[147] Historian of medicine Charles Rosenberg once described epidemics operating as a form of 'dramaturgy',[148] and the present coronavirus has been no exception. The myth that the economy must come first was swiftly shattered in countries that had hitherto subscribed to Thatcherite 'there is no alternative' dogma.[149] While some have styled the pandemic as a 'portal' to a post-neoliberal future,[150] others have concluded more pessimistically that post-COVID-19 futures will more likely be an instance of never letting a serious crisis go to waste.[151]

[141] Mark Fisher, *Capitalist Realism: Is There No Alternative?* (Zero Books 2009) 2 (describing the 'widespread sense that not only is capitalism the only viable political and economic system, but that it is now impossible to even *imagine* a coherent alternative to it').

[142] Robert Shiller, *Narrative Economics: How Stories Go Viral and Drive Major Economic Events* (Princeton University Press 2019); Jens Beckert, *Imagined Futures: Fictional Expectations and Capitalist Dynamics* (Harvard University Press 2016).

[143] Suresh Naidu, Dani Rodrik, and Gabriel Zucman, 'Economics After Neoliberalism' *Boston Review* (15 February 2019) (discussing a willingness to subordinate textbook economic efficiency to other values such as democratic rule and egalitarian relationships among citizens).

[144] Mariana Mazzucato, *The Entrepreneurial State: Debunking Public vs Private Sector Myths* (Penguin 2015) 7–8.

[145] Mariana Mazzucato, *The Value of Everything: Making and Taking in the Global Economy* (Penguin 2018) xviii.

[146] Jedediah Britton-Purdy et al, 'Building a Law-and-Political-Economy Framework: Beyond the Twentieth-Century Synthesis' (2020) 129(6) *Yale Law Journal* 1784, 1792 ('understanding that the economy is always already political in both its origin and its consequences … [and requiring] attentiveness to the ways in which economic and political power are inextricably intertwined with racialized and gendered inequity and subordination').

[147] Anthea Roberts and Nicholas Lamp, 'Is the Virus Killing Globalization? There's No One Answer' *Barron's* (15 March 2020).

[148] Charles Rosenberg, 'What Is an Epidemic? AIDS in Historical Perspective' (1989) 118 *Daedalus* 1; Priscilla Wald, *Contagious: Cultures, Carriers, and the Outbreak Narrative* (Duke University Press 2008).

[149] Adam Tooze, 'Coronavirus has shattered the myth that the economy must come first' *The Guardian* (20 March 2020).

[150] Arundhati Roy, 'The pandemic is a portal' *Financial Times* (3 April 2020).

[151] Philip Mirowski, *Never Let a Serious Crisis Go to Waste: How Neoliberalism Survived the Financial Meltdown* (Verso 2013).

This narrative dissensus is a microcosm of the challenges that attend storytelling in the Anthropocene.[152] Climate change has been described by Dipesh Chakrabarty as presenting formidable challenges to several metanarratives of humanist history.[153] The Dark Mountain Project offers a useful corrective in this respect.[154] A network of writers and artists and activists, the Project's manifesto is a striking paean to counterstorytelling:

> We believe that the roots of these crises lie in the stories we have been telling ourselves. We intend to challenge the stories which underpin our civilisation: the myth of progress, the myth of human centrality, and the myth of our separation from 'nature'. These myths are more dangerous for the fact that we have forgotten they are myths. We will reassert the role of storytelling as more than mere entertainment. It is through stories that we weave reality ... We will celebrate writing and art which is grounded in a sense of place and of time. Our literature has been dominated for too long by those who inhabit the cosmopolitan citadels.[155]

Should international lawyers—those quintessential inhabitants of the cosmopolitan citadels—be entrusted with the task of forecasting the future of the international economy? Two notes of caution must be advanced. Faith in progress often imperils forecasting regarding the future of capitalism,[156] and international lawyers are perennial sinners in that respect.[157] More fundamentally, even heterodox modes of knowledge production in international economic law demand to be understood not as oppositional to the neoliberal social context in which they are produced, but as 'part and parcel of that context'.[158]

Learning from the Dark Mountain Project's warning about the myth of progress, one approach would be to imagine the future by 'projecting ourselves into it, adopting its standpoint, [and then] ... retroactively insert[ing] into its past (the past of the future) counterfactual possibilities'.[159] Science fiction might be called

[152] Amitav Ghosh, *The Great Derangement: Climate Change and the Unthinkable* (University of Chicago Press 2016) 8 ('Are the currents of global warming too wild to be navigated in the accustomed barques of narration?').

[153] Dipesh Chakrabarty, 'The Climate of History: Four Theses' (2009) 35(2) *Critical Inquiry* 197.

[154] The Dark Mountain Project, *Walking on Lava: Selected Works for Uncivilised Times* (Chelsea Green Publishing 2017).

[155] https://dark-mountain.net/about/manifesto/ (accessed on 6 July 2020).

[156] Francesco Boldizzoni, *Foretelling the End of Capitalism: Intellectual Misadventures Since Karl Marx* (Harvard University Press 2020) 225–31.

[157] Martti Koskenniemi, 'The Subjective Danger of Projects of World Community' in Antonio Cassese (ed), *Realising Utopia: The Future of International Law* (Oxford University Press 2012) 3.

[158] Jana Bacevic, 'Knowing Neoliberalism' (2019) 33(4) *Social Epistemology* 380, 389 ('It is perfectly possible to engage in ever-more-sophisticated analyses of the nature of the "neoliberal beast" from within its belly').

[159] Slavoj Zizek, *First as Tragedy, Then as Farce* (Verso 2009) 151. For a useful application see Ingo Venzke, 'International Law and the Spectre of Inequality' (Amsterdam University Press 2019).

in aid as a means of anticipating different economic futures,[160] perhaps more productively in its dystopian rather than utopian variants. As science fiction author cum international law theorist China Miéville noted:[161]

> Utopias are necessary but not only are they insufficient: they can, in some iterations, be part of the ideology of the system, the bad totality that organises us, warms the skies, and condemns millions to peonage on the garbage scree.

David Scott once observed that it is 'precisely when the future has ceased to be a source of longing and anticipation that the past has become such a densely animated object of enchantment'.[162] Although the ongoing appeal of the turn to history in international law shows no sign of abating, international lawyers must also seek to cultivate a sense of an ending.[163] International lawyers should approach the crystal ball with humility, remembering to distinguish between the progress narratives of the profession and their own political posture. Failure to forecast the future altogether likely involves capitulation to the pernicious path-dependencies of management consultants involved in scenario planning—a dystopian prospect indeed.

V Polyphonic International Law

Novelist Chimamanda Ngozi Adichie once described the 'danger of a single story'.[164] Without proper scrutiny, the 'single story' can constitute an invisible frame.[165] The formidable analytic purchase of counterstorytelling is to render that frame visible and other frames viable.[166] Counterstorytelling is less invested in endorsing a hermeneutic of suspicion than affirming a 'right to narrate'.[167] The

[160] William Davies (ed), *Economic Science Fictions* (Goldsmiths Press 2018); Orna Ben-Naftali and Zvi Triger, 'The Human Conditioning: International Law and Science-Fiction' (2018) 14(1) *Law, Culture and the Humanities* 6. See also the literature on Afrofuturism: Alondra Nelson, 'Introduction: Future Texts' (2002) 20(2) *Social Text* 1.

[161] China Miéville, 'The Limits of Utopia' in Thomas More, *Utopia* (Verso 2016) 16–17.

[162] David Scott, *Omens of Adversity: Tragedy, Time, Memory, Justice* (Duke University Press 2014) 13.

[163] Frank Kermode, *The Sense of an Ending* (Oxford University Press 1967).

[164] https://www.ted.com/talks/chimamanda_ngozi_adichie_the_danger_of_a_single_story (accessed 6 July 2020).

[165] Delgado, 'Storytelling for Oppositionists and Others' (n 49) 2413 ('They are like eyeglasses we have worn a long time'); Michel-Rolph Trouillot, *Silencing the Past: Power and the Production of History* (Beacon Press 2015) xxiii ('The ultimate mark of power may be its invisibility; the ultimate challenge, the exposition of its roots').

[166] Friedrich Nietzsche, *On the Genealogy of Morals* (Penguin 2013) 112 ('There is *only* a perspective seeing, *only* a perspective 'knowing'; and the *more* affects we allow to speak about one thing, the *more* eyes, different eyes, we can use to observe one thing, the more complete will our 'concept' of this thing, our 'objectivity' be').

[167] Homi K Bhabha, 'The Right to Narrate' (2020) 38 *Harvard Design Magazine* (affirming the 'dialogic right to address and be addressed, to signify and be interpreted, to speak and be heard').

aesthetic aspiration might be to achieve a kind of polyphony, with texts comprising a multiplicity of voices that do not merge into a singular perspective.[168] Polyphony in practice requires learning how to listen without 'interrupting, negating, minimizing, or inserting a dominant narrative'.[169] In an earlier article on narration in international law, I urged international lawyers to foster multi-perspectival narration as a 'valiant effort to narrate without silencing, without consuming the voices of others'.[170] I conclude this one by renewing an appeal for insurgent storytelling against all modalities of domination—past, present, and future.

[168] Mikhail Bakhtin, 'Theory and History of Literature v8' in *Problems of Dostoevsky's Poetics* (University of Minnesota Press 1984). See eg Svetlana Alexievich, *Second-Hand Time* (Fitzcarraldo Editions 2017) (powerfully assembling a chorus of individual monologues regarding the post-Soviet condition). Cf Rose Sydney Parfitt, 'Newer is Truer: Time, Space, and Subjectivity at the Bandung Conference' in *Bandung, Global History, and International Law* (n 114) 49, 64 (noting the risk that 'polyphony' can become 'cacophony').

[169] Milton Reynolds, 'Shifting Frames: Pedagogical Interventions in Colorblind Teaching Practice' in Kimberlé Crenshaw et al (eds), *Seeing Race Again: Countering Colorblindness Across the Disciplines* (University of California Press 2019) 352, 367–68.

[170] Windsor (n 41) 768.

14
Revisiting the Memory of Solferino: Knowledge Production and the Laws of War

Eyal Benvenisti and Doreen Lustig[*]

I Introduction

During the course of the second half of the 19th century, the rules regulating the conduct of armies during hostilities were internationally codified for the first time. The conventional narrative attributes the codification of the laws of war to the campaign of civil society, especially that of the founders of the Red Cross—Henry Dunant and Gustav Moynier. In what follows, we problematize this narrative and trace the history of the construction of this knowledge. We explore how the leading figures of the Red Cross, who were aware of the shortcomings of their project, were nonetheless invested in narrating its history as a history of success. Their struggle to control the narrative would eventually confer the International Committee of the Red Cross (ICRC) with considerable interpretive and agenda-setting authority in the realm of the laws of war. We dwell on the meaning of this conscious exercise in knowledge production and its normative ramifications.

The teaching of international humanitarian law often includes a narrative on successive codification efforts beginning in the mid-19th century. Jean-Jacques Rousseau's ideas are said to have gained widespread acceptance and the canonical story suggests that 19th-century European governments espoused such humanitarian ideals.[1] This rendition is central in popularized narratives of the ICRC's history. Historian John F. Hutchinson argues that two types of work predominate this history: 'heroic popular biographies of Henry Dunant' or 'institutional histories [of Red Cross organizations]',[2] in which the authors 'take essentially the same

[*] We thank Jennifer Trigell and Matilda Gillis for excellent research assistance. This research was supported by the Israeli Science Foundation (Grant No 1474/20).

[1] For an influential and sophisticated account of the influence of such humanitarian ideals on the codification of the laws of war and their relation to democratization processes see Geoffrey Best, *Humanity in Warfare* (Columbia University 1980) 128–214.

[2] John F Hutchinson, 'Rethinking the Origins of the Red Cross' (1989) 63 *Bulletin of the History of Medicine* 557, 557.

Eyal Benvenisti and Doreen Lustig, *Revisiting the Memory of Solferino: Knowledge Production and the Laws of War* In: *International Law's Invisible Frames.* Edited by: Andrea Bianchi and Moshe Hirsch, Oxford University Press. © Eyal Benvenisti and Doreen Lustig 2021. DOI: 10.1093/oso/9780192847539.003.0015

approach, portraying these events [the signing of the Geneva Convention and creation of the Red Cross] as a triumph for humanitarianism, an example of what can be done by one individual standing alone against state and bureaucracies'.[3]

The canonical story often begins with the 1862 book titled *Un Memoire de Solferino*,[4] which was written by a then unknown author (Henry Dunant) and circulated in Parisian salons. Dunant's account of tending to injured soldiers following the Battle of Solferino in 1859 went into great hyperbolic detail regarding the brutal fate of wounded French and Habsburg soldiers and recalled how the wounded from both sides, over 30,000 of them, inundated local hospitals and churches. Lacking food and water, and any doctors to treat them, they died 'without a word of consolation'.[5] The publication inspired the Geneva Society for Public Welfare, based in Geneva, in 1863 to establish the Red Cross and promote the first Geneva Convention of 1864 and thereby inaugurate what later would be called international humanitarian law. As the product of private initiative, the international humanitarian law codification movement is portrayed as a story of civil society success. This story further emphasizes the universality of the Red Cross and the progressive nature of its codification endeavours.

In section II of this chapter we problematize the key propositions of the canonical story.[6] We consider the contribution of civil society initiatives. We suggest that while civil society efforts served as an important *catalyst* for the intergovernmental codification of the laws of war, civil society actors were ultimately excluded from the actual law-making process. We then question the universality attributed to the ICRC's mission and describe how national societies conceived themselves as serving the interests of states. We interrogate the gap between the codified law and the actual practice of the belligerents, and suggest that the codified law reflected and entrenched, rather than altered, existing practices. Finally, we interrogate the reference to 'humanitarian' in the ICRC narrative and compare it to the multi-faceted meaning of the term and its adequacy in reflecting the codified law at the time.

Section III is dedicated to the processes that rendered the exclusion of civil society invisible in the framing of this narrative. We trace the construction of knowledge by Moynier, Dunant, and the Red Cross Society from the espousal of Dunant's initiative in 1863 and until the early years of the 20th century, when Dunant received the first Nobel Peace Prize (1901) and Moynier did not. We tell the story of 'the Solferino myth': the construction of the narrative of success of the ICRC's codification efforts against all odds.

[3] ibid.

[4] Jean Henry Dunant, *Un Souvenir de Solférino* (J-G Fick 1862).

[5] ibid 60.

[6] On the influence of myth-busting for the promotion and challenging of legal projects see Matthew Windsor, 'Narrative Kill or Capture: Unreliable Narration in International Law' (2015) 28 *Leiden Journal of International Law* 743.

Section IV concludes by addressing an unresolved tension: if governments were able to exclude civil society from the law-making processes of the laws of war and sidelined humanitarian concerns, how and why has the narrative on the history of international humanitarian law as a history of humanitarianism and its victories won out? We cautiously speculate that governments were either indifferent to or supportive of the heroic narrative since it conferred democratic and humanistic legitimacy to their, otherwise, exclusionary project. At the same time, the construction of the Solferino myth of bottom-up humanitarianism promoted the humanitarian ethos of the ICRC and probably facilitated the organization's rise to prominence as a key actor in the regulation of the laws of war. A realist reading of this counter-history may demonstrate the ways in which the construction of the Solferino myth could advance the interests of governments and of the ICRC itself. But this could also be read as a tale about the transformative impact of legal narratives. Dunant's and Moynier's efforts to reconstruct the narrative of 'the myth of Solferino' may have facilitated the possibility of future interpreters to deviate from the original text and promote the interests of those who were excluded from its codification process.

II Problematizing the International Humanitarian Law Narrative

The primary online guide of the ICRC, the ICRC Casebook Project, 'How Does Law Protect in War',[7] describes how '[t]he inception of modern international humanitarian law dates back to the battle of Solferino'. The guide further chronicles how Dunant's book paved the way to the 1864 Geneva Convention, in which, '[f]or the first time, States agreed to limit—in an international treaty open to universal ratification—their own power in favour of the individual and, also for the first time, war was subject to written, general law. Modern international humanitarian law was born'.[8] Indeed, progress narratives are relatively common in international legal scholarship.[9] It is therefore not surprising that various histories of the international humanitarian law field emphasize the 'heroic popular biographies of Henry Dunant',[10] 'the triumph for humanitarianism',[11] and the long evolutionary history from the earlier mid-19th century attempts to codify the laws of war until the present day. Like other progress narratives in international law, the progress

[7] Marco Sassoli and others, 'How Does Law Protect in War?' (ICRC 2020) https://casebook.icrc.org/ (accessed 23 November 2020).

[8] Marco Sassoli and others, 'Fundamentals of International Humanitarian Law' (ICRC 2020)https://casebook.icrc.org/law/fundamentals-ihl (accessed 23 November 2020).

[9] Tilmann Altwicker and Oliver Diggelmann, 'How is Progress Constructed in International Legal Scholarship?' (2014) 25 *European Journal of International Law* 425.

[10] Hutchinson (n 2) 557.

[11] ibid.

narratives of international humanitarian law chronicle a history of events that fall along 'an invisible line of progress' and is characterized by 'discipline optimism'.[12]

A paradigmatic example of the heroic narrative appears in the part of the ICRC Casebook that is devoted to the 'Fundamentals of IHL':

> The codification of IHL began 150 years ago precisely because the international community found the actual practice of belligerents unacceptable, and custom is—despite all modern theories—also based on the actual practice of belligerents.

This statement imparts several propositions: (a) that the codification of international humanitarian law was promoted by 'the international community' that is distinct from the belligerents, presumably alluding to the role of civil society; (b) that the ICRC itself was the embodiment of a universal/transnational civil society effort; (c) that the codified law was different from actual state practice prevailing at the time; (d) and, finally, that the codified law was 'humanitarian' as opposed to the 'unacceptable practice' prevailing during that period. The following sections are dedicated to the analysis of each of these propositions, as far as they refer to the origins of the ICRC's leading role, rather than to its leadership during the post-First World War era. We do not prod here the additional proposition that the codification of international humanitarian law began with the 1864 Geneva Convention and not earlier, before Solferino and the Red Cross.[13]

A International Humanitarian Law as a Bottom-up Initiative?

The idea of helping the sick and the wounded in war was not particularly original in the 1860s. In the period leading up to those years, tending to soldiers was regulated by the so-called cartels—ie ad hoc agreements upon which governments agreed—and complemented by various civil society initiatives.[14] Earlier, before the

[12] Windsor (n 6) 743, 748, referring to Oliver Diggelmann, 'The Periodization of the History of International Law' in B Fassbender and A Peters (eds), *The Oxford Handbook of the History of International Law* (Oxford University Press 2012) 1008; David Koller, ' . . . and New York and The Hague and Tokyo and Geneva and Nuremberg and . . .: The Geographies of International Law' (2012) 23 *European Journal of International Law* 97, 100. See also Gerry Simpson, 'The Sentimental Life of International Law' (2015) 3 *London Review of International Law* 3.

[13] On this topic see Adam Roberts, 'Foundational Myths in the Laws of War: The 1863 Lieber Code, and the 1864 Geneva Convention' (2019) 20 *Melbourne Journal of International Law* 1. On the 1856 Paris Declaration as 'the milestone in the codification of the laws of war' see also Eyal Benvenisti and Doreen Lustig, 'Monopolizing War: Codifying the Laws of War to Reassert Governmental Authority' (2020) 31 *European Journal of International Law* 127).

[14] For a study of the history of the treatment of the sick and wounded in international wars 300 years before the Geneva Convention see Ernst Julius Gurlt, *Zur Geschiechte der Internationalen und Freiwilligen Krankenpflege im Kriege* (F C W Vogel 1873) 800–21, 833–45. On the practice of 'cartels' see also Travers Twiss, *The Law of Nations Considered as Independent Political Communities, on the Rights and Duties of Nations in Time of War* (Oxford University Press 1861) 352–55.

Napoleonic Wars (1803–15), soldiers were professionals, expensive to train, and therefore adequately protected and cared for.[15] The introduction of universal conscription during the Napoleonic wars made vast numbers of inexperienced soldiers available and thus expendable in the eyes of army generals: '[T]he French Revolution relegated the medical services to the bottom of the quartermaster-generals' list of concerns.'[16] But this very turn to national conscription alongside the press, the telegraph, the steamship, and the rail brought the wars of the 1850s—the Crimean and Italian Wars—much closer to European homes and raised wider public concern over the suffering of soldiers on the battlefield. These sentiments were then translated to humanitarian demands by different civil society initiatives. During the period between the Crimean and the Franco-Prussian war, civil society initiatives of various kinds, some of which were inspired by the peace movements, introduced humanitarian concerns over suffering in war into public discourse and forged transnational coalitions and civil-society based initiatives to regulate war. Their humanitarian zeal is often mentioned as a key catalyst for the introduction of the laws of war.[17]

Indeed, the early bottom-up attempts to codify the laws of war led to the first Geneva Convention of 1864. The involvement of civil society in the Geneva Convention was two-fold. First, the project was initiated by civil society agents rather than state representatives, and was drafted in their presence and active involvement. Secondly, the realization of the Convention envisioned civil society as responsible for the actual care for wounded soldiers. However, the signing of the 1864 Geneva Convention would be the last occasion in the 19th century on which civil society activists would be permitted to set the agenda and initiate codification in the context of the laws of war. Subsequent codifying conventions, while perhaps prompted by civil society initiatives, would pre-empt and even subvert their goals. Thus, beyond the codification aspect, the European governments' turn to the codification of international humanitarian law through inter-state agreements could be read as an attempt *to suppress* the institutional vision embodied in their initiatives: the possibility of institutionalizing international law regulated by public conventions and civil society organizations rather than in secret agreements between governments.[18]

The history of the exclusion of civil society from the codification of the laws of war would continue in later codification projects. The Red Cross initiative to update the Geneva Convention in 1868 was eclipsed by the Russian invitation

[15] See Pierre Boissier, *From Solferino to Tsushima: History of the International Committee of the Red Cross* (Henry Dunant Institute 1985) 125–38.

[16] François Bugnion, 'Birth of an Idea: The Founding of the International Committee of the Red Cross and of the International Red Cross and Red Crescent Movement: From Solferino to the Original Geneva Convention (1859–1864)' (2012) 94 *International Review of the Red Cross* 1299, 1312.

[17] Best (n 1).

[18] We develop this argument in greater detail in Benvenisti and Lustig (n 13).

to St Petersburg later that year. Thomas Erskine Holland reflected later[19] how the efforts made by 'the enthusiastic friends of the [1864 Geneva] convention' to add to its stipulations 'a long list of new ones'[20] faltered, as too few delegates attended the Geneva meeting and all eyes were set on the ensuing convention in St Petersburg.[21] From what would become the St Petersburg Declaration onwards, governments would pre-empt civil society initiatives and exclude their members from participation in the drafting processes. Indeed, as we have showed elsewhere, a pressing concern of European governments arriving in Brussels for an 1874 conference was to exclude civil society representatives from the taking part in their meetings.[22] Therefore, while the immediate precursor to the Russian invitation to the Brussels conference was a proposal of a French 'International Society for the Amelioration of the Condition of POWs', with which Henry Dunant was associated,[23] the Society's presence was vetoed by the Germans whose precondition for attending the Brussels Conference was the exclusion of civil society representatives. The Germans believed that those private actors were 'notorious enemies of the German Reich'[24] and specifically singled out the Society (Dunant's new project) as one that must be excluded.[25] Baron Jomini, a general in the Russian Army, stated in his opening speech to the Brussels Conference that, even though private societies took the initiative, it seemed preferable to the Imperial Government that the matter be solved 'by the Governments themselves, because it trenches on their rights and their interests'.[26] The Conference participants agreed at the outset that only state representatives would take part.[27] In fact, their deliberations were supposed to be confidential.[28] As we argue elsewhere, since civil society posed a threat to the governmental monopoly over international regulation and codification, the

[19] Thomas Erskine Holland, 'A Lecture on the Brussels Conference of 1874, and Other Diplomatic Attempts to Mitigate the Rigour of Warfare: Delivered at All Souls College' (10 May 1876).

[20] ibid 8.

[21] ibid.

[22] Benvenisti and Lustig (n 13) 154–55.

[23] Boissier (n 15) 288–89; Georges Werner, 'Les prisonniers de guerre (Vol 21)' (Collected Courses of the Hague Academy of International Law 1928)http://dx.doi.org/10.1163/1875-8096_pplrdc_A9789028605824_01 (accessed 25 November 2020).

[24] Letter from unknown author to Bernhard von Bülow, State Secretary of the Foreign Office (7 July 1874) (R 901/28961 No 17 of the German Foreign Office, National Archives in Berlin) ('... the members of the society are highly politicized, and have offended the German Emperor himself ... The members of the society are notorious enemies of the German Reich') (author's translation).

[25] Letter from Bernhard von Bülow, State Secretary of the Foreign Office and Georg von Kameke, Minister of War, to William I, German Emperor (18 July 1874) (R 901/28961 No 46, the German Foreign Office, National Archives in Berlin) (author's translation).

[26] Opening speech, Actes de la Conférence de Bruxelles de 1874, sur le projet d'une convention internationale concernant la guerre (Librairies des Publications Législatives, A Wittersheim and Cie 1874) Protocol No 2, at 7.

[27] ibid 3, 14–15.

[28] The German Ambassador to Belgium believed someone in the French Government had leaked the protocols to Gambetta, who published them in his journal *La République Française*. Letter from Friedrich von Perponcher-Sedlnitzky, German Ambassador to Belgium, to Bernhard von Bülow, State Secretary of the Foreign Office (24 August 1874) (folder R 901/28963 No 8, the German Foreign Office, National Archives in Berlin).

turn to inter-state international law-making was meant, inter alia, to assist governments in securing their authority as the sole regulators of the international terrain (and at the same time consolidate their power domestically).[29]

A similar concern towards civil society involvement in international law codification was shared among the elitist cadre of international lawyers who founded the *Institut de Droit International* and also represented governments in international conferences. In particular, they opposed the initiatives of leaders of the peace movement to involve broader segments of civil society (ie including non-experts) in the process of international law-making. Leading figures from the peace societies were planning a 'Senate of Jurists' that would elaborate a code of international law, with a view to having it accepted by governments. They envisioned that, following the meeting of the Senate of Jurists, a large popular peace congress would convene and 'give their work publicity'.[30] In June 1873, the Belgian jurist Gustave Rolin-Jaequemyns wrote to the Reverend James B Miles, Secretary of the American Peace Society, noting their disagreements on certain points, 'particularly on the practical utility of Peace Societies', and clarifying that the objective of the meeting at Ghent (where the *Institut* would be set up) 'will not be directly the preparation of a code of international law, but only the establishment of an international institute for the study and promotion of International Law'.[31]

B *The 'International Community' of the Red Cross against 'Savage Patriotism'*

When the ICRC was founded, it evoked the idea of a universal Christian charity, which was intended to challenge bottom-up 'savage patriotism'.[32] In July 1870, Moynier wrote:

> The essentially international feature of the societies under the aegis of the Red Cross is the spirit that moves them, the spirit of charity . . . The societies constitute a living protest against the savage patriotism that stifles any feeling of pity for a suffering enemy. They are working to pull down barriers condemned by the conscience of our times, barriers that fanaticism and barbarity have raised and still too often strive to maintain among the members of the human family.[33]

[29] For further discussion on this dimension see Benvenisti and Lustig (n 13)164–68.

[30] Irwin Abrams, 'The Emergence of the International Law Societies' (1957) 19 *Review of Politics* 361, 364.

[31] Gustave Rolin-Jaequemyns to James B Miles (7 June 1873). American Peace Society MSS, quoted by Abrams (n 30) 370.

[32] David Forsythe, 'The ICRC as Seen Through the Pages of the Review, 1869–1913: Personal Observations' (2018) 100 *International Review of the Red Cross* 45, 49.

[33] Gustave Moynier, 'Du double caractère, national et international, des sociétés de secours' (1870) 1(4) *Bulletin International des Sociétés de Secours aux Militaires Blessés* 159, 160.

The Franco-Prussian War (July 1870–January 1871) would belie this hopeful belief. Soon, 'fledgling National Societies were at each other's throats'.[34] François Bugnion observed that during this conflict:

> The Societies of the belligerent States engaged in spreading the most poisonous propaganda, moved by the 'savage patriotism' that the International Committee had just denounced; and even some Societies of neutral countries did not hesitate to enter the fray. So violent were the recriminations and so deep the wounds that it took the International Committee thirteen years of patient effort to persuade the National Societies to meet again.[35]

To distance itself from actions of national societies, the ICRC, now called the International Committee,[36] was 'remarkably consistent' in stressing the decentralized nature of the Red Cross network.[37] In 1870, Moynier had stated that each national society was independent and manifested 'self- government', whereas the International Committee was merely 'the intermediary' between these independent units.[38]

Following the turbulent experience of the Franco-Prussian war, charity became increasingly militarized as the relationship between states, their armies and national committees grew even closer. Instead of regarding themselves as 'autonomous providers of contingent and supplementary help to the wounded of many nations', national societies 'began to think of themselves as the auxiliaries of a standing military organization that served the interests of one particular state'.[39] The Red Cross movement continued to rely on governmental support.[40]

> [T]hey depended on the backing of their national authorities and the support of public opinion; to muster the resources they needed for their work, they were obliged to appeal just as much to patriotism as to humanitarian feelings. They were too much a part of national life to be reasonably expected to stand aloof when their countries were fighting for survival.[41]

[34] François Bugnion, 'The Composition of the International Committee of the Red Cross' (1995) 35 *International Review of the Red Cross* 427, 430.

[35] ibid.

[36] Until it settled on this title in 1875, the ICRC was using a number of different titles. See François Bugnion, *The International Committee of the Red Cross and the Protection of War Victims* (ICRC and Macmillan 2003) 9.

[37] Forsythe (n 32) 57.

[38] Moynier (n 33).

[39] Hutchinson (n 2) 179. In 1906, the Geneva Convention (1864) was formally revised to recognize the role of aid societies as auxiliaries to the military forces: ibid 150. See also Forsythe (n 32) 20.

[40] Steven R Ratner, 'Law Promotion Beyond Law Talk: The Red Cross, Persuasion, and the Laws of War' (2011) 22 *European Journal of International Law* 459 (discussing the 'unconventional strategy' of the ICRC that entails secret communications with warring parties, ambiguity in conveying their message to them and, at times, persuasion without asserting legal arguments).

[41] Bugnion (n 34) 430.

This major trend towards militarization was just the beginning. Long before the First World War broke out, many national societies had 'become organizations that, in the mind of governments and peoples alike, existed principally for the purpose of war', distinct from international movements that advocated for peace and disarmament.[42] Louis Appia, one of the ICRC founders, expressed his concern to Moynier in 1873 that the Red Cross would be absorbed 'by militarism and official conformity'.[43] Shai Dromi postulates that national societies used nationalism as a form of 'symbolic capital' to establish themselves in their home jurisdiction, even if it was 'seemingly at odds with their cosmopolitan aspirations'.[44] Boissier writes that, following the Franco-Prussian war,

> Divided within itself, its faith badly shaken, misunderstood by the public and irritant to national governments, the Red Cross entered into the most serious crisis of its entire history … Indeed, perhaps all that remained was a façade. Its two main pillars, goodwill between the national societies and the prestige of the Geneva Convention, were crumbling.[45]

It would take decades and the first Hague Peace Conference of 1899 for the Red Cross movement to regain a sense of purpose. In fact, at the Vienna Conference, which included all Red Cross Societies in 1897, the delegates inserted an article to state that '[t]he Assembly cannot consider any proposal laid before it liable to lead to discussion of the Geneva Convention'.[46] Moynier conceded that the time since 1868 was a 'période d'arrèt et d'observation',[47] 'although not a period of inaction'.[48] After a rejection of his proposal to revise the Geneva Convention in 1874 by the national societies of Russia, Germany, and even Switzerland, Moynier turned his efforts to the *Institut de Droit International*.[49]

Among lawyers at the *Institut* his efforts were more successful. Together with other members of the *Institut* he studied the Brussels Declaration of 1874 and proposed suggestions on how to reword the Brussels Declaration.[50] This exercise

[42] Hutchinson (n 2) 150.

[43] Quoted in Roger Boppe, *L'homme et la Guerre: le Docteur Louis Appia et les Débuts de la Croix-Rouge* (J Muhlethaler 1959) 170.

[44] Shai Dromi, 'For Good and Country: Nationalism and the Diffusion of Humanitarianism in the Late Nineteenth Century' (2016) 64 *Sociological Review Monographs* 79, 79.

[45] Boissier (n 15) 272.

[46] ibid 359 ff.

[47] Gustave Moynier, *Rappel Succinct de l'activité déployée par le Comité International de la Croix-Rouge à Genève Pendant les Quarante Premières Années de son Existence (1863 à 1904) Présenté à ce Comité le 17 Octobre 1904* (publication du Comité international de la Croix-Rouge (Imp Soullier) 1905) 63.

[48] ibid 64.

[49] André Durand, 'The Role of Gustave Moynier in the Founding of the Institute of International Law (1873)' (1994) *International Review of the Red Cross* 543.

[50] G Moynier, 'Annexes au rapport qui précède: projet de texte révisé de la déclaration de Bruxelles' (1875) 7 *Revue de droit international et de législation comparée* 514.

yielded a report suggesting improvements to the Brussels text in the following year.[51] The excesses during the Russian-Turkish war of 1877 prompted Moynier to convince the *Institut* to issue an urgent appeal to the belligerent states to comply with the laws of war,[52] to be followed in 1877 with a more elaborate text on the Application of the Law or Nations to the War of 1877 Between Russia and Turkey.[53] With a sense of urgency and opportunity, in 1878, Moynier was tasked by the *Institut* to survey the military codes that had been adopted by armies, a mission he completed in time for the Brussels session of September 1879. In view of the harsh events of the recent war and the disappointing findings of Moynier's report, the *Institut* tasked the commission he led as rapporteur to propose a 'Practical Manual of the Laws of War',[54] a task completed within a few months and which culminated, with a few minor modifications,[55] in the 1880 Oxford Manual.

1. The codified law entrenched existing state practices

The significance of the 1864 Geneva Convention was limited in key respects. First, it did not deal with state practice *during* warfare but with the treatment of the wounded and dead *after* the end of battle. Secondly, it was costless. Armies were not required to invest resources in caring for the wounded and sick. States were not obliged to take any steps to develop national aid societies to aid the wounded. Indeed, the official position of the Red Cross from its inception, seeking to avoid confrontation with European governments, did not promote a humanitarian agenda that would impose significant burdens on governments. This approach was criticized by the British post-Crimean War campaigner, Florence Nightingale:

> I need hardly say that I think its view most absurd—just such as would originate in a little state like Geneva, which never can see war. They tend to remove responsibility from Governments... it would be an error to revert to a voluntary system, or to weaken the military character of the present system by introducing voluntary effort, unless such an effort were to become military in its organization.[56]

Instead of modifying state practice, the subsequent codifications following the Geneva Convention often reflected and entrenched the practice of the powerful state parties. The lofty humanitarian sentiment reflected in the preamble of the 1868 St Petersburg Declaration could not hide the fact that the Declaration

[51] ibid 553.

[52] ibid 556. See also M Albéric Rolin, 'Notices Nécrologiques: M Gustave Moynier' Institut de Droit International Annuaire (tome XXIV 1911) 442, 444–48.

[53] Institut de Droit International, 'Application du Droit des Gens à la guerre de 1877 entre la Russie et la Turquie—Observations et vœux' (1877-Zur-04).

[54] Annuaire Institut, Tomes III and IV 1879–80, 326–27.

[55] Jean Graven, *Le difficile progres du regne de la justice et de la paix internationales par le droit* (A Pedone 1970) 372.

[56] Quoted in Hutchinson (n 2) 40. See also Roberts (n 13) 32–33.

formally prohibited only the use of projectiles that the participating armies had either never obtained or, in the case of Russia, had unilaterally prohibited. The Brussels Declaration, later reflected in the Hague Regulations of 1899 and 1907,[57] endorsed the most controversial aspects of Prussian and French government practices during the Franco-Prussian War.[58]

2. International humanitarian law and the humanitarian project

The history of the laws of war is often conceived in evolutionary terms; towards 'greater humanitarianism'.[59] Competing historical genealogies of the term notwithstanding, the intellectual origins of the term 'humanitarianism' can be traced to the mid-18th century.[60] Thomas Haskell famously analysed humanitarianism as concern for others.[61] Indeed, until the 1860s humanitarianism was associated with attempts to relieve suffering in various contexts yet not on the battlefield: 'to remedy the plight of such disparate groups as Negro slaves, abandoned children, penitent prostitutes, and even chimney sweeps'.[62]

The motivation of those who initiated the codification at the 1864 Geneva Convention was more focused; they sought to limit unnecessary suffering of combatants, as opposed to the plight of civilians writ-large.[63] Furthermore, the Geneva initiative was not concerned with the promotion of peace or the abolition of war. Dunant considered war inevitable and justified and focused his attention on the conduct of armies *during* war. His main concern was not to abolish war but rather to confront the grave magnitude of suffering inflicted by contemporary warfare.[64] By limiting the 'concern for distant others' to the plight of soldiers in times of war, the Red Cross' pragmatic approach to war stood in stark contrast to earlier strands of the peace movement.[65]

[57] For the German delegates of the first Hague Peace Conference of 1899, the proposed text reflected the Brussels law and hence added nothing of significance see Benvenisti and Lustig (n 13) 165–66.

[58] Benvenisti and Lustig (n 13) 154–64.

[59] Frédéric Mégret, 'Theorizing the Laws of War' in Anne Orford and Florian Hoffman (eds),*The Oxford Handbook on the Theory of International Law* (Oxford University Press 2016) 762, 769.

[60] Andrew Porter, 'Trusteeship, Antislavery and Humanitarianism' inAndrew Porter (ed), *The Oxford Handbook of the British Empire, Volume III: The Nineteenth Century* (Oxford University Press 1999) 198. See also Michael Barnett, *Empire of Humanity: A History of Humanitarianism* (Cornell University Press 2011) 52.

[61] Thomas Haskell, 'Capitalism and the Origins of the Humanitarian Sensibility, Part 1' (1985) 90 *American Historical Review* 339, 345, 353. See also Thomas Haskell, 'Capitalism and the Origins of the Humanitarian Sensibility, Part 2' (1985) 90 *American Historical Review* 547–66.

[62] Hutchinson (n 2) 557.

[63] John Fabian Witt compares Dunant's concept of suffering to Francis Lieber's. See John Fabian Witt, Two Concepts of Suffering in War' in Austin Sarat (ed), *Knowing the Suffering of Others* (University of Alabama Press 2012) 135–36.

[64] Dunant (n 4) 116.

[65] Many of the members of the Red Cross were also involved in peace societies and Moynier himself was a founding member of Frédéric Passy's *Ligue internationale et permanente de la Paix.* On the relationship between the Red Cross and the Peace Societies and the ways in which Moynier conceived of that relationship see Andre Durand, 'Gustave Moynier and the Peace Societies' (1996) 36 *International Review of the Red Cross* 532.

Moynier regarded the treatment of the wounded by voluntary societies as an opportunity to civilize armies, especially in light of the menace of popular governments.[66] The main objective of the Geneva initiative of the 'Committee of Five' was the project of 'humanizing' war rather than working towards the illusory goal of its eradication.[67]

The 1864 Geneva treaty thus served as a signalling device for concerned citizens over their fate in times of war, while allocating the cost of actually treating the sick and the wounded to volunteer societies. This may sound like an optimal deal for the convening parties but, just a few years later, the concerns over control and enforcement would eclipse some of its presumed benefits. The flagrant violations of the Convention during the Franco-Prussian war proved the concerns over discipline and enforcement were valid if not underestimated.[68] These violations buried the limited humanitarian promise embedded in the 1864 treaty for years to come. Unlike the approach of the British during the Crimean War, which led to the establishment of official medical services, and despite the public outcry resulting from Dunant's important book, the Geneva Convention stopped short of imposing any positive obligations on state parties.[69]

Later codifications of the laws of war were similarly limited in their humanitarian aspirations. The 1868 St Petersburg Declaration merely paid lip service to humanitarianism with lofty and celebratory remarks, and subjected humanitarian aspirations to military necessity,[70] with little practical significance.[71] In the 1874

[66] John F Hutchinson, *Champions of Charity: War and the Rise of the Red Cross* (Routledge 1996) 21.

[67] As Dunant argued in *La Charité sur les Champs de Bataille suites du Souvenir de Solferino et résultats de la conférence internationale de Genève* (1864) 6: 'La guerre, si elle est inévitable, doit être faite avec le moins de barbarie possible.' In opening the conference, General Dufour proclaimed: 'Malgré les efforts philanthropiques des congrès de la paix—efforts auxquels l'on peut témoigner tout le respect et la sympathie qu'ils méritent, sans se faire illusion sur le peu de succès qu'ils ont quelque chance d'obtenir,—tant que les passions humaines subsisteront, et cela menace de durer encore longtemps, il y aura des guerres sur celle terre. Il faut donc, plutôt que de poursuivre la chimère de leur suppression, pour être vraiment utile à l'humanité, s'attacher à en rendre les conséquences moins terribles, si possible, en venant en aide de la manière la plus efficace à ceux qui sont chargés par leur position de porter secours à ces misères, leur fournir le concours des bras qui leur manquent, et cela sans qu'il en résulte d'embarras préjudiciables au commandement des armées. Tel est le problème à résoudre dont nous parlions tout à l'heure.' Compte rendu de la réunie à Genève les 26, 27, 28, et 29 octobre 1863 pour étudier les moyens de pourvoir a l'insuffisance du service sanitaire dans les armées en campagne (Jules-Guillaume Kick 1863) 5.

[68] For detailed descriptions see Boissier (n 15) 252.

[69] Amanda Alexander demonstrated how the protection of civilians as such would become central to the codification of the laws of war at a later stage, during the inter-war period. Amanda Alexander, 'A Short History of International Humanitarian Law' (2015) 26 *European Journal of International Law* 109, 113. Boyd van Dijk challenged 'the literature's rigid understanding of the bifurcation between human rights and humanitarian law and demonstrated how human rights thinking became instrumentalized to strengthen the protection of victims of war; Common Article 3 represents the first binding post-1945 international legal provision that tried to break with absolute state sovereignty in domestic and colonial affairs'. Boyd van Dijk, 'Human Rights in War: on the Entangled Foundations of the 1949 Geneva Conventions' (2018) 112 *American Journal of International Law* 553, 582.

[70] David Luban, 'Military Lawyers and the Two Cultures Problem' (2013) 26 *Leiden Journal of International Law* 315.

[71] Benvenisti and Lustig (n 13) 141–44.

Brussels Declaration, the targeting of civilians was not prohibited, except for undefended towns (whose targeting was bound to lack significant military value).[72] 'The principle of distinction'—one of the two pillars of international humanitarian law—was not incorporated into the texts of the Geneva, St Petersburg, and Brussels instruments. While Moynier introduced that principle to the Oxford Manual, prohibiting the destruction of public *and private* property unless demanded by 'an imperative necessity of war',[73] the subsequent 1899 Hague Regulations omitted reference to private property when prohibiting excessive harm to 'the enemy's property'.[74] In the years following 1874, civilians of the opposing side would be regarded as 'enemy civilians', assumed to bear allegiance to the enemy by their nationality. As such, for the duration of the war, trade with them was prohibited,[75] their property would be subject to seizure,[76] and they could even be interned,[77] forced to remain in a besieged town,[78] or become the target of bombardment (on the premise that their suffering might lead to their government's surrender).[79] As noted by Amanda Alexander, the law during this period, inspired by the Lieber Code, conceived of civilians as part of their state and thus also as an enemy.[80] Lastly, the ICRC refrained for a considerable and critical time from supporting the international regulation of civil wars.[81] It was only in 1876 that Moynier, speaking on behalf of the ICRC, changed his mind regarding the applicability of the laws of war to internal armed

[72] ibid 161–64.

[73] See art 32(b) of the Oxford Manual. The obligation to prevent excessive harm to civilians and civilian objects appeared also as a sort of chapeau to art 33 addressing bombardments of defended towns: 'Si l'on ne conteste pas aux belligérants le droit de recourir au bombardement contre les forteresses et autres lieux dans lesquels l'ennemi s'est retranché, des considérations d'humanité exigent que ce procédé de coercition soit entouré de quelques tempéraments, qui en restreignent autant que possible les effets à la force armée ennemie et à ses moyens de défense.'

[74] Article 23 (g) of the Regulations Respecting the Laws and Customs of War on Land, Annex to the Convention (II) with Respect to the Laws and Customs of War on Land and its annex: Regulations concerning the Laws and Customs of War on Land (The Hague, 29 July 1899).

[75] Martin Domke, *Trading with the Enemy in World War II* (Central Book Company 1943); Arno A Blum, Max Rosenbaum, and Herbert S Baron, *The Law Relating to Trading with the Enemy* (Solicitors' Law Stationery Society 1940); Charles H Huberich, *The Law Relating to Trading with the Enemy: Together with a Consideration of the Civil Rights and Disabilities of Alien Enemies and of the Effect of War on Contracts with Alien Enemies* (Baker, Voorhis 1918).

[76] Arnold D McNair and Arthur D Watts, *The Legal Effects of War* (4th edn, Cambridge University Press 1966) 332; Martin Domke, *The Control of Alien Property* (Central Book Company 1943); Francis A Mann, 'Enemy Property and the Paris Peace Treaties' (1948) 64 *Law Quarterly Review* 492.

[77] Convention (IV) relative to the Protection of Civilian Persons in Time of War (Geneva, 12 August 1949) art 41.

[78] *United States v Wilhelm von Leeb and Others*, The High Command Case, US Military Tribunal (Nuremberg, 27–28 October 1948).

[79] Benvenisti and Lustig (n 13) 162.

[80] Amanda Alexander, 'The Genesis of the Civilian' (2007) 20 *Leiden Journal of International Law* 359, 363.

[81] See discussion of the ICRC Meeting of 17 February 1863, minutes reprinted and translated in Jean S Pictet, 'The Foundation of the Red Cross: Some Important Documents' (1963) 3 *International Review of the Red Cross* 63, 67; Sandesh Sivakumaran, *The Law of Non-International Armed Conflict* (Oxford University Press 2012) 30.

conflict, in response to Turkey's refusal of to apply the Convention in its war with Serbia, a Christian state.[82]

III Knowledge Construction—Resuscitating the Memory of Solferino, Dunant, and Geneva after 1874–1910

By the end of the Franco-Prussian war, it had become evident that the Geneva Convention had failed its first major test. Both the French army Medical Corps and the French Aid Society were ill-prepared for the conflict. Few in the army knew about the Geneva Convention and were prepared to comply with its terms.[83] Moreover, the Red Cross symbol was repeatedly abused by French civilians,[84] and members of the French National Society found it necessary to give up using the symbol when they realized insurgents in Paris 'used the sign of neutrality ... to facilitate espionage'.[85] Even though it demanded so little, the Geneva Convention was regarded as a dismal failure by the end of the war. The very idea of amending its provisions by introducing a new convention was readily dismissed as unrealistic. And yet, Moynier was heavily invested in the construction of the history of the Red Cross and what would eventually become the myth of Solferino. This was a steep uphill battle to resuscitate the story of Solferino and inculcate its legacy.

A Moynier's Struggle to Salvage the ICRC's Legacy

The Franco-Prussian war led Moynier to concede that moral sanctions may not suffice to secure the humanitarian cause. In 1872, following the experience of the Alabama arbitral tribunal, he presented a proposal for the establishment of an international criminal tribunal, to no avail.[86] In a subsequent publication, while admitting that the Geneva law was violated in the Franco-Prussian war, Moynier chose an alternative route. He offered a rosy interpretation of the Convention's

[82] Benvenisti and Lustig (n 13) 157.

[83] Greg Seltzer, 'The American Ambulance in Paris, 1870-1871' (2009) 6 *Madison Historical Review* 1, 5. By contrast, rather than haphazardly improvising their provision of aid, the Red Cross Society in Berlin was thoroughly prepared well in advance: 'III. Sociétés de secours' (1873) 4(16) *Bulletin International des Sociétés de Secours aux Militaires Blessés* 171, 222.

[84] Gustave Moynier, 'La Convention de Geneve Pendant la Guerre Franco-Allemande' (1873) 4(14) *Bulletin International des Sociétés de Secours aux Militaires* 23.

[85] 'Le Comité Français a Versailles Pendant l'Insurrection de Paris' (1873) 4(15) *Bulletin International des Sociétés de Secours aux Militaires Blessés* 152, 153.

[86] Gustave Moynier, 'Note sur la Création d'une Institution Judiciaire Internationale Propre à Prévenir et à Réprimer les Infractions à la Convention de Genève' (1872) 3(11) *Bulletin International des Sociétés de Secours aux Militaires Blessés* 122. But Moynier's proposal failed to attract the needed support of governments or international lawyers. For further analysis see Christopher Keith Hall, 'The First Proposal for a Permanent International Criminal Court' (1998) 38 *International Review of the Red Cross* 57.

legacy: the Geneva Convention was too harshly and unfairly critiqued. In his opinion, most misuses and abuses of the Convention were attributable to the negligence of some (particularly the belligerent governments), and the ignorance of others.[87] He further noted that it was the first time that the Geneva Convention was used; the war was prolonged and the combatants were overly excited.[88] Nevertheless, Moynier still claimed that '[t]his baptism of fire has consolidated rather than undermined' the Geneva Convention.[89] Despite the above-mentioned problems that that conflict posed for the movement, Moynier asserted that 'the Convention has emerged victorious from the formidable trial to which it has been subjected'.[90]

The convening of the Brussels Conference (with its resulting declaration) posed additional challenges. Moynier was hoping that the states negotiating the Brussels Declaration would formally invite the Red Cross representatives to air their thoughts and concerns.[91] Before the conference, on 20 June 1874, Moynier sent a circular to the national societies, in which he urged them to use their influence within their respective governments to adopt the position he articulated on behalf of the Red Cross.[92] In particular, he wanted to ensure that the core text of the Geneva Convention was considered in negotiations and that the Brussels Conference was postponed until findings on the application of the Convention during the Franco-Prussian war were available.[93]

While Moynier's hopes of influencing the Brussels Declaration were eventually shattered, he revelled in the fact that the Brussels text did not address the Geneva Convention and hence left the Geneva initiative intact.[94] He triumphantly declared that his circular to the national societies and their successive efforts probably influenced decisions made in Brussels.[95] The Russian Government 'did us the honor of officially transmitting our circular to its representatives in Brussels, who proposed and received support that it should be examined carefully', and the President of the Conference, Baron Jomini, read the circular before the Grand Committee, which was composed of one representative from each state. Overall, Moynier concluded, the ICRC achieved 'the desired result' since '[o]ur wish to keep intact the text of the 1864 Convention was fully realized'.[96] Several states, he said, including Sweden,

[87] Moynier (n 77) 51, 53 (most abuses that were pointed out would not have occurred had the belligerent governments taken appropriate measures to prevent or repress them).
[88] ibid 54.
[89] ibid 53.
[90] ibid 52.
[91] Moynier (n 47) 67.
[92] ibid.
[93] ibid 68.
[94] ibid.
[95] Gustave Moynier, 'La Convention de Genève à la Conférence de Bruxelles' (1875) 6(21) *Bulletin International des Sociétés de Secours aux Militaires Blessés* 9, 9.
[96] ibid.

Germany, and Switzerland, explicitly insisted upon preserving the integrity of the Geneva Convention.[97]

Several years later, in 1903,[98] and then again in 1905,[99] writing his memoires after Dunant had received the Nobel Peace Prize in 1901, Moynier narrated the history of the laws of war as driven by civil society humanitarian sensibilities. Pledging that his account was 'carefully staying in line with the most scrupulous historical truth',[100] Moynier effectively spun a narrative of the ICRC, himself and (to a lesser degree)[101] Dunant as primary actors in the codification of the international humanitarian law. While Dunant was depicted as the visionary, Moynier had the role of the builder of the organization. Dunant 'opened people's eyes, touched the hearts of those who were otherwise indifferent and engaged with intellectual and moral groups on the subject',[102] and Moynier transformed this aspiration into reality. In his memoir, Moynier claims that he took the practical steps of organizing a group to revolutionize the conduct of warfare, beginning with a debate that he initiated at the Geneva Society of Public Utility, which he chaired for several years and which hosted the first Geneva Conference in 1863.[103]

Through their involvement in drafting the Geneva Convention in August 1864, Moynier described the International Committee of the Red Cross as having 'contributed more than anybody' to the principles underpinning the law of nations and without whom the old customs of war would still prevail.[104] Although that assembly in Geneva was a formal one for state parties, two members of the International Committee—General Dufour and Moynier—were included in the Swiss mission. Moynier asserts that they were given the greatest consideration, since they were left to organize or direct the work of the Conference and they authored the draft Convention (drawing upon their own knowledge), which was submitted for the plenipotentiaries' approval.[105] Furthermore, the International Committee was also credited with coaxing states to become signatories to the Geneva Convention: when

[97] ibid 9–10.

[98] Gustave Moynier, *La Fondation de la Croix-Rouge: Mémoire Présenté au Comité International* (Du Comité International de la Croix-Rouge 1903) 4.

[99] Moynier (n 47). The publication lists 'MOYNIER, Gustave, président effectif, membre (associé étranger) de l'Institut de France, président d'honneur de l'Institut de Droit internationa;. and DUNANT, Henry, secrétaire (démissionnaire le 25 août 1867).

[100] Moynier (n 92) 3.

[101] Moynier (n 47) 53. The publication lists 'MOYNIER, Gustave, président effectif; and DUNANT, Henry, secrétaire (démissionnaire le 25 août 1867). In the publications of the comité international in 1867, 1868, 1873, and in 1884, Dunant is not mentioned (except on the list of the comité in 1884) as 'Dunant, Henry, Secrétaire. (Démissionnaire le 25 août 1867'). In LA PART de COMITÉINTERNATIONAL de la CROIX-ROUGE dans L'HISTOIRE de la CONVENTION DE GENÈVE (Isaac Soullier 1900), Dunant is mentioned once, as a traveller with connections in high places who managed to secure the support of Napoleon III for convening the Geneva Conference in 1863 (at pp 7–8).

[102] ibid.

[103] ibid 5.

[104] ibid 28.

[105] ibid 27.

the Austro-Prussian war of 1866 broke out, the Committee 'multiplied its efforts at that time and had the joy of obtaining the signatures of five of the belligerents',[106] and was occasionally assisted by governments in gathering signatories.[107] The publication of the ICRC—the *Bulletin International des Sociétés de la Croix-Rouge* first appearing in 1869—and the library Moynier created ('a true nineteenth-century documentation centre')[108] attest to the Committee's various and innumerable efforts to advance its cause and create and preserve knowledge about its legacy.

B Henry Dunant and the Creation of the Myth of Solferino

Dunant, having been forced to leave the Red Cross and Geneva in 1867, remained active in the following years, promoting, without much success, the protection of soldiers during war. He initiated and led several civil society initiatives, such as the Universal Association for the Welfare or Citizens under Arms (1870). His experiences during the Franco-Prussian war led him to establish and lead the Universal alliance for Order and Civilization (1871) concerned especially with the protection of prisoners of war.[109] This initiative served as one of the catalysts for the Russian initiative to convene the state-only convention in Brussels in 1874.[110]

Subsequently, impoverished and increasingly depressed, Dunant settled in a hospital in the Swiss village of Heiden. He complained that the world had forgotten him and his cause, and was determined to revive his campaign.[111] Trying to regain attention and support, a chance meeting with a local journalist in 1895 led to temporary relief from obscurity,[112] and, ultimately, a book that appeared in 1897 helped Dunant gain worldwide recognition as 'the founder of the Red Cross and the originator of the Geneva Convention'.[113] This book was the culmination of five years of toiling over 'countless letters, notes and documents supplied by Dunant'[114]

106 Gustave Moynier, note sur les travaux de comité international, foundateur de l'oeuvre des secours aux militaires blessés, lue a la conférence internationale de Berlin 7 (1869).

107 ibid 175.

108 Ismaël Raboud, Matthieu Niederhauser, and Charlotte Mohr, 'Reflections on the Development of the Movement and International Humanitarian Law Through the Lens of the ICRC Library's Heritage Collection' (2018) 100 *International Review of the Red Cross* 143, 149.

109 Boissier (n 15) 286–87.

110 Benvenisti and Lustig (n 13) 162.

111 Caroline Moorehead, *Dunant's Dream: War, Switzerland, and the History of the Red Cross* (Harper Collins 1998) 162–63.

112 ibid 162.

113 'Begründer des Roten Kreuzes und Urheber der Genfer Konvention' (as appearing on the title page): Rudolf Müller, *Entstehungsgeschichte des Roten Kreuzes und der Genfer Konvention* (Greiner and Pfeiffer 1897) 90 (mit Unterstutzung ihres Begrunders J H Dunant). The book does not contain critique of Moynier, except a few minor snubs, such as where Moynier is said to have been upset by the fact that the Committee had assigned Dunant to be the chair of the Drafting Committee of the Geneva Convention in tribute to 'the founder of the work'.

114 As told by Manfred Müller, the author's son: Manfred Müller, 'Henry Dunant and Rudolf Müller' (1972) 12 *International Review of the Red Cross* 547.

to Rudolf Müller, a Stuttgart schoolteacher who had become Dunant's admirer and confidant.

Once published, Müller circulated the book widely 'to principalities and ministries, and also to outstanding figures in Germany and abroad'.[115] This book also served as the basis for the campaign to bestow the inaugural Nobel Peace Prize on Dunant. To achieve that goal, Müller and Dunant's other supporters had to make the case that Dunant's work was directly connected to peace.[116] Müller wrote to one of the members of the Prize Committee that '[i]n everything he has undertaken, Henry Dunant's constant aim was to encourage peace and brotherhood amongst peoples. Everybody is agreed that Dunant has done more for 'mutual understanding amongst nations' than any of his contemporaries'.[117] Hans Daae, Müller's colleague, translated this long letter into Norwegian and published it under the title of 'Dunant's Work for Peace'.[118]

Eventually, Dunant was awarded the first Nobel Peace Prize, together with the prominent peace activist Frédéric Passy. Dunant was acknowledged for the establishment of the ICRC in 1863 and for leading the adoption of the Geneva Convention in 1864. The award reasoned that Dunant was responsible for inculcating the idea 'that all wounded soldiers in a land war should be treated as friends'.[119] The announcement continued triumphantly: '[T]he organization he had created grew, and the underlying ideas won gradual acceptance.'[120] The award thus identified the ICRC with the successful promotion of peace and humanitarianism.

In subsequent years, the ICRC itself would endorse the narrative of its role in promoting humanitarianism and the major codification efforts since 1864.[121] Pierre Boissier, one of the prominent historians of the ICRC, reflected back at the Conventions of 1899, 1906, and 1907, describing how they all

> owe much to the Red Cross. Not only because it originated the written laws of war, but because, without waiting for the legislator to intervene, it had time and again shown the way, demonstrating how belligerents could come to an agreement on various points. It was the Red Cross, too, that had on several occasions prepared the diplomatic conferences and ensured their success.[122]

[115] ibid.

[116] Willy Heudtlass, 'J Henry Dunant and the events leading to the award of the first Nobel Peace Prize' (1964) 4 *International Review of the Red Cross* 283.

[117] ibid 289.

[118] ibid.

[119] 'Nobel Peace Prize 1901: Jean Henry Dunant' (Norwegian Nobel Institute)https://www.nobelpeaceprize.org/Prize-winners/Prizewinner-documentation/Jean-Henry-Dunant-Frederic-Passy (accessed 25 November 2020).

[120] ibid.

[121] On the role of the ICRC in the formation of 'the myth of international humanitarian law' during the 1960s see Page Wilson, 'The Myth of International Humanitarian Law' (2017) 93 *International Affairs* 563, 567–69.

[122] Boissier (n 15) 366, 381.

IV The Beneficiaries of the ICRC's Knowledge Construction

In this chapter, we hoped to demonstrate the construction of the myth of Solferino. We sought to open a space for an alternative understanding of the history of the Geneva Convention as a humanitarian and successful endeavour and challenge the centrality of the Red Cross in shaping the early codification of the laws of armed conflict.[123] The history of the Franco-Prussian war and its legal outcome, the Brussels Declaration, were anathema to the peace movement, the Red Cross, and international lawyers who sought to promote humanitarianism. While their humanitarian sensibilities were important catalysts of the turn to codification, they were coopted by powerful European governments and were excluded from participating in the law-making process. Nevertheless, Moynier and Dunant managed to salvage their legacy and reconstruct the myth of Solferino. In subsequent years, the great influence of the Franco-Prussian war on the content and form of the laws of war would be conveniently forgotten, and the Brussels Declaration, if mentioned at all, would be belittled as having failed to produce a legally binding text.

How did the myth of Solferino gain traction? If governments were the actual codifiers of the earlier laws of war, having successfully excluded civil society from the law-making process, why did they remain agnostic to the construction of this narrative? Furthermore, how should we understand the myth of Solferino—should we conceive of it as a subversive story that disrupted the victory of powerful nations by inciting civil society and empowering activists worldwide or as a hegemonic tale, favouring the interests of the ICRC while compatible with the interests of the powerful?

A realist perspective may consider the heroic narrative on the myth of Solferino convenient to ruling elites. Governments were probably driven to the negotiation table because of civil society critique and the threat Geneva posed to their monopoly over the regulation of the laws of war. Maintaining the image of the battle of Solferino of 1859 as the motivation for governmental elites' codification effort by casting aside Brussels in favour of Geneva, could allow leaders to appear gracious and compassionate. The Franco-Prussian war exposed the extent to which the aristocratic rule in continental Europe had become fragile. Against this backdrop, the myth of Solferino could potentially have a legitimizing effect and thus seem consonant with the interests of European governmental elites.

Furthermore, deferring to the less radical and cooperative Red Cross as embodying civil society and as a compass of humanitarianism may have deflected some of the grass roots resistance governments experienced during those years. In response to the transnational character of many of the challengers—socialists, communists, workers' associations, feminists, anarchists, nihilists,[124] the myth of

[123] As noted by Mathew Windsor in this volume, '[a]cknowledging the narrativity of international law enables us to "open up our usual stories", making the "space for new ones to be told" ' See ch 13 above.

[124] Bertrand Taithe, *Citizenship and Wars: France in Turmoil 1870–1871* (Routledge 2001) 135.

Solferino, with the ICRC at the helm, held the potential of securing the stature of the Red Cross as a central, if not *the* central civil society institution in the promotion and protection of the laws of war.

The narrative's focus on the Red Cross as the ultimate representative of civil society (perhaps together with the Institute du Droit International) may have contributed to its eminence and special role as an active developer and interpreter of the laws of war. Such prominence may have positioned the Red Cross in an unusually dominant position in comparison to other civil society actors in the development, interpretation, and codification of international humanitarian law.

Beyond these readings of the role and meaning of the construction of the *Myth of Solferino*, Moynier's imagined narrative may have enabled future interpreters of the law to deviate from the original textual intention and promote the interests of the many. Judges and jurists in later generations would interpret the law to serve humanitarian goals.[125] Ironically, judicial interpretation endorsing the humanitarian aspects in these sources might prove more democratic than the original elitist formation of the laws of war.

[125] On the judicial evolution of the principle of military necessity toward the proportionality test (as part of 'the "civilianization" of the laws of war') see Luban (n 65) 339–47. On 'the conflict between the "IHL camp", which emphasizes the humanitarian aim of the *jus in bello* and the "LOAC camp", which wishes to point out that the Law of Armed Conflict is primarily designed to regulate the relations between fighting armies and therefore must take military concerns seriously into account' see also Eyal Benvenisti, 'The Legal Battle to Define the Law on Transnational Asymmetric Warfare' (2010) 20 *Duke Journal of Comparative & International Law* 339, 348.

15

Knowledge Production, Big Data, and Data-driven Customary International Law

*Tamar Megiddo**

I Introduction

In a 2018 article published in the *American Journal of International Law*, BS Chimni argued that customary international law has historically served and continues to advance the interests of Global North capitalist countries. One of the article's key arguments is 'that the non-availability of the state practice of third world countries, and also the paucity of scholarly writings on the subject, allows the identification of rules of CIL primarily on the basis of state practice of advanced capitalist nations and the opinions of their scholars'.[1] J. Patrick Kelly has voiced a similar argument with respect to determinations of *opinio juris* (the second constitutive element of customary international law in addition to state practice), where anecdotal evidence of the legal positions of Northern countries were the key evidence used in the process of customary international law determination.[2] He, too, emphasized the decisive role of 'academic and judicial elites'[3] in making customs and decried customary international law's 'democracy deficit'.[4]

The process of determining that a customary international norm has been created or has evolved is commonly understood to depend on empirical findings regarding the actions (practice) and legal positions (*opinio juris*) of states. The process of producing knowledge about customary international law therefore involves the collection and identification of relevant facts and evidence, their analysis and interpretation as well as a final conclusion as to whether sufficient evidence indicates that a norm was created or has changed, and as to its content. Arguably, the

* Thanks to Alon Jasper, Mor Mitrani and Renana Keidar and the participants of the Hebrew University's International Law Forum's 2018 Year in Review conference for helpful comments and conversations.

[1] BS Chimni, 'Customary International Law: A Third World Perspective' (2018) 112 *American Journal of International Law* 1, 6.

[2] J. Patrick Kelly, 'The Twilight of Customary International Law' (1999) 40 *Virginia Journal of International Law* 449, 472–73.

[3] ibid 519.

[4] ibid 519–20.

Tamar Megiddo, *Knowledge Production, Big Data, and Data-driven Customary International Law* In: *International Law's Invisible Frames*. Edited by: Andrea Bianchi and Moshe Hirsch, Oxford University Press. © Tamar Megiddo 2021.
DOI: 10.1093/oso/9780192847539.003.0016

modes of producing this knowledge may have implications for the final conclusions. If one relies on an unrepresentative or otherwise biased sample of evidence, or if certain actors are unable to participate in the process of knowledge production, the conclusion of the process may be biased in various ways, too.

International law scholarship is currently seeing a turn to big data and data-driven research. Although this shift has been pioneered by compliance scholars, it is international lawyers' recent shift to data-driven research for spotting trends in bilateral treaty-making,[5] jurisprudence,[6] and, in collaboration with activists and journalists, collecting information on war crimes through open-source investigations,[7] which may be the bellwether for a new era in studying the creation and development of customary international law as well. By 'data-driven' I am referring not only to research whose conclusions are purported to derive entirely from data without making any prior assumptions, but also to a mode of investigating the development of customary international law by systematically testing hypotheses on large amounts of data, as distinct from doing so through anecdotal, unsystematic surveys.

Assuming that the pledge to give equal weight to the practice and *opinio juris* of all sovereign states is genuine, this chapter suggests that an emergent data-driven customary international law methodology has the potential of remedying customary international law's democratic deficit. Transnational collaborations and data crowd-sourcing have the potential to increase both data availability and data diversity. Moreover, technology facilitates transnational collaborations which allow actors from the Global South to participate in customary international law research together with Northern actors. In such circumstances, Southern scholars' proficiency in languages other than English and their expertise in the legal systems of Global Southern countries becomes a competitive advantage for them as data producers and analysers.

Consequently, the creation of larger, more diverse, and more representative datasets on which to test customary international law queries also carries the potential of reducing concerns of a sampling bias. Use of text-as-data computerized

[5] Wolfgang Alschner and Dmitriy Skougarevskiy, 'Mapping the Universe of International Investment Agreements' (2016) 19 *Journal of International Economic Law* 561 (analysing international investment treaties to identify the system's rule-makers and contagion patterns); Alexander Thompson, Tomer Broude, and Yoram Z Haftel, 'Once Bitten, Twice Shy? Investment Disputes, State Sovereignty, and Change in Treaty Design' (2019) 73 *International Organization* 859 (analysing the effects of states' experience in international dispute settlement proceedings on their subsequent treaty-making); Adam S Chilton and Eric A Posner, 'Why Countries Sign Bilateral Labor Agreements' (2018) 47 *Journal of the Learning Sciences* 45 (analysing why states enter into bilateral labour agreements).

[6] Joost Pauwelyn and Krzysztof Pelc, 'Who Writes the Rulings of the World Trade Organization? A Critical Assessment of the Role of the Secretariat in WTO Dispute Settlement' (2019) https://papers.ssrn.com/abstract=3458872 (analysing the influence of the WTO secretariat on the Dispute Settlement Body's rulings).

[7] 'The Yemen Project: Open Source Investigations and the Law of War' *Just Security* (23 September 2019) https://www.justsecurity.org/66258/the-yemen-project-open-source-investigations-and-the-law-of-war/.

content analysis methods may further diminish bias in interpretation or analysis. Moreover, applying machine learning algorithms to big datasets may generate hitherto unconsidered hypotheses regarding customary norms which could later be vetted by human researchers. However, this optimism should be qualified given the resources and scientific sophistication still required to produce, collect, and analyse big datasets, which may render data-driven customary international law once more a methodology used mainly by actors from richer, more developed countries. It should further be qualified given scholarship on the prevalent and non-transparent biases of these technologies.[8]

The chapter begins by discussing the historical production of customary international law, its biases, and concerns. Thereafter, it introduces the concept of knowledge-production, and argues that a new methodology of data-driven customary international law knowledge production is emerging, and may attenuate concerns associated with existing customary international law methodologies. However, data-driven customary international law also raises some concerns, which I discuss in the conclusion.

II Historical Production of Customary International Law

Article 38(1)(b) of the Statute of the International Court of Justice (ICJ) defines international custom 'as evidence of a general practice accepted as law'.[9] It is widely accepted that this definition is composed of two elements: state practice and *opinio juris*,[10] and evidence is required of both elements in order to pronounce that a norm of customary nature has crystallized into binding law.[11]

[8] Scholars studying machine learning algorithms have long raised concerns that biased training data and coding make this improvement questionable. See eg Safiya Noble, *Algorithms of Oppression: How Search Engines Reinforce Racism* (NYU Press 2018); Virginia Eubanks, *Automating Inequality: How High-Tech Tools Profile, Police and Punish the Poor* (St Martin's Press 2019).

[9] Statute of the International Court of Justice, annexed to the UN Charter, art 38(1)(b); cf with the identical art 38(1)(b) of the Court's predecessor under the League of Nations system, Statute of the Permanent Court of International Justice (16 December 1920).

[10] Regarding *opinio juris*, the ICJ distinguished actions 'motivated by considerations of courtesy, convenience or tradition, and not by any sense of legal duty'. Only the latter form of practice can serve as a basis for the determination of a customary international norm. *North Sea Continental Shelf (Germany v Denmark, Germany v Netherlands)* (Judgment) [1969] ICJ Rep 3, para 77.

[11] *The Case of the SS 'Lotus' (France v Turkey)* (Judgment) [1927] PCIJ Series A-No 10, 18 ('The rules of law binding upon States therefore emanate from their own free will as expressed in conventions or by usages generally accepted as expressing principles of law and established in order to regulate the relations between these co-existing independent communities or with a view to the achievement of common aims'); *North Sea Continental Shelf* (n 10) 44 ('State practice, including that of States whose interests are specially affected, should have both extensive and virtually uniform in the sense of the provision invoked; and should moreover have occurred in such a way as to show a general recognition that a rule of law or legal obligation is involved').

Scholars have differentiated between 'traditional' and 'modern' approaches to custom.[12] Whereas the traditional approach places emphasis on inductive reasoning from evidence of state practice and is in this sense more descriptive, the modern approach stresses *opinio juris* and is more normative and deductive.[13] Modern custom is associated with a shift in the ICJ's jurisprudence towards recognizing the possibility of more rapidly crystallizing custom, conditioned on 'a very widespread and representative participation',[14] including by 'specially affected states'.[15] The ICJ has also considered resolutions made at international fora as evidence for determining the development of custom.[16] While such resolutions may theoretically be more representative of states, critics have pointed out that states' consent to resolutions is not necessarily equivalent to their consent to binding norms.[17] The shift towards modern practice has made the kind of evidence which may support a claim of state practice much closer to that supporting a claim of *opinio juris*.[18]

However, despite its pronounced emphasis on the importance of ensuring constant and uniform,[19] or at least widespread and representative practice of states, scholars have long noticed that the ICJ and its predecessor, the Permanent Court of International Justice (PCIJ), have in fact often relied on an anecdotal, unsystematic survey of practice by states—if any.[20] Moreover, when evidence of state practice was weighed by the Court, this evidence was often derived from the practice of Global North rich countries, and particularly these states which have the resources

[12] See eg Anthea Elizabeth Roberts, 'Traditional and Modern Approaches to Customary International Law: A Reconciliation' [2001] 95 *American Journal of International Law* 757 (2001).

[13] ibid 762; Chimni (n 1) 3.

[14] Also see *Asylum Case (Columbia v Peru)* (Judgment) [1950] ICJ Rep 266, 276 ('The Colombian Government must prove that the rule invoked by it is in accordance with a constant and uniform usage practiced by the States in question, and that this usage is the expression of a right appertaining to the State granting asylum and a duty incumbent on the territorial State').

[15] *North Sea Continental Shelf* (n10) paras 73–74.

[16] See eg *Military and Paramilitary Activities (Nicaragua v US)* (Judgment) [1986) ICJ Rep 14, paras 188–89 (hereinafter 'Nicaragua v. US'). Legality of the Threat or Use of Nuclear Weapons (Advisory Opinion) [1996] ICJ Rep 226, paras. 70–73; Legal Consequences of the Separation of the Chagos Archipelago from Mauritius in 1965 (Advisory Opinion) [2019] ICJ Rep 95, paras 150–160.

[17] Kelly (n 2) 520–21.

[18] In the International Law Commission's latest Draft Conclusions on CIL, evidence for state practice were suggested to include: 'diplomatic acts and correspondence; conduct in connection with resolutions adopted by an international organization or at an intergovernmental conference; conduct in connection with treaties; executive conduct, including operational conduct "on the ground"; legislative and administrative acts; and decisions of national courts.' Evidence for *opinio juris* included: 'Official statements: PM speeches, Foreign ministries declarations, formal/diplomatic documents and reports, court decisions, legal opinions, military manuals, accession to treaties, acquiescence.' International Law Commission, 'Draft Conclusions on Identification of Customary International Law, with Commentaries' (2018) at ss 6.2, 10.2.

[19] *Asylum Case* (n 14) 276.

[20] '[m]ost customs are found to exist on the basis of practice by fewer than a dozen states'. See Roberts (n 12) 767 ('Conclusions [re inductive identification of *opinio juris*—TM] are drawn by scholars and courts based on a few incidents of state practice with little attention to practices or views of the broader international community'). Kelly (n 2) 470–71.

to document and publish their practice and legal positions.[21] Furthermore, international law scholars have been accused of following in the Courts' footsteps.[22]

Indeed, as early as the seminal *Lotus* case, the PCIJ has relied on the practice of only a handful of Northern countries' domestic court decisions.[23] In the *Wimbledon* case, it found a customary norm of neutrality of international canals based only on the Suez and Panama Canal Treaties, whose parties included chiefly European powers and the United States (US), as well as Russia, Turkey, and Panama.[24] In addition to these, William Wooster cites the *Nottebohm* and *Asylum* cases as leaving unclear what evidence was relied on.[25] And Kelly also points out that on various occasions the ICJ only rehearsed the elements required for the formation of customary international law, without actually discussing any evidence of them, including in the *Nicaragua Case* and the *Lybia v Malta* decision.[26] Even in the seminal *North Sea Continental Shelf* case the ICJ considered only 15 cases of border delimitations cited by the parties[27] to reject the argument that a new customary law had crystallized on delimitation of the continental shelf.[28]

When a small sample of evidence is considered, a non-randomized or non-representative selection of evidence creates a bias and undermines the claim for an inductive process.[29] Anthea Roberts dubs these evidentiary practices 'procedural inadequacies'.[30] As already noted, they also reflect entrenched substantive biases in the data that serves to ground determinations regarding the development and crystallization of customary international law norms. And, indeed, Roberts reports critiques by new, developing, and socialist states who have objected to customs since these have been 'created by wealthy European and Imperialist powers'. To them, customary international law is 'hegemonic, ideologically biased, and a legitimating force for the political and economic status quo'.[31]

As noted, the evidentiary bias may occur not only as a result of greater attention to rich Northern countries, but also as a result of the greater sophistication and

[21] William Thomas Worster, 'The Inductive and Deductive Methods in Customary International Law Analysis: Traditional and Modern Approaches' (2013) 45 GJIL 445, 497; Roberts (n 12) 767; See similarly Kelly (n 2) 474.

[22] Kelly (n 2) 470–71.

[23] *Lotus Case* (n 11) 28–30; Roberts (n 12) 768.

[24] *The Case of SS Wimbledon (UK and Others v Germany)* (Judgment) [1923] PCIJ Ser A No 1, 235, 25–28.

[25] Worster (n 21) 502; *Nottebohm Case (Liechtenstein v Guatemala)* (Judgment) [1955] ICJ Rep 4; *Asylum Case* (n 14) 277.

[26] Kelly (n 2) 476–77; *Nicaragua v US* (n 16) paras 98–108 (discussing the *(Lybia v Malta)* elements of CIL but citing evidence for neither); *Case Concerning the Continental Shelf* (Judgment) [1982] ICJ Rep 18, 30 (determining that a UN Convention on the Law of the Sea provision on the Exclusive Economic Zone supports the conclusion that the norm according to which the continental shelf of 200 miles is exclusively controlled has become customary without any reference to state practice).

[27] *North Sea Continental Shelf* (n 10) para 75.

[28] ibid para 77.

[29] Worster (n 21) 496–98.

[30] Roberts (n 12) 768.

[31] ibid 768.

resources they may have to collect and publish their practice.[32] The evidentiary bias is further coupled with an English-language bias, which places an increased burden on non-English speaking countries to collect and publish, as well as translate their practice.[33] Therefore, there is less data on the practice and *opinio juris* of Global South countries.[34] Chimni links these evidentiary and language biases with a tendency to downplay the importance of representativeness, for instance, by requiring only a 'sufficiently representative' sample, which would ultimately lead to less weight granted to the third world.[35]

This is the case for scholarly work as well. As Kelly notes, '[t]he practices and attitudes of Japan, China and the many nations of Africa, Asia, and Latin America are virtually ignored in the Western literature. Even the use of Continental sources is generally limited to the decisions of international tribunals and other sources available in English'.[36] Kelly therefore concludes that customs are made by the 'academic and judicial elites',[37] and views both traditional and modern customary international law methodologies as suffering from a 'democracy deficit'.[38]

These critiques point to several problems with the production of knowledge regarding customary international law: The first is an issue at the level of *data availability*: there appears to be more data, and more accessible data (including with respect to language capacity of those engaged in data collection) from rich, Northern, English-speaking countries. A second and related issue is that of *data representativeness*, as the dataset is biased towards such states. A third issue has to do with the *identity of the actors participating* in data-generation, collection, and analysis, where, arguably, a similar bias exists towards Northern or Northern-educated lawyers, especially with respect to scholars working to identify customary norms.[39]

After briefly introducing the concept of knowledge production, I apply this framework to the emerging methodology of data-driven customary international law.

[32] Kelly (n 2) 472–73; See eg the recently launched resource *GPIL—German Practice in International Law* https://gpil.jura.uni-bonn.de/.

[33] Kelly adds: 'In part, this is a result of our lack of facility in foreign languages, but it also reveals a peculiar chauvinism that is incompatible with the concept of customary law. there is an unspoken assumption that the practices, theories, and perspectives of the United States and the United Kingdom, each of which have been paramount powers in distinctive periods of international law, have preeminent weight. The practices of non-Western cultures are just not taken seriously'; Kelly (n 2) 473.

[34] Chimni (n 1) 25–26.

[35] ibid 22 (referring to the International Law Association's Final Report of the Commission on Formation of Customary [General] International Law, Statement of the Principles Applicable to the Formation of General Customary International Law [2000]).

[36] Kelly (n 2) 472–73.

[37] ibid 519.

[38] ibid 519–20.

[39] As Chimni explains, the voice of third-world scholars has been less central historically, and today it remains underrepresented in the scholarship working to identify customary international law since many of them write critique rather than construction of customary international law Chimni (n 1) 25–26.

III Knowledge Production and Big Data

In their seminal work on knowledge production, Michael Gibbons and co-authors make the case that a new way of knowledge production has been born. This new mode 'affects not only what knowledge is produced but also how it is produced; the context in which it is pursued, the way it is organized, the reward systems it utilises and the mechanisms that control the quality of that which is produced'.[40] Although Gibbons and his co-authors aim to describe a new mode of scholarly knowledge production (which they dub 'Mode 2'), their insights are also applicable to the investigation of the elements of customary international law, which is not dissimilar to academic investigation of the social, political, and legal practice of state actors.

Gibbons and co-authors describe Mode 2 as one of transdisciplinary research, and as involving multiple contributors which bring different skills and experience, a fact which makes the process more reflexive and impacts the quality of research.[41] Mode 2's heterogeneity and organizational diversity are marked by an increasing number of sites of knowledge production, the various ways of linking these sites (including electronically, socially, or through informal networks), and the ultimate differentiation and specialization of these sites.[42] However, Mode 2 knowledge production is characteristically transient and research groups are often not firmly institutionalized: work groups come together and dissolve when the project is completed.[43] Nonetheless, the organization and communication pattern remains as a matrix on which other groups can be established in the future.[44] Finally, Mode 2 knowledge production is often sensitive to the social impact of research, and takes it into account in defining the problem and setting research priorities.[45] Writing in 1994, Gibbons and others nonetheless viewed the development of information and communication technologies as key in allowing 'socially distributed knowledge production systems' across institutional boundaries, and across the globe.[46]

This form of decentralized collaborative knowledge production can also support the creation of big databases, encompassing data from multiple, diverse sources. Rob Kitchin has defined big data as huge in volume; high in velocity; diverse in

[40] M Gibbons and others, *The New Production of Knowledge* (Sage Publications 1994) v.

[41] ibid v, 3–8, although not all of Mode 2's attributes appear in every instance of it: ibid 8. Contrasting the two modes of knowledge production, the authors explain that Mode 1 deals with problems set in the context of a particular academic community, is disciplinary, characterized by homogeneity and hierarchy, and tends towards preservation. By contrast, Mode 2 is carried out in the context of application, it is transdisciplinary and characterized by heterogeneity, heteroarchy, and transiency and it is more socially accountable and reflexive in its quality control. See ibid 3.

[42] Gibbons and others (n 40) 6.

[43] ibid 6.

[44] ibid 6.

[45] ibid 7.

[46] ibid 10.

variety; exhaustive in scope; fine-grained in resolution and uniquely indexical in identification; relational in nature; and flexible, holding the traits of extensionality and scalability.[47] Others have suggested that there are actually various types of big data, some of which may reflect only some of the characteristics offered by Kitchin: 'not all will be equally large, not all will involve fast and real-time data availability, and not all will include an all-encompassing wide range of information.'[48] Rather, Connelly and others have focused on the fact that big datasets are often 'found' rather than 'made' by researchers, and are then repurposed for use in research.[49]

Furthermore, big data analytics may facilitate insights that are 'born from the data', as opposed to hypotheses that are identified first and then tested on the dataset. These are insights drawn from machine learning that scans the data and automatically 'mines' it for patterns, subsequently producing predictive models based on its analysis.[50] The degree to which research can genuinely be purely data-driven is a highly debatable issue,[51] and one I would like to bracket in the present discussion. One reason to bracket this discussion is the fact that knowledge production that aspires to be purely data-driven relies heavily on identifying correlations between bits of evidence, whereas customary international law requires causation, even if only constructive causation, between *opinio juris* and state practice. As Fulvio Mazzocchi explains, on the one hand such data-driven research can tell us *that* something is happening, that a recurring phenomenon or a trend are apparent in the data, but it cannot tell us *why* something is happening: what is the cause.[52] Identification of customary international law, on the other hand, requires that one shows not only that states acted in a certain way, but also that such action was guided by said state's self-perception of being legally obligated to act in that manner.[53]

This chapter therefore explores the degree to which big data and data analytics may impact the examination of whether state practice and *opinio juris* are evidenced in a manner that justifies a conclusion that a new customary international norm has crystallized.[54]

[47] R Kitchin, 'Big Data, New Epistemologies and Paradigm Shifts' (2014) 1 Big Data and Society 1, 1–2.

[48] R Connelly and others, 'The Role of Administrative Data in the Big Data Revolution in Social Science Research' (2016) 59 *Social Science Research* 1, 2–3.

[49] ibid 3.

[50] Kitchin (n 47) 2.

[51] F Mazzocchi, 'Could Big Data Be the End of Theory in Science?' (2015) 16 *EMBO Reports* 1250, 1250.

[52] ibid 1252.

[53] *Asylum Case* (n 14) 286 (rejecting certain suggestions of state practice as sufficient basis for finding a customary norm because they seem to have been guided by 'considerations of convenience or simple political expediency', rather than 'dictated by any feeling of legal obligation').

[54] Mazzocchi (n 51) 1252.

IV Data-driven Customary International Law

As Wolfgang Alschner explains, '[o]ne of the greatest promises of computation methods lies in providing better tools to establish customary law'.[55] This part of the chapter surveys a handful of early attempts to harness big-data and data analytics in order to draw conclusions on the development or crystallization of customary norms. It is striking, however, that most of these examples eventually do not draw such conclusions. Despite recognizing that using the data to draw conclusions on customary international law formation is warranted, scholars tend to stop at compiling and describing the dataset and leave it to readers or other researchers to draw their own conclusions.

A Just Security

In the early morning hours of 14 April 2018, the US, the United Kingdom (UK), and France launched an aerial attack against targets in Syria[56] said to have been connected to its chemical weapons programme. This attack followed the Assad regime's chemical attack on the town of Douma a week earlier, on 7 April, which reportedly caused the death of 70 people. Of the three attacking countries, the UK was the only one explicitly to offer a legal justification for the attacks, qualifying them as humanitarian intervention.[57] The US asserted the legality of its actions, but refrained from providing a legal basis for this assertion.[58] France

[55] Wolfgang Alschner, 'The Computational Analysis of International Law' (2019) 17 https://papers.ssrn.com/abstract=3428762.

[56] Helene Cooper, Thomas Gibbons-Neff, and Ben Hubbard, 'Trump Launches Strikes on Syrian Targets' *New York Times* (14 April 2018) 1.

[57] Prime Minister's Office, 'Policy Paper: Syria action—UK Government Legal Position' (14 April 2018) https://www.gov.uk/government/publications/syria-action-uk-government-legal-position/syria-action-uk-government-legal-position.

3. The UK is permitted under international law, on an exceptional basis, to take measures in order to alleviate overwhelming humanitarian suffering. The legal basis for the use of force is humanitarian intervention, which requires three conditions to be met:
   (i) there is convincing evidence, generally accepted by the international community as a whole, of extreme humanitarian distress on a large scale, requiring immediate and urgent relief;
   (ii) it must be objectively clear that there is no practicable alternative to the use of force if lives are to be saved; and
   (iii) the proposed use of force must be necessary and proportionate to the aim of relief of humanitarian suffering and must be strictly limited in time and in scope to this aim (i.e. the minimum necessary to achieve that end and for no other purpose).
4. The UK considers that military action met the requirements of humanitarian intervention in the circumstances of the present case.

[58] Helene Cooper, 'Mattis Wanted Congressional Approval Before Striking Syria. He Was Overruled' *New York Times* (17 April 2018) ('The French, the United Kingdom, the United States, allies, all NATO

merely said it acted in accordance with the 'principles and values' of the UN Charter.[59]

The repercussions of the bombings were also evident in the international legal blogosphere, where scholars were quick to offer legal analyses of the legality of the attacks.[60] A particularly interesting contribution by Alonso Gurmendi Dunkelberg and co-authors appeared on the blog *Just Security*. This post introduced a project of mapping and categorizing the different responses of states to the allied attacks in Syria, in an attempt to discern the extent of states' support of the attacks and to distill their legal position.[61] The goal was to try to ascertain not just the political atmosphere towards the attacks, but also, as the authors put it, 'the legality of the use of force in such circumstances'.[62] Statements of states in response to the attack, the authors hypothesized, could either (1) reassert a well-established rule of international law (presumably, the prohibition on the use of force enshrined in the UN Charter); (2) express *opinio juris* for the formation or evolution of a customary norm (for instance, a new customary exception allowing the use of force in cases of humanitarian intervention); or (3) serve to express agreement (or lack thereof) with the practice of UN member states, which is pertinent to interpretation of the Charter in accordance with the Vienna Convention on the Law of Treaties.[63]

Indeed, as we know from the ICJ's decision in *Nicaragua*, a breach of international law which is justified by a state's reliance on 'a novel right or an unprecedented exception ... might, if shared in principle by other States, tend towards modification of a customary international law'.[64] Furthermore, according to the International Law Commission's latest draft conclusions on the identification

allies, we worked together to maintain the prohibition on the use of chemical weapons,' Mr Mattis said at the Pentagon. 'We did what we believe was right under international law, under our nation's laws'); Ambassador Nikki Haley, US Permanent Representative to the United Nations, Remarks at UNSC Emergency Session (14 April 2018) https://mr.usembassy.gov/remarks-at-an-emergency-un-security-council-meeting-on-syria/ ('We acted to deter the future use of chemical weapons by holding the Syrian regime responsible for its atrocities against humanity').

[59] Intervention de M François Delattre, Représentant permanent de la France auprès des Nations unies—Conseil de sécurité (14 Avril 2018) https://onu.delegfrance.org/Syrie-le-silence-n-est-plus-une-solution (Translation by *Just Security* blog: 'Our action is in full conformity with the objectives and values enshrined in the United Nations Charter').

[60] Kevin John Heller, 'The Coming Attack on Syria Will Be Unlawful' *Opinio Juris* (12 April 2018) http://opiniojuris.org/2018/04/12/the-coming-attack-on-syria-will-be-unlawful/.

[61] Alonso Gurmendi Dunkelberg and others, 'Mapping States' Reactions to the Syria Strikes of April 2018' *Just Security* (22 April 2018) https://www.justsecurity.org/55835/mapping-states-reactions-syria-strikes-april-2018-a-comprehensive-guide/.

[62] ibid.

[63] Vienna Convention on the Law of Treaties (opened for signature 23 May 1969, entered into force 27 January 1980) 1155 UNTS 331, art 31(3) ('There shall be taken into account, together with the context: (a) Any subsequent agreement between the parties regarding the interpretation of the treaty or the application of its provisions; (b) Any subsequent practice in the application of the treaty which establishes the agreement of the parties regarding its interpretation; (c) Any relevant rules of international law applicable in the relations between the parties').

[64] *Nicaragua v US* (n 16) para 20.

of customary international law, statements made on behalf of states can serve as evidence of *opinio juris*.[65] Moreover, if such statements are expressed in a way qualifying as diplomatic acts and correspondence, they could also serve as evidence of state practice.[66]

The post on *Just Security* was authored by academics and practitioners from Peru, the US, the Philippines, and Finland. They canvassed, initially, about 100 states for responses to the attack and were able to identify responses of 56 states and two intergovernmental organizations. Where official translation was unavailable, they produced it themselves with the further assistance of several other researchers, who presumably speak additional languages or otherwise had access to additional responses by states. Furthermore, the authors asked the readers of the blog to alert them to pronouncements by additional states and promised to update the post. Some such additional information and discussion of how to appropriately categorize various states' responses was evident in Twitter threads, and one may presume that additional information was communicated privately to the authors.[67] Gurmendi and his collaborators updated the post at least twice, with the most recent update covering over 130 states and analysing the responses of 82 states and two intergovernmental organizations, and sporting more nuanced maps, tables, pie charts, and gifs and a more elaborate analysis of states' responses.

This mode of data-driven customary international law knowledge production was reiterated in another *Just Security* post published following the January 2020 US–Iran uses of force in Iraq which culminated in the assassination of Iranian Major-General Qassem Suleimani, the Iraqi military commander Abu Mahdi al-Muhandis, and the injury of US service members.[68] Here, once again, the authors collected and published reactions of states to the use of force, stressed that 'States' reactions may, if accompanied by legal opinions, contribute to the formation and interpretation of customary international law and the UN Charter', and invited readers to point them towards additional evidence they may have missed. They note that the initial collection already builds on data shared by the public international law community on Twitter.

Neither post drew final conclusions on whether, in fact, customary international law on *jus ad bellum* or *jus in bello* has evolved following these instances. They seem to view their role as producing the evidence and providing the big dataset that others could subsequently utilize for analysis of the evolution in the content of norms. Nevertheless, both projects have benefited from improved data availability

65 International Law Commission (n 18) Conclusion 10.2.
66 ibid Conclusion 6.2.
67 On file with author.
68 Mehrnusch Anssari and Benjamin Nußberger, 'Compilation of States' Reactions to U.S. and Iranian Uses of Force in Iraq in January 2020' *Just Security* (22 January 2020) https://www.justsecurity.org/68173/compilation-of-states-reactions-to-u-s-and-iranian-uses-of-force-in-iraq-in-january-2020/.

and improved data representativeness, thanks to the transnational collaboration they sponsored and facilitated. They were able swiftly to collect large amounts of raw data from multiple jurisdictions, languages, and types of documents, through the participation of contributors from multiple countries in the Global South as well as North, and publish it in open source form, for anyone to share and utilize.

B Efrony and Shany

Another example relying on big data to discern developments in customary international law on *jus ad bellum*, as well as *jus in bello*, is a recent article by Dan Efrony and Yuval Shany. Seeking to evaluate whether and to what degree the Tallinn Manual 2.0 on the International Law Applicable to Cyber Operations is accepted by states, Efrony and Shany use big datasets and data analytics to make observations on 'state practice and *opinio juris* in relation to cyber operations and on the extent to which they accept the Tallinn Rules as a normative point of reference'.[69] To extract such evidence, the authors created a database of known cyberattacks by using the services of a web-search company which scanned the web, including social media, for reports of cyberattacks. They then cross-referenced the results with two other depositories of known cyber incidents. From the resultant database, they then selected 11 case studies that matched stipulated criteria and contained information about state practice and *opinio juris* in relation to cyber operations.[70]

Therefore, utilizing a host of technological tools, the authors were able to survey and analyse large amounts of data from across the web, and identify and extract the most relevant cases for research. These included responses to attacks from victim states in both the Global North and South. They point out, interestingly, that states repeatedly choose to avoid acknowledging the attacks, to avoid attributing responsibility for them, and even to avoid relying on a right to countermeasures, which is proposed by the Tallinn Manual 2.0. The authors therefore conclude that the Tallinn Manual 2.0 seems not (or perhaps not yet) to have become 'universally regarded as an acceptable basis for articulating the norms of international law governing cyberoperations'.[71] In other words, on their exploration of whether a customary international norm has emerged which reflects acceptance of the Tallinn Manual 2.0 as an agreed framework covering cyber operations, the authors' data-driven research yields the answer: no, or at least: not yet.

[69] Dan Efrony and Yuval Shany, 'A Rule Book on the Shelf? Tallinn Manual 2.0 on Cyber Operations and Subsequent State Practice' (2018) *112 American Journal of International Law* 583, 585.
[70] ibid 595.
[71] ibid 585.

C Bilateral Treaty Studies

In two additional cases, researchers built big datasets of thousands of bilateral treaties and applied various computational content analysis tools to the data, searching for similar provisions or other recurring patterns. The use of bilateral treaties for identification of customary international law is not obvious. As the International Law Commission explains, 'the existence of similar provisions in a number of bilateral or other treaties ... does not necessarily indicate that a rule of customary international law is reflected in such provisions'.[72] Nevertheless, as the commentary also notes, the existence of a corresponding rule of customary international law, whether one reflective of a previously crystallized norm, or one generated by the repetition in multiple bilateral treaties, remains a possibility.[73]

Eliott Ash and Omri Marian built a dataset of 4,052 bilateral tax treaties, including also 16 model tax treaties published by different international organizations. They then used natural language processing to seek consensus on legal rules on bilateral tax among states. Although they 'stop short of concluding that a customary international law of taxation exists', they believe that their findings 'lend some support to such arguments'.[74]

Similarly, although Alschner and Dmitry Skougarevskiy acknowledge that treaty language homogeneity has in the past been used to discern the customary nature of legal rules, their investigation of language consistency among international investment treaties does not include any subsequent analysis of its consequence for customary international law.[75]

Therefore, as with the *Just Security* posts, these authors stop short of utilizing their big datasets to draw conclusions on the creation or evolution of customary norms. Nevertheless, they are fully cognizant that drawing such conclusions based on the data collected is quite plausible.

D Discussion

Big data and data analytics are paving the way for a new method of producing knowledge on customary international law. This new method has potentially significant implications with respect to the doctrine, the academic research, and the legal practice of international law.

In the examples discussed above, data availability is increased by the advances in technology. This is evident on several levels. First, the internet greatly increases

[72] International Law Commission (n 18) 145–46.

[73] ibid.

[74] Elliott Ash and Omri Y Marian, 'The Making of International Tax Law: Empirical Evidence Using Natural Language Analysis' (2017) 16 https://papers.ssrn.com/abstract=2994217.

[75] Alschner and Skougarevskiy (n 5) 7.

and renders easier a researcher's access to the primary materials required for customary international law research. Take, for instance, the official statements of states. Such statements are now regularly posted on the websites of ministries of foreign affairs or shared through social network accounts of various office holders or official agencies. When carrying significance for international law, statements are sometimes further circulated by scholars and practitioners within global online epistemic communities through social media or by reporters through traditional mass media. Access is also made easier to secondary materials in various languages, ranging from academic scholarship to press reports on states' statements or on their actions, and it is facilitated further by freely available automated translating software. These abundant sources of information are accessible to any internet user. Using unstructured machine learning algorithms to scan the official websites of key ministries or of mass media and extract data may further boost data-gathering efforts.[76] Relying on web-search specialists, as Efrony and Shany did, further enhances one's ability to extract relevant data from publicly available information.

Secondly, various online platforms now facilitate transnational collaborations involving multiple participants from a diversity of geographical locations, thus creating socially distributed knowledge production systems across an increasing number of sites. As the Covid-19 experience has shown, while not delivering on many other important aspects of conference participation, video conferencing at least facilitates greater inclusivity and ease of including participants from diverse geographical locations and backgrounds. Collaborations such as the one behind the *Just Security* projects are able to bridge significant language and access barriers, harnessing the diverse skills and expertise of collaborators. They allow researchers familiar with the legal and political context of a particular domestic system to not just collect data, but also to generate a more nuanced and accurate interpretation of its meaning in context. Consequently, knowledge produced about customary international law through such collaborations is based not only on a much bigger dataset, but also on data that is more trustworthy, as well as more diverse—representing more states, geographical regions, political systems, and languages. Furthermore, by crowd-sourcing data—such as by inviting the *Just Security* blog's readership to contribute to the dataset—participating researchers are able to canvass even more states and enlarge their basis for analysis.

Thirdly, and as a consequence, the increased availability of data and the increased diversity of the data sources and of the actors participating in its production have the potential to lead to significant improvement in data representativeness. Finally, by providing open access to their data, collaborators also encourage additional researchers to make use of the data, and potentially fact check or challenge their

[76] Alschner (n 55) 12.

interpretation or analysis of the data, giving rise to a reflexive process and thereby improving the quality of the data and its analysis.

In addition to data gathering, the analysis of data is also significantly enhanced by technology. The use of technology at this stage can range from facilitating the communication and joint work of researchers to producing sophisticated computerized analysis of the data. At the data analysis stage too, the facility of remote, transnational collaboration made possible by the internet, social networks, and software that allows for collaborative sharing of data, analysis, and writing, is key. In other words, even if customary international law researchers opt for human analysis of big datasets rather than computerized content analysis, this effort is made much easier thanks to technology and facilitates diversity of those participating in the effort of analysis. Teams can thus split tasks, share information, consult each other and compare results with ease. Researchers can code, count, search for patterns, run regressions on structured data or otherwise analyse the data themselves.

However, technology's role in the analysis can be more enhanced, with the use of a variety of computerized analysis methods. Different natural language processing (NLP) tools can be used to identify certain predetermined keywords; to scan for recurrent regular expressions across texts; to pick up co-occurrence of words; to conduct sentiment analysis of texts (using a dictionary of tone-signalling words); to cluster similar documents together, or to classify them into groups.[77]

To understand the implications of these tools of customary international law research, take, for instance, sentiment analysis. Building a dictionary of words signalling a sentiment of legal obligation, researchers can use sentiment analysis tools to scan vast text corpora for indications of *opinio juris*. Of course, the output can serve merely as a first stage, which is then followed and vetted by human interpretation and analysis.

Moreover, automated content analysis methods can also be useful in finding patterns across large text corpora, and identifying recurrent patterns that may have been missed.[78] Such pattern analysis can therefore be used to identify candidate customary international law norms which are indicated by recurrent appearances in the data, or which are coupled with positive-tone legal obligation word signals. Revealing candidate customary international law norms in this manner may suggest norms that researchers had not thought to test or verify, and which can now be systematically analysed.

Such pattern searching can also be achieved through supervised machine learning, 'teaching' a computer to scan and extract customary international law-relevant data from defined sources by first 'training' it on data that was manually coded by the researcher. As Alschner explains, '[w]hat makes this technology so successful is that, in contrast to algorithms that mimic human reasoning by

[77] ibid 7–10.
[78] ibid 12.

specifying explicit rules (if A occurs, do B), the algorithm finds rules implicitly by learning the relationship between input and output autonomously'.[79] The algorithm can therefore both work at a scale beyond that of human researchers and identify themes unnoticed by them. Finally, pattern scanning could further be attained through unsupervised machine learning, for instance, by producing topic models.[80]

V Conclusion

Big data and data analytic tools have the power to revitalize the identification of customary international law formation and evolution. This new data-driven customary international law methodology has implications for scholars and practitioners alike.

Data-driven customary international law research allows for the gathering and processing of vast amounts of data, using a diversity of human and automated tools. Even if computer interpretation of legal documents is reasonably thought to be inferior to human interpretation, the ability to process huge amounts of information carries alternative benefits that should not be understated. Systematic analysis is able to mine and include in its evaluation more countries resulting in greater representation to poorer, non-Northern countries, which do not have the resources to document, translate, and publish their opinions or practice into English. It therefore carries significant promise in attenuating contemporary Northern/English-language bias in customary international law research. This is even more so the case when data-driven customary international law is coupled with technology-induced transnational collaborations which further give voice to scholars, activists, or practitioners from such countries. Data-driven customary international law can therefore promote customary international law research that is more representative and egalitarian, and that is in keeping with the fundamental principle of sovereign equality.

However, data-driven customary international law cannot solve all that is flawed in current customary international law methodologies. It is likely that even with more collaborative researches, improved translation tools, and automated scanning and pattern searching, smaller, poorer and non-English speaking states will remain under-represented, if only for not having the resources to engage and form positions on the diversity of international law developments at any given time.

Moreover, engaging in sophisticated data-driven research requires resources and training which once more limit the pool of customary international law researchers to those able to obtain such resources or training. In other words, this

[79] ibid 11.
[80] ibid 12.

fact may give greater power to actors from rich, developed countries to conduct data-driven customary international law studies and consequently to influence the evolution of customary international law—whether as academics or practitioners.

Finally, one should note that the efficacy of natural language processing and other computational content analysis software is not consistent in quality across different languages. This may once more introduce bias into the process of evidence gathering and analysis. It is therefore important to make sure that we do not just relocate the hurdles to inclusion of Global South perspectives behind opaque algorithmic walls, and act to mitigate algorithmic biases as well.

16

Going by the Book: What International Law Textbooks Teach Us Not to Know

Ana Luísa Bernardino[*]

I Introduction

Textbooks typically constitute international law students' first encounter with the discipline, playing a significant and lasting role in shaping the vocabulary, identity, and perception of generations of international lawyers. Their function, however, is not limited to introducing novices to the field, as they are also routinely relied upon by established professionals and international adjudicatory bodies,[1] in so far as they are taken to represent uncontroverted knowledge about international law. Textbooks constitute the discipline of international law in both senses of the term: they constitute international law as an autonomous field of study, but they also constitute the discipline of international law in the sense of deeply influencing what one thinks about and what one does as an international lawyer.

Being privileged vehicles for the establishment and dissemination of the official point of view of the discipline,[2] textbooks determine the fields' authoritative definitions, the questions one may legitimately ask within and about international law, or how international legal claims can be articulated. By telling us what to think about, and what the questions and topics 'of relevance' to international law are,

* I am especially grateful to Andrea Bianchi, BS Chimni, Dorothea Endres, Moshe Hirsch, Abhimanyu George Jain, Luíza Leão Soares Pereira, Phil Saengkrai, Ingo Venzke, and Fuad Zarbiyev for their valuable comments on earlier drafts.

[1] Sondre T Helmersen, 'The Use of Scholarship by the WTO Appellate Body' (2016) 7 *Goettingen Journal of International Law* 309; Sondre Torp Helmersen, 'Finding "the Most Highly Qualified Publicists": Lessons from the International Court of Justice' (2019) 30 *European Journal of International Law* 509; Thomas Schultz and Niccolò Ridi, 'Arbitration Literature' in Thomas Schultz and Federico Ortino (eds), *The Oxford Handbook of International Arbitration* (OUP 2020) 14. Schultz and Ridi conclude that most works cited in investment scholarship in the period spanning from 2008 to 2018 are textbooks. More generally, on textbooks as complex professional discourse involving different dimensions of social interaction see Ken Hyland, *Disciplinary Discourses: Social Interactions in Academic Writing* (The University of Michigan Press 2004) 107.

[2] B S Chimni, 'An Outline of a Marxist Course on Public International Law' in Susan Marks (ed), *International Law on the Left: Re-Examining Marxist Legacies* (CUP 2008) 55. As Chimni writes, 'it is the textbook on CIL [contemporary international law] that is the most influential vehicle in disseminating the MILS [mainstream international law scholarship] world-view, especially in the Third World'.

Ana Luísa Bernardino, *Going by the Book: What International Law Textbooks Teach Us Not to Know* In: *International Law's Invisible Frames*. Edited by: Andrea Bianchi and Moshe Hirsch, Oxford University Press. © Ana Luísa Bernardino 2021.
DOI: 10.1093/oso/9780192847539.003.0017

textbooks inevitably determine the things we do not think about.[3] In addition to discrete blind spots in any given area of international law, textbooks also contain what Asia Friedman has aptly termed 'blind *fields*',[4] which, in the context of this study, would include areas such as international finance, international labour law, or development law, which are understood to be outside the realm of expertise of a 'generalist' international lawyer, beyond the scope of the discipline's jurisdiction, or simply another sub-field of international law which is generally perceived to merit less attention.[5] In so doing, textbooks ensure that international lawyers share not only the same grammar but also, and perhaps more importantly, the same ignorance or unawareness.

More than any other genre of international legal scholarship, textbooks thus provide an ideal (and hitherto undertheorized) object of examination to explore what international lawyers as a community are socialized into attending and disattending. Thus, despite their blatant materiality (indeed, most of them would be difficult to miss, with their many hundreds of pages), international law textbooks constitute 'invisible frames' within the meaning given to this expression by editors of this book.[6]

In a nutshell, this chapter treats textbooks as invisible frames of broader processes of discursive socialization that determine what falls within the frame of the discipline and what is 'out-of-frame'.[7] It builds on literature on cognitive sociology, which explores the processes through which we, as a collective, are socialized into attending to certain things, while pushing others to the background. The purpose is not to provide *errata* for major public international law textbooks, but rather to show how inclusions and omissions serve as enablers for current international legal discourse.

[3] Rod Hill and Tony Myatt, *The Economics Anti-Textbook: A Critical Thinker's Guide to Microeconomics* (Zed Books 2010) 2–3. As Hill and Myatt write: '[T]extbooks are necessarily selective. They must include and emphasize some things and exclude or downplay others. They ask certain questions and not others. They place some topics and questions in the forefront, and put others in the background or leave them out entirely. Those decisions usually reflect implicit, not explicit, value judgements about what is interesting and important. No "objective" account is possible.' See also Eviatar Zerubavel, *Hidden in Plain Sight: The Social Structure of Irrelevance* (Oxford University Press 2015) 62.

[4] Asia Friedman, 'Cultural Blindspots and Blind Fields: Collective Forms of Unawareness' in Wayne H Brekhus and Gabe Ignatow (eds), *The Oxford Handbook of Cognitive Sociology* (OUP 2019) 467.

[5] Similarly see Jan Klabbers, 'On Epistemic Universalism and the Melancholy of International Law' (2018) 29 *European Journal of International Law* 1057, 1058–59. Klabbers writes: '[T]here are ... thousands of taxation conventions in force, yet tax law is rarely considered as international law. Likewise, the International Labour Organization may have sponsored some 200 labour conventions and another 200 or so recommendations, but labour law is rarely considered as international law. The Refugee Convention may be the single most applied convention on earth, but refugee and asylum law are at best budding branches of international law. Nationality law may boast to be among the first topics addressed by the Permanent Court of International Justice, but it is still, almost a century later, rarely regarded as international law.'

[6] Andrea Bianchi and Moshe Hirsch, 'Introduction' to this volume.

[7] On the concept of 'out-of-frame' activity see Erving Goffman, *Frame Analysis: An Essay on the Organization of Experience* (Northeastern UP 1974) 201.

This chapter starts by analysing textbooks as engines of sociomental control, that is, tools that delimit what is relevant in the field of international law and what international lawyers as a community think about (section II). Section III examines how the unarticulated theoretical assumptions of textbooks ensure that they are not commonly experienced as frames, but rather unmediated representations of reality. In section IV, I turn to the importance of analysing the silences of international law textbooks. Finally, section V discusses international law textbooks' hidden curriculum, in the sense given to the concept by critical pedagogy theorist Henry Giroux. Section VI concludes.

II Textbooks as Engines of Sociomental Control

What we see, hear or pay attention to in international law is not merely a function of our eyes and ears, but rather involves cognitive processes, since we are trained and socialized into seeing or deeming certain things noteworthy. As Ludwik Fleck remarks 'only a small minority of students independently notice something new without having their attention explicitly drawn to it, and that even then only a few see it immediately as it is shown to them. They first learn to see.'[8] As readers of international law textbooks, for instance, we are taught that studying international law involves studying *texts, cases, and materials,* not structures, power and discourses.

Textbooks of international law teach us to see distinct issues as 'relevant' to international law. The flip side of this is that the socialization operated by textbooks involves a parallel loss of ability to see what does not fit neatly into the narrow confines of this frame.[9] As Eviatar Zerubavel writes, '[d]etermining what others should consider relevant is a major form of *sociomental control.* It is thus teachers, for example, who determine what students are required to read as well as what are the "main ideas" on which they ought to focus while reading and what are the mere "minor details" they should actually ignore as irrelevant.'[10]

While textbooks may not causally determine what international lawyers specifically *think*, they are extremely influential in demarcating what international lawyers should *think about.*[11] Textbooks thus offer a common language which, despite not being able to solve disagreements about the law, circumscribes the perimeter

[8] Ludwik Fleck, 'On the Crisis of "Reality"' in Robert S Cohen and Thomas Schnelle (eds), *Cognition and Fact: Materials on Ludwik Fleck* (D Reidel Publishing Company 1986) 48.

[9] Ludwik Fleck, 'Scientific Observation and Perception in General' in Robert S Cohen and Thomas Schnelle (eds), *Cognition and Fact: Materials on Ludwik Fleck* (D Reidel Publishing Company 1986) 62–63.

[10] Zerubavel (n 3) 62 (original emphasis).

[11] Similarly see Hill and Myatt (n 3) 4: '[T]extbooks are not only trying to teach you how to think ("like an economist"), they are also trying to tell you what to think about.'

within which disagreement takes place: they make sure that we generally agree on the things we disagree about. This observation is particularly significant because telling us what to think about is a way of telling us what *not* to think about, as Zerubavel has persuasively shown.[12] These textbooks teach one how to think like an international lawyer, how to identify an 'international legal problem', the kind of questions one poses when faced with such a problem, as well as the kind of answers one can give to such questions. For instance, while international lawyers may not agree about the status or characteristics of the different sources of international law, they generally agree that the doctrine of the sources of international law is a topic of major relevance to the discipline, in contrast to the domestic legal realm where it is commonly experienced as a non-issue.[13]

Textbooks linger excessively on knowledge of the rules and principles of international law to the detriment of all other considerations.[14] There is a significant amount of importance given to discussions of the findings of courts in contemporary textbooks, without any discussion as to the practical outcome of the case or its real-life implications. Take, for example, the standard treatments of the *Reparation for Injuries* advisory opinion[15] which invariably features in discussions of international legal personality of international organizations.[16] Textbooks describe the factual circumstances of the case and the holding of the International Court of Justice (ICJ) concluding, inter alia, that the UN had the capacity to bring a claim against Israel. There is no discussion, however, about what happened once the advisory opinion was rendered. Did the UN actually bring a claim against Israel? If so, in what forum? What was the outcome? Was the case settled instead? All those elements are deemed to be of little importance when compared with the determinations of the ICJ.

Textbooks also play a role in determining what *counts* as 'general international law'. One textbook, for instance, argues that, while investment law forms part of general international law, the same would not be true for trade law because

> [I]nvestment law is about importing capital, while trade is about movement of goods and services across borders; investment attracts protection under

[12] Zerubavel (n 3) 71.

[13] See eg 'The Future of Public International Law and of the International Legal System in the Circumstances of Today' Special Report by Sir Gerald Fitzmaurice, *Livre du Centenaire*, Institut de droit international 1873–1973, 251: '[A]lthough on the domestic plane there may still remain uncertainty as to what the law *is* (for statutes, judicial decisions, etc., have to be interpreted and applied) there is never any uncertainty as to *what is law*. On the international plane there may be uncertainty on both heads.'

[14] ibid 75.

[15] *Reparation for Injuries Suffered in the Service of the United Nations* (Advisory Opinion) [1949] ICJ Rep 1949, 174.

[16] Alexander Orakhelashvili, *Akehurst's Modern Introduction to International Law* (8th edn, Routledge 2019) 112–13; Patrick Daillier, Mathias Forteau, and Alain Pellet, *Droit International Public* (9th edn, LGDJ 2009) 661–62; Jean Combacau and Serge Sur, *Droit International Public* (13th edn, LGDJ 2019) 772.

> general international law rules regarding the treatment of aliens. Trade law is about the access to market conditions which are purely treaty-based requirements having no analogue under general international law. Investment law does not directly regulate the access of a foreign investor to a domestic market.[17]

In this way, textbooks operate in a similar fashion to what Jacques Rancière termed the 'partage du sensible', policing our perceptual fields through 'a distribution of what is visible and what is not, of what can be heard and what cannot … an intervention in the visible and the sayable'.[18] Rancière's instructive example involves the orders of police officers: 'Move along! There's nothing to see here!'[19] Pages of textbooks of international law are not unlike such police orders, dividing up what there is to be seen and unseen in the world of international law. One particularly illuminating example is found in the index of the most recent edition of *Brownlie's Principles of International Law.* Readers who search for the entry 'colonialism' are readily directed to 'see decolonialization'.[20] The message is quite clear: there is nothing to see on colonialism, let's move along, forget international law's complicity with colonial violence and contemporary forms of neocolonialism, and redirect the readers' attention to the decolonization movement and the 1960 Declaration on the Granting of Independence to Colonial Countries and Peoples as the definitive mark of the end of colonialism.

Our disciplinary training imposes a certain gaze on the world, allowing us to see certain things and to miss others. Part of this specific way of seeing things is exactly what makes international lawyers a distinct professional group. As one textbook notes, '[international law] is characterized by a well-marked frame of mind: a way of thinking that differs from other disciplines'.[21] The reason why textbooks and other 'invisible frames' work so powerfully is that we do not experience them as such. As Klinkenborg writes, '[y]ou don't even notice what you notice … [b]ecause nothing in your education has taught you that what you notice is important.'[22] And yet, 'the criteria used for deciding what matters themselves matter', as Susan Marks points out.[23]

[17] Orakhelashvili (n 16) 407.
[18] Jacques Rancière, *Dissensus: On Politics and Aesthetics* (Steven Corcoran tr, Continuum 2010) 37.
[19] ibid.
[20] James Crawford, *Brownlie's Principles of Public International Law* (9th edn, OUP 2019) 752.
[21] Giovanni Distefano, *Fundamentals of Public International Law: A Sketch of the International Legal Order* (Brill Nijhoff 2019) xii.
[22] Veryl Klinkenborg, *Several Short Sentences About Writing* (Vintage Books 2012) 36.
[23] Susan Marks, *The Riddle of All Constitutions: International Law, Democracy, and the Critique of Ideology* (OUP 2003) 121.

III Representing International Law without the Intermediation of Theory

Textbooks are extremely powerful vehicles which embody the foundational and (for the most part) uncontested premises of the discipline.[24] As the work of Ludwik Fleck reminds us, 'handbook science formulates the genuine core of the system of opinions of a discipline. It is impersonal, presents itself as secure and substantiated knowledge, which is taken as the basis for all further work of the thought-collective.'[25] This explains the flagrant homogeneity of international law textbooks: these works follow broadly the same structure, cover a similar range of topics, and do not differ significantly in the arguments and examples put forward.[26] The author of a recent textbook attests to this when he candidly acknowledges that 'writing a textbook is hardly a revolutionary act'.[27]

There is, indeed, a sense in which textbooks are barely original, as they simply put together the accumulated knowledge of the field which claims to faithfully represent the reality of international law at a given time. As the United States Supreme Court stated in *Paquete Habana*, these works are relied on 'not for the speculations of their authors concerning what the law ought to be, but for trustworthy evidence of what the law really is'.[28] Textbooks foster the idea that they put forward accurate descriptions of a reality independent of the theoretical assumptions that its particular author espouses.[29] It is not uncommon to read statements in textbooks to the effect that '[t]he reality of international law—whatever its theoretical underpinnings—is clearly that of . . .'.[30] In the words of Fleck, '[t]he textbook changes the subjective judgment of the author into a proven fact'.[31] Textbooks are the codification of the discipline's common sense.[32] They are taken to reflect

[24] Hyland (n 1) 104.

[25] Robert S Cohen and Thomas Schnelle, 'Introduction' in Robert S Cohen and Thomas Schnelle (eds), *Cognition and Fact: Materials on Ludwik Fleck* (D Reidel Publishing Company 1986) xxix.

[26] Andrea Bianchi, *International Law Theories: An Inquiry into Different Ways of Thinking* (OUP 2016) 22.

[27] Gleider Hernández, *International Law* (OUP 2019) vi.

[28] *The Paquete Habana*, 175 US 677 (1900). Similarly, Anthea Roberts, *Is International Law International?* (OUP 2017) 32. Roberts states that textbooks 'are not generally meant to be polemic, but are typically understood as providing an account of what international law "is" rather than what the author thinks it "should be" '.

[29] China Miéville, *Between Equal Rights: A Marxist Theory of International Law* (Brill 2005) 2. Miéville argues that 'the bulk of [literature on international law] consists of textbooks, in which theoretical assumptions are generally unacknowledged and implicit'.

[30] Crawford (n 20) 15.

[31] Ludwik Fleck, 'The Problem of Epistemology' in Robert S Cohen and Thomas Schnelle (eds), *Cognition and Fact: Materials on Ludwik Fleck* (D Reidel Publishing Company 1986) 108. Fleck continues: 'It will be united with the entire system of science, it will henceforward be recognized and taught, it will become a foundation of further facts and the guiding principle of what will be seen and applied until a new developmental wave will wash it away.'

[32] Arnulf Becker Lorca, 'International Law in Latin America or Latin American International Law? Rise, Fall, and Retrieval of a Tradition of Legal Thinking and Political Imagination' (2006) 47 *Harvard International Law Journal* 283, 287.

self-evident truths that are commonly shared by the different actors engaged in international legal affairs as a result of processes of socialization where the studying of these textbooks plays a major role. The basis for such self-evidence is produced by these works themselves through rhetorical labour[33] evident not least in the language that these books employ: '[a]s demonstrated . . .',[34] '[i]t is no longer possible to deny that . . .',[35] 'there is little evidence, even from the most progressive perspective, that . . .'.[36]

Treating theory merely for decorative purposes, as Gerry Simpson writes,[37] textbooks repress overt admissions of their theoretical assumptions, thus reinforcing their roles as producers of common sense. For instance, one textbook encourages readers to 'leave behind the glacial uplands of juristic abstraction',[38] claiming that, on a given issue, 'theoretical constructions have done much to obscure realities.'[39] Another textbook, while briefly discussing different theories of international law, hastily reminds its readers that those theories have 'limited relevance for the actual practice of States and the problems that have to be solved in daily life.'[40] A leading French textbook of 1709 pages dedicates half a page to 'post-modernism' and 'the critical school', including feminist approaches and critical legal studies.[41] These works aim to teach us not to know that they themselves lie on a given theory which remains 'unmarked' and 'taken for granted' as it forms part of the orthodoxy of the field. Indeed, works that explicitly acknowledge the theoretical underpinnings that underlie their pages remain the exception.

Such hostility to theory is instrumental in furthering the idea that textbooks set out *the* reality of international law. To borrow Berger and Luckmann's expression, textbooks form part of 'structures of plausibility',[42] they are tools of 'reality maintaining'. Any deviation from the reality built by textbooks may be given a negative ontological status.[43] Questioning that an internationally wrongful act is grounded on two elements of attribution and breach of an international obligation, or that custom is based on two elements of practice and *opinio juris* will likely earn an international law student (or professional) ridicule,[44] which helps to explain

33 See Stanley Fish, *Think Again: Contrarian Reflections on Life, Culture, Politics, Religion, Law, and Education* (Princeton UP 2015) 140 (arguing that clarity is a rhetorical achievement).

34 Crawford (n 20) 16.

35 ibid.

36 ibid.

37 Gerry Simpson, 'On the Magic Mountain: Teaching Public International Law' (1999) 10 *European Journal of International Law* 70, 79.

38 Crawford (n 20) 47.

39 ibid 101.

40 Orakhelashvili (n 16) 15.

41 Daillier, Forteau, and Pellet (n 16) 94.

42 ibid 154.

43 Peter L Berger and Thomas Luckmann, *The Social Construction of Reality: A Treatise in the Sociology of Knowledge* (Anchor Books 1967) 114.

44 ibid 155: 'The plausibility structure is also the social base for the particular suspension of doubt without which the definition of reality in question cannot be maintained in consciousness. Here specific social sanctions against such reality-disintegrating doubts have been internalized and are ongoingly

why textbooks are shockingly homogenous. Few people would dare to dispute a *textbook example*.

IV The Silences of Textbooks

In a now classic piece, published in 1999, Hilary Charlesworth noted that '[a]ll systems of knowledge depend on deeming certain issues as irrelevant or of little significance', thus concluding that 'the silences of the discipline are as important as its positive rules and rhetorical structures'.[45] Despite their claim to comprehensiveness, international law textbooks are no exception in this regard.[46] Such claim to comprehensiveness, sometimes made in the titles of these works,[47] is key to reinforcing the frames through which we come to learn international law, facilitating the assumption that certain things are not 'international law'. One of textbooks' most insidious repression might very well be the repression of the idea that they are repressing anything at all. Studying what textbooks do not teach is therefore just as important as examining what is included in them. As Pierre Macherey writes: '[T]he book is not self-sufficient; it is necessarily accompanied by *a certain absence*, without which it would not exist ... the explicit requires the implicit: for in order to say anything, there are other things *which must not be said*'.[48] There is thus merit to analysing what is ignored in the most influential contemporary textbooks of international law, as well as the 'ignorance of that ignorance and of the economic and social conditions that make it possible'.[49]

However, selectivity and the exclusions it implies may be the very reason why we are able to grasp any concept at all: selectivity may be a necessary condition for the possibility of knowledge.[50] This is why Nietzsche argued that the will to knowledge

reaffirmed. Ridicule is one such sanction. As long as he remains within the plausibility structure, the individual feels himself to be ridiculous whenever doubts about the reality concerned arise subjectively.'

[45] Hilary Charlesworth, 'Feminist Methods in International Law' (1999) 93 *American Journal of International Law* 379, 381.

[46] Similarly see Hill and Myatt (n 3) 2–3: 'Textbooks are necessarily selective. They must include and emphasize some things and exclude or downplay others. They ask certain questions and not others. They place some topics and questions in the forefront, and put others in the background or leave them out entirely. Those decisions usually reflect implicit, not explicit, value judgements about what is interesting and important.' See also Martti Koskenniemi, *From Apology to Utopia: The Structure of International Legal Argument* (CUP 2005) 14: 'Public international law contains a wide range of more or less loosely connected themes. Any attempt to look at it as a whole will necessarily entail privileging some of those themes and downplaying the importance of others.'

[47] Ademola Abass, *Complete International Law: Text, Cases, and Materials* (2nd edn, OUP 2014).

[48] Pierre Macherey, *A Theory of Literary Production* (Geoffrey Wall tr, Routledge 1978) 95 (original emphasis).

[49] Pierre Bourdieu, *Pascalian Meditations* (Richard Nice tr, Stanford UP 2000) 15.

[50] Alexander Nehamas, *Nietzsche: Life as Literature* (Harvard UP 1985) 49: 'We do not, and cannot, begin (or end) with "all the data." This is an incoherent desire and an impossible goal. "To grasp everything" would be to do away with all perspective relations, it would mean to grasp nothing, to misapprehend the nature of knowledge. If we are ever to begin a practice or an inquiry we must, and want to,

fundamentally hinges upon the will to ignorance, for in order to be able to know anything, there are certain things we must ignore, relegate to the background, or leave unquestioned.[51] Studying the omissions of textbooks, however, remains crucial for at least three reasons.

First, it is important to study the exact processes by which certain things come to be silenced in international law textbooks. As Pierre Schlag notes, 'much of the elite academic efforts to produce expert knowledge of the law might be usefully understood as *efforts not to know*, as elaborate academic strategies to avoid taking cognizance of career-arresting phenomena'.[52] Secondly, what comes to be included or excluded at any given time is subject to change.[53] Exclusions are inevitable in their occurrence but not in their contours. The boundaries of inclusion/exclusion constantly shift and vary across times and places. Authors writing in the 19th and early 20th centuries, for instance, speak of a 'science of international law'[54] and clearly divide the discipline into the sub-fields of war and peace.[55] Contemporary textbooks virtually always cover the principle of the non-use of force, but some do not include international humanitarian law as a separate chapter.[56] One should thus analyse what is precisely excluded at one point in time in a given place and the circumstances and causes behind each exclusion. Thirdly, given that attention is socially organized, the fact that textbooks writers do not discuss a given issue may

leave unasked many questions about the world.' Similarly see Eviatar Zerubavel, *The Fine Line: Making Distinctions in Everyday Life* (University of Chicago Press 1991) 1; Robert N Proctor, 'Agnotology: A Missing Term to Describe the Cultural Production of Ignorance (and Its Study)' in Robert N Proctor and Londa Schiebinger (eds), *Agnotology: The Making and Unmaking of Ignorance* (Stanford UP 2008) 7: '[I]nquiry is always selective. We look *here* rather than *there* … and the decision to focus on this is therefore invariably a choice to ignore that. Ignorance is a product of inattention, and since we cannot study all things, some by necessity—almost all, in fact—must be left out' (original emphasis).

[51] Friedrich Nietzsche, *The Will to Power* (Walter Kaufmann and RJ Hollingdale trs, Vintage Books 1967) 328, § 690. In a similar vein, Friedrich Nietzsche, *On the Genealogy of Morals and Ecce Homo* (Walter Kaufmann and RJ Hollingdale trs, Vintage 1989) 57–58: 'Forgetting is no mere *vis inertiae* as the superficial imagine; it is rather an active and in the strictest sense positive faculty of repression, that is responsible for the fact that what we experience and absorb enters our consciousness as little while we are digesting it (one might call the process "inpsychation") as does the thousandfold process, involved in physical nourishment—so-called "incorporation" … The man in whom this apparatus of repression is damaged and ceases to function properly may be compared (and more than merely compared) with a dyspeptic—he cannot "have done" with anything.' See also Nehamas (n 50) 49.

[52] Pierre Schlag, 'The Knowledge Bubble: Something Amiss in Expertopia' in Justin Desautels-Stein and Christopher Tomlins (eds), *Searching for Contemporary Legal Thought* (CUP 2017) 429.

[53] Markus Schroer, 'Sociology of Attention: Fundamental Reflections on a Theoretical Program' in Wayne H Brekhus and Gabe Ignatow (eds), *The Oxford Handbook of Cognitive Sociology* (OUP 2019) 428–29.

[54] TA Walker, *The Science of International Law* (CUP 1893).

[55] See eg L Oppenheim, *International Law: A Treatise, vol I: Peace* (Longmans, Green and Co 1905); L Oppenheim, *International Law: A Treatise, vol II: War and Neutrality* (Longmans, Green and Co 1906); John Westlake, *International Law, Part I: Peace* (CUP 1904); John Westlake, *International Law, Part II: War* (CUP 1907).

[56] See eg Crawford (n 20); Martin Dixon, Robert McCorquodale, and Sarah Williams, *Cases and Materials on International Law* (6th edn, Oxford University Press 2016).

very well determine that this particular matter will never cross the minds of a significant group of international lawyers.

V Textbooks' Hidden Curriculum

Textbooks not only allow students to apprehend the formal rules and structures of the international legal system, but also give them implicit lessons on a myriad of different topics, such as whose knowledge counts in international law, what is the place of certain states in international affairs, or what it means to be a successful international lawyer. Alongside the orthodox presentation of the rules of international law, there is also, to use Giroux's well-known concept, a *hidden curriculum* being transmitted to readers of textbooks, that is, lessons which 'although not openly intended, [students] do, in fact, learn'.[57] These publications are thus extremely successful in redirecting the focus of attention of the community to certain things. There is, as Elizabeth Mertz writes, '[h]idden beneath the apparent content of a lesson . . . a deeper message about how the world operates, about what kind of knowledge counts, about who may speak and how to proceed—a cultural epistemology that is quietly conveyed through classroom language'.[58]

Unlike textbooks in other disciplines, the common international law textbook spills much ink in addressing critiques of international law and claiming the relevance and autonomy of the discipline. First, authors justify that international law is in fact law. Indeed, one salient feature of the majority of international law textbooks is a staunch defence of the relevance and importance of the discipline in international affairs against criticism that either international law is not a legal system or not enough of a deterrent on state behaviour. Critiques of international law are dismissed as extreme or facile.[59] As B.S. Chimni points out, the stories of resistance to the international law's violent structures are not told.[60] Since most textbook writers (like most international lawyers) are normatively committed to international law,[61] it is no surprise that they over-inflate the role that international

[57] Jane R Martin, 'What Should We Do with a Hidden Curriculum When We Find One?' (1976) 6 *Curriculum Inquiry* 135, 136. Similarly see Louis Althusser, *On the Reproduction of Capitalism: Ideology and Ideological State Apparatuses* (Verso 2014) 51.

[58] Elizabeth Mertz, *The Language of Law School: Learning to 'Think Like a Lawyer'* (OUP 2007) 23.

[59] ibid 16–17. Crawford writes that: '[C]ritics of international law have tended to approach the subject in extreme ways—by dismissing the project entirely, or by attributing to the agencies of reform almost magical powers.' He continues, '[I]t is easy to be sceptical of the claims of international law given the discrepancies between the power of states, the complexity of modern military systems and, more generally, the scope of the enterprise of international relations. It is also facile.' See also Daillier, Forteau, and Pellet (n 16) 96–104; Combacau and Sur (n 16) 33.

[60] BS Chimni, 'Teaching, Research and Promotion of International Law in India: Past, Present and Future' (2001) 5 *Singapore Journal of International & Comparative Law* 368, 374–75.

[61] David W Kennedy, 'A New World Order: Yesterday, Today, and Tomorrow' (1994) 4 *Transnational Law & Contemporary Problems* 329, 335: 'At a minimum, such lawyers see themselves and their work *favoring* international law and institutions in a way lawyers working in many other fields do not—to work for a bank is not to be *for* banking. Law professors who teach international law are understood to favor

law plays in world affairs. Perhaps most tellingly, one textbook author claims that '[m]etaphorically speaking, [public international law] is to law what Formula 1 is to ordinary car racing'.[62]

These authors then point to examples of international law's potential as a force for good, presenting 'political decolonization' or 'the moratorium on the hunting of the great whales' as important achievements of international law.[63] The effectiveness and relevance of international law is also generally defended in the introductory chapters of textbooks by reference to the system of international aerial transport, international postal services, or trade in goods.[64] Interestingly, none of these topics is generally seen as deserving any treatment in the later chapters of the textbook, which are reserved for the 'core' themes of international law, such as use of force, human rights, or state responsibility. The message to be retained is, indeed, that international law is effective and makes much of the world go around smoothly. The allegedly most informative examples of the effectiveness and relevance of international law are, however, considered to be of lesser relevance and unworthy of discussion in a textbook, since they relate to more mundane forms of international cooperation, the less glamorous sides of the profession. International lawyers want to be seen as indispensable fighters for international peace and justice, not the smooth operation of international postal services.

Besides delimiting the field of the 'noteworthy', textbooks also determine a number of hierarchies of relevance. The most conspicuous example relates to the vast majority of textbooks' treatment of the topic of the relationship between international law and municipal law. Virtually none of the most influential textbooks cover non-OECD member countries. The specific ways in which the treatment of different countries is presented also merits further reflection. One leading textbook, for example, devotes its first section to the United Kingdom's approach, with another section dedicated to the United States', and a final section to 'Other Countries'.[65] The preface of another textbook also explains how it has been updated to include references to decisions of courts in the 'US ... the UK ... the Netherlands ... *and elsewhere*'.[66] Only a couple of powerful states are deemed to be worthy of discussion and even naming.[67]

its development, to believe in its efficacy, to see their pedagogic practice as persuasion and defense of international public order.'

[62] Distefano (n 21) xii.

[63] James Crawford, *Brownlie's Principles of Public International Law* (8th edn, Oxford University Press 2012) 18–19. The reference to decolonization was removed in the most recent edition of the textbook. On textbooks' narrative of progress see BS Chimni, *International Law and World Order: A Critique of Contemporary Approaches* (2nd edn, CUP 2017) 53–55.

[64] Dixon, McCorquodale, and Williams (n 56) 1; Jan Klabbers, *International Law* (2nd edn, CUP 2017) 3; Crawford (n 20) 14.

[65] Malcolm N Shaw, *International Law* (8th edn, CUP 2017) 96 ff.

[66] Crawford (n 20) xvii (emphasis added).

[67] Anthea Roberts, *Is International Law International?* (OUP 2017) 165.

Furthermore, a quick survey of the titles of international law textbooks also sheds some light on cognitive defaults, the marked and unmarked perceptual fields of the majority of international lawyers.[68] Zerubavel gives the example of the need to qualify *male* nurses, as opposed to the 'female nurse' counterpart, which is considered redundant, as conventionally unmarked or taken-for-granted. Similarly, textbooks written by Global North scholars are commonly titled as 'International Law' *tout court*, contrary to textbooks written in the Global South, some of which more modestly present themselves as an angled account of international law.[69]

It appears that only textbooks written outside the mainstream tradition and/or written by Global South scholars will ask questions such as 'Is International Law Eurocentric?'[70] or 'given that international law admittedly centres on European interests . . . how can . . . [an] African or developing country use it for its own (non-European) interests?'[71] Other textbooks brush off critiques of Eurocentrism, claiming that whilst international law might have been Eurocentric decades ago, that is no longer the case now. Some go even further stating that: '[I]n terms of intellectual history, international law was European *in origin*, *although the Europe in question was large*, extending to the whole Mediterranean, to Russia and the Near East . . . At this time Europe was not chauvinistic in defining membership of the international system. For example, the Ottoman Empire was accepted as a valid participant as early as 1649.'[72]

In the first pages of some textbooks, we also find glossaries filled with a number of Latin maxims. Students who had hitherto been trained in a civil law and Roman-based legal systems will feel at home, while all others soon realize that certain traditions matter more than others. Those first pages will also normally contain a table of legal instruments. The order in which such instruments appear is not without consequence. In one textbook, the table is titled 'table of treaties *and other international instruments*'.[73] Despite what may be discussed later when analysing Article 38 of the Statute of the ICJ, through these and other indications, students will already grasp (perhaps unbeknownst to them) the idea that treaties occupy a prominent place in international law, all else falling under the miscellaneous category of 'other international instruments'. The order of the first tables of textbooks equally determines a hierarchy of relevance between treaties, case law, and scholarly pieces, among others. The same consideration applies to the table of contents

[68] Eviatar Zerubavel, *Taken for Granted: The Remarkable Power of the Unremarkable* (Princeton UP 2018).

[69] I am grateful to Fuad Zarbiyev for this point. See eg Dunia P Zongwe, *International Law in Namibia* (Langaa Research & Publishing CIG 2019); Dejo Olowu, *International Law: A Textbook for the South Pacific* (Lulu 2010); John Dugard and others, *International Law: A South African Perspective* (Juta 2011).

[70] Zongwe (n 69) 29.

[71] ibid 4.

[72] Crawford (n 20) 4 (emphasis added).

[73] ibid xviii (emphasis added).

and the relative importance the specific author attributes to different subtopics of international law. While such orders may strike as harmless at first sight, they bear important consequences. Just like Georges Perec wrote, while the order of the alphabet may be

> arbitrary, inexpressive and … neutral,… the mere fact that there is an order no doubt means that, sooner or later and more or less, each element in the series becomes the insidious bearer of a qualitative efficient. Thus a B-movie will be thought of as 'less good' than another film which, as it happens, no one has yet thought of calling an 'A-movie'.[74]

Textbooks of international law also contribute to perpetuating certain stereotypes in international relations.[75] Some authors speak of 'major states',[76] implying that some are minor. One of the most influential textbooks discusses the relevance of a failure to act in ascertaining the existence of a rule of customary international law with the example that 'Chad consistently fails to send a man to the moon'.[77] At the time of writing, there are, to be precise, 192 UN member countries that have consistently failed to send a person to the moon.

VI Conclusion

This chapter has analysed some of the most influential international law textbooks as invisible frames that importantly shape the knowledge production in the discipline, foreshadowing some things international lawyers forfeit when they go by the book. I have examined how textbooks delimit what is relevant to international law and function as powerful instruments of sociomental control, defining the issues we think about as international lawyers and consequently what we do not think about. As important frames of the discipline, they police our perceptual world, determining what is visible and what is invisible, the sayable, and the unsayable.

The chapter also set out to explore how textbooks, by establishing the common sense of the discipline, are able to present *the* world of international law. Fostering a widely shared collective identity and corresponding thought-styles, the *partial*

[74] Georges Perec, 'Think/Classify' in Philip Terry (ed), *The Penguin Book of Oulipo* (Penguin Books 2019) 181–82.

[75] On the pernicious character of textbook stereotypes see Ann Althouse, 'Lying Woman, the Devious Prostitute, and Other Stories from the Evidence Casebook' (1993) 88 *Northwestern University Law Review* 914. Discussing the dangers of stereotypes in international law through the lens of cognitive sociology and social cognition see Moshe Hirsch, 'Cognitive Sociology, Social Cognition and Coping with Racial Discrimination in International Law' (2019) 30 *European Journal of International Law* 1319, 1329 ff.

[76] Shaw (n 65) 59; Daillier, Forteau, and Pellet (n 16) 75–78.

[77] Shaw (n 65) 59.

reality textbooks create,[78] promote, or simply rely on is reified and presented as the sole and full reality,[79] shrouding the various exclusions that underlie them and denying them the recognition of their existence. In the same way that naming certain things makes them real, one of the most efficient ways to deny something its existence is precisely to expurgate it from everyday language, to relegate it to silence.

Finally, this chapter has analysed the question of the hidden curriculum of textbooks, specifically focusing on some hierarchies of relevance established by these works as implicit lessons to be assimilated by their readers.

Further research can unpack other functions of textbooks in the universe of knowledge (and ignorance) production in international law. For instance, textbooks do not only set out the foundational myths of the discipline and reproduce the field's stereotypes; they also establish the social groups and social roles that are organized within the profession.[80] Indeed, textbook-writing in international law involves a 'symbolic struggle for the production of common sense', to borrow Bourdieu's terminology.[81] Contrary to what may be the case in other disciplines, in international law there is a significant amount of symbolic capital and prestige associated with textbooks, to the extent that textbook writers are generally glorified in the discipline. The authority of this small group of white, male, middle-aged scholars in the discipline is, in large measure, constituted by the publication of a textbook with an influential publishing house. Richard Posner gives the example of high school physics students who believe that the author of their textbook, and not Einstein, had discovered the theory of relativity.[82] Similarly, students who are first exposed to an international law textbook might too readily credit all ideas contained therein to its author. Even if this first impression may be displaced the further one advances in one's studies of international law, these 'masters' of international law maintain their god-like status, given the nature and rhetorical apparatus of textbooks.[83]

[78] Fleck, 'The Problem of Epistemology' (n 31) 112.

[79] Hayden White, 'The Value of Narrativity in the Representation of Reality' (1980) 7 *Critical Inquiry* 5, 14.

[80] Ken Hyland, 'Academic Discourse' in Ken Hyland, and Brian Paltridge (eds), *The Bloomsbury Companion to Discourse Analysis* (Bloomsbury 2013) 171–172; Ken Hyland, *The Essential Hyland: Studies in Applied Linguistics* (Bloomsbury 2018) 3. Similarly see Yves Dezalay, 'La Production Doctrinale Comme Objet et Terrain de Luttes Politiques et Professionnelles' in Yves Poirmeur and Alain Bernard (eds), *La Doctrine Juridique* (PUF 1993).

[81] Pierre Bourdieu, *In Other Words: Essays Towards a Reflexive Sociology* (Matthew Adamson tr, Stanford UP 1990) 135.

[82] Richard A Posner, *The Little Book of Plagiarism* (Knopf Doubleday Publishing Group 2009) 19.

[83] See Jonathan Potter, *Representing Reality: Discourse, Rhetoric and Social Construction* (SAGE Publications 1996) 10. Potter argues that 'academic writing tends to draw on textual forms—tropes—which construct a god-like, all-seeing, all-knowing, all-comprehending stance, which is at the same time disinterested and fair'.

Wittgenstein famously observed that: '[T]he aspects of things that are most important for us are hidden because of their simplicity and familiarity.'[84] It is hoped that this chapter has made one thing clear: neither the simplicity nor the familiarity of textbooks should prevent international lawyers from appreciating their significant role in the constitution of the discipline of international law.

[84] Ludwig Wittgenstein, *Philosophical Investigations* (GEM Anscombe tr, Basil Blackwell 1986) 129.

Index

For the benefit of digital users, indexed terms that span two pages (e.g., 52–53) may, on occasion, appear on only one of those pages.

Wherever possible in the case of topics with many references, these have either been divided into sub-topics or only the most significant discussions of the topic are listed. Because the entire work is about 'international law', the use of this term (and certain others which occur constantly throughout the book) as entry points has been minimized. Information will be found under the corresponding detailed topics.